Lecture Notes in Computer Science 5237

Commenced Publication in 1973
Founding and Former Series Editors:
Gerhard Goos, Juris Hartmanis, and Jan van Leeuwen

Andrei Popescu-Belis   Rainer Stiefelhagen (Eds.)

Machine Learning for Multimodal Interaction

5th International Workshop, MLMI 2008
Utrecht, The Netherlands, September 8-10, 2008
Proceedings

 Springer

Volume Editors

Andrei Popescu-Belis
IDIAP Research Institute, Centre du Parc
Rue Marconi 19, Case Postale 592, 1920, Martigny, Switzerland
E-mail: andrei.popescu-belis@idiap.ch

Rainer Stiefelhagen
Universität Karlsruhe (TH), Interactive Systems Labs
Am Fasanengarten 5, 76131 Karlsruhe, Germany
E-mail: stiefel@ira.uka.de

Library of Congress Control Number: Applied for

CR Subject Classification (1998): H.5.2-3, H.5, I.2.6, I.2.10, I.2, D.2, K.4, I.4

LNCS Sublibrary: SL 3 – Information Systems and Application, incl. Internet/Web
and HCI

ISSN   0302-9743
ISBN-10   3-540-85852-0 Springer Berlin Heidelberg New York
ISBN-13   978-3-540-85852-2 Springer Berlin Heidelberg New York

Springer is a part of Springer Science+Business Media

springer.com

© Springer-Verlag Berlin Heidelberg 2008
Printed in Germany

Typesetting: Camera-ready by author, data conversion by Scientific Publishing Services, Chennai, India
Printed on acid-free paper   SPIN: 12513789   06/3180   5 4 3 2 1 0

Preface

The series of workshops on Machine Learning for Multimodal Interaction (MLMI) celebrates this year its fifth anniversary. On this occasion, a number of innovations have been introduced in the reviewing and publication procedures, while keeping the focus on the same scientific topics.

For the first time, the reviewing process has been adapted in order to prepare the proceedings in time for the workshop, held on September 8–10, 2008, in Utrecht, The Netherlands. The 47 submissions received by the Program Committee were first reviewed by three PC members each, and then advocated by an Area Chair. Overall, 12 oral presentations (ca. 25% of all submissions) and 15 poster presentations were selected. Authors were given one month to revise their papers according to the reviews, and the final versions were briefly checked by the two Program Co-chairs. Both types of presentation have been give equal space in the present proceedings.

The 32 papers gathered in this volume cover a wide range of topics related to human-human communication modeling and processing, as well as to human-computer interaction, using several communication modalities. A significant number of papers focus on the analysis of non-verbal communication cues, such as the expression of emotions, laughter, face turning, or gestures, which demonstrates a growing interest for social signal processing. Yet, another large set of papers targets the analysis of communicative content, with a focus on the abstraction of information from meetings in the form of summaries, action items, or dialogue acts. Other topics presented at MLMI 2008 include audio-visual scene analysis, speech processing, interactive systems and applications.

A special session on user requirements and evaluation of multimodal meeting browsers/assistants was organized, with a separate submission track, resulting in the five papers gathered in the last part of these proceedings. The goal of the session was to put together the lessons learned from several large projects involving meeting technology – partly the same projects that launched the MLMI series. The session included short presentations of user requirements and evaluation studies, introduced by a related keynote talk, and followed by a plenary discussion.

MLMI 2008 featured four keynote talks, focusing on theory, applications, and evaluation. The organizers would like to express their gratitude to the invited speakers: Maja Pantic, from the Imperial College London and the University of Twente; Catherine Pelachaud, from the Montreuil University of Technology and INRIA Rocquencourt; Mark Sanderson, from the University of Sheffield; and Stephen Von Rump, CEO of HeadThere, Inc., San Francisco, CA.

The number of MLMI satellite events keeps growing every year. The following events were associated to MLMI 2008: the AMI Career Day, an opportunity for young scientists to talk to representatives of companies working on meeting technology and prepare the next steps of their careers; the above-mentioned special session on user requirements and evaluation of multimodal meeting browsers/assistants; a workshop on the evaluation of automatic speech recognition systems for Dutch; an interproject meeting on the evaluation of space-time audio processing; and a student poster session.

To conclude, we would like to warmly thank all the members of the Program Committee, the Area Chairs, and the people involved in the workshop organization, in particular David van Leeuwen (TNO). We are grateful to Hervé Bourlard (Idiap Research Institute) and Steve Renals (University of Edinburgh) for their constant support. MLMI 2008 acknowledges sponsoring from the AMIDA Integrated Project, which is funded by the European Commission under the Information Society Technologies priority of the sixth Framework Program, and from the IM2 National Center of Competence in Research, which is funded by the Swiss National Science Foundation.

June 2008   Andrei Popescu-Belis
                                                           Rainer Stiefelhagen

Organization

Organizing Committee

Andrei Popescu-Belis	Idiap Research Institute (Program Co-chair)
Rainer Stiefelhagen	University of Karlsruhe (Program Co-chair)
David van Leeuwen	TNO (Organization Chair)
Anton Nijholt	University of Twente (Special Sessions Chair)

Workshop Organization

Songfang Huang	University of Edinburgh (Proceedings)
Jonathan Kilgour	University of Edinburgh (Webmaster)
Marjolein Klootwijk	TNO (Secretary)
Suzanne Schrijvers-van der Klip	TNO (Secretary)
Josef Žižka	Brno University of Technology (Webmaster)

Program Committee

Jan Alexandersson	DFKI
Tilman Becker	DFKI
Samy Bengio	Google Inc.
Hervé Bourlard	Idiap Research Institute
Lukas Burget	Brno University of Technology
Nick Campbell	ATR
Jean Carletta	University of Edinburgh
Rolf Carlson	KTH
Jan "Honza" Černocký	Brno University of Technology
Trevor Darrell	MIT
John Dines	Idiap Research Institute
Gerald Friedland	ICSI
Sadaoki Furui	Tokyo Institute of Technology
John Garofolo	NIST
Daniel Gatica-Perez	Idiap Research Institute
Thomas Hain	University of Sheffield
Mary Harper	University of Maryland
James Henderson	University of Geneva
Hynek Hermansky	Idiap Research Institute
Simon King	University of Edinburgh
Michael Kipp	DFKI
Denis Lalanne	University of Fribourg
David van Leeuwen	TNO (Organization Chair)

Yang Liu	University of Texas at Dallas (Area Chair)
Stéphane Marchand-Maillet	University of Geneva
Jean-Claude Martin	LIMSI-CNRS
Helen Meng	Chinese University of Hong Kong
Luděk Müller	University of West Bohemia
Anton Nijholt	University of Twente (Area Chair)
Fabio Pianesi	FBK-IRST (Area Chair)
Andrei Popescu-Belis	Idiap Research Institute (Program Co-chair)
Wilfried Post	TNO
Gerasimos Potamianos	IBM T.J. Watson (Area Chair)
Steve Renals	University of Edinburgh
Gerhard Sagerer	University of Bielefeld (Area Chair)
Nicu Sebe	University of Amsterdam
Elizabeth Shriberg	SRI and ICSI
Pavel Smrž	Brno University of Technology
Rainer Stiefelhagen	University of Karlsruhe (Program Co-chair)
Jean-Philippe Thiran	EPFL
Matthew Turk	UCSB
Enrique Vidal	Universidad Politécnica de Valencia
Steve Whittaker	University of Sheffield
Jie Yang	CMU

Sponsoring Programs, Projects and Institutions

Programs:

- European Commission, through the Multimodal Interfaces objective of the Information Society Technologies (IST) priority of the sixth Framework Program.
- Swiss National Science Foundation, through the National Center of Competence in Research (NCCR) Program.

Projects:

- AMIDA, Augmented Multiparty Interaction with Distance Access, http://www.amiproject.org
- IM2, Interactive Multimodal Information Management, http://www.im2.ch

Institutions:

- TNO, Netherlands Organisation for Applied Scientific Research, http://www.tno.nl
- SIKS, Dutch Research School for Information and Knowledge Systems, http://www.siks.nl
- FIT BUT, Faculty of Information Technology, Brno University of Technology, http://www.fit.vutbr.cz

Table of Contents

III   Social Signal Processing

IV   Human-Human Spoken Dialogue Processing

V   HCI and Applications

VI   User Requirements and Evaluation of Meeting Browsers and Assistants

Visual Focus of Attention in Dynamic Meeting Scenarios

Michael Voit[1] and Rainer Stiefelhagen[2]

[1] Fraunhofer IITB, Karlsruhe
michael.voit@iitb.fraunhofer.de
[2] Interactive Systems Labs, Universität Karlsruhe (TH)
stiefel@ira.uka.de

Abstract. This paper presents our data collection and first evaluations on estimating visual focus of attention during dynamic meeting scenes. We included moving focus targets and unforeseen interruptions in each meeting, by guiding each meeting along a predefined script of events that three participating actors were instructed to follow. Further meeting attendees were not introduced to upcoming actions or the general purpose of the meeting, hence we were able to capture their natural focus changes within this predefined dynamic scenario with an extensive setup of both visual and acoustical sensors throughout our smart room. We present an adaptive approach to estimate visual focus of attention based on head orientation under these unforeseen conditions and show, that our system achieves an overall recognition rate of 59%, compared to 9% less when choosing the best matching focus target directly from the observed head orientation angles.

1 Introduction

Smart rooms, or smart spaces, proclaim proactive computer services in unobtrusive sensor environments. Knowing at all times, who enters the room, who interacts with whom and where all people reside and look at, allows interfaces to adapt for personal needs and input modalities to relate to context and semantics. Research in this area covers both the fundamental fields of (multiview) visual and acoustical perception, such as face identification [1], gaze recognition [2,3,4], speech detection [5] and speaker localization [6] or audio-visual multi-person tracking and identification [7,8], as well as the combination of all modalities in order to allow higher-level observations and summarizations, as for example in transcribing meetings [9] or analyzing floor control and interaction patterns [9]. One particular cue for modeling (inter-)actions between a group of people or understanding actions and occupations of observed meeting participants and group members, is to understand their visual focus and deduce the respective attentional target they focus on. By means of recognizing objects, colleagues are working on together, or the recognition of a group's joint attention towards a specific speaker during an observed lecture, smart room systems obtain one further cue to modeling a scene's context and individual behavior.

A. Popescu-Belis and R. Stiefelhagen (Eds.): MLMI 2008, LNCS 5237, pp. 1–13, 2008.

To follow eye-gaze and obtain knowledge about one's viewing direction, head orientation usually acts as an approximation to allow non-intrusive sensor setups as applied in our described environment. Due to individual head turning styles, gaze and head orientation tend to differ and a direct interpretation from observed head rotations to a discrete set of focus targets is not always possible as studies and evaluations show [10,11,12]. Measured head rotations are therefore mostly used to describe individually shifted means around predefined focus targets, which, recently in combination with multimodal cues such as presentational slide changes or speech activity [13] both increase recognition rate and allow analysis of group activities or role models during meetings, but still limit the applicational area to a predefined set of non-moving focus targets around a table.

In [14], we extended our system to estimate visual focus of attention from monocular views during recorded meetings [12] to using multi-view head orientation in order to allow for a sensorless work area on the meeting table. Applying the motivation for unrestricted behavior and dynamic scenes to the recorded settings and peoples' focus, we now collected a new dataset, in which a number of scripted events - such as people entering and leaving the room, or phones ringing in the room - were introduced, in order to provoke attention shifts of the meeting participants from their ongoing work. Hence, all meetings contain a varying set of participants and different seating positions as well as the introduction of new objects and moving targets.

2   Dataset

The dataset we recorded consists of 10 meeting videos in total. Each video is approximately 10 min. long and starts with each participant entering the room and finally ends with all persons leaving the room again. For introducing dynamic events and behavior and ensuring the same over all videos, each video consists of three acting participants, that followed a predefined script and a varying number (one or two) of unaware persons, whose attention was to be distracted by different kinds of interruptions, unforeseen persons walking through the room in different trajectories or newly introduced objects.

2.1   Sensor Setup

The sensor setup we recorded with, consisted of 4 fixed cameras in the upper corners of the room, each recording with a resolution of 640 × 480 pixels and 15 frames per second. The purpose of these cameras is to obtain a coarse view of the whole room, for allowing people to move and behave as naturally as possible and walk around and interact with each other without being limited by a predefined setup and a restricted sensor range. The camera array was extended with a panoramic view from a fisheye lens camera that was installed on the ceiling (same specifications). For a complete recording of the scenery and its context, audio was recorded by means of four T-shaped microphone arrays, each installed on every wall of the room (northern, western, southern and eastern side), allowing

Fig. 1. Example scene of one meeting video. Shown are two out of four camera views from the room's upper corners and the panoramic view, captured from the ceiling. In this scene, interrupting person P04 passes the meeting-table towards the entrance door and walks in between the projection screen and person P00 sitting in front of it, working on his notebook.

for the inclusion of audio source localization, and one table-top microphone for speech recognition and acoustical context modelling.

2.2 Dynamic Meetings

We defined a predefined set of events in a script, that were initiated and followed by all actors in each recorded meeting. The remaining participants were unaware of what was to happen during the recordings, hence, their observed reaction was spontaneous and unplanned. Each meeting consisted of three acting participants and one or two participants that were not aware of the scripted events and the exact purpose of the data collection. To obtain groundtruth information about head orientation and position, one of the unaware persons was wearing a magnetic motion sensor (Flock of Birds, Ascension Technologies) on top of his or her head, calibrated along the room's (hence global) coordinate system. All persons were tagged with respect to their seating position in counter-clockwise order around the meeting table and/or acting role during the meeting: The person sitting at the table's northern edge was named P00, the person to the west P01, the person at the southern edge, always wearing the magnetic sensor was named P02 and the person at the eastern edge P03. The fourth person, called P04 was chosen to interrupt the meeting from time to time, hence entering and leaving the room multiple times and not being bound to one particular seat around the table. The seating positions and roles of all acting persons were changed and rotated during the recordings to prevent repetitive patterns.

In general, the used script followed the particulars given below:

- Person P02 is to be seated beforehand, calibrated along the room's coordinate system. Persons P00, P01 and P03 enter the room successively, meet and greet at the table before sitting down.
- All participants start a discussion about 'Computer Vision' in general and a possible reason for the current meeting.
- The interrupting person P04 enters the room, recognizes the meeting and spontaneously grabs a nearby chair to join it. One of the yet seated participants needs to make room for the additional member, hence his or her

seating position changes - a new person is therefore added around the table, the seating positions disturbed temporarily.

– After a small talk, person P04 stands up, moves his or her chair and leaves the room on either of two possible ways around the table.
– One acting member (P00, P01 or P03) stands up, walks towards the projection screen and starts to give a presentation. Thereby, the presenter gesticulates in front of the screen, changing position in front of it and explains the bullet points listed on the presented slide. All remaining participants were instructed to make notes on the notebooks in front of them on the table and interrupt the presentation with questions and own discussion.
– Person P04 enters the room again, walks towards 'Desktop-Computer 2', sits down and starts working. P04 chooses either way of walking through the room and thus interrupts the presentation for a short amount of time.
– The presenter walks to a nearby placed camera, grabs it, walks back to being in front of the screen and meeting table and introduces the camera before placing it on top of the table for everyone to examine and holding it. The presentation continues.
– The presenter sits down, back onto his or her previous seat. The meeting continues.
– Person P04 starts to play a loud, interrupting sound, initiated from his or her current location in front of 'Desktop-Computer 2'. P04 suddenly stands up, apologizes to the meeting group and rushes to turn the loudspeakers off. P04 then rapidly leaves the room. The meeting continues.
– A cellphone, previously placed inside a cupboard, suddenly starts to ring. Person P04 enters the room, interrupts the meeting by asking if anybody has seen his or her cellphone and follows the ringing sound towards the cupboard. He or she grabs the cellphone, shows it to the meeting participants, turns it off and leaves the room with it. The meeting continues.
– The printer starts to output papers. Person P04 enters the room again, walks to the printer and while shaking and pretending to repair it, P04 complains loudly about a pretended malfunction. P04 grabs papers and leaves the room. The meeting continues.
– All meeting participants, except P02 wearing the sensor, stand up, shake hands and leave the room.

2.3   Annotated Focus Targets

Considering abovely scripted events, a minimum focus target space can be set up with the following:

– Persons P00, P01, P02, P03 and P04 (as available and participating)
– Entrance to the room
– Meeting Table (further, each individual's notebook on top of the table)
– Projection Screen (for during the presentation)
– Camera (that is being introduced during the presenter's talk)

Fig. 2. Camera 1's view of a recorded meeting scene during a short presentation, given by person P00. Person P02, sitting opposite to the presenter, is wearing the magnetic motion sensor to capture her true head orientation, depicted by the red (x), green (y) and blue (z) coordinate axes. All *axis aligned bounding boxes* of focus targets we annotated, visible from this view, are highlighted in white.

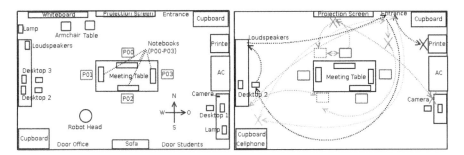

Fig. 3. Left: Overview of annotated focus targets throughout the meeting room. Right: Observed trajectories of all meeting participants. Rather than only gathering meetings with fixed seating positions, participants were advised to walk throughout the entire room, to distract the visual focus of the remaining meeting members.

- Loudspeakers (interrupting the meeting by outputting a disruptive sound)
- Cupboard enclosing the later-on interrupting cellphone
- Printer

For completing the list of potential targets, such as surrounding tables, chairs, working places or cupboards, the room's interieur was completely modeled in 3D: The position and bounding box of each object was measured and head bounding boxes of all meeting participants were annotated for every camera view and every frame recorded. The head bounding boxes were used to triangulate 3D positions of the corresponding heads' centroids in room coordinates and provide basis for future estimation of head orientation for all participants. In addition, the magnetic motion sensor provided groundtruth information about the head orientation for person P02 with approx. 30Hz. Person P02 was always made sure to be one of the unaware meeting participants. All in all, a total of 36 targets were made available for the annotation process, classifying each meeting participant's visual focus. As can be seen in Fig. 3, air conditioning, all chairs and sofas, desktop PCs and cupboards were included as potential targets, too. Even a small robot head we used for different experiments was considered as a potential target due to its position near the meeting table. Fig. 4 depicts a distribution of all annotated objects and persons for how often they were focused throughout the entire dataset by either meeting participant and thus provides a complete overview of all included focus targets. An example of a meeting, with some of the targets being highlighted, can be seen in Fig. 2.

3   Estimating Visual Focus of Attention

3.1   Target Modeling

Due to targets moving, we decided to describe each object and person by its *axis aligned bounding box* in 3D space (see Fig. 2). In order for targets to be able to be focused, their box must overlap or intersect with the respective person's viewing frustum. This viewing cone was defined to open up 60° horizontally and 50° vertically. A potential target F_i thus lies within the viewing frustum, if its axis aligned bounding box contained at least one point $P_i = (x, y, z)$ on its shell within that cone. For gaining that *representational point P_i*, we computed the nearest point (by its euclidean distance) on the box, relative to the head orientation vector. P_i either resembles a true intersection or a point on the box' edges. P_i is verified to reside within the viewing cone - targets outside the viewing frustum are ignored, their likelihood to be focused was set to 0.

3.2   Baseline: Choosing the Nearest Target

A comparative baseline is established by classifying for target F_i, who seems to be nearest to the observed head orientation. Hence, we distinguished targets by their euclidean distance, computed with their respective representative points P_i and the head pose vector.

3.3   An Adaptive Focus Model

We adopted the described visual focus model presented in [15], which summarizes a linear correlation between the corresponding gaze angle α_G towards the target and the observable head turning angle α_H when focusing on it:

$$\alpha_H = k_\alpha \cdot \alpha_G \qquad (1)$$

We analyzed this relation for dynamic and moving persons and objects by computing α_H based on the annotations we made upon our dataset and all

Targets / Persons	P00	P01	P02	P03	P04	Mean
P00	0.06	20.66	24.39	18.22	8.05	15.82
P01	19.54	0.00	14.32	26.38	8.87	13.91
P02	18.79	12.08	0.07	11.59	5.72	9.62
P03	16.47	20.32	13.55	0.00	6.44	12.09
P04	9.37	10.55	6.52	7.72	0.00	7.63
Notebook P00	8.07	1.45	0.29	0.52	0.11	2.09
Notebook P01	0.36	6.37	0.41	0.52	0.18	1.84
Notebook P02	0.14	0.22	8.75	0.67	0.00	2.40
Notebook P03	0.35	0.56	0.82	10.61	0.01	2.70
Notebook P04	0.00	0.00	0.00	0.02	0.09	0.01
Printer	1.48	0.24	0.31	0.09	8.38	1.30
Ceiling	0.23	0.13	0.00	0.08	0.00	0.09
Whiteboard	0.02	0.01	0.10	0.04	0.24	0.06
Robot Head	0.25	0.10	0.11	0.08	0.16	0.13
Desktop 3	0.37	0.03	0.45	0.16	1.88	0.42
Desktop 2	3.52	0.11	0.34	0.19	34.79	4.40
Desktop 1	0.24	0.10	0.11	0.07	0.03	0.12
Meeting-Table	2.80	3.70	2.54	2.01	2.89	2.79
Entrance	0.76	1.11	1.15	0.98	3.89	1.31
Cupboard (North)	0.20	0.08	0.04	0.02	0.21	0.09
Cellphone	0.36	0.52	0.11	0.13	1.87	0.44
Floor	2.79	1.53	0.19	0.99	5.63	1.74
Door Students	0.17	0.02	0.00	0.16	0.20	0.09
Sofa	0.16	0.25	0.00	0.14	0.45	0.17
Lamp (South-East)	0.00	0.01	0.03	0.00	0.00	0.01
Armchair	0.00	0.03	0.01	0.00	0.13	0.02
Chair P04	1.14	0.57	0.04	0.45	1.36	0.60
Lamp (North-West)	0.05	0.00	0.00	0.06	0.00	0.02
Camera	4.10	6.17	7.73	5.04	0.00	5.29
Cupboard (South)	0.91	0.49	0.21	0.31	3.16	0.74
Door Office	0.22	0.15	0.00	0.03	0.03	0.09
Sensor Stool	0.02	0.18	0.00	0.07	0.34	0.10
Projection Screen	6.36	11.83	17.20	12.30	2.52	11.27
Loudspeakers	0.46	0.26	0.18	0.32	1.80	0.45
Small Table	0.09	0.08	0.03	0.00	0.49	0.09
Air Conditioning	0.14	0.06	0.02	0.01	0.05	0.05
Sum	100.00	100.00	100.00	100.00	100.00	100.00

Fig. 4. Distribution of visually focused targets. Each column depicts the focus distribution for the person sitting at the respective position (P00, P01, P02, P03, P04). Each row describes one single focus target.

targets representational points P_i described in 3.2. A measured mapping coefficient k_α could thus be obtained with

$$k_\alpha = \frac{\alpha_H}{\alpha_G} \tag{2}$$

As depicted in Fig. 6 and intuitively assumed, k_α's value does not stay fixed throughout the observations, but rather changes, depending on the dynamics in the observed scene. Its variance can be described as rather high, changing from positive to negative values, adapting to focus changes that happen over time. The presented camera view in Fig. 6 shows the recorded scene during the highlighted time range in k_α's plot. Its values were computed for person P02 (left person in the images), who is positioned at the table's southern edge, wearing the magnetic motion sensor on her head and being one of the unaware meeting participants. The scene shows all participants meeting at the table, greeting each other. P02's focus changes from Person P03 (standing to the right at the table's western edge, with an approximate horizontal gaze angle of $+60°$) to person P00 (standing right in front of her to the north, at approximately $-10°$ horizontally). While looking at P03, head orientation was measured to intersect with the target, hence the mapping factor of 1.0. During focus change to P00, head pose slowly adapted to the observable gaze change, but stopped at approximately $+3°$: the mapping coefficient k_α changed to a value of -3 to shift the head vector onto the target's real position at $-10°$. Fig. 5 shows an exemplary depiction of this process: Depicted are three targets to focus on. In the top row of the image, focus changes quickly between targets 2 and 3. Due to the rapid interaction, head orientation slows down right between the two persons and eye gaze is used to overcome the difference to focus on the particular target. A fixed mapping coefficient would map target 2's position towards target 3 and target 3's position even further away. If only this kind of interaction is given, a static model interprets the shifted position of target 2 successively and classifies correctly for person 2, even though its position seems rather shifted. The bottom row shows a successive focus change between targets 1 and 2. Here, using the same fixed mapping coefficient would map target 2's position towards target 3 again (but not as far as in the top row) and target 1's position towards target 2. A static model trained with these head observations, would assume target 2's gaze angle to lie nearer in front than the static model trained with observations from the top image. Further, the fixed mapping coefficient clearly shows, that head orientation, when focusing on target 1, is clearly mapping into the wrong direction. It needs to adapt to a lower value. The example shows, how the region of interaction and interest influences the necessary transformation value and should be due to adapt.

To better model the dynamics in mapping, we defined a discrete set of possible coefficients (k_α, k_β) for mapping horizontal and vertical head orientation α_h and β_H, and reweighed them by means of the most likely focus target F_i's a-posteriori probability, given the corresponding mapping:

$$\pi_{(k_\alpha, k_\beta),t} = \gamma \cdot \pi_{(k_\alpha, k_\beta),t-1} + (1 - \gamma) \cdot \arg\max_{F_i} p(F_i | \Phi_{k_\alpha, k_\beta}) \qquad (3)$$

The mapping coefficient pair (k_α, k_β) with highest weight is chosen for mapping head pose and finally classifying for the target, that shows maximum a-posteriori probability.

Since most coefficients might intersect with a target, hence return a high likelihood for the given transformation, each target includes an a-priori factor for stating the probability of actually focusing it or changing focus towards it.

In general, the a-posteriori likelihood is defined by

$$p(F_i | \Phi_{k_\alpha, k_\beta}) = \frac{p(\Phi_{k_\alpha, k_\beta} | F_i) \cdot P(F_i)}{p(\Phi_{k_\alpha, k_\beta})} \qquad (4)$$

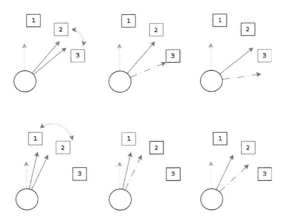

Fig. 5. Top row: Focus changes back and forth between target 2 and target 3 (high-lighted red): when focusing target 2 (middle image), a fixed mapping coefficient $0 < k_\alpha < 1$ maps head orientation (solid arrow) onto target 3 (dashed arrow). The gaze angle to target 3's is put even further away than its real position (right image). Bottom row: successively happening focus change between target 1 and target 2: while in the top row, when focusing target 2, head pose tends to cluster towards target 3, here, its corresponding head orientation can be observed between target 1 and 2. Furthermore, target 1's mapped gaze position is shifted towards the second target, instead of backwards to its real origin.

with $\Phi_{k_\alpha, k_\beta} = (\frac{\alpha_H}{k_\alpha}, \frac{\beta_H}{k_\beta})$ being the adapted head orientation with the horizontal rotation α_H, transformed with the mapping factor k_α and β_H being the vertical head rotation transformed with k_β.

The a-posteriori probability of a target F_i is composed of different factors that describe possible models of the scene's context. By now, we simply include the likelihood of looking at this target in the last n frames and secondly a change of pose to the target in the current frame T:

$$P(F_i) = \frac{1}{n} \sum_{t=T-n}^{T-1} (p_t(F_i|(\Phi_t))) \cdot \varphi(\frac{\partial(\angle(\Phi, F_i)))}{\partial t}) \qquad (5)$$

The angular difference $\angle(\Phi, F_i)$ describes the distance between the real head orientation and target F_i's representational point P_i. If the head is rotated towards a target F_i, the angular difference decreases, hence its derivation $\frac{\partial(\angle(\Phi, F_i))}{\partial t}$ over time shows peaks of negative values and implies a more likely focus change towards that particular target.

3.4 Experimental Evaluation

We reduced the target space to meeting participants, meeting table and projection screen only. This included 88% of all focused objects as annotated in Table 4 and reduces complexity both for these first evaluations and annotations,

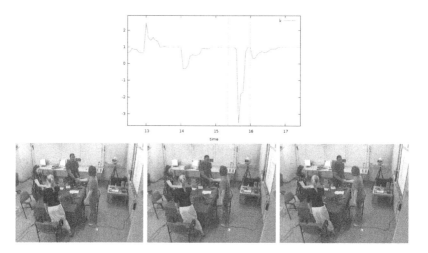

Fig. 6. Respective plot of person P02's mapping coefficient k_α and the corresponding scene in the meeting to the highlighted time window in the plot: Person P02 is standing to the left in the images. Her mapping coefficient k to project the horizontal head orientation to its respective gaze-angle does not stay fixed over time (as visible in the plot). Values of 1 depict, that head orientation points directly to the target and intersected its axis aligned bounding box. The strong variance in the highlighted time window depicts a focus change to person P00 standing in front of her and shows that head orientation not always points behind gaze angles, but depending on the direction focus changes are happening from, might also point ahead of the targets' true positions. Thus, k needs be adapt to a much lower value to map head pose to a lower gaze angle.

Table 1. Recognition rates on the described dataset for person P02. Four different approaches are compared (three direct mappings with a fixed mapping coefficient k_α respectively and our adaptive approach with a variable k_α). The constant mapping factor $k_\alpha = 0.72$ was computed as being the mean mapping coefficient when mapping the observed head orientation to the annotated targets. Head orientation was measured with a magnetic motion sensor.

Mapping	Meeting 1	Meeting 2	Meeting 3	Meeting 4	Mean
Direct Mapping ($k_\alpha = 1$)	54%	49%	**57%**	51%	53.5%
Direct Mapping ($k_\alpha = 0.5$)	53%	49%	43%	55%	49.5%
Direct Mapping ($k_\alpha = 0.72$)	53%	52%	48%	51%	50%
Adaptive Mapping ($\gamma = 0.95$)	**58%**	**59%**	55%	**61%**	**59%**

which are still happening and take a lot of time to define all object and person positions. At the current time writing this paper, all of the videos are annotated for all persons' corresponding visual focus, but only four videos provide the positions and bounding boxes of above mentioned targets. Due to missing upper body annotations for all remaining participants, our evaluations only included estimating focus for person P02, wearing the magnetic motion sensor, whose body orientation was always made sure to show towards the projection screen.

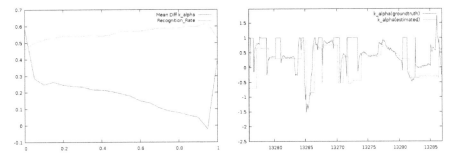

Fig. 7. Left image: Recognition Rate (upper green plot) and mean difference of estimated k_α to groundtruth k_α (lower red plot), with respect to increasing adaption factor γ. A value of $\gamma = 1.0$ describes that the scores π_{k_α} are not adapted at all. In this case, the constant mapping coefficient $k_\alpha = 0.72$ was used, which showed to be the measured mean mapping factor over all videos for person P02. Right image: Groundtruth (red plot) versus estimated (green plot) mapping values k_α in a 30sec. long scene.

The low numbers clearly show the difficulty of the task, especially of this particular setting we chose for meetings: Person P00's seat is right in front of the projection screen. Reliantly distinguishing between the two targets is only possible, if either of them is ignored for any reason (possibly due to person P00 sitting a lot nearer and thus overlapping too much of the viewing frustum towards the screen) or context is further taken into account for understanding whether the interest relies on a person sitting in front of the screen or the screen directly behind.

Clearly visible from the results however is, that an adaptive mapping of head pose to the respective focus target increases the recognition rate in almost every case. The only exception shows to be video 3, where a direct interpretation of head pose seems to perform slightly better than a variable (or even fixed with different values) mapping. This might be due to the fact, that this person mostly used its eye gaze to focus on targets - head orientation stayed fixed for most of the time. During the video, our system kept the mapping coefficient relatively constant due to the missing head movements. Especially, rapid focus changes between two targets were more or less completely ignored by our system: Where in the remaining videos slightly head rotations towards the respective targets were observable, here, only gaze was used to switch back and forth - hence, our approach only recognized one target focused during this time; due to the mapped head orientation often the wrong one during these interactions. Further, especially moving targets, for example person P04 passing by in between the meeting table and the projection screen as depicted in Fig. 1, only distracted person P02's visual focus by quick eye movements, instead of letting head orientation follow that respective trajectory. The focus did not change for more than fractions of frames, it was kept on the previous target all the time. However, the a-priori likelihood described in equation 5 includes the derivation of the difference between head pose and a target's gaze angle. This derivation even shows peaks, if head orientation stays fixed and the target passes by, since then, the angular distance decreases down to the point where head pose and the trajectory intersect. This factor seems to provide a possible basis for recognizing focus changes, but does not allow to distinguish between *real* focus changes and moving objects or persons only. In the example of person P02 during meeting video 3, the interrupting person shows high likelihoods for being focused at when walking only through the room, even though head pose stayed fixed. The focus change here, is enforced to be recognized, even though in this case it does not happen at all.

Hence, general questions that are to be answered in future work (especially as soon as the complete dataset annotation process is finished) are, how head orientation correlates to moving targets and if a fitting user model for this perception can be found during meetings (do people tend to follow behind the target's trajectory or do they rather estimate the trajectory in advance and adapt to movement changes?) as well as how several focus targets merge into one single group of interest for particular meeting members or objects instead of distinguishing between every single item. Future work also includes the fast estimation of upper body orientation to easily recognize every meeting member's resting position and initial head orientation when looking straight forward. This cue, also should show strong correlation to group behavior and allow focus target abstractions by separating persons into groups, analyzing group roles and including multi-person focus of attention and region of interests with respect to individual groups and their interactions.

4   Conclusion

In this paper we presented our work on enhancing the estimation of visual focus of attention in group meetings: We collected a new dataset to include dynamic scenes and moving persons and objects. The dataset contains recordings of meetings from the beginning where all participants enter the room and follows a predefined script of events that three acting meeting members in the recordings were to follow and suprise further attending and unaware participants with. The sensor setup both contains visual recordings from wideangle cameras in the room's upper corners and a panoramic camera on the ceiling as well as audio recordings from T-shaped microphone arrays and one table-top microphone on top of the meeting table. All recordings were annotated for the participants' head bounding boxes, everybodies' visual focus of attention and the complete room's interieur in 3D by means of bounding boxes of each object and allowed target that was annotated. Secondly, we described and evaluated our first system to estimate visual focus of attention for one person on moving targets and achieved an overall mean recognition rate of 59%. We compared our approach to interpreting head orientation as the actual gaze direction and mapping its vector onto the first-best matching, nearest corresponding focus target and our enhancements showed an overall increase in recognition rate by almost 9%. Current and ongoing work and research include the analysis of the targets' movements, adding a correlation model to moving focus targets and extending the target space to all annotated objects in the room. Further, in order to adopt our approach on every meeting participant, independent of his or her movement, research on estimating upper body orientation is due to be done and combined with estimating head orientation and a fully automate multi-person tracking and identification.

References

1. Ekenel, H., Fischer, M., Stiefelhagen, R.: Face recognition in smart rooms. In: Popescu-Belis, A., Renals, S., Bourlard, H. (eds.) MLMI 2007. LNCS, vol. 4892, Springer, Heidelberg (2008)
2. Voit, M., Nickel, K., Stiefelhagen, R.: Head pose estimation in single- and multi-view environments - Results on the CLEAR 2007 benchmarks. In: Stiefelhagen, R., Bowers, R., Fiscus, J.G. (eds.) CLEAR 2007 and RT 2007. LNCS, vol. 4625. Springer, Heidelberg (2007)
3. Head orientation estimation using particle filtering in multiview scenarios. In: Stiefelhagen, R., Bowers, R., Fiscus, J.G. (eds.) CLEAR 2007 and RT 2007. LNCS, vol. 4625. Springer, Heidelberg (2007)
4. Lanz, O., Brunelli, R.: Joint bayesian tracking of head location and pose from low-resolution video. In: Stiefelhagen, R., Bowers, R., Fiscus, J.G. (eds.) CLEAR 2007 and RT 2007. LNCS, vol. 4625. Springer, Heidelberg (2007)
5. Maganti, H.K., Motlicek, P., Gatica-Perez, D.: Unsupervised speech/non-speech detection for automatic speech recognition in meeting rooms. In: Proceedings of IEEE International Conference on Acoustics, Speech, and Signal Processing (ICASSP) (2007)
6. Maganti, H.K., Gatica-Perez, D.: Speaker localization for microphone-array-based asr: the effects of accuracy on overlapping speech. In: Proceedings of IEEE International Conference on Multimodal Interfaces (ICMI) (2006)
7. Bernardin, K., Stiefelhagen, R.: Audio-visual multi-person tracking and identification for smart environments. In: Proceedings of ACM Multimedia (2007)
8. Lanz, O., P.C., Brunelli, R.: An appearance-based particle filter for visual tracking in smart rooms. In: Stiefelhagen, R., Bowers, R., Fiscus, J.G. (eds.) CLEAR 2007 and RT 2007. LNCS, vol. 4625. Springer, Heidelberg (2007)
9. Chen, L., Harper, M., Franklin, A., Rose, R.T., Kimbara, I.: A multimodal analysis of floor control in meetings. In: Renals, S., Bengio, S., Fiscus, J.G. (eds.) MLMI 2006. LNCS, vol. 4299. Springer, Heidelberg (2006)
10. Freedman, E.G., Sparks, D.L.: Eye-head coordination during head-unrestrained gaze shifts in rhesus monkeys. Journal of Neurophysiology 77, 2328 (1997)
11. Wang, X., Jin, J.: A quantitative analysis for decomposing visual signal of the gaze displacement. In: Proceedings of the Pan-Sydney area workshop on Visual information processing, p. 153 (2001)
12. Stiefelhagen, R.: Tracking focus of attention in meetings. In: Proceedings of IEEE International Conference on Multimodal Interfaces (ICMI), p. 273 (2002)
13. Ba, S., Odobez, J.: Multi-party focus of attention recognition in meetings from head pose and multimodal contextual cues. In: International Conference on on Acoustics, Speech, and Signal Processing (ICASSP) (2008)
14. Voit, M., Stiefelhagen, R.: Tracking head pose and focus of attention with multiple far-field cameras. In: International Conference on Multimodal Interfaces (ICMI) (2006)
15. Ba, S., Odobez, J.: A cognitive and unsupervised map adaptation approach to the recognition of focus of attention from head pose. In: Proceedings of International Conference on Multimedia and Expo (ICME) (2007)

Fast and Robust Face Tracking for Analyzing Multiparty Face-to-Face Meetings

Kazuhiro Otsuka and Junji Yamato

NTT Communication Science Labs.,
3-1, Morinosato-Wakamiya, Atsugi-shi, 243-0198, Japan
{otsuka,yamato}@eye.brl.ntt.co.jp

Abstract. This paper presents a novel face tracker and verifies its effectiveness for analyzing group meetings. In meeting scene analysis, face direction is an important clue for assessing the visual attention of meeting participants. The face tracker, called STCTracker (Sparse Template Condensation Tracker), estimates face position and pose by matching face templates in the framework of a particle filter. STCTracker is robust against large head rotation, up to ± 60 degrees in the horizontal direction, with relatively small mean deviation error. Also, it can track multiple faces simultaneously in real-time by utilizing a modern GPU (Graphics Processing Unit), e.g. 6 faces at about 28 frames/second on a single PC. Also, it can automatically build 3-D face templates upon initialization of the tracker. This paper evaluates the tracking errors and verifies the effectiveness of STCTracker for meeting scene analysis, in terms of conversation structures, gaze directions, and the structure of cross-modal interactions involving head gestures and utterances. Experiments confirm that STCTracker can basically match the performance of from the user-unfriendly magnetic-sensor-based motion capture system.

Keywords: Meeting analysis, face tracking, multiparty conversation, dynamic Bayesian network, multimodal interaction, GPGPU, CUDA.

1 Introduction

Face-to-face conversation is the most basic forms of communication in our life and is used for conveying/sharing information, understanding others' intention/emotion, and making decisions. To enhance our communication capability, the automatic analysis of conversation scenes is a basic technical requisite for effective teleconferencing, meeting archival/summarization, and to realize communication via social agents/robots. In the face-to-face setting, people exchange not only verbal messages but also nonverbal messages. The nonverbal messages are expressed by nonverbal behaviors in multimodal channels such as eye gaze, facial expressions, head motion, hand gesture, body posture and prosody [1]. Among the nonverbal messages/behaviors, eye gaze is especially important because it has various roles such as monitoring others, expressing one's attitude/interest, and regulating conversation flow [2]. However, gaze direction during natural

A. Popescu-Belis and R. Stiefelhagen (Eds.): MLMI 2008, LNCS 5237, pp. 14–25, 2008.
© Springer-Verlag Berlin Heidelberg 2008

conversation is difficult to measure directly. Face direction is often used as an alternative to gaze, because it is relatively easy to measure. Also face direction is not just an alternative; by itself it is a useful indicator of people's attention to others during meetings. In addition, the temporal changes in face direction indicate head gestures such as nodding. Therefore, face direction is an important cue for analyzing meetings.

For measuring face direction, visual face/head tracking has been the gold standard because it is not intrusive, unlike contact-type motion sensors. So far, several research groups have been trying to develop face tracking systems to capture human communicative behaviors. As a pioneering work, Stiefelhagen et al. developed a head pose detector based on a neural network [3]. Its advantage is that it can work with small faces captured by omni-directional cameras. Recently, his group extended the scope of their neural-network-based head pose detector to cover multi-view images captured by multiple cameras in their smart room, to widen the range of human positions detectable, and head pose in the room [4]. Unfortunately, due to its use of a neural network, its performance heavily relies on the training process, which requires large training images of various head poses of different people. Luis et al. proposed a stereo-based face tracking system for human-robot interaction [5]. Their tracker employed the gradient search strategy based on both image intensity and depth from stereo cameras. Moreover, the Bayesian filter framework has been exploited to track head location and pose in images from a single camera [6] and from multiple cameras [7]. The advantage of their trackers [6][7] is that it can cover a wide range in head pose. However, it can not provide precise head pose angles, because they quantize head pose into a few discrete states.

Although many face/head trackers have been developed so far, no really practical and comprehensive system suitable for automatic meeting analysis has been realized. This is because meeting scene analysis entails many difficulties such as large head rotation, occlusions, drastic changes in facial expressions, opening/closing mouth, and person independency problem. For example, meeting participants often turn their head to look at person sitting on their right/left during a meeting. This kind of head rotation is often large enough that many existing trackers are unable to follow it. Moreover, the tracker must be precise/accurate enough to differentiate which of several people sitting close together is the intended gaze target. Furthermore, the tracker needs to handle multiple faces simultaneously, unlike personal man-machine interfaces; the demands placed on computational resources also hamper realtime meeting analysis.

To tackle these problems, the authors have been developing a new face tracker called STCTracker (Sparse Template Condensation Tracker) [8][9]. The purpose of this paper is to verify its effectiveness for meeting analysis, a target set by the authors for estimating conversation structures ("who is talking to whom"), gaze pattern ("who is looking at whom"), and interaction structures ("who responds to whom"); a large part of the analysis has been based on head pose measurements from magnetic sensors[10][11]. This paper targets situations in which each meeting participant is captured by a separate monocular camera. STCTracker is robust against large head rotation and can track multiple faces simultaneously in real-time. The key to its robustness is its combination of robust template matching and multiple hypothesis generation/testing in the particle filter framework. Its speed is achieved by utilizing the power of modern GPUs (Graphics Processing Units); the parallel architecture of recent GPUs perfectly matches the parallelism available in particle filtering. In addition, it can automatically build 3-D face templates when tracking starts. Experiments confirm that STCTracker can basically match the face direction measurement performance of magnetic-based sensors.

This paper is organized as follows. Section 2 presents our face tracker and evaluates its performance. Section 3 verifies the effectiveness of the tracker in terms of conversation scene analysis. Section 4 presents our conclusion and discussions.

2   Fast and Robust Face Tracker: STCTracker

For measuring face directions, we introduce the Sparse-Template Condensation tracker, we named it STCTracker. This tracker was originally proposed by Matsubara and Shakunaga [12] and we first applied it to conversation scene analysis [13]. Recently, the authors enhanced it into a more robust, accurate, and faster tracker for following multiple faces [8][9]. This section first overviews STCTracker, and then describes two key improvements: the face model and accelerated tracking. Finally, a performance evaluation is presented.

2.1   Overview of STCTracker

The basic idea of STCTracker is combining template matching with particle filtering. Figure 1 shows the framework of STCTracker. In contrast to traditional template matching, which assesses all pixels in a rectangular region, sparse template matching focuses on a sparse set of feature points within a template region, called the sparse template (Fig. 2(b)). The state of a template, which represents the position and pose of the face, is defined as a 7 dimensional vector consisting of 2-DOF translation on the image plane, 3-DOF rotation, scale (we assume weak-perspective projection), and an illumination coefficient. The particle filter, also known as the Condensation algorithm, is used to sequentially estimate the posterior density of the template state, which is represented as a particle set.

As illustrated in Figure 1, the STCTracker consists of initialization, update, diffusion, and display. First, the initialization stage detects faces in images, generates templates, and initializes the particles. The update stage calculates particle weight based on the likelihood of observation, which is defined using matching error between input images and the template whose state is assigned by each particle; higher weight is given to particles with smaller matching error. More specifically, the likelihood value is defined as the inverse of the matching error. The matching error is a function of the summation of difference in image intensity values between each feature point in the face template and the corresponding pixel of the input image. Here, a robust function is used in the calculation of matching error to alleviate adverse effect from outlier points caused by occlusions. The resulting particle distribution represents the posterior distribution of

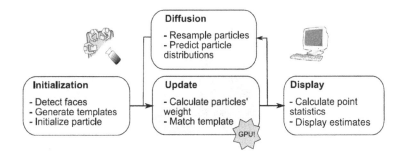

Fig. 1. Framework of STCTracker

template states. The diffusion stage resamples particles and predicts the particle distribution at the next time step. The update stage and diffusion stage are alternately repeated for each image frame. The display stage calculates point statistics from the posterior particle distribution output by the update stage.

STCTracker has the advantages of speed owing to the sparseness of the feature points and robustness owing to robust template matching combined with multiple-hypothesis generation/testing by the particle filter framework. Although the face model (template) is rigid, it can accept a certain amount of facial deformation caused events such by utterances and expression changes.

2.2   3-D Face Template and Automatic Initialization

The original STCTracker employed a flat plane as the shape model, as a rough approximation of the human face surface [12,13]. Due to the shape differences between the flat plane and the human face, tracking was essentially unstable and inaccurate estimates were output. In addition, the original STCTracker needed manual initialization, i.e. detection of target face and manual setting of the initial position and pose of the target before tracking.

Authors' new STCTracker solves these two problems simultaneous by introducing the 3D face model and automatic initialization stage, as illustrated in Figure 2. First, a new face is detected by using a face detector (Step 1); we employ the Viola & Jones boosting algorithm [14]. Step 1 is repeated until frontal face(s) are found. The minimum face size applicable for tracking is about 50×50 pixels. There is no limit on maximum face size. Note that face size does not affect the speed of tracking due to the sparseness of the face template. Next, the Active Appearance Model (AAM) [15] is used to locate facial parts and contours from the facial subimages detected in step 1 (Step 2). AAM represents the combination of eigen face textures and eigen face shapes, both of which were built from a set of training samples with hand-marked facial landmarks (Fig. 2(a)). Next, in step 3, a set of feature points (Fig. 2(b)) is extracted from each facial region surrounded by a facial contour determined by AAM fitting. The feature points are located at the local minimum/maximum of image intensities and straddle the zero-cross boundaries of images. Usually, the number of

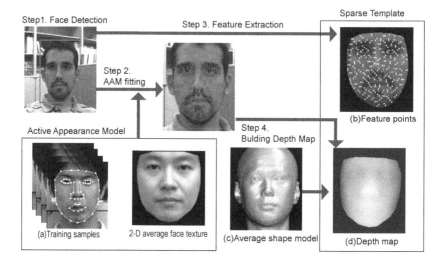

Fig. 2. 3-D face model and automatic initialization process

feature points is $100 \sim 200$. Finally, the depth value of each feature point is retrieved from a personalized depth map (Fig. 2(d)), which is created by morphing an average shape model (Fig. 2(c)) so that the facial landmark points and those of the AAM fitted model coincide. Note because AAM fitting is 2 dimensional and does not include any depth information, we assume that the morphed average 3-D face shape provides a good approximation of the actual face shape. The facial template consists of a set of feature points whose attributes include 3-D position (2-D location on facial sub-image and depth value) and corresponding image intensity.

After the initialization process, steps 1 to 4 in Fig. 2, M particles of each face to be tracked are randomly selected and their state-space values filled with random values uniformly distributed around the initial position. Note, AAM fitting is used only for initialization, not for tracking itself. Tracking is based on the fixed face model (facial template) for each person.

2.3   Speed Boost by GPU

The particle filter algorithm itself is computationally expensive, but the weight computation (updating stage in Fig. 1) is the main bottleneck, and so we execute it on a GPU, Graphics Processing Unit. Especially, we use NVIDIA's CUDA (Compute Unified Device Architecture [16]) environment which allows the GPU to be viewed as a data-parallel computing device that operates as a coprocessor to the main CPU. Weight calculation of each particle is an independent process, as is the matching error calculation for each feature point. Our method exploits these independencies to utilize the parallel processing offered by the GPU. The atomic computation (called a *kernel* in GPU computing) performs the following operations. First, the 3D transformation of each feature point as estimated by

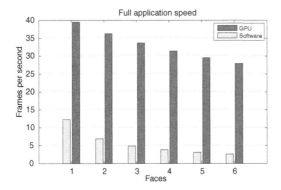

Fig. 3. Speed of the full application: comparing processing speed of the GPU version to a serial CPU-only version. Video 1024x768, ≈230 feature points per face, and 1000 particles per face.

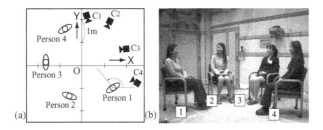

Fig. 4. Overview of scene. (a)plan view of participants' location, (b)whole view of participants.

each of the particles, and then the feature point gray level is compared against the resulting point in the full image. The sum of all those comparisons for each feature point results in the weight of each one of the particles. This is our output stream: the collection of weight values of all particles. For more detail see [9].

2.4 Performance Evaluation of Face Tracking

Speed. Fig. 3 shows a comparison of the speeds achieved by the CPU-only version and the GPU version of the same STCTracker. The developed software (a mixture of C++ and CUDA) was tested on an Intel Core 2 Duo 2.66GHz host system with 2GB RAM, with a NVIDIA GeForce 8800GTX GPU. The results indicate an important speed boost compared to the CPU-only version of the algorithm, especially when using a large number of particles and/or tracking multiple faces simultaneously. The boost makes the tracker eminently suitable for real-time processing in a standard PC platform, e.g. analysis of group meetings.

Accuracy. We targeted meeting scenes as shown in Fig. 4; bust-shot images of each person were captured by separate cameras, indicated by $C_1 \sim C_4$ in Fig. 4(a). Image size was 640×480 pixels and face size was about 170×170 pixels.

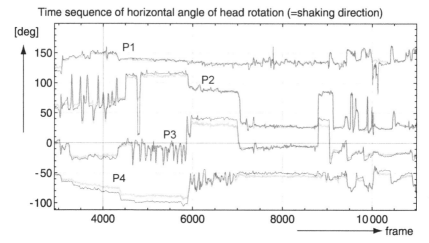

Fig. 5. Time sequence of horizontal angle of head rotation [deg]. Thin solid (read) lines: tracker result, Thick pale (blue) lines : sensor output. 1[frame]=1/30[sec]

We applied STCTracker to each person's video offline separately. The tracking speed was about 28[frame/sec] for each person with 10000 particles[1]. Also, as post-processing, a wavelet denoising technique [17] was applied to each component of face position and pose, in order to reduce jitter. Fig. 5 shows the time series data of horizontal head azimuth angle (horizontal rotation) obtained with our face tracker; the azimuth angle is defined as the angle between world coordinate X and the frontal direction of face, as shown in Fig. 4(a). Fig. 5 also shows the corresponding sensor output from magnetic-based 6-DOF sensors (POLHE-MUS Fastrak™), which were attached to the subjects' heads with hair bands. For a more acccurate comparison, a bias was added to each STCTracker output so that it had the same average as the sensor output. [2] Fig. 5 confirms that tracking data well replicated the sensor output.

Table 1 shows tracking error in the metric of mean deviation, the average value of absolute difference between tracking-based and sensor-based sequences.

---

[1] We decided to use 10000 particles for more accurate tracking than 1000 particles, assuming offline processing of prerecorded video. In contrast, Fig. 3 uses 1000 particles, because this yields faster tracking for realtime applications while still maintaining reasonable accuracy.

[2] Originally, the face direction measurement obtained by STCTracker is relative to the camera coordinate system; the rotation angle is 0.0 when the face points directly at the camera (= frontal face = face pose at initialization). However, the target video was captured using uncalibrated cameras, and no information is available to link the measured values to global coordinates. Therefore, we decided to add a uniform bias to the horizontal rotational component for comparison purposes. Note that measurements relative to unknown camera coordinates are still useful for the meeting analysis proposed by the authors in [10][11]. It can infer "who is looking at whom" in a self-organizing manner given prior knowledge on the seating order of participants; absolute face directions in global coordinates are not necessary.

Table 1. Accuracy of facial direction estimates in mean deviation [deg]. Azimuth = horizontal rotation = head shaking direction, Elevation = vertical rotation = head nodding, Roll = in-plane rotation = head tilting.

	Azimuth [deg]	Elevation [deg]	Roll [deg]
With denoising	3.59	3.21	1.29
Without denoising	3.68	3.30	1.32

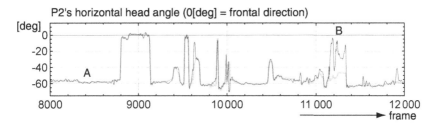

Fig. 6. A part of person 2's sequence in Fig. 5. 0[deg] corresponds to frontal face direction. Thin solid (read) lines : tracker result, Thick pale (blue) lines : sensor output.

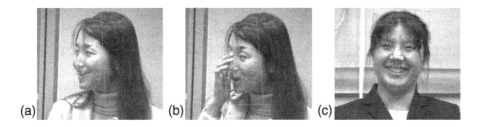

Fig. 7. Snapshot of tracking results. (a)profile view = turning sideway (corresponds to part A in Fig. 6), (b)partial occlusion (corresponds to part B in Fig. 6), (c)laughing.

The length of data was about 5 minutes. These tracking errors are fairly small compared to the dynamic range of head rotation, especially horizontal head rotation. These results also confirmed that the denoising applied decreases the error.

Robustness. To show the robustness of STCTracker against large head turn, Fig. 6 shows a part of person 2's horizontal head angles over time. Fig. 7(a) shows snapshots of the templates during tracking at the time indicated by part A in Fig. 6. From Fig. 6 and Fig. 7(a), it is confirmed that STCTracker is robust against significant head rotation (about 60[deg]), when the target keeps looking at another sitting on his right or left. In the meeting situation, partial occlusions can occur when a person covers his/her face with their hand(s), as shown in Fig. 7(b), which corresponds to part B in Fig. 6; the tracking results are significantly degraded due to the occlusion. But, tracking itself continues and the correct

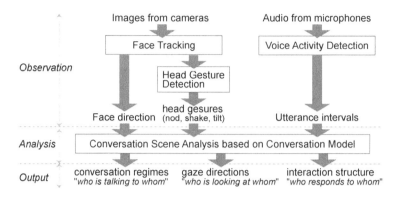

Fig. 8. Flow of multimodal meeting analysis

track is recovered when the occlusion passes. STCTracker is also robust against changes in facial expression from the one in the registered template, as shown in Fig. 7(c).

3   Meeting Analysis Based on Face Tracking

This section applies STCTracker to a method of meeting analysis, which the authors proposed in [11]. A comparison against sensor-based analysis confirms the effectiveness of the proposed face tracker.

3.1   Overview: Automatic Inference of Nonverbal Cross-Modal Interactions in Meeting

This framework was proposed for analyzing cross-modal nonverbal interactions in multimodal face-to-face conversation; its goal is to determine "who responds to whom, when, and how", from multimodal cues including gaze, head gestures, and utterances. We formulated this problem as the probabilistic inference of the causal relationship among participants' behaviors involving head gestures and utterances. Fig. 8 shows the flow of the analysis. First, from the images obtained with cameras, face tracking is done to yield the temporal sequence of face directions. From the sequence, head gestures such as nodding, shaking, and tilting are detected. The voice activity of each participant is detected from audio signals captured by lapel microphones. From the observed nonverbal behaviors, face directions, head gestures, and utterances, conversation scene analysis is conducted based a conversation model to estimate conversation regimes, gaze directions, and interaction structures. The conversation regimes represent the global status of conversations, and indicate "who is talking to whom". Here, for 4 person conversation, the conversation regime has 11 discrete states: 4 convergence regimes (monologue), 6 dyad-link regimes (dialogue between each pair), and 1 divergence regime (no organized conversation). The gaze directions indicate "who is

Table 2. Accuracy of head gesture detection [%]

	Data 1			Data 2		
	Precision	Recall	Hit	Precision	Recall	Hit
Tracking-based	57.2	81.1	76.8	69.7	62.0	81.0
Sensor-based	60.0	86.6	73.3	75.1	60.3	77.2

Table 3. Quantitative evaluation of meeting analysis. frame-based hit ratio [%]. (a)Gaze directions, (b)Conversation regimes, (c)Reaction targets.

	Data 1			Data 2		
	(a)Gaze	(b)Regime	(c)Reaction	(a)Gaze	(b)Regime	(c)Reaction
Tracking-based	75.0	84.2	95.0	67.1	52.8	91.0
Sensor-based	69.4	72.5	95.9	69.0	55.1	91.4

looking at whom"; there are 4 discrete states for each person (looking at one among others, or avert gaze from everyone). The interaction structures indicate "who responds to whom"; the state of interaction structure is defined for each utterance and gesture intervals; spontaneous or reaction toward another. Our conversation model is a hierarchical probabilistic model; the structures of interactions are probabilistically determined from high-level conversation regimes and gaze directions. The estimation is done using the Markov chain Monte Carlo method. See the details in [11].

3.2 Experiments

This paper targets the same data set as used in [11]; group discussions by 4 women, 2 sessions, about 5 minutes each. Model parameters were the same as used in [11].

Head Gesture Detection. Head gesture intervals are detected by the wavelet-based gesture detector proposed in [11]. We targeted nodding, shaking, and tilting. The detection was based on the denoised sequences of head pose output by STCTracker. We employ head pose components consisting of azimuth (horizontal rotation), roll (in-plane rotation), and y coordinate (vertical axis on image plane). The reason why we use the y coordinate instead of elevation (vertical rotation) as used in [11] is that the elevation sequences include significant amounts of noise which hamper accurate gesture detection; the y coordinate is more stable and well reflects vertical head rotation like nodding. Table 2 shows the accuracy of gesture detection using the measures of frame-based precision, recall, and hit ratio. Table 2 suggests that tracking-based gesture detection is moderately successful at this stage of development and that it is useful for meeting analysis. Also, it confirms that tracking-based detection generally has lower performance than sensor-based detection. One possible reason is that small nods (almost invisible) were eliminated by the denoising post process.

Evaluations of Meeting Analysis. Table 3 shows the results of a quantitative evaluation of gaze direction and conversation regimes as determined from

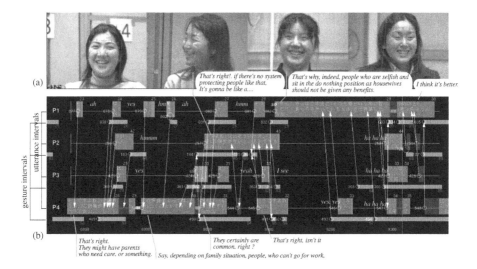

Fig. 9. Temporal visualization. (a)Tracking result (indicated with mesh), (b)Interaction network (rectangles : utterance intervals, line segments: gesture intervals, arrows: reaction target).

tracking-based and sensor-based analysis. Table 3(a) lists how often the estimated and manually annotated gaze directions coincided. Table 3(b) lists how often the conversation regimes were correctly estimated (ground truth provided by manual annotation). Table 3(c) shows how often the reaction targets ("who responds to whom") were correctly estimated (ground of manual annotation). Table 3 confirms that tracking-based analysis is comparable to sensor-based analysis, and can sometimes even outperform the sensor-based technique.

Fig. 9 shows the temporal structure of interactions; how the meeting evolved over time[3]. It includes face images with tracking results, detected utterance intervals (rectangles), detected gesture intervals (line segments below utterances), and interaction structure (thin arrows [4]). Fig. 9 confirms that head gesture intervals are reasonably well detected by using tracking-based face direction sequences, and that the resulting interaction structures were inferred successfully.

4   Conclusion and Discussion

This paper introduced a novel face tracker called STCTracker and verified its effectiveness in meeting scene analysis. The speed and robustness of STCTracker will contribute to opening up new fields in realtime multimodal meeting analysis. Future works include the following. In this paper, the image of each meeting participant is captured by a separate camera. To avoid this restrictive setting,

---

[3] Movies are available from http://www.brl.ntt.co.jp/people/otsuka/MLMI2008.html

[4] An arrow runs from person A's reaction to the person B's behavior that triggered A's reaction.

we are now working on an omni-directional camera system that can capture a complete view with just a single image. Other challenging problems include enhanced robustness against illumination changes and occlusions. In meetings, people often cover their face by their hands. Furthermore, we are working on facial expression recognition based on STCTracker [18].

References

1. Argyle, M.: Bodily Communication, 2nd edn. Routledge, London, New York (1988)
2. Kendon, A.: Some functions of gaze-direction in social interaction. Acta Psychological 26, 22–63 (1967)
3. Stiefelhagen, R., Yang, J., Waibel, A.: Modeling focus of attention for meeting index based on multiple cues. IEEE Trans. Neural Networks 13(4) (2002)
4. Voit, M., Stiefelhagen, R.: Tracking head pose and focus of attention with multiple far-field cameras. In: Proc. ICMI 2006 (2006)
5. Morency, L.P., Rahimi, A., Checka, N., Darrell, T.: Fast stereo-based head tracking for interactive environment. In: Proc. IEEE FG 2002, pp. 375–380 (2002)
6. Gatica-Perez, D., Odobez, J. M., Ba, S., Smith, K., Lathoud, G.: Tracking people in meetings with particles. Technical Report IDIAP-RR 04-71, IDIAP (2004)
7. Ba, S.O., Odobez, J.M.: A probabilistic head pose tracking evaluation in single and multiple camera setups. In: Proc. CLEAR 2007 (2007)
8. Lozano, O.M., Otsuka, K.: Simultaneous and fast 3D tracking of multiple faces in video by GPU-based stream processing. In: Proc. IEEE ICASSP 2008, pp. 713–716 (2008)
9. Lozano, O.M., Otsuka, K.: Real-time visual tracker by stream processing – simultaneous and fast 3D tracking of multiple faces in video sequences by using a particle filter. Journal of VLSI Signal Processing Systems (accepted)
10. Otsuka, K., Takemae, Y., Yamato, J., Murase, H.: A probabilistic inference of multiparty-conversation structure based on Markov-switching models of gaze patterns, head directions, and utterances. In: Proc. ACM ICMI 2005, pp. 191–198 (2005)
11. Otsuka, K., Sawada, H., Yamato, J.: Automatic inference of cross-modal nonverbal interactions in multiparty conversations. In: Proc. ACM ICMI 2007, pp. 255–262 (2007)
12. Matsubara, Y., Shakunaga, T.: Sparse template matching and its application to real-time object tracking. IPSJ Trans. Computer Vision and Image Media 46(SIG9), 60–71 (2005) (in Japanese)
13. Otsuka, K., Yamato, J., Murase, H.: Conversation scene analysis with dynamic Bayesian network based on visual head tracking. In: Proc. IEEE ICME 2006, pp. 949–952 (2006)
14. Viola, P., Jones, M.: Robust real-time face detection. Intl. Journal of Computer Vision 57(2), 137–154 (2004)
15. Edwards, G.J., Taylor, C.J., Cootes, T.F.: Interpreting face images using active appearance models. In: Proc. IEEE FG1998, pp. 300–305 (1998)
16. NVIDIA: NVIDIA CUDA (compute unified device architecture) programming guide ver.1.0 (2007), http://developer.nvidia.com/object/cuda.html
17. Donoho, D.L.: De-noising by soft-thresholding. IEEE Trans. Inf. Theory 41(3), 613–627 (1995)
18. Kumano, S., Otsuka, K., Yamato, J., Maeda, E., Sato, Y.: Pose-invariant facial expression recognition using variable-intensity templates. In: Yagi, Y., Kang, S.B., Kweon, I.S., Zha, H. (eds.) ACCV 2007, Part I. LNCS, vol. 4843, pp. 230–239. Springer, Heidelberg (2007)

What Does the Face-Turning Action Imply in Consensus Building Communication?

Tetsuro Onishi, Takatsugu Hirayama, and Takashi Matsuyama

Graduate School of Informatics, Kyoto University
Yoshida-honmachi, Sakyo-ku, Kyoto, Japan
{t-onishi,hirayama}@vision.kuee.kyoto-u.ac.jp, tm@i.kyoto-u.ac.jp

Abstract. When talking with someone, we convey intention to each other by verbal and non-verbal behaviors. In consensus building dialogue, the participants need to understand whether they agree or disagree. They reiterate confirmation of partner's internal state (agreement/disagreement) and reaction for it. In this study, we considered that the timing of listener's reaction for the confirmation by a speaker reflects listener's internal state, therefore analyzed the multimodal timing structures between the confirmation and the reaction by utterance and body motion. Especially, we focused on an action that the speaker turns his face toward the listener as the confirming action and analyzed how it influences the timing structures. As the results, we confirmed that the timing structures relate to the internal state and the relations are controlled by *face-turning* action.

1 Introduction

In recent years, many researchers have developed user support systems based on the human-machine interaction. We are currently designing an interactive system that supports the human-human task-oriented dialogue making a travel plan or selecting a gift. The system needs to estimate user's internal state, such as intention, through his behaviors in order to serve sensible information or recommend desired goods. We human basically interact using speech in the dialogue. Speech is the revealed information, and it is consciously controlled. Therefore, speech can express intention falsely. It is hard for us and the system to estimate real internal state from speech acculately. In this study, we focus on non-verbal behaviors. Humans cannot control to express their internal state perfectly, and real internal state shows through non-verbal behaviors unconsciously [1].

Body motion, such as head rotation, facial expression, and gesture, and prosody of speech are non-verbal behaviors. We focus on a behavior that a speaker turns his face toward a listener (*face-turning* action) to confirm listener's internal state in the task-oriented dialogue. What does the *face-turning* imply in the dialogue? Humans tend to turn their gaze on the dialogists to observe reaction [2,3]. The listener's reaction with body motion would reflect the internal state because the gazing by the speaker captures the listener's body action. We also consider that the *face-turning* often induces the reaction (sometimes requests the reaction). It

A. Popescu-Belis and R. Stiefelhagen (Eds.): MLMI 2008, LNCS 5237, pp. 26–37, 2008.

would be a powerful signal to elicit the internal state. We focus on a specific internal state, which is listener's agreement/disagreement with an intention expressed by the speaker. The state is the most primordial one built up in the task-oriented dialogue. The participants of the dialogue need to understand whether they agree or disagree, and then reach a consensus. They reiterate confirmation of agreement/disagreement and reaction for it, with occasional *face-turning*.

Temporal feature is also non-verbal media, which is a feature in the orthogonal dimension to the non-verbal behaviors. Some researchers have argued that the internal state is expressed in the timing of speech response more than in the prosody of speech [4,5]. They, however, analyzed only speech and ignored influences of body motion which has important function in face-to-face communication, on the timing of response. We analyze the relations between the internal state and the timing structures based on both utterance and body motion, i.e. multimodal timing structures. The listener may unconsciously reflect his internal state to the timing of the reaction by utterance and body motion for the speaker's confirmation with the *face-turning*.

In this paper, we make some hypotheses about how the multimodal timing structures relate to respondent's internal state (agreement/disagreement), and test the hypotheses by analyzing video data and audio signals recorded in some consensus building dialogues. Especially, we focus on how the *face-turning* influences the timing structures, and discuss the meaning of the *face-turning* to confirm partner's intention in the consensus building communication.

2   Relations between the Timing of the Reaction for the Confirmation and the Respondent's Internal State

2.1   Dialogue Components of Consensus Building

Consensus building dialogue is a kind of task-oriented dialogue. The dialogue usually consists of some exchanges. In this study, we address an exchange composed of *Confirmation* and *Reaction* by speech and body action, which is a primordial framework to convey agreement/disagreement. *Confirmation* is an action that starts a new exchange, represents intention, and confirms agreement/disagreement of the partner. *Reaction* is an action that reacts to *Confirmation*. Fig.1 shows an example of the exchange.

Various body motions occur with utterance of *Confirmation* and *Reaction*. These are non-verbal behaviors that emphasize and supplement verbal behaviors. We focus on some body motions based on head rotation. *Face-turning* is one of the typical body motions denoting *Confirmation* because its actor can observe

Speaker A : I want to go to the Netherlands. How about you?   *: Confirmation*

Listener B : Nice! I'm interested in *Eredivisie*.   *: Reaction*

Fig. 1. An example of the exchange

partner's behaviors reflecting the internal state, and it often induces *Reaction*. Nodding, head-inclining, head-shaking, and *face-turning* are the typical body motions denoting *Reaction*. They can express agreement/disagreement.

2.2   Timing Structures between the Confirmation and the Reaction by Utterance and Body Motion

Given the situation where speaker A confirms agreement/disagreement of listener B and B reacts to the confirmation, we have four timing structures, $\mathbf{I_{UU}}$, $\mathbf{I_{MU}}$, $\mathbf{I_{UM}}$, and $\mathbf{I_{MM}}$ expressing the interval between utterance $\mathbf{U}$ and body motion $\mathbf{M}$ of the two dialogists (see Fig.2). The details on the definition of the timing structures are described below. $T(\mathbf{E}_t^X)$ denotes the time when an event $\mathbf{E}_t$ caused by dialogist X occurs. $\mathbf{E}_s$ and $\mathbf{E}_e$ represent the start and end point of $\mathbf{E}_t$, respectively. $\mathbf{U}(cnf)$, $\mathbf{U}(rct)$, $\mathbf{M}(cnf)$, and $\mathbf{M}(rct)$ denote utterance of *Confirmation*, utterance of *Reaction*, face-turning of *Confirmation*, body motion of *Reaction*, respectively.

The timing structure $\mathbf{I_{UU}}$, which is the interval between the end time of utterance of *Confirmation* by speaker A and the start time of utterance of *Reaction* by listener B, is described as

$$\mathbf{I_{UU}} = T\left(\mathbf{U}\left(rct\right)_s^B\right) - T\left(\mathbf{U}\left(cnf\right)_e^A\right). \tag{1}$$

Intention of speech is often revealed at the end time of its utterance. We consider $T(\mathbf{U}(cnf)_e^A)$ as the base time of $\mathbf{I_{UU}}$.

The timing structure $\mathbf{I_{MU}}$, which is the interval between the start time of *face-turning* of *Confirmation* by speaker A and the start time of utterance of *Reaction* by listener B, is described as

$$\mathbf{I_{MU}} = T\left(\mathbf{U}\left(rct\right)_s^B\right) - T\left(\mathbf{M}\left(cnf\right)_s^A\right). \tag{2}$$

Listener B can observe *face-turning* by speaker A at the start time of it. We consider $T(\mathbf{M}(cnf)_s^A)$ as the base time of $\mathbf{I_{MU}}$. Here, *face-turning* of *Confirmation* is defined below. When *face-turning*, $\mathbf{M}^*$, satisfies all of the following equations:

$$\begin{cases} T(\mathbf{M}_s^*) \geq T\left(\mathbf{U}(cnf)_s\right) & \text{(3a)} \\ T(\mathbf{M}_s^*) \leq T\left(\mathbf{U}(rct)_s\right) & \text{(3b)} \\ T(\mathbf{M}_s^*) \leq T\left(\mathbf{M}(rct)_s\right), & \text{(3c)} \end{cases}$$

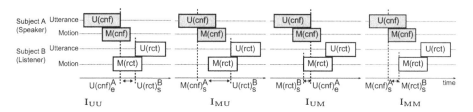

Fig. 2. Timing structures

the $\mathbf{M}^*$ is regarded as $\mathbf{M}(cnf)$. If some *face-turnings* satisfy these conditional equations, the latest one is regarded as $\mathbf{M}(cnf)$. Note that $\mathbf{I_{MU}}$ is always positive value because of satisfying eq.(3b).

The timing structure $\mathbf{I_{UM}}$, which is the interval between the end time of utterance of *Confirmation* by speaker A and the start time of body motion of *Reaction* by listener B, is described as

$$\mathbf{I_{UM}} = T\left(\mathbf{M}\left(rct\right)_s^B\right) - T\left(\mathbf{U}\left(cnf\right)_e^A\right). \tag{4}$$

The body motion of *Reaction* is defined below. When *face-turning*, nodding, head-inclining, or head-shaking, $\mathbf{M}^*$, satisfies the following conditional equation:

$$T\left(\mathbf{U}\left(cnf\right)_s\right) \leq T(\mathbf{M}_s^*) \leq T\left(\mathbf{U}\left(rct\right)_e\right), \tag{5}$$

and also satisfies either one of the following conditional equation:

$$\begin{cases} T\left(\mathbf{U}\left(cnf\right)_e\right) - T(\mathbf{M}_s^*) \leq 500\text{msec} & \text{(6a)} \\ T\left(\mathbf{U}\left(rct\right)_s\right) - T(\mathbf{M}_s^*) \leq 500\text{msec}, & \text{(6b)} \end{cases}$$

the $\mathbf{M}^*$ is regarded as $\mathbf{M}(rct)$. If some body motions satisfy the conditional equations, the earliest one is regarded as $\mathbf{M}(rct)$.

The timing structure $\mathbf{I_{MM}}$, which is the interval between the start time of *face-turning* of *Confirmation* by speaker A and the start time of body motion of *Reaction* by listener B, is described as

$$\mathbf{I_{MM}} = T\left(\mathbf{M}\left(rct\right)_s^B\right) - T\left(\mathbf{M}\left(cnf\right)_s^A\right). \tag{7}$$

Note that $\mathbf{I_{MM}}$ is always positive value because of satisfying eq.(3c).

2.3 Relations between the Timing Structures and the Respondent's Internal State

Some researchers have argued that the respondent unconsciously controls the timing structure $\mathbf{I_{UU}}$ as the negative response timing is later than the positive one in the task-oriented dialogue [4]. The respondent would also control the timing of utterance, $\mathbf{I_{UU}}$, according to agreement/disagreement with the partner. We make the first hypothesis as the following:

Hypothesis 1: Relation between $\mathbf{I_{UU}}$ and the Internal State
$\mathbf{I_{UU}}$ based on *Reaction* with disagreement is later than agreement.

Although the dialogists basically use speech to convey information to each other, they emphasize and supplement it by body motion except in some situations[1]. The body motion has often unignorable effects on the dialogue. Especially, *face-turning* of *Confirmation* denotes the action to observe some behaviors by the respondent, and would also suggest the action to induce some reactions reflecting his internal state. The respondent may control $\mathbf{I_{UU}}$ more explicitly than **Hypothesis1**. We make the second hypothesis as the following:

---

[1] Telephone is one of exceptive situations.

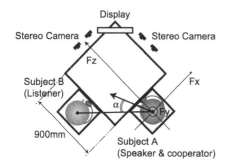

Fig. 3. Dialogue environment

Fig. 4. Captured images

Hypothesis 2: Variations of I_{UU} by Face-Turning

Face-turning of *Confirmation* increases the difference between I_{UU} of agreement and disagreement supporting **Hypothesis1**.

The timing structures based on the respondent's body motion, I_{UM} and I_{MM} would be controlled as well as I_{UU}. We make the third hypothesis below:

Hypothesis 3: Relations between I_{UM}, I_{MM} and the Internal State

I_{UM} and I_{MM} based on *Reaction* with disagreement are later than agreement. *Face-turning* of *Confirmation* increases the differences between I_{UM}, and I_{MM} of agreement and disagreement.

In order to test these hypotheses, we analyze video data and audio signals recorded in some consensus building dialogues, and clarify how the respondent controls I_{UU}, I_{UM}, I_{MU}, and I_{MM} in the following situations:

(s1) agreement-*Reaction* for *Confirmation* by only utterance,
(s2) disagreement-*Reaction* for *Confirmation* by only utterance,
(s3) agreement-*Reaction* for *Confirmation* by utterance and *face-turning*,
(s4) disagreement-*Reaction* for *Confirmation* by utterance and *face-turning*.

3   Construction of Dialogue Corpus

3.1   Recording the Consensus Building Dialogue

We constructed a dialogue corpus to analyze the four situations described in section 2.3. The dialogue task was either-or quiz. Fig.3 shows the overview of dialogue environment. A display which shows the task and two alternatives was set at the corner of the square desk, and two subjects interacted side by side in order to make them produce *face-turning* obviously.

To evenly analyze the four situations, we regulated experimental conditions by introducing an experimental cooperator to either subject. Just before they started the dialogue, the experimenter presented the quiz to each subject, and queried about the answer to only a real subject as preliminary survey. Then, the experimenter instructed the cooperator what to do according to the answer, e.g. *Confirmation* by only utterance expressing agreement with the answer. The real subject could not sense the instruction. The experimenter also made the cooperator say "If I choose among them, I like XXX" in the dialogue, to regulate speech of *Confirmation* under constant speech rate and prosody. XXX is either alternative depending on the answer. In addition, it is important to keep a regular timing, $\mathbf{I_{cnf}}(= T(\mathbf{M}(cnf)_s) - T(\mathbf{U}(cnf)_e))$, between utterance and body motion of *Confirmation*. We investigated the distribution of $\mathbf{I_{cnf}}$ by preliminary experiments. $\mathbf{I_{cnf}}$ was mostly distributed between -750 and 0msec. We trained the cooperator to do *face-turning* according to the timing and also analyzed only experimental data which satisfy the following conditional equation: -750msec $\leq$ $\mathbf{I_{cnf}} \leq$ 0msec.

It is not natural to make the cooperator produce the regulated behavior frequently in a dialogue. We made a rule that the experimenter chooses a preceding speaker of the dialogue and the cooperator produces the behavior once in the first exchange only when he is chosen. We analyzed only this first exchange.

We had 13 pairs of dialogists of the same sex with friendships[2]. We conducted each experiment based on situation (s1) $\sim$ (s4) twice every pair, i.e. we recorded 104 dialogues[3].

3.2 Extraction of Utterance and Body Motion Events

Each subject wore a directional headset microphone. Stereo cameras were set on the opposite side of each subject as shown in Fig.3. The resolution of the video data was 1024×768pixel and the frame rate was 30fps. The sampling rate of the audio signals was 44.1kHz.

Extraction of Utterance Events

We detected the start and end of utterances deleting non-verbal sounds, such as laugh and cough, by using the sound processing tool "Wavesurfer" [4]. If there was the silent interval longer than 400msec, we regarded it as a pause between utterances. We labeled each utterance *Confirmation*, *Reaction*, and *Others*.

Extraction of Body Motion Events

Face-turning, nodding, head-inclining, and head-shaking were extracted by measuring the amount of head rotation and head translation. We defined the subject coordinate system whose origin is the centroid of subject's head positions shown in Fig.3. F_z-axis of the system is a horizontal line from the origin to the center of baseline of the stereo camera, F_y-axis is a vertical line for F_z from the origin, and F_x-axis is an orthogonal line to both F_y-axis and F_z-axis. We measured the amount on the system. Let α be an angle between the subject's head rotation vector around F_y-axis and the vector from the subject to another. We defined the time when the temporal differentiation of α goes under/over a certain threshold

---

[2] 13 pairs are the subset combination of 4 cooperators and 13 real subjects.
[3] 13 pairs $\times$ 4 situations $\times$ 2.
[4] http://www.speech.kth.se/wavesurfer/

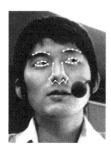

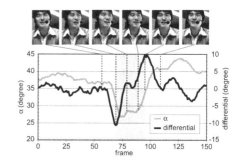

Fig. 5. Facial feature points extracted by AAM

Fig. 6. Extracted interval of *face-turning*

as the start/end time of *face-turning*. We also extracted nodding, head-inclining, and head-shaking based on the amount of head rotation around F_x-, F_z-, and F_y-axis, respectively. We defined the time when the absolute amount of the temporal differentiation of head rotation around each axis goes over a certain threshold as the start/end time of each body motion.

The amount of head rotation and translation were estimated as below. Firstly, we applied AAM (Active Appearance Model [6]) to captured face images (Fig.4) in order to obtain 2-D positions of facial feature points as shown in Fig.5. Secondly, we applied the stereo measurement method [7] to 2-D positions of the points in order to obtain 3-D positions of them. Thirdly, we obtained the amount of head rotation and translation by solving the minimization problem,

$$\min_{\mathbf{R},\mathbf{T}} \sum_{i=1}^{n} \| \mathbf{Q}' - (\mathbf{R}\mathbf{Q} + \mathbf{T}) \|^{2}, \tag{8}$$

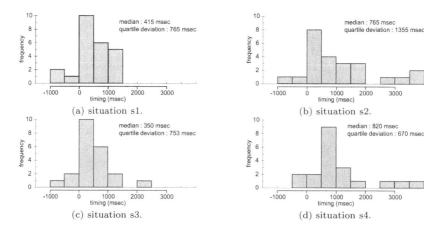

(a) situation s1.

(b) situation s2.

(c) situation s3.

(d) situation s4.

Fig. 7. Histograms of $\mathbf{I_{UU}}$

where n is the number of the facial feature points, $\mathbf{Q}'$ denotes a 3×1 vector which has 3-D position of capturing facial feature point i, $\mathbf{Q}$ denotes that of the face model which was constructed from the first frame of the captured image sequences, $\mathbf{R}$ denotes a 3×3 rotation matrix, and $\mathbf{T}$ denotes a 3×1 translation vector. We used the algorithm based on singular value decomposition method (SVD) to solve eq.(8) [8]. The algorithm applies SVD to $\mathbf{Q}\mathbf{Q}'^{T}(= \mathbf{U}\mathbf{S}\mathbf{V}^{T})$. The head rotation, $\mathbf{R}$, was calculated as $\mathbf{R} = \mathbf{V}\mathbf{U}^{T}$. And then the head translation, $\mathbf{T}$, was measured by the difference between centroid of the 3-D points of capturing face and the face model. Fig.6 shows an example of extracted *face-turning*.

Manual Compensation of Extracted Events
We used the annotation tool "Anvil" [9] and compensated some start/end times of utterance and body motion.

4 Analysis of Relations between the Timing Structures and the Internal State and Test of the Hypotheses

4.1 Analysis of the Timing Structures on the Reaction by Utterance

At first, we analyze the timing structures $\mathbf{I_{UU}}$ and $\mathbf{I_{MU}}$ on utterance of *Reaction*. The utterance occurred for each utterance of *Confirmation* in the whole of the experiments. The number of samples for situation (s1), (s2), (s3), and (s4) were 24, 24, 22, and 20, respectively.

Distributions of $\mathbf{I_{UU}}$
The distributions of $\mathbf{I_{UU}}$ resulted from the dialogue corpus are shown in Fig.7. We focus on the median and the quartile deviation extracted from the distributions to eliminate outliers from sample statistics. The medians of timings of agreement- and disagreement-*Reaction* for *Confirmation* without *face-turning* were 415msec and 765msec, respectively. The quartile deviations of their timings were 765msec and 1355msec, respectively. Each peak of the distributions was between 0 and 500msec.

And the medians of timings of agreement- and disagreement-*Reaction* for *Confirmation* with *face-turning* were 350msec and 820msec, respectively. The quartile deviations of their timings were 753msec and 670msec, respectively. The peak timing of the distribution of disagreement-*Reaction* (500 $\sim$ 1000msec) was later than that of agreement-*Reaction* (0 $\sim$ 500msec).

Distributions of $\mathbf{I_{MU}}$
The distributions of $\mathbf{I_{MU}}$ are shown in Fig.8. $\mathbf{I_{MU}}$ has distributions and statistics similar to $\mathbf{I_{UU}}$ because we regulated $\mathbf{I_{cnf}}$ within a defined span as described in section 3.1.

Test of Hypothesis 1
The timing of disagreement-*Reaction* for *Confirmation* without *face-turning* was later than that of agreement. This result supports **Hypothesis 1**. However, the

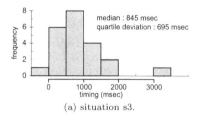
(a) situation s3.

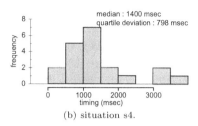
(b) situation s4.

Fig. 8. Histograms of $\mathbf{I}_{MU}$

Table 1. Occurrence frequency of $\mathbf{M}(rct)$

situation	frequency of $\mathbf{M}(rct)$ / frequency of $\mathbf{U}(cnf)$
s1	14 / 24 (58.3%)
s2	20 / 24 (83.3%)
s3	18 / 22 (81.8%)
s4	9 / 20 (45.0%)

result of the median test does not show significant difference between medians of their timings (significant probability $p = 0.56$).

Test of Hypothesis 2

The timing of disagreement-*Reaction* for *Confirmation* with *face-turning* was later than that of agreement, as well as the timing structure without *face-turning*. The result of the median test shows significant difference between medians of their timings ($p = 0.013$). The difference was significantly increased by *face-turning* because of not significant difference in case of *Confirmation* without *face-turning*. This result supports **Hypothesis 2**.

4.2   Analysis of the Timing Structures on the Reaction by Body Motion

We analyze the timing structures $\mathbf{I}_{UM}$ and $\mathbf{I}_{MM}$ on body motion of *Reaction*. The body motion did not occur for every utterance of *Confirmation* in the whole of the experiments. Table 1 shows frequency of the occurrence in each experimental situation.

Distributions of $\mathbf{I}_{UM}$

The distributions of $\mathbf{I}_{UM}$ are shown in Fig.9. Agreement-*Reaction* occurred more frequently between 0 and 2000msec. Disagreement-*Reaction* tended to occur frequently in two parts of span ($0 \sim 1000$msec and 2500msec $\sim$).

The medians of timings of agreement- and disagreement-*Reaction* for *Confirmation* without *face-turning* were 820msec and 770msec, respectively. The quartile deviations of their timings were 720msec and 2925msec, respectively. And the medians of timings of agreement- and disagreement-*Reaction* for *Confirmation*

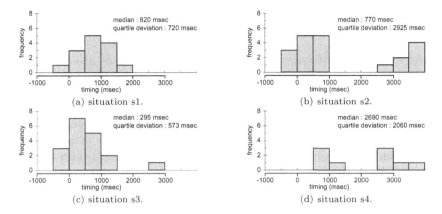

Fig. 9. Histograms of I_{UM}

with *face-turning* were 295msec and 2690msec, respectively. The quartile deviations of their timings were 573msec and 2060msec, respectively.

Distributions of I_{MM}

The distributions of I_{MM} are shown in Fig.10. I_{MM} has distributions and statistics similar to I_{UM} because we regulated I_{cnf}.

Test of Hypothesis 3

Although distributions of I_{UM} and I_{MM} were similar to I_{UU} and I_{MU}, sample numbers of the distributions were less and uneven as shown in Table 1. We shelve test of **Hypothesis 3** by the statistical significant difference.

Table 1 shows that the body motion tends to occur as below.

⋆ For *Confirmation* without *face-turning*, the respondent more frequently produces body motion in case of disagreement-*Reaction* than agreement-*Reaction*.
⋆ For *Confirmation* with *face-turning*, the respondent more frequently produces body motion in case of agreement-*Reaction* than disagreement-*Reaction*.

We discuss the reason of this tendency in the next section.

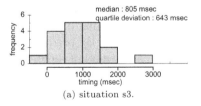
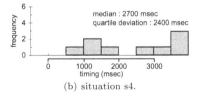

Fig. 10. Histograms of I_{MM}

5   Discussion–What Does the Face-Turning Action Imply in Consensus Building Communication?

We first consider the reason why agreement-*Reaction* occurred at early timing, based on the discussion by Fujiwara *et al.* [4]. If the respondent reacts at late timing, his partner may imagine that he is not sure which is better. The respondent, therefore, wants to convey agreement to his partner soon. In case of disagreement-*Reaction*, the respondent needs to choose his words with full respect for his partner and think how to *Reaction* in order to make the partner understand his intention. Therefore, disagreement-*Reaction* occurred at late timing. Also, the timing structure must be an implicit rule to express agreement/disagreement.

We confirmed that *face-turning* of *Confirmation* increased the difference between the timing of agreement- and disagreement-*Reaction*. Based on the approach-avoidance model by Argyle *et al.* [2], we consider that the *face-turning* suggests the approach action. Therefore, the respondent produced agreement-*Reaction*, which is regarded as the approach response, at earlier timing and he produced disagreement-*Reaction*, which is regarded as the avoidance response, at later timing. Also, the *face-turning* often induces the reaction. This inducibility can be confirmed from a result that the quartile deviation of timings of disagreement-*Reaction* for *Confirmation* with *face-turning* (Fig.7(d)) was much smaller than that without *face-turning* (Fig.7(b)). The *face-turning* has the potency inducing the partner to react by utterance within a certain temporal interval. Through these results, we consider that the *face-turning* controls the timing of partner's reaction and elicits his internal state. The dialogists can build up a sense of dialogue timing by producing the explicit event of *face-turning*.

As shown in Table 1, the *face-turning* promoted the body motion suggesting agreement and restrained the motion suggesting disagreement. When the listener receives *Confirmation* without *face-turning*, he is not pressured by partner's observation. Therefore, he does not need to express agreement by using body motion excessively. On the other hand, he produces the motion suggesting disagreement unconsciously. In case of *Confirmation* with *face-turning*, it is a kind of *Reaction* with disagreement that he does not produce the motion. He nods to convey agreement to the partner excessively, and he often suggests disagreement without the motion. *Face-turning* opens new dialogue channel of body motion, and it is possible to change the meaning of producing the motion.

It is difficult to detect false agreement/disagreement, i.e. lie, when confirming partner's intention without *face-turning*, because the timing of agreement-reaction is almost the same as that of disagreement-reaction. By producing the *face-turning*, the dialogists can observe the reaction by body motion and estimate partner's real agreement/disagreement by sensing the timing of the reaction. We actually turn our face toward partner when we cannot understand partner's internal state and want to understand the state surely in daily communication. *Face-tuning* is an action to probe partner's mind[5].

---

[5] We have proposed a new proactive human-machine interaction model, *Mind Probing*.

6 Conclusion

We made some hypotheses about the relations between the timing of the listener's reaction for the confirmation of his internal state by the speaker and the state. We analyzed some consensus building dialogues by an experimental cooperator and a subject to test the hypotheses. Especially, we focused on the action that the speaker turns his face toward the listener as the confirming action and analyzed how it influences the timing structures.

As the results, the timing of the reaction by utterance suggesting disagreement was later than that of agreement, and the *face-turning* increased the difference between the timing of the reaction suggesting agreement and disagreement. We consider that the *face-turning* is a trigger to make the dialogists build up a sense of dialogue timing. The *face-turning* also promoted the body motion suggesting agreement and restrained the motion suggesting disagreement. It was contrary to result for the confirmation without *face-turning*. This result must be a feature of dialogue opening the dialogue channel of body motion.

In future work, we need to increase the size of the dialogue corpus and evaluate reliability of these results. We will design the human-machine interaction system able to estimate user's internal state based on findings of this work.

Acknowledgments. This work is in part supported by Grant-in-Aid for Scientific Research of the Ministry of Education, Culture, Sports, Science and Technology of Japan under the contract of 18049046.

References

1. Jacobs, T.J.: On Unconscious Communications and Covert Enactments: Some Reflections on Their Role in the Analytic Situation. Psychoanalytic Inquiry 21, 4–23 (2001)
2. Argyle, M., Dean, J.: Eye Contact, Distance and Affiliation. Socimetry 28, 289–304 (1965)
3. Kendon, A.: Some Function of Gaze-direction in Social Interaction. Acta Psychological 26, 22–63 (1967)
4. Fujiwara, N., Itoh, T., Araki, K.: Analysis of Changes in Dialogue Rhythm due to Dialogue Acts in Task-oriented Dialogues. In: Matoušek, V., Mautner, P. (eds.) TSD 2007. LNCS (LNAI), vol. 4629, pp. 564–573. Springer, Heidelberg (2007)
5. Yoshida, M., Miyake, Y.: Relationship between Utterance Dynamics and Pragmatics in the Conversation of Consensus Building Process. In: Proceedings of the 15th IEEE International Symposium on Robot and Human Interactive Communication, pp. 641–645 (2006)
6. Cootes, T.F., Edwards, G.J., Taylor, C.J.: Active Appearance Model. In: Proceedings of European Conference on Computer Vision, vol. 2, pp. 484–498 (1998)
7. Hartley, R., Zisserman, A.: Multiple View Geometry in Computer Vision. Cambridge University Press, Cambridge (2004)
8. Arun, K.S., Huang, T.S., Blostein, S.D.: Least-squares Fitting of Two 3-d Point Sets. IEEE Transactions on Pattern Analysis and Machine Intelligence 9(5), 698–701 (1987)
9. Kipp, M.: Gesture Generation by Imitation - From Human Behavior to Computer Character Animation. Dissertation.com. Boca Raton, Florida (2004)

Distinguishing the Communicative Functions of Gestures
An Experiment with Annotated Gesture Data

Kristiina Jokinen[1], Costanza Navarretta[2], and Patrizia Paggio[2]

[1] University of Tartu and University of Helsinki
kristiina.jokinen@helsinki.fi
[2] University of Copenhagen, CST
costanza@hum.ku.dk, patrizia@cst.dk

Abstract. This paper deals with the results of a machine learning experiment conducted on annotated gesture data from two case studies (Danish and Estonian). The data concern mainly facial displays, that are annotated with attributes relating to shape and dynamics, as well as communicative function. The results of the experiments show that the granularity of the attributes used seems appropriate for the task of distinguishing the desired communicative functions. This is a promising result in view of a future automation of the annotation task.

1 Introduction

The purpose of this paper is to present the results of a machine learning experiment conducted on multimodal data annotated by means of the MUMIN coding scheme (Allwood et al. 2007).

An increasing number of research projects and research initiatives concern themselves with the development of annotated multimodal corpora, i.e. annotated resources where the various modalities involved in human interaction, or human-computer interaction, are recorded and annotated at many different levels (Martin et al. 2007). The MUMIN framework is intended as a general tool for the study of multimodal human behaviour, and focuses on specific communicative aspects of this behaviour, thus providing a complementary and important perspective to frameworks dedicated to detailed analyses of the physical characteristics of gestures. It could also be used to add a layer of functional gesture interpretation to large state-of-the-art multimodal corpora such as those built in the AMI (Carletta 2007) and CHIL (Mostefa et al. 2007) projects.

In the machine learning experiment described here, we investigate how well the annotation categories relating to the gesture shape and dynamics can be used to distinguish different functional categories of gesture types. Our immediate goal is to find an indication of whether these features have the correct granularity in this respect. More generally, machine learning of the functional categories can pave the way to the automation of this type of annotation.

A. Popescu-Belis and R. Stiefelhagen (Eds.): MLMI 2008, LNCS 5237, pp. 38–49, 2008.
© Springer-Verlag Berlin Heidelberg 2008

We start by briefly explaining the MUMIN coding scheme in Section 2; then we describe the datasets used in the experiment in Section 3; we present the results in Section 4 and conclude in Section 5.

2   The MUMIN Coding Scheme

The MUMIN coding scheme, developed in the Nordic Network on Multimodal Interfaces MUMIN, is a general framework for the study of gestures (it covers at the moment hand gestures, facial displays and body posture) in interpersonal communication. The framework focuses on the role played by multimodal expressions for feedback, turn management and sequencing. This focus, as we shall see, drives the selection of gestures to be annotated as well as the choice of available annotation attributes. The framework builds on previous studies of feedback strategies in conversations (Clark and Schaefer 1989, Allwood et al. 1992), research on non-verbal behaviour (Duncan and Fiske 1977, Kendon 2004, McNeill 1992) and work where verbal feedback has been categorised in behavioural or functional terms (Allwood 2001a and 2001b, Allwood and Cerrato 2003, Cerrato 2007). The MUMIN scheme is neutral with respect to the tool used to carry out the annotation. Since it consists of a number of hierarchically organised attributes, it can easily be implemented in different formalisms. In this study, we have used the ANVIL tool (Kipp 2001).

The annotation work consists of a number of preliminary steps i.a. finding appropriate video material, implementing the coding scheme as required by the annotation tool chosen and transcribing the speech of the dialogue participants. The actual gesture annotation proceeds then by selecting gestures that have a communicative function relating to either feedback, turn management or sequencing[1] (possibly several functions at the same time). In this study, we will focus on feedback and turn management. Sequencing, which is intended to capture the role played by gestures in discourse structuring and segmenting, is more relevant for monologues and narratives than for the type of interaction targeted in this study.

Then each gesture is assigned several labels relating to its communicative function(s), shape and dynamics as well as semiotic type. If there is a relation with another cooccurrent gesture or speech, this is also annotated by means of a so-called crossmodal attribute, not considered here. Below we briefly describe the categories available in the MUMIN coding scheme, especially the functional categories used in this study. A detailed description and discussion is provided in Allwood et al. (2007). The categories for the annotation of feedback, turn management and semiotic types are listed in Table 1. For feedback, a basic distinction is made between Give and Elicit (whether the speaker is giving feedback to the interlocutor or asking for feedback). In both cases, there is a Basic attribute that says whether there is only acknowledgement of perception, or whether there are signs of having or not having understood the message that is being conveyed. An additional attribute is related to whether the feedback is one of acceptance or

---

[1] In other words, not *all* gestures are selected for annotation.

Table 1. Functional annotation features and semiotic types

Behaviour	Attribute	Value
Feedback Give	Basic	ContactPerception (CP),
		ContactPerceptionUnderstanding (CPU)
	Acceptance	Accept, Non-accept
	Additional emotion/Attitude	Happy, Sad, Surprised, Disgusted,
		Angry, Frightened, Other
Feedback Elicit	Basic	CPU, CP
	Acceptance	Accept, Non-accept
	Additional emotion/Attitude	Happy, Sad, Surprised, Disgusted,
		Angry, Frightened, Other
Turn Management	Turn gain	Turn take, Turn accept
	Turn end	Turn yield, Turn offer, Turn complete
	Turn hold	Turn hold
Semiotic type	Indexical	Deictic, Non-deictic (e.g.: beats)
	Non-indexical	Iconic, Symbolic

Table 2. Annotation features for facial displays

Behaviour	Attribute	Value
Face	General face	Smile, Laugh, Scowl, Other
	Eyebrow movement	Frown, Raise, Other
	Eye movement	Extra-Open, Close-Both
		Close-One, Close-Repeated, Other
	Gaze direction	Towards-Interlocutor, Up,
		Down, Sideways, Other
	Mouth openness	Open mouth, Closed mouth
	Lip position	Corners up, Corners down,
		Protruded, Retracted
	Head movement	Down, Down-Repeated, BackUp,
		BackUp-Repeated, BackUp-Slow,
		Forward, Back, Side-Tilt, Side-Tilt-Repeated,
		Side-Turn, Side-Turn-Repeated, Waggle, Other

refusal. A third option is to add a value for Emotion. Turn management is coded by the three general features Gain, End and Hold. An additional dimension concerns whether the turn changes in agreement between the speakers or not, thus giving rise to different values for Gain and End. The semiotic categories are based on Peirce (1931). They correspond roughly to pointing gestures (Indexical Deictic); beats (Indexical Non-deictic); gestures expressing a semantic feature by similarity, including metaphoric gestures (Iconic); and emblems (Symbolic). Table 2 shows the features available in MUMIN to describe shape and dynamics of facial displays (hand gestures and body posture features are also part of the scheme but were not considered for this experiment). The categories are intentionally coarse-grained, in that we only want them to be specific enough to be able to distinguish and characterise non-verbal expressions that have a feedback, turn management and sequencing function.

3   The Annotated Data

Two datasets were used in this study, one containing Danish multimodal data and one Estonian. Additional case studies are presented in Allwood et al. (2007).

3.1 The Danish Data

The Danish data used in the experiment consist of a one minute clip from an interview from Danish television. The dialogue between a male interviewer and an actress was transcribed and then all the gestures were annotated independently by two experienced coders. The purpose of producing this first version of the data was to test the reliability of the coding scheme, which proved in fact quite good in that we obtained k scores (Carletta 1996) between .7 and .96 for most of the attributes[2].

To produce the dataset used in the machine learning experiment, the coding manual was slightly revised and the inconsistencies found in the first version were evened out on the basis of the revised guidelines. Since the video clip contains many close-ups of the faces of the two dialogue participants, in many cases the hands and the body are not visible, so that most of the annotated gestures in these data concern facial displays. Therefore only the annotation of facial displays is considered in the machine learning experiment described in this paper.

3.2 The Estonian Data

The Estonian dialogue consists of two half-an-hour long scenario-based conversations. In the first one, the task was to discuss the design of a new school building, and the three participants assumed the roles of an architect, a building designer, and a council representative. In the second scenario, the task was to discuss the inspection of the new school building and the participants had the roles of an architect, a project manager, and a council representative. The participants were three students. Although the dialogues were based on controlled scenarios, the participants behaved naturally, and we can assume that their non-verbal activity (hand gestures, and facial expressions) is representative for the current purposes.

Two video clips about 2 minutes each from each dialogue were selected for annotation, and they were annotated by a non-expert, native Estonian speaker, who first went through a short introductory course on the topic. The annotation was then checked by the expert annotator.

The annotation scheme was based on a slightly modified version of the MU-MIN annotation scheme. The eye and eyebrow movement as well as lip and mouth opening were left out since the video was not considered accurate enough for these annotations. The tag names were also slightly modified so as to make them easier to be remembered; their meaning, however, remained the same and the annotations can thus be compared with the Danish ones.

4 Experimenting with Machine Learning

4.1 The Hypothesis

The machine-learning experiments were set up to investigate how well the selected attributes could distinguish different functional categories of facial and

---

[2] See Allwood et al. (2007) for a discussion.

gesture categories. Our immediate goal is to find an indication of whether the attributes concerning gesture shape and dynamics have the correct granularity in this respect. But a more general related question is whether in future the functional annotation could be automated at least partly. Given the fact that data on the gesture shape and dynamics can be obtained through the use of cameras and sensors, this is clearly a very relevant question.

4.2   The Setup

We used the Weka software package (Witten and Frank 2005) and performed various experiments on the following attribute classes: feedback, semiotic type, and turn management.

Table 3. Input statistics

	no. face displays	no. face attributes
DK	51	7
Est	89	7
Total	140	7

The input statistics are given in Table 3. In order to be able to combine the annotations from both datasets, the attributes were simplified as already explained. The list for facial displays is shown below in the format used in WEKA:

```
@relation face
@attribute General-Face{Neutral,Smile,Laugh,Sulk,Other}
@attribute Gaze {None,Interlocutor,Up,Down,Side,Other}
@attribute Head {Static,Nod,Nod-R,Jerk,Forward,Backward,
          Side-Tilt,Side-Tilt-R,Side-Turn,Shake,Waggle,Other}
@attribute Emotion-Attitude {Neutral,Happy,Sad,Surprised,
          Disgusted,Angry,Frightened,Certain,Uncertain,Interested,
          Disappointed,Satisfied,Other}
@attribute Feedback {None,CPU,CP,Accept,Non-accept,Elicit,Emphasis}
@attribute Semiotic {None,Index-Deictic,Index-Non-deictic,Iconic,
          Symbolic}
@attribute Turn {None,Take,Accept,Yield,End,Hold}
```

There are two main differences with respect to the MUMIN model, in addition to the already mentioned missing attributes for Eyebrow, Eye, Mouth and Lip. One is the use of null values (Neutral and None) in cases where some of the attributes have not been given a value in the annotation; the other is an apparently different set of Feedback attributes. In reality, although the set used in the experiment has less expressive power (only one value can be chosen to the Feedback attribute contrary to the original MUMIN model where several Feedback values can be

Table 4. Simplified feedback attributes

MUMIN attributes	Simplified attributes
FeedbackGive-Basic-CPU	CPU
FeedbackGive-Basic-CP	CP
FeedbackGive-Basic-CPU/Acceptance-Accept	Accept
FeedbackGive-Basic-CPU/Acceptance-Non-accept	Non-accept
FeedbackElicit-Basic-CPU	Elicit
-	Emphasis

instantiated at the same time), the two attribute sets are comparable, as shown in Table 4. The Feedback value Emphasis was meant to pick up cases were the speaker especially emphasises the content of her contribution. The hypothesis was that this kind of behaviour would cooccur with the Semiotic-type=Index-Non-deictic, i.e. with beats. Although the Estonian data seems to support this, emphasis also seems to occur with other semiotic types.

4.3   Classification

The classification experiments give us information about the predictive power of the attribute set, i.e. how well the given attributes predict the functional class in each case. We experimented with different classification algorithms provided in Weka (Support Vector Machines, Decision Trees, and Naive Bayes), and the best results were produced with the SVM. The classification results below are based on the SMO (Sequential Minimal Optimization, Platt 1998) version of the algorithm which is implemented in Weka. The experiments used linear kernel, and ten runs with 10-fold classification.

Table 5. The classification accuracy of communicative functions on the Estonian and Danish data

Facial displays		
Dataset	ZeroR	SVM
Estonian		
feedback	46.11(+/- 3.75)	69.86(+/-16.43)
semiotic type	56.25(+/- 2.20)	82.22(+/-19.74)
turn	70.83(+/- 5.44)	73.06(+/-14.93)
Danish		
feedback	45.00(+/- 8.50)	86.33(+/-13.37)
semiotic type	72.67(+/- 9.66)	92.33(+/- 9.94)
turn	62.67(+/- 6.44)	80.33(+/-13.37)
Both combined		
feedback	30.71(+/- 3.45)	64.29(+/- 8.25)
semiotic type	62.14(+/- 3.45)	81.43(+/- 9.04)
turn	67.86(+/- 3.76)	72.86(+/- 6.56)

As the baseline, we used the accuracy results from Weka's ZeroR, which predicts the mode for a nominal class, i.e. the most frequent attribute value, and the accuracy is thus the frequency of the particular most frequent category.

For the three classes, the accuracy results (= percentage of correctly classified elements of the whole input set) are as in Table 5. On the confidence level 0.01, Feedback and Semiotic type using all datasets (Estonian, Danish as well as the combined data set) can be predicted more accurately than the baseline. On a lower confidence level 0.05, the accuracy is significantly better than the baseline on all datasets except for the Turn attribute in the Estonian and the combined data.

4.4   Clustering

We also experimented with Weka's Expectation-Maximization algorithm to investigate if the annotated gestures and facial expressions exhibit any meaningful patterns on the basis of the annotation features. The EM algorithm compares the data points and their similarity and clusters the most similar points together while trying to maximize the overall probability of the cluster distributions so that the clusters are the most different ones. Thus there is no need to provide any particular number of clusters in advance, because the algorithm forms these on the basis of the probability distribution of the individual features.

The results are similar to those reported in Jokinen and Ragni (2007): the clustering of facial data produced a number of patterns. First of all, in the Danish data, the facial data group into three clusters (see Fig. 1) which seem to correspond to Feedback values of Accept (cluster 0), CP or No feedback (Cluster 1) and Elicit (Cluster 2). Since CP can be considered a rather mild feedback, where no understanding signs are given, it makes sense for it to cluster together with No feedback. Accept and Elicit, on the other hand, are very different, so it is reassuring to see that they make up distinct clusters.

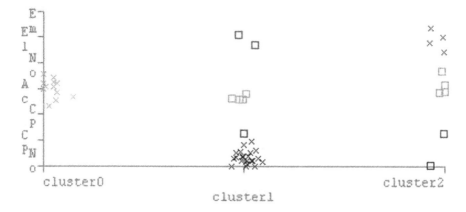

Fig. 1. Feedback clusters in the Danish data. The attributes on the y axis are from the top: Emphasis, Elicit, Non-accept, Accept, CPU, CP and No-feedback.

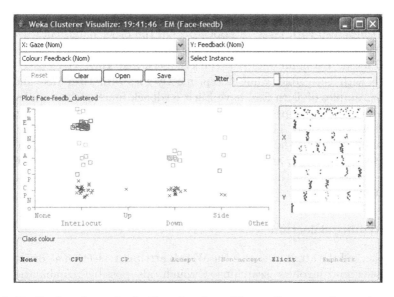

Fig. 2. Feedback and gaze in the Estonian data. The attributes on the y axis are from the top: Emphasis, Elicit, Non-accept, Accept, CPU, CP and No-feedback.

The clustering data also show some interesting correspondences between Feedback and Turn attributes and other, especially non-functional attributes. In particular, both the Danish and the Estonian datasets exhibit a relation between Feedback and other attributes, and the Estonian data set between Turn and other attributes.

To start with feedback, the following patterns emerge in the Danish data between Gaze and Feedback: gaze to Interlocutor seems to coincide with Accept while gaze to Side, Other or Down corresponds to No feedback. Also Head and Feedback pattern together: nods are accompanied by Accept, while side-turns and side-tilts have No feedback. Head is usually Jerk or leaning Forward if Feedback is Elicit. It must be remembered that the data only show gesture behaviour in two subjects: therefore, these patterns may only concern these two specific individuals. However, both the gaze patterns and the head movements also confirm our intuitions about the way in which feedback is expressed.

If we now look at feedback in the Estonian data, we see that Nod and Accept go together as in the Danish study. However, side-turns as well as Head Forward seem to be used with CPU and Elicit. This could be an interesting difference in the facial feedback strategies. Whether this is due to individual differences, different cultures or the different communicative situations, however, cannot be established on the basis of this very limited experiment. Still considering feedback in the Estonian data, interesting and plausible correspondences emerge between Feedback and Gaze as shown in Fig. 2. With Elicit the gaze is always towards the interlocutor, although Gaze Interlocutor also occurs together with other feedback functions. The same tendency can be noticed in the combined datasets as well. Acceptance feedback often occurs together with Gaze Down, and sometimes also with Gaze Interlocutor. On the other hand, Gaze Down is also present with CPU in addition to Accept. Finally, interesting correspondences are found in the Estonian data between Feedback and Turn. Here CPU seems to coincide with Turn Hold, while Accept mostly goes with Turn Take and Turn Hold. All examples of Turn End have Elicit feedback function (this makes a lot of sense: the speaker stops talking and asks for feedback) although Elicit also occurs when Turn Hold. Looking at Turn and Gaze, Turn End goes together with Gaze Interlocutor (the speaker looks at the interlocutor to ask for feedback when releasing the turn), and Gaze Down goes rather systematically with Turn Hold (by not looking at the interlocutor, the speaker makes it harder for them to interrupt).

4.5   Attribute Selection

We also checked the attributes with the Weka's attribute selection algorithm. Attribute selection involves searching through all possible combinations of

Table 6. 10-fold cross validation for facial displays

category	average merit		average rank		attribute
Danish Feedback	51.049	+- 3.605	1.2	+- 0.4	5 Turn
	45.487	+- 5.31	1.8	+- 0.4	3 Head
	27.423	+- 1.998	3	+- 0	2 Gaze
	21.907	+- 1.58	4.1	+- 0.3	6 Semiotic
	17.598	+- 2.109	4.9	+- 0.3	4 Emotion-Attitude
	6.773	+- 0.868	6	+- 0	1 General-Face
Danish Turn	59.165	+-14.128	1.3	+- 0.9	4 Emotion-Attitude
	51.14	+- 3.215	1.9	+- 0.3	7 Feedback
	32.386	+- 3.667	3.3	+- 0.46	3 Head
	32.124	+- 5.985	3.5	+- 0.67	1 General-Face
	18.268	+- 2.908	5	+- 0	2 Gaze
	7.2	+- 0.724	6	+- 0	6 Semiotic
Estonian Feedback	90.891	+-11.137	1	+- 0	3 Head
	58.222	+- 6.309	2.1	+- 0.3	6 Turn
	42.375	+- 7.228	3.2	+- 0.6	7 Emotion-Attitude
	39.892	+- 2.63	3.7	+- 0.46	2 Gaze
	22.126	+- 1.722	5	+- 0	4 Semiotic-Type
	9.252	+- 1.757	6	+- 0	1 General-Face
Estonian Turn	58.094	+- 5.762	1	+- 0	5 Feedback
	35.177	+- 4.741	2.2	+- 0.4	3 Head
	32.263	+- 5.409	2.8	+- 0.4	2 Gaze
	12.754	+- 1.454	4.3	+- 0.46	4 Semiotic-Type
	9.992	+- 2.196	4.7	+- 0.46	7 Emotion-Attitude
	1.468	+- 0.098	6	+- 0	1 General-Face
Both Feedback	155.533	+- 9.533	1	+- 0	3 Head
	95.075	+- 7.603	2.2	+- 0.4	5 Turn
	79.858	+- 5.603	3.3	+- 0.9	2 Gaze
	74.585	+- 5.531	3.8	+- 0.6	6 Semiotic
	64.378	+-10.952	4.7	+- 0.64	4 Emotion-Attitude
	21.258	+- 2.781	6	+- 0	1 General-Face
Both Turn	133.485	+-37.22	1.3	+- 0.9	4 Emotion-Attitude
	94.752	+- 6.475	1.9	+- 0.3	7 Feedback
	61.957	+- 5.825	2.9	+- 0.3	3 Head
	26.711	+- 3.925	4	+- 0.45	2 Gaze
	20.951	+- 3.864	5.1	+- 0.54	1 General-Face
	17.415	+- 1.828	5.8	+- 0.4	6 Semiotic

attributes in the data so as to find which subset of attributes works best for prediction. This task involves two algorithms, one to search the attributes and the other to evaluate the algorithm. We used the Chi-square attribute evaluation, together with the built in Ranker. The results for the two classes Feedback and Turn Management using 10-fold cross validation are in Table 6. These data show that the Head features are quite important to discriminate between Feedback types in both datasets, and especially in the Estonian data. We have already noted the cooccurrence of Nod and Feedback Accept values in both cases. To distinguish between Turn values, on the other hand, the Head features are less important than Feedback in both datasets. This points at the possibility that feedback is a more general category than turn management. The most discriminating attribute in the Danish data is in fact Emotional attitude, which seems to indicate that the interaction in the Danish video is more emotional.

5   Conclusion

In this paper we presented the MUMIN categories for the annotation of the communicative functions of gestures in multimodal corpora, with focus on feedback and turn management. Then we described various machine learning experiments conducted to investigate the adequacy of the annotation categories in distinguishing the various functions of facial displays, and to see whether the attributes for gesture shape and dynamics have the appropriate granularity. The experiments were run using Weka (Witten and Frank, op. cit.) on datasets extracted from Danish and Estonian annotated conversations.

The results of the classification experiments indicate that feedback and semiotic type in our datasets can be predicted more accurately than the baseline (results in Weka's ZeroR) in most cases. The results of clustering indicate correspondences between feedback and turn attributes on the one hand and nonfunctional attributes on the other – correspondences which confirm intuitions on the cooccurrence of certain gesture types and particular communicative functions. Similarly, the analysis of attribute selection in Weka indicates that head features are more important to distinguish feedback categories than to discriminate between turn values.

Although the obtained results are only tentative because of the limited size of the datasets, they indicate that machine learning algorithms can be usefully applied on data extracted from multimodal corpora annotated according to the MUMIN scheme. They also show that the granularity of the attributes for the annotation of facial displays seems appropriate for the task of distinguishing the desired communicative functions. An important aspect we haven't considered is modelling of the context in which the gestures occur. It is a well-known fact that gestures (like in fact speech) may be ambiguous out of context. Therefore, taking into account preceding gestures as well as the speech context is likely to produce more accurate and realistic results. This will be done in future work.

In spite of these limitations, the results of the experiment are encouraging given the fact that the granularity of gesture annotation is quite coarse, and therefore relatively easy to annotate. In fact, coarse-grained gesture annotation has also been adopted in large corpus building projects such as the already cited AMI and CHIL, so the issue of whether such granularity is enough has general interest. Another related issue is whether the MUMIN functional categories can be linked to automatically recognised form features. Since manual annotation is costly and time-consuming, several projects have started using cameras and sensors for automated annotation, e.g. Campbell (2008) and Douxchamps and Campbell (2008). Thus, this is clearly a very relevant future possibility in which our annotation scheme may prove a useful starting point.

References

Allwood, J.: Dialog Coding – Function and Grammar. Gothenburg Papers. In: Theoretical Linguistics. Department of Linguistics, vol. 85, Gothenburg University (2001a)

Allwood, J.: The Structure of Dialog. In: Taylor, M., Bouwhuis, D., Nel, F. (eds.) The Structure of Multimodal Dialogue II, pp. 3–24. Amsterdam, Benjamins (2001b)

Allwood, J., Cerrato, L.: A study of gestural feedback expressions. In: Paggio, P., et al. (eds.) Proceedings of the First Nordic Symposium on Multimodal Communication, pp. 7–22 (2003)

Allwood, J., Nivre, J., Ahlsén, E.: On the Semantics and Pragmatics of Linguistic Feedback. Journal of Semantics 9, 1–26 (1992)

Allwood, J., Cerrato, L., Jokinen, K., Navarretta, C., Paggio, P.: The MUMIN coding scheme for the annotation of feedback, turn management and sequencing phenomena. In: Martin, J.C., et al. (eds.) Multimodal Corpora for Modelling Human Multimodal Behaviour. Special issue of the International Journal of Language Resources and Evaluation, vol. 41(3–4), pp. 273–287. Springer, Heidelberg (2007)

Campbell, N.: Tools and Resources for Visualising Conversational-Speech Interaction. In: LREC 2008, Marrakesh, Morocco (2008)

Carletta, J.: Assessing agreement on classification tasks: the kappa statistics. Computational Linguistics 22(2), 249–254 (1996)

Carletta, J.: Unleashing the killer corpus: experiences in creating the multi-everything AMI Meeting Corpus. In: Language Resources and Evaluation, vol. 41(2), pp. 181–190. Springer, Heidelberg (2007)

Cerrato, L.: Investigating Communicative Feedback Phenomena across Languages and Modalities. PhD Thesis in Speech and Music Communication, Stockholm, KTH (2007)

Clark, H.H., Schaefer, E.F.: Contributing to Discourse. Cognitive Science 13, 259–294 (1989)

Douxchamps, D., Campbell, N.: Robust real-time tracking for the analysis of human behaviour. In: Popescu-Belis, A., Renals, S., Bourlard, H. (eds.) MLMI 2007. LNCS, vol. 4892. Springer, Heidelberg (2008)

Duncan Jr., S., Fiske, D.W.: Face-to-Face Interaction: Research, Methods and Theory. John Wiley & Sons/Lawrence Erlbaum, Mahwah (1977)

Jokinen, K., Ragni, A.: Clustering experiments on the communicative properties of gaze and gestures. In: Proceeding of the 3rd. Baltic Conference on Human Language Technologies, Kaunas (2007)

Kendon, A.: Gesture, Cambridge (2004)

Kipp, M.: Anvil – A Generic Annotation Tool for Multimodal Dialogue. In: Proceedings of Eurospeech 2001, pp. 1367–1370 (2001)

Martin, J.C., Paggio, P., Kuenlein, P., Stiefelhagen, R., Pianesi, F. (eds.): Multimodal Corpora for Modelling Human Multimodal Behaviour. Special issue of the International Journal of Language Resources and Evaluation, vol. 41(3–4). Springer, Heidelberg (2007)

McNeill, D.: Hand and Mind: What Gestures Reveal About Thought. University of Chicago Press, Chicago (1992)

Mostefa, D., Moreau, N., Choukri, K., Potamianos, G., Chu, S.M., Tyagi, A., Casas, J.R., Turmo, J., Cristoforetti, L., Tobia, F., Pnevmatikakis, A., Mylonakis, V., Talantzis, F., Burger, S., Stiefelhagen, R., Bernardin, K., Rochet, C.: The CHIL audiovisual corpus for lecture and meeting analysis inside smart rooms. In: Language Resources and Evaluation, vol. 41(3-4), pp. 389–407. Springer, Heidelberg (2007)

Peirce, C.S.: Elements of Logic. In: Hartshorne, C., Weiss, P. (eds.) Collected Papers of Charles Sanders Peirce, vol. 2, Harvard University Press, Cambridge (1931)

Witten, I.H., Frank, E.: Data Mining: Practical machine learning tools and techniques, 2nd edn. Morgan Kaufmann, San Francisco (2005)

Platt, J.: Sequential minimal optimization: A fast algorithm for training support vector machines. Technical Report MSR-TR-98-14, Microsoft Research (1998)

Optimised Meeting Recording and Annotation Using Real-Time Video Analysis

Paul Chippendale and Oswald Lanz

FBK-irst
chippendale@fbk.it, lanz@fbk.it

Abstract. The research detailed in this paper represents the confluence of various vision technologies to provide a powerful, real-time tool for human behavioural analysis. Gesture recognition algorithms are amalgamated with a robust multi-person tracker based on particle filtering to monitor the position and orientation of multiple people, and moreover to understand their focus of attention and gesticular activity. Additionally, an integrated virtual video director is demonstrated that can automatically control active cameras to produce an optimum record of visual events in real-time.

Keywords: Person Tracking, Gestures, Head Orientation, Active Camera.

1 Introduction

The manual annotation and analysis of human interactions, 'who does what' during a meeting for example, is a time-consuming and laborious task. The creation of transcriptions and subsequent data mining from such a huge data-set is always open to ambiguities, as one transcriber will notice or interpret events that another will overlook. The Holy Grail for annotators would be the creation of a fully automated, accurate and consistent tool that effortlessly provides a complete and comprehensive breakdown of which people being monitored did what, where and when.

This topic is being addressed with increasing research effort and the CHIL and AMI European projects [1,2] are two prime examples. However, when a scene is complex and the number of people to be observed is large, the problem becomes computationally constraining. Due to the enormous complexity of the systems involved in people monitoring, in this paper we will only present the integration of video technologies, however an analysis of appropriate audio technologies and their integration with vision tools can be found in [3]. Needless to say, a wealth of information can be gleaned from the observation of non-verbal communications [4].

To visually monitor human gestures and interactions effectively, the exact location of all participants and their head orientations must be ascertained. For decades, extensive research has been conducted on multi-person tracking from video sources, however a robust solution that can handle many of the scientific challenges present in natural scenes such as occlusions, illumination changes and high-dimensional motion is hard to realise. Particle filter tracking [5] is a promising and robust approach that can now be implemented in real-time thanks to advances in computing power. The

A. Popescu-Belis and R. Stiefelhagen (Eds.): MLMI 2008, LNCS 5237, pp. 50–61, 2008.
© Springer-Verlag Berlin Heidelberg 2008

positions of multiple people in the environment can be tracked down to an average error of less than 10cm, even under heavy occlusion. Along with knowledge of body position, a person's body posture (e.g. standing, sitting, etc.) should also be monitored. These additional parameters can also be obtained from the same tracker by increasing the state-space, at the cost of increased complexity.

The tracking of body parts (as opposed to the whole) has also received a great deal of attention over the years. For applications such as gesture recognition, there are inherent minimum observable size constraints; tiny movements potentially providing valuable information could otherwise go undetected. Therefore, to ensure that adequate images are available for gesture recognition, active cameras are crucial.

There are two main approaches commonly employed for the driving/steering of active cameras in a multi-person environment. The first requires a skilled human operator(s) to steer all cameras simultaneously towards the multiple participants. The second requires the complete integration of a robust person tracker to automatically handle camera allocation and steering in real-time.

In this paper the various technologies we developed[1] to automatically annotate visually-apparent human behaviour will briefly be explained and proven through real life experimentation. We will show how these were integrated to produce a cohesive system that provides a real-time output of target position, focus of attention, fidgeting activity and static arm gestures, to name but a few. We will illustrate how information flows around the system and how we might infer some basic human activities. In addition we will demonstrate how our system can create optimal visual recordings for multiple targets by steering active cameras using body position and head orientation.

2 System Architecture

The system is composed of three types of modules: those which process images and output features (denoted in Fig. 1. by a rectangle); those which take features as inputs and combine these to make others (denoted by an oval); and those which receive features as an input and act upon them (denoted by a diamond).

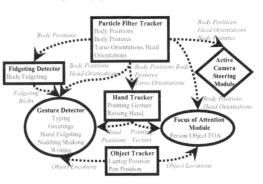

Fig. 1. System Schematic

2.1 Particle Filter Based Location and Pose Tracker

Classical solutions to vision based location and pose tracking factorise the problem into background suppression, morphological noise filtering and blob classification. They usually require the engineering of complex cascades of low-level filters whose behaviour is difficult to understand and which require the tuning of many parameters to particular scene conditions. We, instead, adopt a principled Bayesian approach to track position and body posture whose core is a *generative likelihood function*. The

[1] This research was funded under EU projects CHIL and NETCARITY.

role of the likelihood is to score a hypothetical target pose by analysing a set of calibrated input images. Pose tracking is then formulated as a stochastic filtering problem, and solved by propagating the best-scored hypotheses according to a simple model of pose dynamics.

For the purpose of this paper, a pose is specified in terms of the target's 2D position on the floor, horizontal torso orientation, torso inclination, head pan and tilt, together with a binary label for sitting and standing. These features have been chosen because they can be extracted from the raw video signal and are of high interest when analysing interactions.

2.1.1 Modelling Pose Appearance

We model the visual appearance of a person using:

- A Coarse, volumetric, description of human body shape for different poses;
- Body part and viewpoint based representation of target colour, in the form of head, torso (articulated about the waist) and legs histograms.

For a given pose hypothesis, the shape model is used to identify the triple of image patches where head, torso and legs are expected to appear under that hypothesis. Within these patches, we use colour histograms to describe the appearance of the body parts. Since histograms summarise their colour statistics, their use in a localisation task offers robustness to small misalignments, slight illumination changes and to noise deriving from non-modelled articulated motion. Part-based definition of the model emphasises appearance independence that usually holds between the different body parts due to skin colour and clothing.

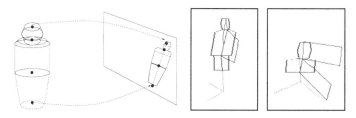

Fig. 2. 3D shape of a standing person and its rendered silhouette. To the right: rendering of a standing pose with an inclined upper body and misaligned head orientation, and a sitting pose.

Fig. 2. shows the part-based 3D target model assembled from a set of rigid cone trunks. To obtain its image projection a quadruple of 3D points is computed which represent the centre of the feet, hips, shoulders and the top of head. These points are projected onto the camera frame using a calibrated camera model. The segments joining these image points define the 'backbone' around which the body profile is drawn with a piece-wise linear offset from this axis. The profile width, W, of the torso and hips changes with the relative orientation, α, of the body to the observer, according to $w(\alpha) = 0.7 + 0.3|cos(\alpha)|$. Similarly, the relative head orientation β is taken into account to modulate the projected head width. The head patch also has a horizontal offset O from the axis which scales as a function of β: $o(\beta) = 0.38 \cdot sin(\beta)$.

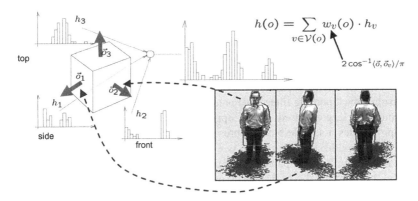

Fig. 3. Reference histogram rendering procedure

For a sitting pose we set the height of the 3D hip centre approximately to the chair height and ignore the legs trunk.

Within the body parts identified by the shape model, the appearance of the target is described by one colour histogram per part. The reference histogram is created for a given pose as depicted in Fig. 3. The basic idea is to record a set of key views of the target prior to tracking, to extract the corresponding descriptions (i.e. colour histograms) for each body part and to then generate the histograms for a new pose and view by interpolation. Given the spatial orientation γ of a body part, the set of neighbouring model views $V(\gamma)$ that point towards the camera is found. Corresponding key view histograms H_v are combined to get the reference appearance by interpolation

$$H(\gamma) = \sum_{v \in V(\gamma)} w_v(\gamma) \cdot H_v \quad \text{with} \quad w_v(\gamma) \propto 2 \cdot \cos^{-1}(\langle \vec{\gamma}, \vec{\gamma}_v \rangle) / \pi .$$

Here $\langle \vec{\gamma}, \vec{\gamma}_v \rangle$ denotes the scalar product between the 3D versors pointing in the direction of pose orientation γ and key view orientation γ_v. This method supports histogram rendering from any viewing orientation, including top-down views. In setups where only lateral views are available (typically cameras placed in the corners of a room) it is sufficient to acquire key view histograms for side views only (like those seen in Fig. 3.), and interpolation is done using the two closest reference views.

2.1.2 Appearance Likelihood

To score a given pose hypothesis, x, on a new input image, I, we extract histograms from the image areas identified by shape rendering. These histograms are then compared to reference histograms rendered as described, using a similarity measure derived from Bhattacharyya-coefficient based distance: if a^h, a^t, a^l, is the area of body part projections and H^h_z, H^t_z, H^l_z and H^h_m, H^t_m, H^l_m denote normalised extracted and modelled histograms, the assigned likelihood value is:

$$\exp\left(-(a^h d^2(H^h_z, H^h_m) + a^t d^2(H^t_z, H^t_m) + a^l d^2(H^l_z, H^l_m)) / 2\sigma^2(a^h + a^t + a^l)\right)$$

with histogram distance d given by (where index i scans all colour bins)

$$d^2(H,K) = 1 - \sum_i \sqrt{H_i K_i}.$$

Parameter σ controls the selectivity of this function and is set empirically to 0.12.

2.1.3 Particle Filtering

An occlusion robust particle filter [5,6] is implemented to jointly track the location and pose of multiple targets based on the appearance likelihood defined above. Particle filtering propagates a sample-based representation of the posterior density over target pose. A pose hypothesis, or *particle*, is embodied by a 7–dimensional vector: (x,y) location, head pan/tilt, body pan/tilt, plus a binary dimension for sitting/standing. The particle set representing the probabilistic estimate at time *t* is projected to time *t+1* by

adding zero-mean Gaussian noise to the components of each particle. After prediction, pose likelihoods are computed on the different views and particle weights are assigned; weighted re-sampling is then finally applied. After enrolment (see below), the initial particle set is sampled from a Gaussian distribution centred in the hot spot position. The probabilistic tracker outputs the expectation over the current, weighted particle set. Fig. 4. shows a typical real-time output.

Fig. 4. Real time particle filter output

2.1.4 Target Detection and Model Acquisition

Reference histograms and shape parameters are acquired prior to tracking, in an enrolment phase. To achieve this without manual intervention a virtual *hot spot* of the scene is continuously monitored using multiple cameras. To enrol, each person visits the hot spot area upon entering. Target detection within this area is based on the matching of extracted image contours and the virtual silhouette of the shape model rendered for different target heights, widths and positions (pose is fixed to standing upright). If the best matching result is above a threshold for a number of consecutive frames, a target is detected. Reference histograms are stored for the best matching result, together with the target's physical width and height (see Fig. 5. for examples).

Fig. 5. Enrolment

2.2 Focus of Attention Module

The majority of the features required to determine focus of attention are automatically derived by the particle filter and object trackers, i.e. target location, head pan and tilt, laptop and pens, however other objects such as table, whiteboard can be manually inputted. The focus of attention of each target is then estimated by projecting a ray from the person's head centroid in the direction of his head orientation and then whatever the ray intercepts first is deemed to be the focus of his attention.

2.3 Hand Tracker

The output of the particle filter tracker can be exploited and fused in a multitude of ways to derive further features. By passing absolute body position, body posture and torso orientation to the hand tracker module and by imposing basic anatomical rules, 3D regions can be postulated which should contain a target's hands and shoulder joints. From the 3D shoulder points, two spherical volumes are described within the environment proportional to the target's body height (see Fig. 6.(a)).

Within these regions, candidate hand blobs are located through the application of a statistical skin model filter, as in [7], created through the prior observation of hundreds of skin regions from our camera video streams. The centroids of appropriately sized skin regions inside the projected spheres are re-projected back into 3D space in the form of a ray originating from the camera's origin. This is conducted for all skin regions pertaining to the same target in each camera; then using an SVD algorithm the minimum distances between rays from other cameras is computed. Providing that the closest intersection distance is small (say < 30cm), and that the hypothesised position of the 3D hand lies inside the spheres, a hypothetical 3D hand position is created. All permutations of skin regions are tested in order to find the best hypotheses, and subsequently these are labelled as left and right hands. Left hands are assumed to be the leftmost with respect to the torso's orientation and likewise rightmost for the right. The same process is repeated for all targets within the room.

2.3.1 Pointing and Hand Raising Detection

The detection and accurate interpretation of dynamic hand gestures is a very challenging task. Gesticular actions vary greatly from one individual to another and it is often difficult to discern exactly when one gesture begins and another ends. Conversely, static gestures (sometimes referred to as postures) such as pointing and the raising of the hand, can be generalised as being periods of static hand postures punctuating periods of temporal hand movement.

To decide whether a gesture relates to pointing, the raising of the hand or neither, we examine the spatial and temporal stability of the hands and their position with respect to the two spheres prescribed.

The first pointing-gesture criterion to be met is based upon its dwell time. The estimated position of the hand, even when it is stationary, will move slightly due to the presence of image noise. To compensate for this, a positional variance of 30cm (roughly equal to 2 hand widths) was empirically selected, thus if the hand centroid does not move more than this during one second the hand is deemed to be stationary.

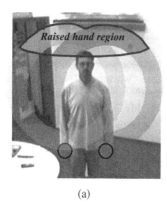 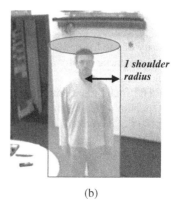

(a)   (b)

Fig. 6. (a) Pointing detection, (b) Fidgeting volume

When a static hand is identified, its Euclidean distance from the shoulder joint is measured. When it lies more than 75% of an arm's length away from the shoulder joint (see Fig. 6.(a)) and it does not lie inside the 3D cylinder seen in Fig. 6.(b) a pointing gesture is detected. Additionally, if the hand is above the head height, then the gesture is deemed to be a raised hand.

2.4 Fidgeting Detector

2.4.1 Hand, Head and Body Fidgeting

Fidgeting is defined as "a condition of restlessness as manifested by nervous movements", and it can reveal important clues about the emotional state and activity of an individual [8]. Using visual means, fidgeting signatures can be detected using techniques such as optical flow or Memory History Images (MHIs) [9]. However, due to ambiguities between the actions say of fiddling with a pair of glasses and writing, it is difficult to be sure which is taking place, unless of course a pen can be detected.

To pinpoint fidgeting, we concentrate our search efforts around the 3D position of the head and hands we project back into the 2D images. In these regions the fidgeting algorithm searches for temporally unstable skin pixels to construct an MHI representing repetitive skin motion. The more often a pixel within a hand or head region changes from skin to non-skin, the brighter the corresponding MHI pixel becomes. In addition to observing periodic motion, the spatial persistence of the hand is also taken into account; this information is provided by the hand tracker.

In a similar fashion, the amount of body fidgeting is also assessed. However, as the colour histogram of the body is only crudely known from the person tracker, in this case a thresholded change in pixel colour over time is used to trigger the MHI.

2.5 Gesture Detector

2.5.1 Nodding and Shaking of the Head

To detect whether a head is nodding or shaking it is sufficient to correlate head fidgeting events with the head information supplied by the particle filter tracker.

Although the fidgeting detector can tell us that a repetitive head movement is taking place, it is not always straightforward to determine whether the head is panning or tilting from the shape of the fidgeting event. To provide the missing information, the pan and tilt values are taken from the head tracker during the past few frames and their trend used to make a joint decision.

2.5.2 Greetings
The location and subsequent detection of greeting gestures is achieved through the projection of imaginary cuboids onto the 2D camera images (see Fig. 10.(a)), which connect pairs of standing targets at mid-torso height that are separated by less than two arm lengths (~2m). Inside the projected cuboid volumes, hand fidgeting events are searched for and if located the hand tracker module is asked to confirm whether both targets roughly share a hand location.

2.6 Object Tracker and Activity Detection

2.6.1 Laptop and Typing
To facilitate the detection of typing events, a simple object tracker is employed to locate potential laptops on the table's surface. The laptop model is a basic one based on a reference colour histogram and shape (based on the average colour gamut and dimensions of several laptops in the lab). To identify a laptop's location, homographic projection is employed using multiple camera images along the plane of the tabletop. Where an appropriate footprint is located, its colour signature is then evaluated.

Typing events are subsequently detected by correlating the position of laptops with the results from the fidgeting detector (see Fig. 10. (b) for an example).

2.6.2 Pen and Writing
In the case of pens, each one that was to be used in the meeting was fitted with two bands of known colours. The pens were then detected using the same algorithm as for skin but with a different colour gamut.

To detect whether writing is taking place, the location of the pen is correlated against hand fidgeting events. To provide further corroborating evidence, temporal frame differencing is employed using the pen colours as an identifying feature.

3 Virtual Video Director

Even with many cameras available, it can often be difficult to manually select (and consistently maintain) a good frontal image for a given number of targets. To address this 'best camera' selection issue, we created a fully automatic means to steer active cameras so as to provide optimal views for all tracked targets at all times.

Our selection strategy computes a camera's 'utility' score, to a given target from two derived metrics. The first is based upon the angular distance between the target's face plane and camera position, in combination with the target's likelihood of occlusion. For each target (e.g. Target A in Fig. 7.) a list of face plane to camera angles

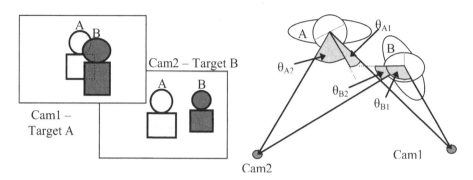

Fig. 7. Camera Utility Score Calculation

is calculated (e.g. θ_{A2} and θ_{A1}). Then, from a simulated pan and tilt configuration orientated towards the centroid of the target's mid-torso, the 3D shape model of the target is projected. Crucially, all other targets are also projected onto the simulated camera view to compute the amount of occlusion of, or overlap with, the considered target. The angular distance is then multiplied with this occlusion factor to compute the camera-to-target utility score. As Fig. 7. shows, Target A is partially occluded in Cam1's view, but is unobstructed in Cam2's, consequently Cam2 is selected (assuming that both have similar angular distance). To avoid excessive camera re-allocation when multiple targets are mobile, we introduced a minimum target-camera pairing duration of three seconds, i.e. after a camera has been instructed to point towards a target it cannot be re-assigned to another target for at least this period.

As facial pixels generally play a more significant role in gesture analysis, a higher importance is placed upon them. Consequently, a further utility factor is calculated by summing and normalising the number of pixels that are unobstructed, multiplying them by a factor relating to the Euclidean angular distance observed and then applying a further factor dependant on whether they belong to the face or torso. Another consideration relates to the current pan, tilt and zoom configuration of each camera relative to the hypothetical configuration that they would have to be at to ideally encapsulate the target in its field of view. This discrepancy is crucial as active cameras can only re-orientate themselves at a finite rate.

The overall utility metric is calculated by adding the two separate considerations together in a weighted manner. This weighting is user-controlled that can place a higher emphasis on a target's viewability from a more consistent camera view rather than providing a better frontal image at the expense of changing cameras more often.

Once the most appropriate, available camera for a target has been selected, it is commanded to point itself to the mid-torso of the target to optimise the images for gesture analysis. If the target moves outside of a central region of the image, a pan or tilt is initiated such to map it onto the image centre. The size of the central region is arbitrary and can be set to a size appropriate for the application, i.e. if the region is small, then the camera will be re-orientated more often. In order to maintain a good size of target in the field of view, the zoom level of the camera is automatically adjusted in accordance with the intra camera-target distance.

4 Human Activity Estimation from Observation Fusion

In this paper a tentative attempt at human activity detection has been made by logically combing the various outputs from the many visual cues from either single or multiple targets in a way shown in Fig. 8. In this way, the spatio-temporal co-incidence of features gives rise to a certain

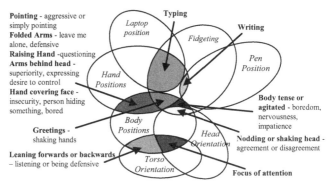

Fig. 8. Integration of features to infer higher level activities

hypothesis about an activity. For example, if a target is fidgeting his hands and they are close to the laptop then he probably typing.

5 Results

Despite compression artefacts and poor resolution, information about face and body pose can be extracted to good precision, an achievement to be rewarded to the generative approach under-taken (a quantitative evalua-tion of head pan precision is available in [10]).

The graph presented in Fig. 9. shows the out-put from the fidgeting module (i.e. head, hand and body fidgeting) during a 15 minute pre-re-corded simulated meeting (see Fig. 10. for example images), for a single tracked target. To provide an optimal ob-servation, the target's

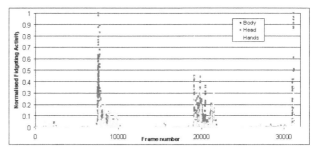

Fig. 9. Results from fidgeting analysis for Target 1

fidgeting levels were measured independently for each of the four cameras, normalised according to camera-target distances, and then the maximum for each feature stored. S can be seen, the graph shows four distinct activity periods: The first coincided with the meeting participants entering the room and greeting one another (Fig. 10a), then seating. The second repre-sented a typing period (Fig. 10b). The third correlated to a period just before the target was expecting to stand and was a little restless. The final peak shows where the target shook hands with the others before leaving.

Fig. 10.(a) illustrates a 3D bounding box pro-jected onto an active camera image in between two targets in order to detect greeting events. Fig. 10.(b) shows a clear example of a captured 'typing' event. As hand activity correlated to the position of the laptop, a typing event was logged.

Fig. 10. Detected events: greeting (a), and typing (b)

To validate the camera allocation policy we acquired image streams from four active cameras centrally mounted on each wall. During acquisition, the cameras were continuously steered towards the same target. To evaluate 'utility' performance, the average size of the face skin blob was calculated using the skin blob detector. Table 1 clearly shows the advantage of best view selection over a fixed camera-to-target allocation. In particular, Fig. 11. shows an interesting situation involving an occlusion successfully handled by the policy. Note that without occlusion reasoning camera (A) would be selected, as it provides the most face-frontal view.

Fig. 11. Active views and tracker output during an occlusion. A predefined camera-to-target allocation may deliver (A), while the selection policy successfully allocated (C).

Table 1. Average face blob size in a fixed camera-to-target allocation vs. optimal selection

Active camera ID	Cam1	Cam2	Cam3	Cam4	Selection
Average face size (pixel)	343	227	367	358	605

6 Conclusions

In this paper we have shown that a real-time system can be created to automatically annotate visually apparent human behaviour. We have also shown how an effective means of selecting and maintaining an ideal camera view can be achieved and how an ideal camera sequence can be created from the automatic steering and selecting of the optimum camera.

Our next steps towards a richer annotated output will be based upon the extraction and fusion of more visual cues (for example, improved posture detection while seated) and integrating other modalities.

References

1. CHIL, Computer. In: the Human Interaction Loop, http://chil.server.de/
2. AMI, Augmented Multi-party Interaction, http://www.amiproject.org/
3. Brunelli, R., Brutti, A., Chippendale, P., Lanz, O., Omologo, M., Svaizer, P., Tobia, F.: 'A Generative Approach to Audio-Visual Person Tracking', Multimodal Technologies for Perception of Humans, Springer LNCS 4122, pp. In: Stiefelhagen, R., Garofolo, J.S. (eds.) CLEAR 2006. LNCS, vol. 4122, pp. 302–9743. Springer, Heidelberg (2007)
4. Fromkin, V., Rodman, R., Hyams, N.M.: 'An Introduction to Language', 7th edn. Heinle & Heinle,
5. Lanz, O.: Approximate Bayesian Multibody Tracking. IEEE Transactions on Pattern Analysis and Machine Intelligence 28(9), 1436–1449 (2006)
6. SmarTrack – a SmarT people Tracker, http://tev.fbk.eu/smartrack/
7. Chippendale, P.: Towards Automatic Body Language Annotation. In: 7th Int. Conference on Automatic Face and Gesture Recognition, Southampton, UK, pp. 487–492 (2006)
8. Zancanaro, M., Lepri, B., Pianesi, F.: Automatic detection of group functional roles in face to face interactions. In: proceedings ICMI 2006, pp. 28–34 (2006)
9. Davis, J.W.: Hierarchical Motion History Images for Recognizing Human Motion. In: IEEE Workshop on Detection and Recognition of Events in Video, p. 39. IEEE, Los Alamitos (2001)
10. Lanz, O., Brunelli, R.: Dynamic Head Location and Pose from Video. In: Proc. IEEE Multisensor Fusion and Integration MFI2006, Heidelberg, Germany (September 2006)

Ambiguity Modeling in Latent Spaces

Carl Henrik Ek[1], Jon Rihan[1], Philip H.S. Torr[1], Grégory Rogez[2],
and Neil D. Lawrence[3]

[1] Oxford Brookes University, UK
{cek,jon.rihan,philiptorr}@brookes.ac.uk
[2] University of Zaragoza, Spain
grogez@unizar.es
[3] University of Manchester, UK
Neil.Lawrence@manchester.ac.uk

Abstract. We are interested in the situation where we have two or more representations of an underlying phenomenon. In particular we are interested in the scenario where the representation are complementary. This implies that a single individual representation is not sufficient to fully discriminate a specific instance of the underlying phenomenon, it also means that each representation is an ambiguous representation of the other complementary spaces. In this paper we present a latent variable model capable of consolidating multiple complementary representations. Our method extends canonical correlation analysis by introducing additional latent spaces that are specific to the different representations, thereby explaining the full variance of the observations. These additional spaces, explaining representation specific variance, separately model the variance in a representation ambiguous to the other. We develop a spectral algorithm for fast computation of the embeddings and a probabilistic model (based on Gaussian processes) for validation and inference. The proposed model has several potential application areas, we demonstrate its use for multi-modal regression on a benchmark human pose estimation data set.

1 Introduction

A common situation in machine learning is the consolidation of two disparate, but related, data sets. Examples include: consolidation of lip movement with cepstral coefficients for improving the quality of robust speech recognition; consolidation of two different language renderings of the same document for cross language information retrieval; and consolidation of human pose data with image information for marker-less motion capture.

Formally, we will consider the situation where we are provided with two data sets, $\mathbf{Y} = [\mathbf{y}_1 \dots \mathbf{y}_N]^\mathrm{T} \in \Re^{N \times D_Y}$ and $\mathbf{Z} = [\mathbf{z}_1 \dots \mathbf{z}_N]^\mathrm{T} \in \Re^{N \times D_Z}$, for which there is some kind of correspondence between each point. For example, each measurement could have been taken at the same time or under the same experimental conditions. We are interested in answering questions about the relationship $\mathbf{z}_n$ and $\mathbf{y}_n$. For example: what is the most likely $\mathbf{z}_n$, given $\mathbf{y}_n$? This question can be answered by direct modeling of the conditional probability $p(\mathbf{z}_n | \mathbf{y}_n)$. However, this distribution can be very complex in practice. If we for example used a regression model, it would only be valid if the

A. Popescu-Belis and R. Stiefelhagen (Eds.): MLMI 2008, LNCS 5237, pp. 62–73, 2008.

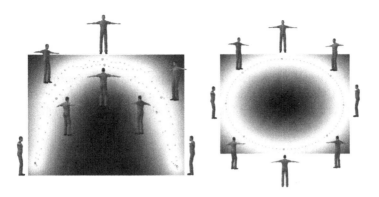

Fig. 1. Latent representation associated with a static pose rotating $360°$ and its corresponding silhouette image features. The x-axis represents the dimension that is common to both spaces. The y-axis is *image feature specific* on the **left** and *pose feature specific* on the **right**. We have also used the GP-LVM model to associate each location in latent space with a likelihood. White represents high and black low regions of likelihood. Note the ambiguities in pose associated with the image feature space (ambiguous poses have similar x and y positions). In the pose space these ambiguities are resolved in the y axis.

relationship between the observations was unimodal, this is often an invalid assumption. Multi-modalities that arise are a manifestation of a non-bijective relationship between y_n and z_n, one that is difficult to express in a standard regression model. We could turn to a model for conditional probability estimation that allows for multi-modalities [13]. However, the nature of the multi-modal relationship is likely to be difficult to learn when the size of the data set is restricted. In this paper we propose an alternative approach, one that is based explicitly on assumptions about the relationship between y_n and z_n. In particular we will assume that the data is generated by a lower dimensional latent variable, X. The approach is similar in character to that of canonical correlation analysis (CCA) with one key difference: the latent space associated with CCA describes only the characteristics of the data that are common to both the representations. We will construct a latent space that represents the *full data set*. We will subdivide the latent space into three *non-overlapping* partitions. One partition will be associated only with the Y data another partition is associated only with the Z data and the remaining partition is associated with the common or shared information between Y and Z. The remaining non-shared or private latent subspaces model information not present in the corresponding observation space. This means when estimating z_n from y_n the private space represents the ambiguities of z_n when presented with y_n.

A simple example of such an ambiguity is given in Figure 1 where the proposed model has been applied to a toy data set of a rotated character. The x-axis direction in both plots is shared for both pose and silhouette. The y-axis in the left plot represents information specific to the silhouette, while in the in the right plot, information specific to the pose. When looking at the information in the x axis only, the pose is ambiguous. However, in the right plot (from the motion capture) the pose is disambiguated on the y-axis, *i.e.* each pose is associated with a single location. The y-axis does not help in disambiguation in the left plot (which encodes silhouette information). Clearly, augmenting the latent space with a direction representing the 'private information' will be vital in disambiguating the pose from the silhouette.

Outline of the paper: In the next section we will present the non consolidating component analysis (NCCA) model for data consolidation, we will then show results on both real and synthetic data in Section 3 followed by conclusions in Section 4.

2   The NCCA Model

Given two sets of corresponding observations $\mathbf{Y} = [\mathbf{y}_1, \ldots, \mathbf{y}_N]^T$ and $\mathbf{Z} = [\mathbf{z}_1, \ldots, \mathbf{z}_N]^T$ where $\mathbf{y}_n \in \Re^{D_y}$ and $\mathbf{z}_n \in \Re^{D_z}$ we wish to characterize the relationship between the data sets through a latent variable model. We will assume that the two data sets can be generated by noise corrupted smooth functions that map from the latent space to the data-spaces in the following way,

$$y_{ni} = f_i^Y\left(\mathbf{x}_n^s, \mathbf{x}_n^Y\right) + \epsilon_{ni}^Y, \quad z_{ni} = f_i^Z\left(\mathbf{x}_n^s, \mathbf{x}_n^Z\right) + \epsilon_{ni}^Z, \tag{1}$$

where $\{y, z\}_{ni}$ represent dimension i of point n and ϵ_{ni}^Y, ϵ_{ni}^Z are sampled from a zero mean Gaussian distribution. The mappings are occurring from a latent space which is split into three parts, $\mathbf{X}^Y = \{\mathbf{x}_n^Y\}_{n=1}^N$, $\mathbf{X}^Z = \{\mathbf{x}_n^Z\}_{n=1}^N$ and $\mathbf{X}^s = \{\mathbf{x}_n^s\}_{n=1}^N$. The first two splits will be associated with variance that is particular to the $\mathbf{Y}$ and $\mathbf{Z}$ spaces. The last split is associated with variance that is shared across the spaces.

Distance preserving approaches to dimensionality reduction typically imply that there is a smooth mapping in the *reverse direction*. In particular, kernel-CCA [4] implicitly assumes that there is a smooth mapping from each of the data-spaces to a shared latent space,

$$x_{ni}^s = g_i^Y\left(\mathbf{y}_n\right) = g_i^Z\left(\mathbf{z}_n\right). \tag{2}$$

However, CCA does not characterize the nature of the other latent subspaces, $\mathbf{X}^Y$ and $\mathbf{X}^Z$. In Section 2.1 we will introduce an algorithm for extracting these spaces which we refer to as the *non-consolidating* subspaces. Underpinning the algorithm will be a further assumption about the non-consolidating subspaces,

$$x_{ni}^Y = h_i^Y\left(\mathbf{y}_n\right), \quad x_{ni}^Z = h_i^Z\left(\mathbf{z}_n\right), \tag{3}$$

where $h_i^Y\left(\cdot\right)$ and $h_i^Z\left(\cdot\right)$ are smooth functions. A graphical representation of the consolidation model is shown in Figure 2. Our approach will be as follows, we will construct a model by assuming the smooth mappings in (2) and (3) hold. We will then validate the model quality through assessing how well the resulting embeddings respect (1). We are inspired in our approach by the suggestion that spectral methods are used to initialize the Gaussian process latent variable model (GP-LVM) in [5] and by the observation of [3] that the quality of an embedding is nicely indicated by the log likelihood of the GP-LVM.

To allow for non-linear relationships in the data we will first represent the observations in kernel induced feature spaces $\Psi_Y : Y \to \mathcal{F}^Y; \Psi_Z : Z \to \mathcal{F}^Z$, by introducing kernels for each feature space, $\mathbf{K}_Y$ and $\mathbf{K}_Z$. The first step in the model is to apply kernel

---

Algorithm 1. NCCA Consolidation

Input:
$\mathbf{Y} = [\mathbf{y}_1, \ldots, \mathbf{y}_N], \ \mathbf{y}_i \in \Re^{D_{\mathbf{Y}}}$
$\mathbf{Z} = [\mathbf{z}_1, \ldots, \mathbf{z}_N], \ \mathbf{z}_i \in \Re^{D_{\mathbf{Z}}}$
$\mathbf{K}_Y, \mathbf{K}_Z$

Stage 1, Learn latent embedding
Find kernel spaces from $\mathbf{K}_y$ and $\mathbf{K}_Z$ by kernel PCA:
1) Apply **CCA** to find shared embedded data $\mathbf{X}^S$, Eq. (8)
2) Apply **NCCA** to find non-shared embedded data
    $\mathbf{X}^Y$ and $\mathbf{X}^Z$, Eq. (9)

Stage 2, Learn mappings, *let J be either Y or Z,*
By GP-regression find:
1) Generative maps: $f^J : [\mathbf{X}^S; \mathbf{X}^J] \rightarrow \mathbf{J}$ Eq. (10)
2) Shared maps: $g^J : \mathbf{J} \rightarrow \mathbf{X}^S$ Eq. (11)
3) Non-shared maps: $h^J : \mathbf{J} \rightarrow \mathbf{X}^J$ Eq. (12)
    See Figure 2

Return:
Pose Estimation: g^Y and f^Z
General Case: All maps learned above.

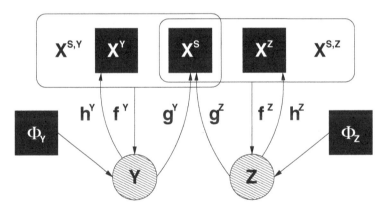

Fig. 2. Graphical model of the NCCA Model. The two observations $\mathbf{Y}$ and $\mathbf{Z}$ are generated from low-dimensional embeddings $\mathbf{X}^{S,Y}$ and $\mathbf{X}^{S,Z}$ indicated by rounded rectangles. The embeddings share a common subspace $\mathbf{X}^S$ representing the shared variance in each observation space. This is variance in $\mathbf{Y}$ and $\mathbf{Z}$ that can be described as a function of $\mathbf{Z}$ and $\mathbf{Y}$ respectively. An additional subspace $\mathbf{X}^Y$ and $\mathbf{X}^Z$ completes the embedding, representing the non-shared variance between the observations. Φ_Y and Φ_Z collects the parameters associated with each mapping.

canonical correlation analysis (CCA) [4] to find the directions of high correlation between the two feature spaces. We therefore briefly review the CCA algorithm. The objective in CCA is to find linear transformations $\mathbf{W}_Y$ and $\mathbf{W}_Z$ maximizing the correlation between $\mathbf{W}_Y \mathbf{Y}$ and $\mathbf{W}_Z \mathbf{Z}$. Applied in the kernel feature space of each observation,

$$\{\hat{\mathbf{W}}_Y, \hat{\mathbf{W}}_Z\} = \mathrm{argmax}_{\{\mathbf{W}_Y, \mathbf{W}_Z\}} \mathrm{tr}\left(\mathbf{W}_Y^{\mathrm{T}}\mathbf{K}_Y^{\mathrm{T}}\mathbf{K}_Z\mathbf{W}_Z\right), \tag{4}$$
$$\mathrm{s.t.} \quad \mathrm{tr}\left(\mathbf{W}_Y^{\mathrm{T}}\mathbf{K}_Y^{\mathrm{T}}\mathbf{K}_Y\mathbf{W}_Y\right) = \mathbf{I}$$
$$\mathrm{tr}\left(\mathbf{W}_Z^{\mathrm{T}}\mathbf{K}_Z^{\mathrm{T}}\mathbf{K}_Z\mathbf{W}_Z\right) = \mathbf{I},$$

the optima is found through an eigenvalue problem. In [4] it is suggested to apply CCA in the dominant principal subspace of each feature space instead of directly in the feature space, this constrains $\mathbf{W}_Y$ and $\mathbf{W}_Z$ to explain only the significant variance. We found this suggestion to be important in practice.

Applying CCA recovers two sets of bases $\mathbf{W}_Y$ and $\mathbf{W}_Z$ explaining the correlated or shared variance between the two feature spaces. However, we wish to represent the full variance of each feature space. To achieve this further sets of bases representing the remaining variance are required. We derive a new algorithm, non consolidating component analysis, for finding these additional bases.

2.1 NCCA

Once a set of basis-vectors in each feature space have been found that describe the shared variance, we need to find directions in each feature space that individually represents the remaining variance of each data space. We therefore proceed by seeking the directions of maximum variance in the data that are *orthogonal* to the directions given by the canonical correlates. We call the following procedure *non-consolidating components analysis* (NCCA). The NCCA algorithm is applied in the same space as CCA, but now we seek the first direction $\mathbf{v}_1$ of maximum variance which is orthogonal to the canonical directions that were already extracted,

$$\mathbf{v}_1 = \mathrm{argmax}_{\mathbf{v}_1} \mathbf{v}_1^{\mathrm{T}}\mathbf{K}\mathbf{v}_1 \tag{5}$$

subject to: $\mathbf{v}_1^{\mathrm{T}}\mathbf{v}_1 = 1$ and $\mathbf{v}_1^{\mathrm{T}}\mathbf{W} = \mathbf{0}$, (here we have temporarily dropped the partition subscript), $\mathbf{W}$ are the canonical directions and $\mathbf{K}$ is the covariance matrix in the dominant principal subspace of the feature space. The optimal $\mathbf{v}_1$ is found via an eigenvalue problem,

$$\left(\mathbf{C} - \mathbf{W}\mathbf{W}^{\mathrm{T}}\mathbf{K}\right)\mathbf{v}_1 = \lambda_1\mathbf{v}_1. \tag{6}$$

For successive directions further eigenvalue problems of the form

$$\left(\mathbf{K} - \left(\mathbf{W}\mathbf{W}^{\mathrm{T}} + \sum_{i=1}^{k-1} \mathbf{v}_i\mathbf{v}_i^{\mathrm{T}}\right)\mathbf{K}\right)\mathbf{v}_k = \lambda_k\mathbf{v}_k \tag{7}$$

need to be solved. Note that we only need the largest eigenvalue for each of these eigenvalue problems which can lead to significant computational savings.

After applying CCA and NCCA we have recovered the following embeddings of the data

$$\mathbf{X}^S = \tfrac{1}{2}\left(\mathbf{W}_Y\mathbf{F}_Y + \mathbf{W}_Z\mathbf{F}_Z\right) \tag{8}$$
$$\mathbf{X}^Y = \mathbf{V}_Y\mathbf{F}_Y; \quad \mathbf{X}^Z = \mathbf{V}_Z\mathbf{F}_Z, \tag{9}$$

where $\mathbf{F}_Y$ and $\mathbf{F}_Z$ represent the kernel PCA representation of each observation space. The latent variables $\mathbf{X}^Y$, $\mathbf{X}^Z$ represent the non shared variance of each feature space and $\mathbf{X}^S$ represents the shared variance.

Our methodology results in a purely spectral algorithm: the optimization problems are convex and they lead to unique solutions. However, these spectral methods are perhaps less useful when it comes to inquisition of the resulting model. The pre-image problem means that handling missing data can be rather involved [9]. Probabilistic latent variable models lack the elegant convex solutions provided by spectral methods, but they facilitate model inquisition. Harmeling [3] has performed a series of embedding experiments for which the ground truth is available. By comparing the embeddings from several different spectral algorithms with the ground truth, a good correpondence between the likelihood of the GP-LVM and the quality of the embedding is shown. Intuitively this is because: if the assumptions in (2) and (3) hold and the manifold has been correctly 'unraveled' (1) should also hold. If (1) holds then the likelihood of the GP-LVM will be high and inferences undertaken with the GP-LVM will be accurate. This allows us to proceed by combining our algorithm with the GP-LVM for model selection and inference.

The NCCA algorithm results in implicit mappings from the observation spaces to the embeddings or, if non function based kernels are used — such as those resulting from the MVU algorithm [14], a mapping can be learned explicitly. However, this leaves us with the pre-image problem [10]. For a given latent location, what is the correct observation? The next stage is, therefore, to build Gaussian process mappings from the latent to the data space. This will result in a combination of GP-LVM models that can be used for any inference tasks in the model. This means that as a post processing step, we learn mappings to regenerate the observations spaces $\mathbf{Y}$ and $\mathbf{Z}$ from the embeddings. We define the $\mathbf{Y}$ and $\mathbf{Z}$ specific latent space as $\mathbf{X}^{S,Y} = [\mathbf{X}^S; \mathbf{X}^Y]$, $\mathbf{X}^{S,Z} = [\mathbf{X}^S; \mathbf{X}^Z]$ respectively. The mappings,

$$f^{\{Y,Z\}} : \mathbf{y}_i = f^Y(\mathbf{x}_i^{S,Y}) + \epsilon_f^Y ; \mathbf{z}_i = f^Z(\mathbf{x}_i^{S,Z}) + \epsilon_f^Z, \tag{10}$$

$$g^{\{Y,Z\}} : \mathbf{x}_i^S = g^Y(\mathbf{y}_i) + \epsilon_g^Y = g^Z(\mathbf{z}_i) + \epsilon_g^Z, \tag{11}$$

$$h^{\{Y,Z\}} : \mathbf{x}_i^Y = h^Y(\mathbf{y}_i) + \epsilon_h^Y ; \mathbf{x}_i^Z = h^Z(\mathbf{z}_i) + \epsilon_h^Z, \tag{12}$$

where $\epsilon_{\{f,g,h\}}^{\{Y,Z\}}$ are samples from zero mean Gaussian distributions, are learned using GP-regression [8].

Note that we have, in effect, created a set of back-constrained GP-LVMs from our data [6]. We could have used the GP-LVM algorithm directly for learning this model, in practice though, the spectral approach we have described is much quicker and has fewer problems with local minima.

2.2 Inference

The proposed model represents two data sets using a low dimensional latent variable. Once the latent representations have been learned we are interested in inferring the location $\mathbf{z}_*$, corresponding to a previously unseen input $\mathbf{y}_*$. The input and the sought output locations latent representation coincide on the shared latent subspace $\mathbf{X}^S$, which can be determined from the input through the mapping g^Y. Therefore, to determine the full location of the corresponding output, it remains to determine the location over the private space associated with the output. However, the private subspace is orthogonal to the input specific latent subspace. This implies $\mathbf{y}_*$ can provide no further information to disambiguate over this space, *i.e.* each location over the private space corresponds to outputs that are ambiguous to the input location. We therefore proceed by finding the most probable $\mathbf{z}_*$'s generated by f^Z for different locations over $\mathbf{X}^Z$. From our model's perspective, this is equivalent to minimizing the predictive variance of f^Z [8] with respect to $\mathbf{x}_*^Z$ under the constraint that $\mathbf{x}_*^S$ is given,

$$\hat{\mathbf{x}}_*^Z = \text{argmax}_{\mathbf{x}_*^Z} \left[k(\mathbf{x}_*^{S,Z}, \mathbf{x}_*^{S,Z}) - k(\mathbf{x}_*^{S,Z}, \mathbf{X}^{S,Z})^{\mathrm{T}} (\mathbf{K} + \beta^{-1}\mathbf{I}) k(\mathbf{x}_*^{S,Z}, \mathbf{X}^{S,Z}) \right].$$
(13)

The optimal $\hat{\mathbf{x}}_*^Z$ is found by optimizing Eq. (13) using gradient based methods. We are looking to find all the locations $\mathbf{z}_*$ that are consistent with a specific $\mathbf{y}_*$. The separation of $\mathbf{Z}$ into shared and non-shared means that the ambiguities are very close in the shared subspace. Therefore, we can explore the different modes by looking for nearest neighbors in the shared subspace and initializing the GP-LVM optimizations from those neighbors.

3   Human Pose Estimation

We now consider the application of the model to human pose estimation. We will first briefly review relevant previous work in this area, much of which has provided the inspiration of our approach. Human pose estimation is the task of estimating the full pose configuration of a human from an image. Due to the high dimensionality of the image representation it is common practice, as a preprocessing stage, to represent each image by a lower dimensional image feature vector. In the simplest case, where there is no ambiguity between the image features and the pose, the relationship can be modeled with regression as was demonstrated by [1]. However, regression models are not sufficient to accurately describe the multi-modalities that we expect to arise as a result of ambiguities associated with common image features. An alternative approach to dealing with the multi-modalities is to use a conditional model over the image feature space given the poses [13]. However, due to the high dimensionality and relative data sparsity care must be taken in choosing the class of conditional models. One solution is to incorporate a low dimensional manifold within the conditional density model, thereby avoiding the curse of dimensionality. This approach is followed by [2,7] who exploit the shared GP-LVM [11] to jointly learn a low dimensional representation of both the image features and the pose space. An advantage of basing the model on the GP-LVM [5] is that it provides a principled probabilistic framework for the resulting inference of pose, easily allowing, for example, the incorporation of dynamical models [2].

A key problem with the application of the shared GP-LVM in this context is that a single latent space is used to explain *all* the variance in the data. Since we know that only a portion of the variance is shared, with the remainder being specific to each data partition, it seems to make much more sense to encode this explicitly. The proposed NCCA model does this by decomposing the latent space into sub-spaces which encode the shared variance and subspaces which encode the variance that is private to each data set. These constraints on the latent spaces lead to much cleaner representation of the ambiguities in practice (as we shall see in Section 3.1). When combining the image features with the motion capture the shared latent space represents the variance in the pose space that can be discriminated from the image feature location. The ambiguities,

Fig. 3. Pose inference from silhouette using two different silhouettes from the training data. From the silhouette in the left image it is not possible to determine the positioning of the legs, this results in an elongated region of high probability in the pose private subspace that describs a full stride. The right image shows a silhouette from which it is not possible to differentiate between the right and the left leg. This results in two clear modes over the non-shared dimensions representing the two possible leg labellings in the silhouette.

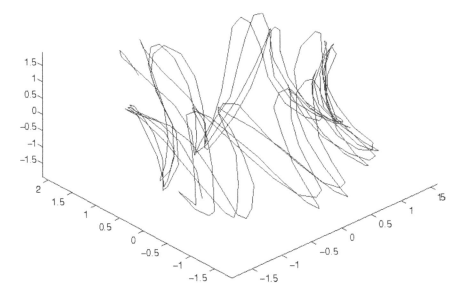

Fig. 4. The pose specific latent representation associated with the HumanEva data. Applying the NCCA algorithm results in a one dimensional shared subspace and a two dimensional pose private space. The larger circle in the embedding is associated with the heading direction while the smaller circles encodes the configuration of arms and legs.

if they exist, therefore necessarily lie in the portion of the latent space that is specific to the motion capture data. As we shall see this makes them much easier to visualize and interpret.

Further, it is likely that a significant amount of the variance in a descriptor does not help in disambiguating the pose. In the shared GP-LVM this information is still encoded

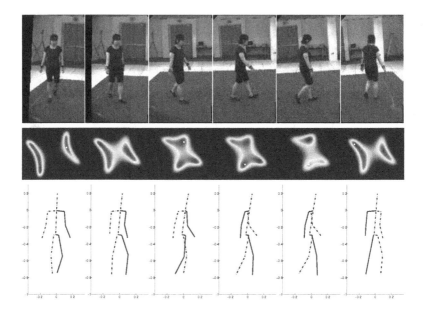

Fig. 5. Pose inference on a sequence of images from the HumanEva data set. Top row: original test set image. Second row: visualisation of the modes in the non-shared portion of the pose specific latent space. Note how the modes evolve as the subject moves. When the subject is heading in a direction perpendicular to the view-plane, it is not possible to disambiguate the heading direction image (1, 2 and 6) this is indicated by two elongated modes. In image $(3 - 5)$ it is not possible to disambiguate the configuration of the arms and legs this gives rise to a set of discrete modes over the latent space each associated with a different configuration. Bottom row: the pose coming from the mode closest to the ground truth is shown. The different types of mode are explored further in Figure 6.

in the model: the shared GP-LVM attempts to model *all* the variance in the data. The NCCA model encodes this information separately, which means it does not influence the inference procedure. This is a key advantage of our model compared to other conditional models, where inference is polluted by estimating this task irrelevant variance.

Once again we direct the reader to Figure 1 to see this effect. The y-axis in the left plot is encoding the spurious information from the image features. It does not help with encoding the true pose. It also is prevented from corrupting the information that arises from the motion capture data (right plot).

3.1 Experiments

We considered a walking sequence from the HumanEva database [12]. There are four cycles in a circular walk, we use two for training and two for testing for the same subject. In the original data the subject is walking in a counter-clockwise direction, to introduce further ambiguities into the data we transform each image and pose to also include the clockwise motion. Each image is represented using a 100 dimensional integral HOG descriptor [15] with 4 orientation bins and the pose space by the $3D$

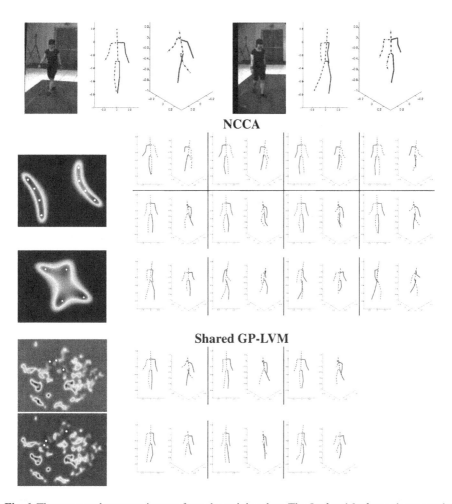

Fig. 6. The top row shows two images from the training data. The $2nd$ and $3rd$ row shows results from infering the pose using the NCCA consolidation, the first column shows the likelihood sampled over the pose specific latent space constrained by the image features, the remaining columns shows the modes associated with the locations of the white dots over the pose specific latent space. **NCCA:** In the $2nd$ row the position of the leg and the heading angle cannot be determined in a robust way from the image features. This is reflected by two elongated modes over the latent space representing the two possible headings. The poses along each mode represents different leg configurations. The top row of the $2nd$ column shows the poses generated by sampling along the right mode and the bottom row along the left mode. In the $3rd$ row the position of the leg and the heading angle is still ambiguous to the feature, however here the ambiguity is between a discrete set of poses indicated by four clear modes in the likelihood over the pose specific latent space. **SGP-LVM:** The $4th$ and $5th$ row show the results of doing inference using the SGP-LVM model. Even though the most likely modes found are in good correspondece to the ambiguities in the images the latent space is cluttered by local minima that the optimization can get stuck in.

locations of 19 major body joints. There are two types of motion in the data, the global motion of the subject moving around in $3D$ space and the local body relative motion, *i.e.* each stride. We assume that each local movement in the training data is possible at all global locations. To decorrelate the two motions we represent the pose space as the sum of a MVU kernel [14] applied to the full pose space and a linear kernel applied on the local motion. The NCCA algorithm with this kernel over the pose space and a MVU kernel over the image features results in a one dimensional shared space explaining 9% and 18% of the variance in the image feature and pose space respectively. To retain 95% of the variance in each observation two dimensions are needed to represent the non-shared variance for both the pose and the image feature space. The pose specific latent space takes the shape of a torus, the larger circle is associated with the heading direction and the smaller circles associated with the stride at that position Figure 4. The total computation time for learning the embedding and the required mappings was about 10 minutes on a Intel Core Duo with 1GB of RAM. In Figure 6 the $2nd$ and $3rd$ row show inference of two different image features from the test data is shown. The inference procedure using 20 nearest neighbor initializations per image took a few seconds to compute.

Shared GP-LVM: The inference procedure in the NCCA model consists of a discriminative mapping followed by the optimization over a sub-set of the pose specific latent space. In comparison to the shared GP-LVM [2,7] the optimization is done over the full latent representation of both image feature and pose. This means that the objective is influenced by how well the latent locations represents variance in the image features that are irrelevant for discriminating the pose. In contrast, the optimization in the NCCA model is done over latent dimensions representing only pose relevant variance. We applied the shared GP-LVM model suggested in [7] to the above data set. To compare models with similar inference complexity we learn a two dimensional shared latent representation of image feature and pose. The optimization on the latent space is initialized by the nearest neighbors in the training data. Note that this is a search in the 100 dimensional image feature space compared to the algorithm we present were the nearest neighbor search takes place in a *one* dimensional space. In Figure 6 the bottom two rows shows the results of applying the Shared GP-LVM to inference the pose of the same images as for the NCCA model.

4   Conclusion

We have presented a practical approach to consolidating two data sets with known correspondences via a latent variable model. We constructed a generative latent variable model for inference and model validation and a spectral algorithm for fast learning of the embeddings, both these interpretations of our model built upon canonical correlation analysis. The resulting model was successful in visualizing the ambiguities on a benchmark human motion data set. Moreover, not only is the presented model fast to train, but also it is efficient in the test phase. Inference is realized by a fast discriminative model that constrains the related generative model. This results in a much simpler estimation compared to previous generative approaches.

References

1. Agarwal, A., Triggs, B.: Recovering 3 d human pose from monocular images. IEEE Transactions on Pattern Analysis and Machine Intelligence 28(1), 44–58 (2006)
2. Ek, C.H., Torr, P.H.S., Lawrence, N.D.: Gaussian process latent variable models for human pose estimation. In: Popescu-Belis, A., Renals, S., Bourlard, H. (eds.) MLMI 2007. LNCS, vol. 4892, pp. 132–143. Springer, Heidelberg (2008)
3. Harmeling, S.: Exploring model selection techniques for nonlinear dimensionality reduction. Technical Report EDI-INF-RR-0960, University of Edinburgh (2007)
4. Kuss, M., Graepel, T.: The geometry of kernel canonical correlation analysis. Technical Report TR-108, Max Planck Institute for Biological Cybernetics, Tübingen, Germany (2003)
5. Lawrence, N.D.: Probabilistic non-linear principal component analysis with Gaussian Process latent variable models. J. Mach. Learn. Res. 6, 1783–1816 (2005)
6. Lawrence, N.D., Quionero-Candela, J.: Local distance preservation in the GP-LVM through back constraints. In: Greiner, R., Schuurmans, D. (eds.) ICML 2006, vol. 21, pp. 513–520. ACM, New York (2006)
7. Navaratnam, R., Fitzgibbon, A., Cipolla, R.: The joint manifold model. In: IEEE International Conference on Computer Vision (ICCV) (2007)
8. Rasmussen, C.E., Williams, C.K.I.: Gaussian Processes for Machine Learning (Adaptive Computation and Machine Learning). MIT Press, Cambridge (2005)
9. Sanguinetti, G., Lawrence, N.D.: Missing data in kernel PCA. In: Fürnkranz, J., Scheffer, T., Spiliopoulou, M. (eds.) ECML 2006. LNCS (LNAI), vol. 4212. Springer, Heidelberg (2006)
10. Scholkopf, B., Smola, A.J.: Learning with Kernels: Support Vector Machines, Regularization, Optimization, and Beyond. MIT Press, Cambridge (2001)
11. Shon, A.P., Grochow, K., Hertzmann, A., Rao, R.P.N.: Learning shared latent structure for image synthesis and robotic imitation. In: Proc. NIPS, pp. 1233–1240 (2006)
12. Sigal, L., Black, M.J.: Humaneva: Synchronized video and motion capture dataset for evaluation of articulated human motion. Brown Univertsity TR (2006)
13. Sminchisescu, C., Kanaujia, A., Li, Z., Metaxas, D.: Discriminative density propagation for 3d human motion estimation. In: Proc. Conf. Computer Vision and Pattern Recognition, pp. 217–323 (2005)
14. Weinberger, K.Q., Sha, F., Saul, L.K.: Learning a kernel matrix for nonlinear dimensionality reduction. In: ACM International Conference Proceeding Series (2004)
15. Zhu, Q., Avidan, S., Yeh, M.C., Cheng, K.T.: Fast Human Detection Using a Cascade of Histograms of Oriented Gradients. CVPR 1(2), 4 (2006)

Inclusion of Video Information for Detection of Acoustic Events Using the Fuzzy Integral

Taras Butko[1,2], Andrey Temko[1,2], Climent Nadeu[1,2], and Cristian Canton[1]

[1] Department of Signal Theory and Communications
[2] TALP Research Center
{butko,temko,climent,ccanton}@gps.tsc.upc.edu

Abstract. When applied to interactive seminars, the detection of acoustic events from only audio information shows a large amount of errors, which are mostly due to the temporal overlaps of sounds. Video signals may be a useful additional source of information to cope with that problem for particular events. In this work, we aim at improving the detection of steps by using two audio-based Acoustic Event Detection (AED) systems, with SVM and HMM, and a video-based AED system, which employs the output of a 3D video tracking algorithm. The fuzzy integral is used to fuse the outputs of the three detection systems. Experimental results using the CLEAR 2007 evaluation data show that video information can be successfully used to improve the results of audio-based AED.

Keywords: Acoustic Event Detection, Fuzzy Integral, Multimodality, Support Vector Machines, Hidden Markov Models, Video 3D Tracking.

1 Introduction

Recently, several papers have reported works on Acoustic Events Detection (AED) for different meeting-room environments and databases e.g. [1] [2] [3]. The CLEAR'07 (Classification of Events, Activities and Relationships) international evaluation database consists of several interactive seminars which, among other things, contain "meeting", "coffee break", "question/answers" activities. The evaluation campaign showed that in that seminar conditions AED is a challenging problem. In fact, 5 out of 6 submitted systems showed accuracy below 25%, and the best system got 33.6% accuracy (see [2] [3] for results, databases and metrics). The single main factor that accounts for those low detection scores is the high degree of overlap between sounds, especially between the targeted acoustic events and speech.

The overlap problem may be faced by developing efficient algorithms that work at the signal level, the model level or the decision level. Another approach is to use an additional modality that is less sensitive to the overlap phenomena present in the audio signal. In this work we aim at including video information in our existing audio-based detection systems using a fusion approach. Actually, the above mentioned seminar databases include both video and audio information from several cameras and microphones hanged on the walls of the rooms.

A. Popescu-Belis and R. Stiefelhagen (Eds.): MLMI 2008, LNCS 5237, pp. 74–85, 2008.

The information about movements and positions of people in a meeting room may be correlated with acoustic events that take place in it. For instance, the sources of events such as "door slam" or "door knock" are associated to given positions in the room; other events such as "steps" and "chair moving" are accompanied with changes of position of participants in the meeting room. Motivated by the fact that the "steps" sound class accounted for almost 35% of all acoustic events in the CLEAR'07 evaluation database, in this work we use video 3D tracking information in order to improve the detection of that particular class.

In our work, *late fusion* is used by combining the decisions from several information sources: two audio-based AED systems, with SVM and HMM, and a VIDEO-based AED system. Fusion is carried out with the Fuzzy Integral (FI) [4] [5], a fusion technique which is able to take into account the interdependences among information sources. Unlike non-trainable fusion operators (*mean, product* [4]) the statistical FI approach can be more beneficial in our challenging task. From the results, FI fusion shows better accuracy than either the single classifiers or the classical Weighted Arithmetical Mean (WAM) fusion operator [4].

The rest of this paper is organized as follows: Section 2 describes video and audio-based systems of AED. The fuzzy integral is described in Section 3. Section 4 presents experimental results and discussions, and Section 5 concludes the work.

2 Acoustic Event Detection Systems

In this work, detection of acoustic events is carried out with one VIDEO-based and two audio-based systems. The use of the three AED systems is motivated by the fact that each system performs detection in a different manner. The video-based system uses information about position of people in the room. The HMM-based AED system segments the acoustic signal in events by using a frame-level representation of the signal and computing the state sequence with highest likelihood. The SVM-based system does it by classifying segments resulting from consecutive sliding windows. The difference in the nature of the considered detection systems makes the fusion promising for obtaining a superior performance.

2.1 Video-Based Detection System for the Class "Steps"

2.1.1 Person Tracking and Multi-object Tracking

Person tracking is carried out by using multiple synchronized and calibrated cameras as described in [6]. Redundancy among camera views allows generating a 3D discrete reconstruction of the space being these data the input of the tracking algorithm. A particle filtering (PF) [7] approach is followed to estimate the location of each of the people inside the room at a given time t. Two main factors are to be taken into account when implementing a particle filter: the likelihood function and the propagation strategy.

Likelihood function $p(z_t|x_t)$ can be defined as the likelihood of a particle belonging to the volume that corresponds to a person. For a given particle j occupying a voxel x_t, its likelihood is formulated as:

$$p(z_t \mid x_t^j) = \frac{1}{\left|C(x_t^j, q)\right|} \sum_{p \in C(x_t^j, q)} d(x_t^j, p) \qquad (1)$$

where $C(\cdot)$ stands for the neighborhood over a connectivity q domain on the 3D orthogonal grid and $|C(\cdot)|$ represents its cardinality. Typically, connectivity in 3D discrete grids can be 6, 14 and 26 and in our research $q=26$ provided accurate results. Function $d(\cdot)$ measures the distance between a foreground voxel p in the neighborhood and the particle.

Challenges in 3D multi-person tracking from volumetric scene reconstruction are basically twofold. First, finding an interaction model in order to avoid mismatches and target merging. Several approaches have been proposed [8] but the joint PF presented in [9] is the optimal solution to multi-target tracking using PFs. However, its computational load increases dramatically with the number of targets to track since every particle estimates the location of all targets in the scene simultaneously. The proposed solution is to use a split PF per person, which requires less computational load at the cost of not being able to solve some complex cross-overs. However, this situation is alleviated by the fact that cross-overs are restricted to the horizontal plane in our scenario (see Fig.1).

Let us assume that there are M independent PF trackers, being M the number of humans in the room. Nevertheless, they are not fully independent since each PF can consider voxels from other tracked targets in either the likelihood evaluation or the 3D re-sampling step resulting in target merging or identity mismatches. In order to achieve the most independent set of trackers, we consider a blocking method to model interactions. Many blocking proposals can be found in 2D tracking related works [9] and we extend it to our 3D case.

The combination of the estimated 3D location together with geometric descriptors allows discarding spurious objects such as furniture and a simple classification of the person's pose as standing or sitting. The performance of this algorithm over a large annotated database [6] showed the effectiveness of this approach.

Fig. 1. Particles from the tracker A (yellow ellipsoid) falling into the exclusion zone of tracker B (green ellipsoid) will be penalized

2.1.2 Feature Extraction and "Steps" Detection

The output of the 3D tracking algorithm is the set of coordinates of all the people in the room, which are given every 40ms. From those coordinates, we have to generate features that carry information correlated with "steps". We assume that information

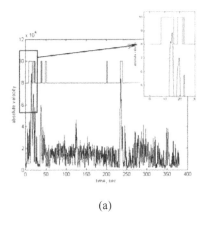
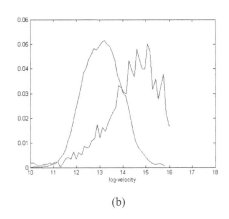

(a)   (b)

Fig. 2. In (a), values of the velocity during one development seminar (bottom) and reference "steps" labels (top). In (b), the histograms of log-velocities for "non-steps" (left hump) and "steps" (right hump).

about movements of people is relevant for "steps" detection. The movements of people in the meeting room can be characterized by a velocity measure. In a 2D plane, the velocity can be calculated in the following way:

$$v = \sqrt{\left(\frac{dx}{dt}\right)^2 + \left(\frac{dy}{dt}\right)^2} \qquad (2)$$

where dx/dt and dy/dt are the values of velocity along x and y axes, respectively. Those values are calculated using a smoothed derivative non-casual filter h applied to the vector of positions of each person in the room. We tried several shapes of the impulse response of the derivative filter; best results were obtained using a linear non-casual filter with the impulse response $h(n) = [-m \ldots -2 \ -1 \ 0 \ 1 \ 2 \ \ldots \ m]$ (zero corresponds to the current value and $L=2*m+1$ is the length of the filter).

Usually more than one person is present in the room, and each person has its own movement and velocity. The maximum velocity among the participants in the seminar is used as a current feature value for "steps"/ "non-steps" detection.

Fig. 2 (a) plots the maximum value of velocity among participants for a 6-min seminar along with the corresponding ground truth labels. From it we can observe that there is certain degree of correspondence between peaks of velocity and true "steps".

The normalized histograms of the logarithm of velocity for "steps" and "non-steps" obtained from development seminars are depicted in Fig. 2 (b), from which can be seen that "steps" are more likely to appear with higher values of velocity.

The jerky nature of the "steps" hump results from a more than 10 times scarcer representation of "steps" with respect to "non-steps" in the development database. These two curves are approximated by two Gaussians via Expectation-Maximization

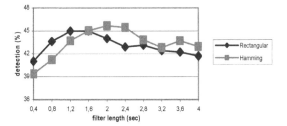

Fig. 3. Detection of "steps" on the development database as a function of the length of the derivative filter (in seconds)

algorithm (EM). During detection on testing data the final decision for "steps"/ "non-steps" classes is made using the Bayesian rule:

$$P(w_j \mid x) = P(x \mid w_j)P(w_j), j=\{1,2\}. \tag{3}$$

where $P(w_1)$ and $P(w_2)$ are prior probabilities for the class "steps" and the meta-class "non-steps" respectively, which are computed using the prior distribution of these two classes in development data and $P(x|w_j)$ are likelihoods given by the Gaussian models.

To have a better detection of "steps" the length L of the derivative filter $h(n)$ and several types of windows applied on $h(n)$ were investigated. According to the results shown in Fig. 3, the best detection of "steps" on development data is achieved with a 2-sec-long derivative filter and a Hamming window.

2.2 SVM-Based AED System

The SVM-based AED system used in the present work is the one that was also used for the AED evaluations in CLEAR 2007 [3] with slight modifications. The sound signal from a single MarkIII array microphone is down-sampled to 16 kHz, and framed (frame length/shift is 30/10ms, a Hamming window is used). For each frame, a set of spectral parameters has been extracted. It consists of the concatenation of two types of parameters: 1) 16 Frequency-Filtered (FF) log filter-bank energies, along with the first and the second time derivatives; and 2) a set of the following parameters: zero-crossing rate, short time energy, 4 sub-band energies, spectral flux, calculated for each of the defined sub-bands, spectral centroid, and spectral bandwidth. In total, a vector of 60 components is built to represent each frame. The mean and the standard deviation parameters have been computed over all frames in a 0.5sec window with a 100ms shift, thus forming one vector of 120 elements.

SVM classifiers have been trained using 1vs1 scheme on the isolated AEs, from two databases of isolated acoustic events, along with segments from the development data seminars, that include both isolated AEs and AEs overlapped with speech. The MAX WINS (pair-wise majority voting) [10] scheme was used to extend the SVM to the task of classifying several classes. After the voting is done, the class with the highest number of winning two-class decisions (votes) is chosen.

2.3 HMM-Based AED System

We formulate the goal of acoustic event detection in a way similar to speech recognition: to find the event sequence that maximizes the posterior probability of the event sequence $W = (w_1, w_2, ..., w_M)$, given the observations $O = (o_1, o_2, ..., o_T)$:

$$W_{max} = argmax\ P(W|O) = argmax P(O|W)P(W).\tag{4}$$

We assume that $P(W)$ is the same for all event sequences.

For building and manipulating hidden Markov models HTK toolkit is used [11]. Firstly, the input signal from a single MarkIII-array microphone is down-sampled to 16 kHz, and 13 FF coefficients with their first time derivatives are extracted, using a Hamming window of size 20-ms with shift 10-ms. There is one HMM for each acoustic event class, with five emitting states and fully connected state transitions. We also used a similar HMM for silence. The observation distributions of the states are Gaussian mixtures with continuous densities, and consist of 9 components with diagonal covariance matrices. The "speech" class is modelled with 15 components as its observation distribution is more complex. Actually, the chosen HMM topology showed the best results during a cross-validation procedure on the development data. Each HMM is trained on all signal segments belonging to the corresponding event class in the development seminar data, using the standard Baum-Welch training algorithm. During testing the AED system finds the best path through the recognition network and each segment in the path represents a detected AE.

3 Fusion of Information Sources

3.1 The Fuzzy Integral and Fuzzy Measure

We are searching for a suitable fusion operator to combine a finite set of information sources $Z = \{1, ..., z\}$. Let $D = \{D_1, D_2, ..., D_z\}$ be a set of trained classification systems and $\Omega = \{c_1, c_2, ..., c_N\}$ be a set of class labels. Each classification system takes as input a data point $x \in \mathfrak{R}^n$ and assigns it to a class label from Ω.

Alternatively, each classifier output can be formed as an N-dimensional vector that represents the degree of support of a classification system to each of N classes. It is convenient to organize the output of all classification systems in a decision profile:

$$DP(x) = \begin{bmatrix} d_{1,1}(x)...d_{1,n}(x)...d_{1,N}(x) \\ ... \\ d_{j,1}(x)...d_{j,n}(x)...d_{j,N}(x) \\ ... \\ d_{z,1}(x)...d_{z,n}(x)...d_{z,N}(x) \end{bmatrix}\tag{5}$$

where a row is classifier output and a column is a support of all classifiers for a class.

We suppose these classifier outputs are commensurable, i.e. defined on the same measurement scale (most often they are posterior probability-like).

Let's denote h_i, $i = 1, .., z$, the output scores of z classification systems for the class c_n (the supports for class c_n, i.e. a column from decision profile) and before defining how

FI combines information sources, let's look to the conventional WAM fusion operator. A final support measure for the class c_n using WAM can be defined as:

$$M_{WAM} = \sum_{i \in Z} \mu(i) h_i$$

$$\text{where } \sum_{i \in Z} \mu(i) = 1 \text{ (additive)}, \ \mu(i) \geq 0 \text{ for all } i \in Z \tag{6}$$

The WAM operator combines the score of z competent information sources through the weights of importance expressed by $\mu(i)$. The main disadvantage of the WAM operator is that it implies preferential independence of the information sources.

Let's denote with $\mu(i, j) = \mu(\{i, j\})$ the weight of importance corresponding to the couple of information sources i and j from Z. If μ is not additive, i.e. $\mu(i, j) \neq [\mu(i) + \mu(j)]$ for a given couple $\{i, j\} \subseteq Z$, we must take into account some interaction among the information sources. Therefore, we can build an aggregation operator starting from the WAM, adding the term of "second order" that involves the corrective coefficients $\mu(i, j) - [\mu(i) + \mu(j)]$, then the term of "third order", etc. Finally, we arrive to the definition of the FI: assuming the sequence h_i, $i=1,..,z$, is ordered in such a way that $h_1 \leq ... \leq h_z$, the Choquet *fuzzy integral* can be computed as

$$M_{FI}(\mu, h) = \sum_{i=1}^{z} [\mu(i,..., z) - \mu(i+1,..., z)] \ h_i \tag{7}$$

where $\mu(z+1) = \mu(\emptyset) = 0$. $\mu(S)$ can be viewed as a weight related to a subset S of the set Z of information sources. It is called *fuzzy measure* for $S, T \subseteq Z$ it has to meet the following conditions:

$\mu(\emptyset) = 0, \mu(Z) = 1$,   Boundary

$S \subseteq T \Rightarrow \mu(S) \leq \mu(T)$,   Monotonicity

For instance, as an illustrative example let's consider the case of 2 information sources with unordered system outputs $h_1=0.4$ and $h_2=0.3$, and corresponding fuzzy measures $\mu(1)=0.6$ and $\mu(2)=0.8$. Note that $\mu(0)=0$ and $\mu(1,2)=1$. In that case, the Choquet *fuzzy integral* is computed as $M_{FI}(\mu,h)= (\mu(1,2)- \mu(1))h_2+ \mu(1)h_1=0.36$.

3.2 Synchronization and Normalization of System Outputs

In order to fuse 3 information sources (SVM-based, HMM-based, and VIDEO-based systems), their outputs must be synchronized in time. In our case, the SVM system provides voting scores every 100ms, the VIDEO system every 40ms, and the HMM system gives segments of variable length which represent the best path through the recognition network. The outputs of the 3 systems were reduced to a common time step of 100ms. For that purpose the output of the VIDEO-based system was averaged on each interval of 100ms, while for the HMM system each segment was broken into 100ms-long pieces.

On the other hand, to make the outputs of information sources commensurable we have to normalize them to be in the range [0 1] and their sum equal to 1.

As it was said in Section 2.2, when the SVM classification system is used alone, after voting, the class with the highest number of winning two-class decisions (votes) is chosen. In case of a subsequent fusion with other classification systems numbers of votes obtained by non-winning classes were used to get a vector of scores for the classes. For the HMM system, each hypothesis of an AE given by the optimal Viterbi segmentation of the seminar is then decoded by the trained HMM models of winning and each non-winning AE class in order to obtain the corresponding log-likelihood values which form vector of scores. In case of VIDEO-based AED system we obtain scores for the two classes "steps" and "non-steps" as the distance between the values of log-velocity and the decision boundary. To make the scores of VIDEO-based and HMM-based systems positive *min-max* normalization [12] is used.

The *soft-max* function is then applied to the vector of scores of each detection system. This function is defined as:

$$q_i\big|_{normalized} = \exp(k * q_i) / \sum_i \exp(k * q_i) \tag{8}$$

where the coefficient k controls the distance between the components of the vector $[q_1, q_2, ..., q_N]$. For instance, in extreme case when $k=0$, the elements of the vector after *soft-max* normalization would have the same value $1/N$, and when $k \rightarrow \infty$ the elements tend to become binary. The normalization coefficients are different for each AED system, and they are obtained using the development data.

4 Experiments and Results

4.1 Database and Metric

In our experiments, the CLEAR'07 evaluation database is used [3]. It consists of 25 interactive seminars, approximately 30min-long that have been recorded by AIT (Athens Information Technology), ITC (Instituto Trentino di Cultura), IBM, UKA (Universität Karlsruhe), and UPC (Universitat Politècnica de Catalunya) in their smart-rooms. In our experiments for development and testing we used only recordings of 3 sites (AIT, ITC, and UPC) because the IBM data is not included in the testing database, and the performance of the video tracking algorithm on the UKA data is very low, due to errors presented in the video recordings (heavy radial distortions in zenithal camera). In other respects, the training/testing division is preserved from CLEAR'07 evaluation scenario.

The AED evaluation uses 12 semantic classes (classes of interest), i.e. types of AEs that are: "door knock", "door open/slam", "steps", "chair moving", "spoon/cup jingle", "paper work", "key jingle", "keyboard typing", "phone ring", "applause", "cough", and "laugh". Apart from the 12 evaluated classes, there are 3 other events present in the seminars ("speech", "silence", "unknown") which are not evaluated.

The Accuracy metric [3] is used in this work and it is defined as the harmonic mean between *precision* and *recall* computed for the classes of interest, where *precision* is number of correct hypothesis AEs divided by total number of hypothesis AEs, and *recall* as number of correctly detected reference AEs divided by total number of reference AEs.

4.2 One-Stage and Two-Stage Fuzzy Integral Approaches

In our case, not all information sources give scores for all classes. Unlike SVM and HMM-based systems, which provide information about 15 classes, the VIDEO-based system scores are given only for the class "steps" and the meta-class "non-steps". Fusion of information sources using the fuzzy integral can be done either by transforming (extending) the score for "non-steps" from the VIDEO-based system to the remaining 14 classes which do not include "steps" or, vice-versa, transforming (restricting) the scores of 14 classes provided by the SVM and HMM-based systems to one score for the meta-class "non-steps". In the former case, the fusion is done at one stage with all the classes. In the latter, a two-stage approach is implemented, where on the first stage the 3 detection systems are used to do "steps"/ "non-steps" classification and on the second stage the subsequent classification of the "non-steps" output of the first stage is done with both SVM and HMM-based systems. The one-stage and two-stage approaches are schematically shown in Fig. 4.

For one-stage fusion (Fig. 4 (a)) the score V of "non-steps" of the VIDEO-based system is equally distributed among the remaining 14 classes assigning to each of them score V before applying *soft-max* normalization. At the first stage of the two-stage approach, all the classes not labeled as "steps" form the "non-steps" meta-class. The final score of "non-steps" is chosen as maximum value of scores of all the classes that formed that meta-class.

For the weights in WAM operator we use uniform class noise model with the detection system [4]. The individual FMs for the fuzzy integral fusion are trained on development data in our work using the gradient descent training algorithm [13]. The 5-fold cross validation on development data was used to stop the training process to avoid overtraining. The tricky point was that during training the algorithm minimizes the total error on development data. As the number of data per each class is non-uniform distributed, during the training process the number of detection mistakes for the most representative classes ("speech", "silence") is decreased at the expense of increasing errors on the classes with lower number of representatives. The final metric scores, however, only 12 classes which are the classes with much smaller number of

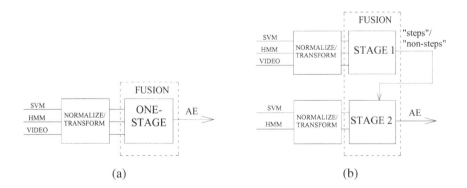

(a)   (b)

Fig. 4. One-stage (a) and two-stage (b) fusion with the fuzzy integral

representatives than e.g. "speech". This way, the FI with the trained FM measure tends to detect correctly the classes that are not scored by the metric. To cope with this problem, we firstly fixed the FM of the classes of no interest ("speech", "unknown", and "silence") to be in the equilibrium state [13] and, secondly, calculate the cross-validation accuracy only for the classes of interest.

4.3 Results and Discussion

The results of first-stage fusion for "steps"/"non-steps" detection are presented in Fig. 5. It can be seen that fusion of SVM and HMM-based systems leads to a small improvement, while in combination with video information the improvement is noticeable. It is worth to mention that 48.1 % of accuracy for "steps" detection would indicate a little worse decision than random choice if the metric scored both "non-steps" meta-class and "steps" class. However, in our case, only the "steps" class is scored and thus 48.1% indicates that not only around 48.1% of "steps" are detected (recall) but also that 48.1% of all produced decisions are correct (precision). On the first stage the FI fusion gives superior results in comparison with WAM fusion. This indicates that a certain interaction between information sources for "steps" detection exists that can not be captured by WAM fusion operator.

The final results of detection of all 15 classes of AEs are presented in Fig. 6. It can be seen that total system accuracy benefits from better recognition of "steps" class. Again in this experiment the FI fusion shows better performance then WAM, resulting in a final accuracy of 40.5%.

One-stage fusion explained in the previous subsection showed lower scores - only 37.9% for WAM and 38.4% with FI. This fact may indicate that in our particular case spreading no-information for classes with missing scores can be harmful and, conversely, to compress the scores of many classes to binary problems can be more beneficial. However, the way of extending/compressing of the scores should be studied in more depth to further support this statement.

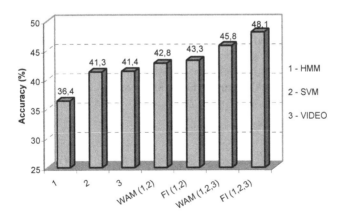

Fig. 5. Accuracy of "steps" detection on the first stage using the fuzzy integral

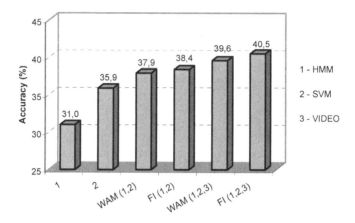

Fig. 6. Total system accuracy based on the first and the second stage fusion

5 Conclusions

In this work, by using data from interactive seminars, we have shown that video signals can be a useful additional source of information to cope with the problem of acoustic event detection. Using an algorithm for video 3D tracking, video-based features that represent the movement have been extracted, and a probabilistic classifier for "steps"/"non-steps" detection has been developed. The fuzzy integral was used to fuse the outputs of both that video-based detector and two audio-based AED systems which use either SVM or HMM classifiers. Results show that video information helps to detect acoustic "steps" events, and future work will be devoted to extend the multimodal AED system to more classes.

Acknowledgements

This work has been funded by the Spanish project SAPIRE (TEC2007-65470). The first author is partially supported by a grant from the Catalan autonomous government. The fourth author has been partially supported by the Spanish Ministerio de Educación y Ciencia, under project TEC2007-66858/TCM.

References

1. Temko, A., Malkin, R., Zieger, C., Macho, D., Nadeu, C., Omologo, M.: CLEAR Evaluation of Acoustic Event Detection and Classification systems. In: Stiefelhagen, R., Garofolo, J.S. (eds.) CLEAR 2006. LNCS, vol. 4122. Springer, Heidelberg (2007)
2. Zhou, X., Zhuang, X., Lui, M., Tang, H., Hasgeawa-Johnson, M., Huang, T.: HMM-Based Acoustic Event Detection with AdaBoost Feature Selection. In: Stiefelhagen, R., Bowers, R., Fiscus, J.G. (eds.) CLEAR 2007 and RT 2007. LNCS, vol. 4625. Springer, Heidelberg (2007)

3. Temko, A., Nadeu, C., Biel, J.-I.: Acoustic Event Detection: SVM-based System and Evaluation Setup in CLEAR 2007. In: Multimodal Technologies for Perception of Humans. LNCS, vol. 4625, pp. 354–363. Springer, Heidelberg (2008)
4. Kuncheva, L.: Combining Pattern Classifiers. John Wiley, Chichester (2004)
5. Temko, A., Macho, D., Nadeu, C.: Fuzzy Integral Based Information Fusion for Classification of Highly Confusable Non-Speech Sounds. Pattern Recognition 41(5), 1831–1840 (2008)
6. López, A., Canton-Ferrer, C., Casas, J.R.: Multi-Person 3D Tracking with Particle Filters on Voxels. In: IEEE ICASSP 2007, pp. 913–916 (2007)
7. Arulampalam., M., Maskell, S., Gordon, N., Clapp, T.: A tutorial on particle filters for online nonlinear/non-Gaussian Bayesian tracking. IEEE Transaction on Signal Processing 50, 174–188 (2002)
8. Lanz, O.: Approximate Bayesian Multibody Tracking. IEEE Transaction on Pattern Analysis and Machine Intelligence 28(9), 1439–1449 (2006)
9. Khan, Z., Balch, T., Dellaert, F.: Efficient particle filter-based tracking of multiple interacting targets using an MRF-based motion model. In: International Conference on Intelligent Robots and Systems (2003)
10. Hsu, C., Lin, C.: A Comparison of Methods for Multi-class Support Vector Machines. IEEE Transactions on Neural Networks, 415–425 (2002)
11. Young, S.J., Evermann, G., Kershaw, D., Moore, G., Odell, J., Ollason, D., Povey, D., Valtchev, V., Woodland, P.: The HTK Book (for HTK Version 3.2). Cambridge University Press, Cambridge (2002)
12. Shalabi, L., Shaaban, Z., Kasasbeh, B.: Data Mining: A Preprocessing Engine. Journal of Computer Science 2(9), 735–739 (2006)
13. Grabisch, M.: A new algorithm for identifying fuzzy measures and its application to pattern recognition. In: IEEE International Conference on Fuzzy Systems, pp. 145–150 (1995)

Audio-Visual Clustering for 3D Speaker Localization

Vasil Khalidov[1], Florence Forbes[1], Miles Hansard[1], Elise Arnaud[1,2],
and Radu Horaud[1]

[1] INRIA Grenoble Rhône-Alpes, 655 avenue de l'Europe, 38334 Montbonnot, France
[2] Université Joseph Fourier, BP 53, 38041 Grenoble Cedex 9, France

Abstract. We address the issue of localizing individuals in a scene that contains several people engaged in a multiple-speaker conversation. We use a human-like configuration of sensors (binaural and binocular) to gather both auditory and visual observations. We show that the localization problem can be recast as the task of clustering the audio-visual observations into coherent groups. We propose a probabilistic generative model that captures the relations between audio and visual observations. This model maps the data to a representation of the common 3D scene-space, via a pair of Gaussian mixture models. Inference is performed by a version of the Expectation Maximization algorithm, which provides cooperative estimates of both the activity (speaking or not) and the 3D position of each speaker.

1 Introduction

In most systems that handle multi-modal data, audio and visual inputs are first processed by modality-specific subsystems, whose outputs are subsequently combined. The performance of such procedures in realistic situations is limited. Confusion may arise from factors such as background acoustic and/or visual noise, acoustic reverberation, and visual occlusions. The different attempts that have been made to increase robustness are based on the observation that improved localization and recognition can be achieved by integrating acoustic and visual information. The reason is that each modality may compensate for weaknesses of the other one, especially in noisy conditions. This raises the question of how to efficiently combine the two modalities in different natural conditions and according to the task at hand.

The first question to be addressed is *where* the fusion of the data should take place. In contrast to the fusion of previous independent processing of each modality [1], the integration could occur at the feature level. One possibility is that audio and video features are concatenated into a larger feature vector which is then used to perform the task of interest [2]. However, owing to the very different physical natures of audio and visual stimuli, direct integration is not straightforward. There is no obvious way to associate dense visual maps with sparse sound sources. The input features in our approach are first transformed into a common representation and the processing is then based on the combination of features in this representation. Within this strategy, we identify two major directions depending on the type of *synchrony* being used. The first one focuses on *spatial synchrony* and implies combining those signals that were observed at

A. Popescu-Belis and R. Stiefelhagen (Eds.): MLMI 2008, LNCS 5237, pp. 86–97, 2008.

a given time, or through a short period of time, and correspond to the same source (e.g. speaker). Generative probabilistic models in [2] and [3] for single speaker tracking achieve this by introducing dependencies of both auditory and visual observations on locations in the image plane. Although authors in [2] suggested an enhancement of the model that would tackle the multi-speaker case, it has not been implemented yet. Explicit dependency on the source location that is used in generative models can be generalized using particle filters. Such approaches were used for the task of single speaker tracking [4, 5, 6, 7, 8] and multiple speaker tracking [7, 9, 10]. In the latter case the parameter space grows exponentially as the number of speakers increases, so efficient sampling procedures were suggested [10], [7] to keep the problem tractable.

The second direction focuses on *temporal synchrony*. It efficiently generalizes the previous approach by making no a priori assumption on audio-visual object location. Signals from different modalities are grouped if their evolution is correlated through time. The work in [11] shows how principles of information theory can be used to select those features from different modalities that correspond to the same object. Although the setup consists of a single camera and a single microphone and no special signal processing is used, the model is capable of selecting the speaker among several persons that were visible. Another example of this strategy is [12] where audio-visual association is performed based on audio and video onsets (times at which sound/motion begins). This model has been successfully tested even in the case of multiple sound sources. These approaches are non-parametric and highly dependent on the choice of appropriate features. Moreover they usually require learning or ad hoc tuning of quantities such as window sizes, temporal resolution, etc. They appear relatively sensitive to artifacts and may require careful implementation.

The second question to be addressed is *which* features to select in order to best account for the individual and combined modalities. A single microphone is easy to set up but it cannot provide spatial localization of sounds. A number of methods rely on complex audio-visual hardware such as an array of microphones that are calibrated mutually and with respect to one or more cameras [6, 8, 10]. Such a microphone array can provide an estimate of the 3D location of each audio source; hence it is at the core of such fusion strategies as partitioned sampling [6]. Here we use a microphone pair to estimate the *interaural time difference* (ITD) which can in turn be used to estimate the 3D azimuth of several sound sources [13].

The advantage of using several cameras are numerous. One may use as many cameras as needed in order to make all parts of a room observable ("smart room" concept). This increases the reliability of visual feature detection because it helps to solve both the occlusion problem and the non fronto-parallel projection problem. Nevertheless, selecting the appropriate camera to be used in conjunction with a moving target can be quite problematic, environment changes require partial or total recalibration. Alternatively, the use of a binocular camera pair allows the extraction of depth information through the computation of stereo disparities. Current audio-visual models do not consider the problem of speaker localization as a 3D problem, although speakers act in a 3D space.

We propose to use a human-like sensor: binaural hearing and binocular vision. It seems that there has been no attempt to use stereoscopic depth cues in combination with binaural cues such as ITD. The advantage of such a agent-centred setup is that it can operate in any type of environment. Another benefit is a symmetric integration of seeing and hearing, in which none of the streams is assumed to be dominant and weighting of the modalities is based on statistical properties of the observed data. The originality of our approach is to embed the problem in the physical 3D space, which is not only natural but has more discriminative power in terms of speaker localization. Our approach makes use of spatial synchrony, but unlike the majority of existing models, performing the binding in 3D space fully preserves localization information so that the integration is reinforced. At the same time we do not rely on image features such as structural templates [10], colour models [6] or face detectors, so that the model becomes more general, flexible and stable. Our approach resembles those based on temporal synchrony in the sense that we recast the problem of how to best combine audio and visual data as the task of finding coherent groups of observations in data. The statistical method for solving this problem is cluster analysis: The 3D positions are chosen as a common representation to which both audio and video observations are mapped, through two Gaussian mixture models.

Our approach has the following main features: (i) a joint probabilistic model, specified through two mixture models sharing some common parameters, captures the relations between audio and video observations, (ii) 3D speaker localization within this framework is defined as maximum likelihood with missing data, and is carried out by a specialized version of the Expectation Maximization (EM) algorithm, (iii) we show that such a formulation results into a cooperative estimation of the 3D positions of multipel speakers as well as the identification of the speakers' activity (speaking or not speaking) using procedures for standard mixture models.

The paper is organized as follows. Section 2 formulates the problem in terms of maximum likelihood with missing data. Section 3 describes the associated generalized EM algorithm. Section 4 describes experiments and results.

2   A Missing Data Model for Clustering Audio-Visual Data

Given a number of audio and visual observations, we address the problem of localizing speakers in a 3D scene as well as determining their speaking state. We will first assume that the number N of speakers is known. Section 4 addresses the question of how to estimate this number when it is unknown. We consider then a time interval $[t_1, t_2]$ during which the speakers are assumed to be static. Each speaker can then be described by its 3D location $s = (x, y, z)^T$ in space. We then denote by $\mathbf{S}$ the set of the N speakers' locations, $\mathbf{S} = \{s_1, \ldots, s_n, \ldots, s_N\}$, which are the unknown parameters to be determined.

Our setup consists of a stereo pair of cameras and a pair of microphones from which we gather visual and auditory observations over $[t_1, t_2]$. Let $\mathbf{f} = \{f_1, \ldots, f_m, \ldots, f_M\}$ be the set of M visual observations. Each of them has *binocular coordinates*, namely a 3D vector $f_m = (u_m, v_m, d_m)^T$, where u and v denote the 2D location in the Cyclopean image. This corresponds to a viewpoint halfway between the left and right cameras, and is easily computed from the original image coordinates. The scalar d denotes the binocular disparity at $(u, v)^T$. Hence, Cyclopean coordinates $(u, v, d)^T$ are associated with each point $s = (x, y, z)^T$ in the visible scene. We define a function $\mathcal{F} : \mathbb{R}^3 \rightarrow \mathbb{R}^3$ which maps s on $\mathbf{f}$:

$$\mathcal{F}(s) = \left(\frac{x}{z}; \frac{y}{z}; \frac{B}{z} \right)^T \qquad \mathcal{F}^{-1}(f) = \left(\frac{Bu}{d}; \frac{Bv}{d}; \frac{B}{d} \right)^T \tag{1}$$

where B is the length of the inter-camera baseline.

Similarly, let $g = \{g_1, \ldots, g_k, \ldots, g_K\}$ be the set of K auditory observations, each represented by an auditory disparity, namely the *interaural time difference*, or ITD. To relate a location to an ITD value we define a function $\mathcal{G} : \mathbb{R}^3 \rightarrow \mathbb{R}$ which maps s on g:

$$\mathcal{G}(s) = c^{-1} \left(\|s - s_{M_1}\| - \|s - s_{M_2}\| \right) \tag{2}$$

Here $c \approx 330 \text{ms}^{-1}$ is the speed of sound and s_{M_1} and s_{M_2} are microphone locations in camera coordinates. We notice that isosurfaces defined by (2) are represented by one sheet of a two sheet hyperboloid in 3D. So given an observation we can deduce the surface that should contain the source.

We address the problem of speaker localization within an unsupervised clustering framework. The rationale is that there should exist groups in the observed data that correspond to the different audio-visual objects of the scene. We will consider mixtures of Gaussians in which each component corresponds to a group or class. Each class is associated to a speaker and the problem is recast as the assignment of each observation to one of the classes as well as the estimation of each class center. The centers of the classes are linked to the quantities of interest namely the speakers 3D localizations. More specifically, the standard Gaussian mixture model has to be extended in order to account for the presence of observations that are not related to any speakers. We introduce an additional background (outlier) class modelled as a uniform distribution, which increases robustness. The resulting classes are indexed as $1, \ldots, N, N + 1$, the final class being reserved for outliers. Also, due to their different nature, the same mixture model cannot be used for both audio and visual data. We used two mixture models, in two different observations spaces (our audio features are 1D while visual features are 3D) with the same number of components corresponding to the number of speakers and an additional outlier class. The class centres of the respective mixtures are linked through common but unknown speaker positions. In this framework, the observed data are naturally augmented with as many unobserved or missing data. Each missing data point is associated to an observed data point and represents the memberships of this observed data point to one of the $N + 1$ groups. The complete data are then considered as specific realizations of random variables. Capital letters are used for random variables whereas small letters are used for their specific realizations. The additional assignment variables, one for each individual observation, take their values in $\{1, \ldots, N, N + 1\}$. Let $A = \{A_1, \ldots, A_M\}$ denote the set of assignment variables for visual observations and $A' = \{A'_1, \ldots, A'_K\}$ the set of assignment variables for auditory observations. The notation $\{A_m = n\}$, for $n \in \{1, \ldots, N, N + 1\}$, means that the observed visual disparity f_m corresponds to speaker n if $n \neq N + 1$ or to the outlier class otherwise. Values of assignment variables for auditory observations have the same meaning.

Perceptual studies have shown that, in human speech perception, audio and video data are treated as class conditional independent [14, 15]. We will further assume that the individual audio and visual observations are also independent given assignment variables. Under this hypothesis, the joint conditional likelihood can be written as:

$$P(\mathbf{f}, \boldsymbol{g} \mid \mathbf{a}, \mathbf{a}') = \prod_{m=1}^{M} P(\boldsymbol{f}_m | a_m) \prod_{k=1}^{K} P(g_k | a_k'). \tag{3}$$

The different probability distributions to model the speakers on one side and the outliers on the other side are the following. The likelihoods of visual/auditory observations, given that they belong to a speaker, are Gaussian distributions whose means respectively $\mathcal{F}(\boldsymbol{s}_n)$ and $\mathcal{G}(\boldsymbol{s}_n)$ depend on the corresponding speaker positions through functions $\mathcal{F}$ and $\mathcal{G}$ defined in (2) and (1). The (co)variances are respectively denoted by $\boldsymbol{\Sigma}_n$ and σ_n^2,

$$P(\boldsymbol{f}_m | A_m = n) = \mathcal{N}\big(\boldsymbol{f}_m | \mathcal{F}(\boldsymbol{s}_n), \boldsymbol{\Sigma}_n\big), \tag{4}$$

$$P(g_k | A_k' = n) = \mathcal{N}\big(g_k | \mathcal{G}(\boldsymbol{s}_n), \sigma_n^2\big). \tag{5}$$

Similarly, we define the likelihoods for an visual/auditory observation to belong to an outlier cluster as uniform distributions:

$$P(\boldsymbol{f}_m | A_m = N + 1) = 1/V \quad \text{and} \quad P(g_k | A_k' = N + 1) = 1/U, \tag{6}$$

where V and U represent the respective 3D and 1D observed data *volumes* (see Sect.4).

For simplicity, we then assume that the assignment variables are independent. More complex choices would be interesting such as defining some Markov random field model to account for more structure between the classes. Following [16] the implementation of such models can then be reduced to adaptive implementations of the independent case making it natural to start with

$$P(\mathbf{a}, \mathbf{a}') = \prod_{m=1}^{M} P(a_m) \prod_{k=1}^{K} P(a_k') . \tag{7}$$

The prior probabilities are denoted by, for all $n = 1, \ldots, N+1$, $\pi_n = P(A_m = n)$ and $\pi_n' = P(A_k' = n)$. The posterior probabilities, denoted by $\alpha_{mn} = P(A_m = n | \boldsymbol{f}_m)$ and $\alpha_{kn}' = P(A_k' = n | g_k)$, can then be calculated, for all $n = 1, \ldots, N+1$, using Bayes' theorem. For $n \neq N + 1$, using (4) and (5) we obtain for each $m = 1, \ldots M$

$$\alpha_{mn} = \frac{|\boldsymbol{\Sigma}_n|^{-1/2} \exp\left(-\frac{1}{2} \|\boldsymbol{f}_m - \mathcal{F}(\boldsymbol{s}_n)\|_{\boldsymbol{\Sigma}_n}^2\right) \pi_n}{\sum_{i=1}^{N} |\boldsymbol{\Sigma}_i|^{-1/2} \exp\left(-\frac{1}{2} \|\boldsymbol{f}_m - \mathcal{F}(\boldsymbol{s}_i)\|_{\boldsymbol{\Sigma}_i}^2\right) \pi_i + (2\pi)^{3/2} V^{-1} \pi_{N+1}} \tag{8}$$

and for each $k = 1, \ldots K$

$$\alpha_{kn}' = \frac{|\sigma_n|^{-1} \exp\left(-(g_k - \mathcal{G}(\boldsymbol{s}_n))^2 / (2\sigma_n^2)\right) \pi_n'}{\sum_{i=1}^{N} |\sigma_i|^{-1} \exp\left(-(g_k - \mathcal{G}(\boldsymbol{s}_i))^2 / (2\sigma_i^2)\right) \pi_i' + (2\pi)^{1/2} U^{-1} \pi_{N+1}'}, \tag{9}$$

where we adopted the notation $\|\boldsymbol{x}\|_{\boldsymbol{\Sigma}}^2 = \boldsymbol{x}^T \boldsymbol{\Sigma}^{-1} \boldsymbol{x}$ for the Mahalanobis distance.

3   Estimation Using the Expectation Maximization Algorithm

Given the probabilistic model defined above, we wish to determine the speakers that generated the visual and auditory observations, that is to derive values of assignment vectors A and A', together with the speakers' position vectors $\mathbf{S}$. The speakers' positions are part of our model unknown parameters. Let Θ denote the set of parameters in our model, $\Theta = \{s_1, \ldots, s_N, \Sigma_1, \ldots, \Sigma_N, \sigma_1, \ldots, \sigma_N, \pi_1, \ldots, \pi_N, \pi'_1, \ldots, \pi'_N\}$. Direct maximum likelihood estimation of mixture models is usually difficult, due to the missing assignments. The Expectation Maximization (EM) algorithm [17] is a general and now standard approach to maximization of the likelihood in missing data problems. The algorithm iteratively maximizes the expected complete-data log-likelihood over values of the unknown parameters, conditional on the observed data and the current values of those parameters. In our clustering context, it provides unknown parameter estimation but also values for missing data by providing membership probabilities to each group. The algorithm consists of two steps. At iteration q, for current values $\Theta^{(q)}$ of the parameters, the *E step* consists in computing the conditional expectation with respect to variables A and A',

$$Q(\Theta, \Theta^{(q)}) = \sum_{\mathbf{a}, \mathbf{a}' \in \{1, N+1\}^{M+K}} \log P(\mathbf{f}, \boldsymbol{g}, \mathbf{a}, \mathbf{a}'; \Theta)\, P(\mathbf{a}, \mathbf{a}'|\mathbf{f}, \boldsymbol{g}, \Theta^{(q)}) \quad (10)$$

The *M step* consists in updating $\Theta^{(q)}$ by maximizing (10) with respect to Θ, i.e. in finding $\Theta^{(q+1)}$ as $\Theta^{(q+1)} = \arg\max_{\Theta} Q(\Theta, \Theta^{(q)})$. We now give detailed descriptions of the steps, based on our assumptions.

E Step. We first rewrite the conditional expectation (10) taking into account decompositions (3) and (7) that arise from independency assumptions. This leads to $Q(\Theta, \Theta^{(q)}) = Q_{\mathcal{F}}(\Theta, \Theta^{(q)}) + Q_{\mathcal{G}}(\Theta, \Theta^{(q)})$ with

$$Q_{\mathcal{F}}(\Theta, \Theta^{(q)}) = \sum_{m=1}^{M} \sum_{n=1}^{N+1} \alpha_{mn}^{(q)} \log(P(\boldsymbol{f}_m|A_m = n; \Theta)\, \pi_n)$$

$$\text{and} \quad Q_{\mathcal{G}}(\Theta, \Theta^{(q)}) = \sum_{k=1}^{K} \sum_{n=1}^{N+1} \alpha_{kn}'^{(q)} \log(P(g_k|A'_k = n; \Theta)\, \pi'_n),$$

where $\alpha_{mn}^{(q)}$ and $\alpha_{kn}'^{(q)}$ are the expressions in (8) and (9) for $\Theta = \Theta^{(q)}$ the current parameter values. Substituting expressions for likelihoods (4) and (5) further leads to

$$Q_{\mathcal{F}}(\Theta, \Theta^{(q)}) = -\frac{1}{2} \sum_{m=1}^{M} \sum_{n=1}^{N} \alpha_{mn}^{(q)} \left(\|\boldsymbol{f}_m - \mathcal{F}(s_n)\|_{\Sigma_n}^2 + \log\left((2\pi)^3 |\Sigma_n| \pi_n^{-2}\right) \right)$$

$$-\frac{1}{2} \sum_{m=1}^{M} \alpha_{m,N+1}^{(q)} \log\left(V^2 \pi_{N+1}^{-2}\right) \quad (11)$$

and $\quad Q_{\mathcal{G}}(\Theta, \Theta^{(q)}) = -\dfrac{1}{2} \displaystyle\sum_{k=1}^{K} \sum_{n=1}^{N} \alpha_{kn}'^{(q)} \left(\dfrac{(g_k - \mathcal{G}(s_n))^2}{\sigma_n^2} + \log(2\pi\sigma_n^2 \pi'^{-2}_{\,n}) \right)$

$$-\frac{1}{2} \sum_{k=1}^{K} \alpha_{k,N+1}'^{(q)} \log(U^2 \pi'^{-2}_{\,N+1}) . \tag{12}$$

M Step. The goal is to maximize (10) with respect to the parameters Θ to find $\Theta^{(q+1)}$. Optimal values for priors π_n and π_n' are easily derived independently of the other parameters by setting the corresponding derivatives to zero and using the constraints $\sum_{n=1}^{N+1} \pi_n = 1$ and $\sum_{n=1}^{N+1} \pi_n' = 1$. The resulting expressions are

$$n = 1, \ldots, N+1, \quad \pi_n^{(q+1)} = \frac{1}{M} \sum_{m=1}^{M} \alpha_{mn}^{(q)} \quad \text{and} \quad \pi_n'^{\,(q+1)} = \frac{1}{K} \sum_{k=1}^{K} \alpha_{kn}'^{(q)} . \tag{13}$$

The optimization with respect to the other parameters is less straightforward. Using a coordinate system transformation, we substitute variables $s_1, \ldots, s_N$ with $\hat{f}_1 = \mathcal{F}(s_1), \ldots, \hat{f}_N = \mathcal{F}(s_N)$. For convenience we introduce the function $h = \mathcal{G} \circ \mathcal{F}^{-1}$ and the parameter-set $\tilde{\Theta} = \left\{ \hat{f}_1, \ldots, \hat{f}_N, \Sigma_1, \ldots, \Sigma_N, \sigma_1, \ldots, \sigma_N \right\}$. Setting the derivatives with respect to the variance parameters to zero, we obtain the empirical variances. Taking the derivative with respect to $\hat{f}_n$ gives

$$\frac{\partial Q}{\partial \hat{f}_n} = \sum_{m=1}^{M} \alpha_{mn} \left(f_m - \hat{f}_n \right)^T \Sigma_n^{-1} + \frac{1}{\sigma_n^2} \sum_{k=1}^{K} \alpha_{kn}' \left(g_k - h(\hat{f}_n) \right) \nabla_n^T \tag{14}$$

where the vector ∇_n is the transposed product of Jacobians $\nabla_n = \left(\dfrac{\partial \mathcal{G}}{\partial s} \dfrac{\partial \mathcal{F}^{-1}}{\partial f} \right)^T_{f = \hat{f}_n}$ which can be easily computed from definitions (1) and (2). The resulting derivation includes a division by d and we note here that cases when d is close to zero correspond to points on very distant objects (for fronto-parallel setup of cameras) from which no 3D structure can be recovered. So it is reasonable to set a threshold and disregard the observations that contain small values of d.

Difficulties now arise from the fact that it is necessary to perform simultaneous optimization in two different observation spaces, auditory and visual. It involves solving a system of equations that contain derivatives of $Q_{\mathcal{F}}$ and $Q_{\mathcal{G}}$ whose dependency on s_n is expressed through $\mathcal{F}$ and $\mathcal{G}$ and is non-linear. In fact, this system does not yield a closed form solution and the traditional EM algorithm cannot be performed. However, setting the gradient (14) to zero leads to an equation of special form, namely the *fixed point equation* (FPE), where the location $\hat{f}_n$ is expressed as a function of the variances and itself. Solution of this equation together with the empirical variances give the optimal parameter set. for this reason we tried the versions of the M-step that iterate through FPE to obtain $\hat{f}_n$. But we observed that such solutions tend to make the EM algorithm converge to local maxima of the likelihood.

An alternative way to search for the optimal parameter values is to use a gradient descent-based iteration, for example, the Newton-Raphson procedure. However, the final value $\tilde{\Theta}^{(q+1)}$ is not necessarily a global optimizer. Provided that the value of Q is improved on every iteration, the algorithm can be considered as an instance of the Generalized EM (GEM) algorithm. The updated value $\tilde{\Theta}^{(q+1)}$ can be taken of the form

$$\tilde{\Theta}^{(q+1)} = \tilde{\Theta}^{(q)} + \gamma^{(q)} \Gamma^{(q)} \left[\frac{\partial Q(\Theta, \Theta^{(q)})}{\partial \tilde{\Theta}} \right]^T_{\Theta = \Theta^{(q)}} \qquad (15)$$

where $\Gamma^{(q)}$ is a linear operator that depends on $\tilde{\Theta}^{(q)}$ and $\gamma^{(q)}$ is a scalar sequence of gains. For instance, for Newton-Raphson procedure one should use $\gamma^{(q)} \equiv 1$ and $\Gamma^{(q)} = -\left[\frac{\partial^2 Q}{\partial \tilde{\Theta}^2} \right]^{-1}_{\Theta = \Theta^{(q)}}$. The principle here is to choose $\Gamma^{(q)}$ and $\gamma^{(q)}$ so that (15) defines a GEM sequence. In what follows we concentrate on the latter algorithm since it gives better results and potentially more flexibility then the FPE formulation.

Clustering. Besides providing parameter estimation, the EM algorithm can be used to determine assignments of each observation to one of the $N + 1$ classes. Observation f_m (resp. g_k) is assigned to class η_m (resp. η'_k) if $\eta_m = \underset{n=1,...N+1}{\operatorname{argmax}} \alpha_{mn}$ (resp. $\eta'_k = \underset{n=1,...N+1}{\operatorname{argmax}} \alpha'_{kn}$). We use this in particular to determine active speakers using the auditory observations assignments η'_k's. For every person we can derive the speaking state by the number of associated observations. The case when all η'_k's are equal to $N + 1$ would mean that there is no active speaker.

4 Experimental Results

Within the task of multi-speaker localization there are three sub-tasks to be solved. First, the number of speakers should be determined. Second, the speakers should be localized and finally, those who are speaking should be selected. The proposed probabilistic model has the advantage of providing a means to solve all three sub-tasks at once. There is no need to develop separate models for every particular sub-task, and at the same time we formulate our approach within the Bayesian framework which is rich and flexible enough to suit the requirements.

To determine the number of speakers, we gather sufficient amount of audio observations and apply the Bayesian Information Criterion (BIC) [18]. This is a well-founded approach to the problem of model selection, given the observations. The task of localization in our framework is recast into the parameter estimation problem. This gives an opportunity to efficiently use the EM algorithm to estimate the 3D positions. We note here that our model is defined so as to perform well in the single speaker case as well as in the multiple speakers case without any special reformulation. To obtain the speaking state of a person we use the posterior probabilities of the assignment variables calculated at the E step of the algorithm.

We evaluated the ability of our algorithms to estimate the 3D locations of persons and their speaking activity in a meeting situation. The audio-visual sequence that we used is a part of the scenario set that was acquired by the experimental setup shown

Fig. 1. This figure shows the mannequin used in our experiments as well as a typical setup. It is equipped with a binaural microphone pair and a camera binocular pair. When the mannequin is moved around, the position and orientation of its head are recorded as well.

in Fig.1. A mannequin with a pair of microphones mounted into its ears and a pair of stereoscopic cameras attached to its forehead, served as the acquisition device. This configuration allows to record data from the perspective of a person, i.e., what a person would hear and see. Each of the recorded scenarios comprised two audio tracks and two sequences of images, together with calibration information[1]. The sequence of interest in our case is a meeting scenario (500 stereo-frames at 25fps), shown on Figure 2[2]. There are 5 persons seating around a table, but only 3 persons are visible. The algorithm was applied to short time intervals that correspond to three video frames. Audio and visual observations were collected within each interval using the following techniques. A standard procedure was used to identify "interest points" in the left and right images [19]. These features were put into binocular correspondence by comparing the local image-structure at each of the candidate points, as described in [20]. The cameras were calibrated [21] in order to define the $(u, v, d)^T$ to $(x, y, z)^T$ mapping (1). Auditory disparities were obtained through the analysis of cross-correlogram of the filtered left and right microphone signals for every frequency band [13]. On an average, there were about 1200 visual and 9 auditory observations within each time interval.

We report here on the results obtained by the versions of the algorithm based on a gradient descent (GD) technique, with Γ being block diagonal. We used $\left[-\partial^2 Q/\partial \hat{f}_n^2\right]^{-1}_{\Theta=\Theta^{(q)}}$ as a block for $\hat{f}_n$, so that the descent direction is the same as in Newton-Raphson method. In the examples that we present we adopted the same video variance matrix Σ for all the clusters, thus there was one common block in $\Gamma^{(q)}$ that performed linear mapping of the form $\Gamma^{(q)}_{\Sigma}(\cdot) = \left(\sum_{n=1}^{N}\sum_{m=1}^{M}\alpha_{mn}^{(q)}\right)^{-1}\Sigma^{(q)}(\cdot)\Sigma^{(q)}$. This direction change corresponds to a step towards the empirical variance value. Analogous blocks (cells) were introduced for audio variances, though, unlike the visual variances, individual parameters were used. We performed one iteration at each M step, as further iterations did not yield significant improvements. The sequence of gains was chosen to be

---

[1] The experimental data are available at
  http://perception.inrialpes.fr/CAVA_Dataset/
[2] Static scenario M1: http://perception.inrialpes.fr/CAVA_Dataset/Site/
  data.html#M1

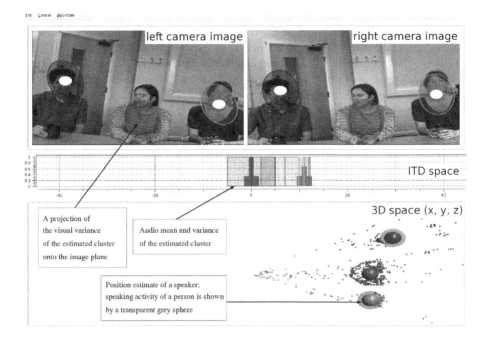

Fig. 2. A typical output of the algorithm: stereoscopic image pair, histogram of ITD observation space and 3D clustering (see text for details)

$\gamma^{(q)} \equiv 1$ (classical GD) and $\gamma^{(q)} = 0.5 + 1/(2(q + 1))$ (relaxed GD). Relaxed GD showed moderate behaviour around the optimal point, which causes slower, but more stable convergence with respect to classical GD. This feature of the relaxed GD could prove to be useful in the case of strong noise. By adjusting $\gamma^{(q)}$ one can improve certain properties of the algorithm, such as convergence speed, accuracy of the solution as well as its dynamic properties in the case of parameters changing through time.

Currently we use the Viola-Jones face detector [22] to initialize the first run of the EM algorithm from visual disparities that lie within faces. But the results of application of BIC criterion to the observations show that it is capable of determining correctly the number of speakers. Hence we do not strongly rely on initial face detection. As we consider the dynamic evolution of the algorithm, the current estimates provide good initializations for the next run of the algorithm.

Figure 2 shows a typical output of our algorithm applied to a time interval. The interest points are shown as dots in the left and right images. The 3D visual observations are shown in x, y, z space, below the images. One may notice that after stereo reconstruction there are both inliers and outliers, as well as 3D points that belong to the background. The histogram representation of the ITD observation space is given in the middle. Transparent ellipses in the images represent projections of the visual covariances corresponding to 3D clusters. The three 3D spheres (blue, red and green) show the locations of cluster centers. Transparent grey spheres surround the current speakers (there are two speakers in this example), also shown with white circles in the image pair. Clusters in the ITD space have a similar representation: the transparent coloured rectangles designate the variances of each cluster, while solid coloured lines drawn at their centres are the corresponding cluster centres. We would like to emphasize the fact that despite the majority of visual observations being located on the central speaker, the influence of the audio data helped to keep the location estimates distinct. At the same time, owing to fine spatial separation of the visual data, the auditory *variances* were adapted rather than the means. This shows the benefits of the combined generative model with respect to separate modality-specific models. The proposed model does not require any explicit modality weighting, as soon as the variances in (14) encode the "reliability" of the observations and the weighting occurs on parameter estimation.

The model was tested on 166 time intervals taken from the meeting scenario with 89 occurences of auditory activity. The soundtrack was labelled manually on the basis of detected onsets and offsets. In total 75 occurences were detected with error probabilities for "missed target" (speaking person detected as non-speaking) and "false alarm" (non-speaking person detected as speaking) being $P_1 = 0.16$ and $P_2 = 0.14$ respectively. Analysis showed that many errors of the first type are due to discretization (frames are processed independently) and proper "dynamic" version of the algorithm could potentially reduce P_1 to 0.08. Currently the auditory observations are collected even when there is no prominent sound, which gives birth to the major part of "false alarm" errors. Such low-energy regions of spectrogram can be detected and suppressed leading to $P_2 = 0.07$. The location estimates for the persons in the middle (green) and on the right (red) lie within their bodies and do not change much. Being accumulated along all chosen time intervals, they form dense clouds of radius 2cm and 4cm respectively. For the person on the left (blue), 97% estimates lie within the body and form the cloud of radius 5cm, though the rest 3% are 10cm away. The reason for this behaviour is, again, the discretization and the problem can be easily resolved by means of tracking. These results show that the model demonstrates reliable 3D localization of the speaking and non-speaking persons present in the scene.

5 Conclusion

We presented a unified framework that captures the relationships between audio and visual observations, and makes full use of their combination to accurately estimate the number of speakers, their locations and speaking states. Our approach is based on unsupervised clustering and results in a very flexible model with further modelling capabilities. In particular, it appears to be a very promising way to address dynamic tracking tasks.

Acknowledgements. The authors would like to thank Heidi Christensen for providing the ITD detection software, as well as Martin Cooke, Jon Barker, Sue Harding, and Yan-Chen Lu of the Speech and Hearing Group (Department of Computer Science, University of Sheffield) for helpful discussions and comments. We would also like to express our gratitude to anonymous reviewers for constructive remarks. This work has been funded by the European Commission under the POP project (Perception on Purpose), http://perception.inrialpes.fr/POP/, number FP6-IST-2004-027268.

References

1. Heckmann, M., Berthommier, F., Kroschel, K.: Noise adaptive stream weighting in audio-visual speech recognition. EURASIP J. Applied Signal Proc. 11, 1260–1273 (2002)
2. Beal, M., Jojic, N., Attias, H.: A graphical model for audiovisual object tracking. IEEE Trans. PAMI 25(7), 828–836 (2003)
3. Kushal, A., Rahurkar, M., Fei-Fei, L., Ponce, J., Huang, T.: Audio-visual speaker localization using graphical models. In: Proc.18th Int. Conf. Pat. Rec., pp. 291–294 (2006)
4. Zotkin, D.N., Duraiswami, R., Davis, L.S.: Joint audio-visual tracking using particle filters. EURASIP Journal on Applied Signal Processing 11, 1154–1164 (2002)
5. Vermaak, J., Ganget, M., Blake, A., Pérez, P.: Sequential monte carlo fusion of sound and vision for speaker tracking. In: Proc. 8th Int. Conf. Comput. Vision, pp. 741–746 (2001)
6. Perez, P., Vermaak, J., Blake, A.: Data fusion for visual tracking with particles. Proc. of IEEE (spec. issue on Sequential State Estimation) 92, 495–513 (2004)
7. Chen, Y., Rui, Y.: Real-time speaker tracking using particle filter sensor fusion. Proc. of IEEE (spec. issue on Sequential State Estimation) 92, 485–494 (2004)
8. Nickel, K., Gehrig, T., Stiefelhagen, R., McDonough, J.: A joint particle filter for audio-visual speaker tracking. In: ICMI 2005, pp. 61–68 (2005)
9. Checka, N., Wilson, K., Siracusa, M., Darrell, T.: Multiple person and speaker activity tracking with a particle filter. In: IEEE Conf. Acou. Spee. Sign. Proc., pp. 881–884 (2004)
10. Gatica-Perez, D., Lathoud, G., Odobez, J.-M., McCowan, I.: Audiovisual probabilistic tracking of multiple speakers in meetings. IEEE trans. Audi. Spee. Lang. Proc. 15(2), 601–616 (2007)
11. Fisher, J., Darrell, T.: Speaker association with signal-level audiovisual fusion. IEEE Trans. on Multimedia 6(3), 406–413 (2004)
12. Barzelay, Z., Schechner, Y.Y.: Harmony in motion. In: IEEE Conf. Comput. Vision Pat. Rec (CVPR), pp. 1–8 (2007)
13. Christensen, H., Ma, N., Wrigley, S.N., Barker, J.: Integrating pitch and localisation cues at a speech fragment level. In: Proc. of Interspeech 2007, pp. 2769–2772 (2007)
14. Movellan, J.R., Chadderdon, G.: Channel separability in the audio-visual integration of speech: A bayesian approach. In: Stork, D.G., Hennecke, M.E. (eds.) Speechreading by Humans and Machines: Models, Systems and Applications. NATO ASI Series, pp. 473–487. Springer, Berlin (1996)
15. Massaro, D.W., Stork, D.G.: Speech recognition and sensory integration. American Scientist 86(3), 236–244 (1998)
16. Celeux, G., Forbes, F., Peyrard, N.: EM procedures using mean-field approximations for Markov model-based image segmentation. Pattern Recognition 36, 131–144 (2003)
17. Dempster, A.P., Laird, N.M., Rubin, D.B.: Maximum likelihood from incomplete data via the EM algorithm (with discussion). J. Roy. Statist. Soc. Ser. B 39(1), 1–38 (1977)
18. Schwarz, G.: Estimating the dimension of a model. The Annals of Statistics 6(2), 461–464 (1978)
19. Harris, C., Stephens, M.: A combined corner and edge detector. In: Proc. 4th Alvey Vision Conference, pp. 147–151 (1988)
20. Hansard, M., Horaud, R.P.: Patterns of binocular disparity for a fixating observer. In: Adv. Brain Vision Artif. Intel., 2nd Int. Symp., pp. 308–317 (2007)
21. Intel OpenCV Computer Vision library,
   http://www.intel.com/technology/computing/opencv
22. Viola, P., Jones, M.: Robust real-time face detection. IJCV 57(2), 137–154 (2004)

A Hybrid Generative-Discriminative Approach to Speaker Diarization

Athanasios K. Noulas[1], Tim van Kasteren[1], and Ben J.A. Kröse[1]

University of Amsterdam,
Kruislaan 403,
1098 SJ Amsterdam,
The Netherlands
{anoulas,tlmkaste,krose}@science.uva.nl
http://staff.science.uva.nl/{anoulas/,tlmkaste/,krose/}

Abstract. In this paper we present a sound probabilistic approach to speaker diarization. We use a hybrid framework where a distribution over the number of speakers at each point of a multimodal stream is estimated with a discriminative model. The output of this process is used as input in a generative model that can adapt to a novel test set and perform high accuracy speaker diarization. We manage to deal efficiently with the less common, and therefore harder, segments like silence and multiple speaker parts in a principled probabilistic manner.

1 Introduction

The objective of speaker diarization is to segment a digital recording in speaker-homogenous parts [12]. Automating this task, enables machines to acquire a better conceptual understanding of a multimodal recording. Furthermore, the output of speaker diarization can be used to improve sentence segmentation [1], and Automatic Speech Recognition (ASR) [8], thus consisting a very important step in analyzing multi-speaker digital recordings. The implementation of a robust system that performs automatic speaker diarization is a formidable task for three reasons. Firstly, in order to be applicable to novel digital recordings, we cannot assume the existence of any speaker-specific training data. Secondly, in order for our system to be robust in different scenarios, we cannot assume knowledge of the microphone locations, or the existence of microphone arrays. Thirdly, if we want to use the output of the framework to improve ASR, we need to segment the digital recording with high precision. If our results have low temporal precision, we will have many segments that contain speech from multiple speakers, and therefore produce low confidence classification and little utility- Cuendet et. al. in [13] showed that increasing the labeling precision of dialog acts by removing the low confidence parts from the training data will increase the ASR performance.

In recent research, there have been many different approaches to speaker diarization. In general, most approaches perform clustering in the audio descriptor space, and expect the clusters discovered to correspond to speaker-homogenous parts. The main problem then lies in dealing with silent parts and multiple-speaker situations, since they both appear for a very small fraction of the digital recording. For example, Laskowski and Schultz, in [8], assign segments of the audio stream to speakers through unsupervised

A. Popescu-Belis and R. Stiefelhagen (Eds.): MLMI 2008, LNCS 5237, pp. 98–109, 2008.

clustering in the audio descriptors space. Using this initial assignment, they learn each person's voice model, and use feature space rotation or sample-level overlap synthesis to deal with multi-speaker parts. With these techniques they use the single-speaker models to predict the distribution of the descriptors coming from the multi-speaker segments. Angueral et.al. in [1], use a preprocessing step to exclude non-speech data from the stream, and use agglomerative clustering in the remaining data to assign each recording segment to the corresponding speaker. In this case, there is an assumption that all speech segments were generated by a single speaker.

In speech recognition or speaker identification, a person's voice is modeled in a generative way [4,6,10]. Furthermore, in [1] and [8], the speaker diarization is evaluated based on the improvement of the ASR, which is performed with a generative model (Hidden Markov Model (HMM)/Gaussian Mixture Model (GMM)). Applying a generative model directly to speaker diarization is much harder.

In general we shall denote the number of participants with P, but for the moment, consider an example recording of two participants. Let's assume that the voice models are given and they are parameterized by θ_1 and θ_2. An audio descriptor at time t, (A_t), can be generated from four different system states, corresponding to one, none, or both of the persons speaking. In general the system state space is of size 2^P. We denote the system state on time t with x_t, which is a binary vector of length P. It is trivial to decide which person most probably generated A_t, by comparing $p(A_t|\theta_p)$ for $p = 1 : P$. However, evaluating the system states is not that straightforward. In order to evaluate $p(A_t|x_t)$ directly, we would need a state-specific distribution. However, some system states appear very rarely in our stream. Thus, we have too little data to learn the parameters of their distribution reliably.

A typical solution in this case is to assume that the state of each participant is independent of the state of the others. Although in a linguistic perspective this is not the case, from a signal processing side of view, it is a very realistic assumption - a person's voice model does not depend on who is speaking at the same time but we do take into consideration the state of the other speakers while we speak. In our example, consider the state where the second person is speaking, this would be:

$$p(A_t|x_t) = \frac{p(x_t|A_t)\,p(A_t)}{p(x_t)} = \prod_{p:1..P} \frac{p(x_t(p)|A_t)\,p(A_t)}{p(x_t(p))} = \prod_{p:1..P} p(A_t|x_t(p)) \quad (1)$$

with $x_t(1) = 0$ and $x_t(2) = 0$.

Assuming the state of different speakers independent of each other, we are left with the formidable task of estimating $p(A_t|x_t(p))$ for $x_t(p) = 0$, which is the probability that a person generated this audio descriptor when they are **not** speaking. This is a quantity which we can not define directly from our data. We can approximate it as a very broad uniform distribution in the feature space, or as the average over all the segments where person p is silent. However, in this case, comparing states which imply a different number of speakers becomes problematic. All speaking segments are more likely to be generated by a voice model than from their average, while all silent segments exhibit the opposite behavior. Thus, we will either assign each segment to an everyone-speaking situation or to a nobody-speaking one.

In section 2 we describe a way to overcome this problem and perform generative speaker diarization, using a simple preprocessing step in which we estimate a distribution over the number of simultaneous speakers on each instant. In section 3 we test two different models for labeling time sequences in the task of determining the number of speakers on each time slice, a HMM and a Conditional Random Field (CRF). In section 4 we show the improvement on speaker diarization on audio streams coming from smart meeting rooms. In section 5 we conclude this paper with a short discussion of the proposed model and the results achieved.

2   Generative Modeling of Multiple Speakers

As described earlier, in a generative approach we need to estimate the probability that the audio descriptor A_t at time t was generated by each system state x_t. Namely we need to compute $p(A_t|x_t)$ which is proportional to $p(x_t|A_t)$. In order to do this, we define a distribution over the number of speakers at time t, $p(n|A_t)$. We describe how we acquire a distribution over the number of speakers for each segment of the recording in section 3

In this case, we can rewrite $p(x_t|A_t)$ as:

$$
\begin{aligned}
p(x_t|A_t) &= \sum_n p(x_t, n|A_t) \\
&= \sum_n p(x_t|A_t, n)\, p(n|A_t) \\
&= \sum_n \frac{p(A_t, n|x_t)p(x_t)}{\sum_x p(A_t, n|x_t)p(x_t)} p(n|A_t) \\
&= \sum_n \frac{p(A_t|x_t)p(n|x_t)p(x_t)}{\sum_x p(A_t|x_t)p(n|x_t)p(x_t)} p(n|A_t)
\end{aligned}
\tag{2}
$$

for clarity of presentation we define as $n_s(x_t)$ a function which returns the number of speakers implied by x_t. At this point, we notice that $p(n|x_t)$ is 1 for n equal to $n_s(x_t)$ and 0 otherwise. Thus we simplify equation 2 in:

$$
p(x_t|A_t) = \frac{p(A_t|x_t)\,p(x_t)}{\sum_{x:n_s(x)=n} p(A_t|x_t)\,p(x_t)} p(n_s(x_t)|A_t)
\tag{3}
$$

Now, from equation 1 we can express $p(A_t|x_t)$ as:

$$
\begin{aligned}
p(A_t|x_t) &= \prod_p p(A_t|\theta_p)^{x_t(p)} Q^{1-x_t(p)} \\
&= [N - n_s(x_t)]\, Q \prod_{p:x_t(p)=1} p(A_t|\theta_p)^{x_t(p)}
\end{aligned}
\tag{4}
$$

where $Q = p(A_t(i)|x_t(j))$ for $x_t(j) = 0$. Assigning the same Q for all speakers j, implies that all the persons affect the audio stream the same way when they do not speak, and it is a reasonable assumption. If we use uniform $p(x_t)$ for all possible states we get:

$$
p(x_t|A_t) = p(n_s(x_t)|A_t) \frac{\prod_{p:x_t(p)=1} p(A_t|x_t)}{\sum_{x:n_s(x)=n} \prod_{p:x_t(p)=1} p(A_t|x_t)}
\tag{5}
$$

Intuitively, we have one unit of probability mass to distribute among the different possible system states. The states are grouped based on the number of speakers that each state implies, and the term $p\left(n_s\left(x_t\right)|A_t\right)$ determines what part of the probability mass is allocated to each group. This part is then distributed among the states of the group through the second term of the product.

3   Modeling the Number of Speakers

The objective of our data preprocessing step is to estimate a distribution over the different numbers of speakers for each segment of the recording. Since the temporal patterns of the data are very important for such a task, we compared two probabilistic models that take into consideration the temporal relationships in our data. A generative one, in the form of a HMM [11], and a discriminative one, in the form of a linear CRF [7].

A HMM is a generative probabilistic model, defined fully by the prior probability of the system to be at each state on the first time slice of the model π; the transition distribution $p\left(n_t|n_{t-1}\right)$ representing the probability of going from state n_{t-1} at time $t-1$ to state n_t, and the observation model that defines the probability that an observation A_t was generated by state n_t, namely $p\left(A_t|n_t\right)$. A graphical representation of a HMM can be seen in figure 1(a).

A linear chain CRF, parameterizes is a discriminative probabilistic model that resembles closely the HMM. As we can see in figure 1(b), the model still consists of a hidden variable and an observable variable at each time step. However, the arrowheads of the edges between the various nodes have disappeared, making this an undirected graphical model. This means that two connected nodes no longer represent a conditional distribution (e.g. $p\left(A_t|n_t\right)$), but instead we speak of the potential between two connected nodes. This potential also represents the chance of observing a specific configuration of its variables, but unlike a probability is not restricted to be a value between 0 and 1.

The potential functions that specify the linear-chain CRF are $\psi(n_t, n_{t-1})$ and $\psi(n_t, A_t)$. For clarity of representation these potential functions are written down using a more uniform notation, which allows different forms of CRFs to be expressed using a common formula. In this work, we adopt the notation of [14] and therefore define:

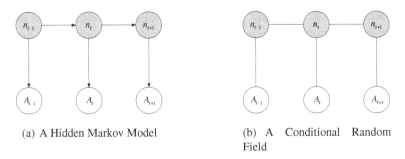

(a) A Hidden Markov Model

(b) A   Conditional   Random
Field

Fig. 1. The two models compared for estimating the number of speakers on each time slice. The grey nodes denote hidden variables, while the white nodes depict observable ones.

$\psi(n_t = i, n_{t-1} = j) = \lambda_{ijk} f_{ij}(n_t, n_{t-1}, A_t)$ in which the λ_{ij} is the parameter value (the actual potential) and $f_{ijk}(n_t, n_{t-1}, A_t)$ is a feature function which in our case can be a binary indicator of whether $n_t = i$ and $n_{t-1} = j$ or it returns the value of the specific feature respectively. The index ij is typically replaced by a one-dimensional index, denoted here with k, so we can easily represent the summation over all the different potential functions.

The essential difference between HMMs and CRFs lies in the way we learn the model parameters. In the case of HMMs the parameters are learned by maximizing the *joint* probability distribution $p(n_{1:T}, A_{1:T})$. The parameters of a CRF are learned by maximizing the *conditional* probability distribution $p(n_{1:T} \mid A_{1:T})$. One of the main consequences of this choice, is that while learning the parameters of a CRF, we avoid modeling the distribution of the observations, $p(A)$. The conditional probability is modeled as:

$$p(n_{1:T}|A_{1:T}) = \frac{1}{Z(A)} \exp\left\{\sum_{k=1}^{K} \lambda_k f_k(n_t, n_{t-1}, A_t)\right\} \tag{6}$$

where $Z(A)$ is the normalization function

$$Z(A) = \sum_{n_t} \exp\left\{\sum_{k=1}^{K} \lambda_k f_k(n_t, n_{t-1}, A_t)\right\} \tag{7}$$

Note that the quantity $p(n_{1:T}|A_{1:T})$ is convex in the λ-space, and we can use any optimization algorithm to obtain the optimal λ values. In our implementation we used the BFGS algorithm [2] which was shown to be the most efficient approach [14].

We trained and tested both our models on 2 hours of data, coming from multiple speakers. In this corpora, coming mainly from interviews and video-conferences, the number of speakers on each time window was set manually. We extracted the 13 first Mel frequency cepstra coefficients, and concatenated their first and second order differences. Thus, a 39 dimensional vector was created for each audio window, while the stream was segmented in 25 ms audio windows with 10 ms overlap. The HMM modeled the generative distribution for different numbers of speakers as a Gaussian mixture model of 15 components with diagonal covariances. The CRF used one feature function per dimension which returned the observation value itself. We selected the preprocessing model for our final framework using 10-fold cross validation on this data. The results achieved under both models can be seen in table 1.

Table 1. Cross validation results (%) acquired on determining the number of speakers

HMM	0	1	2	3	4	CRF	0	1	2	3	4
0	**88.38**	6.79	0.543	2.71	1.56	0	**82.74**	10.05	0.95	3.73	2.51
1	23.98	**49.04**	9.17	13.17	4.61	1	18.07	**60.59**	14.6	5.91	0.81
2	10.32	14.94	**33.08**	17.32	24.32	2	2.64	25.40	**41.50**	21.8	8.55
3	15.89	23.43	16.03	**21.12**	23.50	3	2.71	8.49	24.86	**38.79**	25.13
4	4.07	9.17	13.17	16.6	**56.92**	4	3.66	3.05	4.75	20.58	**67.93**

The CRF performed much better than the HMM, and therefore it was preferred for our final implementation. The main diagonal of the confusion matrixes contains the accuracy per class, and CRF was able to distinguish multiple speaker states much better. It is interesting to notice that the two diagonals near the central one, highlighted with a gray background in table 1, contain the main mass of classifications. This is reasonable, since when on person is speaking there are long pauses, and while two or more people are speaking it is often the case that only 2 of them are active over such a small time window of 25ms.

Finally, it is important to notice that the number of speakers on a time slice can be estimated using parameters trained with speaker-independent data. Therefore, a discriminative approach, like the CRF, which requires labeled data, can also be used. In actual speaker diarization, described in section 4, we require speaker-specific voice models, without assuming the existence of any labeled speaker-specific data. Thus, we can only use a generative approach, and learn the parameters of each person's model directly from our test data, using the Expectation Maximization algorithm [3].

4   Inference for Speaker Diarization

The distribution on the number of speakers of each time-slice, acquired from the pre-processing step, is used as observation in our speaker diarization model. The graphical representation of the proposed probabilistic model can be seen in figure 2 and comes in the form of a HMM. The generative choice here is necessary, since we want to learn the parameters of our model directly from our training data.

In the proposed approach, we assume a recording containing P persons. Therefore, the possible system states take values from a discrete space of 2^P values. We represent these states as binary vectors, with the pth element being 1 if the corresponding person is speaking and 0 otherwise. We assume a uniform prior probability for the system being

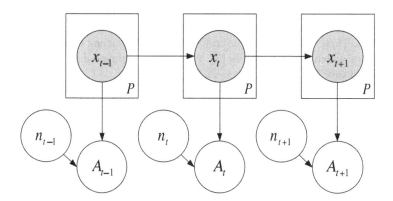

Fig. 2. The model used for learning and inference during speaker diarization. Notice that node $X(p)$ is repeated P times at each time slice. The state of different persons at a specific time slice t ($X_t(p)$) are interdependent since they are parents of the same observable node A_t, but they are independent at the transition phase.

in any state at the beginning of the stream. The transition matrix, A, is of size $2^P \times 2^P$, with the element A_{ij} corresponding to the probability $p(x_t = j | x_{t-1} = i)$. This creates a very number of parameters $(2^P(2^P - 1))$, with some specific state transitions becoming very improbable, or even never appearing in a given recording. We reduce the number of necessary parameters to $2P$ assuming that the transition of each person's state is independent of the others. In principle, humans perceive the changes in the state of their co-speakers and act based on this, but in practice this simplification works well. Thus we denote with A_p^1 the probability that person p will remain speaking in a system transition $(p(x_t(p) = 1 | x_{t-1}(p) = 1))$, and A_p^0 that person p will remain silent, and we get:

$$A_{ij} = p(x_t = j | x_{t-1} = i) = \prod_p p(x_t(p) | x_{t-1}(p)) \tag{8}$$

where we need to learn $2P$ A_p parameters. Finally, the observation model defines the probability that a specific observation was generated from a given system state, $p(A_t | x_t)$. We acquire this using Bayes Rule:

$$p(A_t | x_t) = \frac{p(x_t | A_t) p(A_t)}{p(x_t)} \tag{9}$$

and assuming uniform priors for all different system states.

5   Learning with the E.M.

The framework presented so far is generic, in the sense that any voice model can be incorporated to model $p(A_t | x_t(p) = 1)$. In our implementation we modeled each participants voice with a 15 component Gaussian mixture model in the feature space. In order to perform speaker diarization as described in section 4, we need to acquire the voice model and the transition probabilities for each person. We acquire these parameters using the E.M. algorithm [3] directly on the test data.

In the E-step, we estimate the expectation of the system to be at a specific state on each time slice. We perform the forward procedure, which estimates $\alpha_i(t) = p(A_{1..t}, x_t = i)$ and the backward procedure that estimates $\beta_i(t) = p(A_{t+1..T} | x_t = i)$ for all time slices. These quantities can be computed efficiently using a recursive formula, more details of which can be found in [3]. We can now estimate the probability of the system to be in state i at t, $\gamma_i(t) = p(x_t = i | A_{1..T})$ as:

$$\gamma_i(t) = \frac{\alpha_i(t)\beta_i(t)}{\sum_{i=1}^{2^P} \alpha_j(t)\beta_j(t)} \tag{10}$$

as well as the probability of the system having a transition from state i to state j at time t, $\xi_{ij}(t) = p(x_t = i, x_{t+1} = j | A_{1..T})$ as:

$$\xi_{ij}(t) = \frac{\gamma_i(t) A_{ij} p(A_{t+1} | x_t = j) \beta_j(t+1)}{\beta_i(t)} \tag{11}$$

In our case, the state of each person is independent of the others. Thus, the probability of a person to be speaking on a specific time slice is $\gamma^p(t) = p(x_t(p) = 1 | A_{1..T})$:

$$\gamma^p(t) = \sum_{i:x_t(p)=1} \gamma_i(t) \tag{12}$$

and the probability of a person transition from state k to l, denoted as $\xi_{kl}^p(t)$

$$\xi_{kl}^p(t) = \sum_{i:x_t(p)=k, j:x_{t+1}(p)=l} \xi_{ij}(t) \tag{13}$$

In the m-step we are going to use these expectations to set the model parameters to the values that maximize the complete-data likelihood. For each person:

$$A_p^0 = \frac{\sum_T \xi_{00}^p}{\sum_T 1 - \gamma^p(t)} \qquad A_p^1 = \frac{\sum_T \xi_{11}^p}{\sum_T \gamma^p(t)} \tag{14}$$

which correspond to the expectation of person p to remain silent or speaking.

The voice model of each person is modeled as a Gaussian mixture model of 15 components. For each component c we need to estimate the mean μ_c^p, covariance Σ_c^p and mixture proportion π_c^p. If we denote with $p_c^p(t)$ the probability that observation A_t was generated from the cth component of the pth person, then

$$p_c^p(t) = \gamma^p(t) \frac{\mathcal{N}(A_t; \mu_c^p \Sigma_c^p)}{\sum_c \mathcal{N}(A_t; \mu_c^p \Sigma_c^p)} \tag{15}$$

where $\mathcal{N}$ denotes the Gaussian kernel. The M-step equations become:

$$\mu_c^p = \frac{1}{N_c} \sum_t p_c^p(t) A_t$$
$$\Sigma_c^p = \frac{1}{N_c} \sum_t p_c^p(t) (\mu_c - A_t(i))^2 \tag{16}$$
$$\pi_c^p = \frac{N_c}{\sum_c N_c}$$

where $N_c = \sum_t p_c^p(t)$. Note here that $(\mu_c - A_t(i))^2$ represents raising element-wise the result in the power of 2, leading to spherical covariance matrices.

6   Results

We applied the proposed model to perform speaker diarization in a 30 minutes audio recording, coming from a smart meeting room. The recording was part of the AMI corpus and comes from the IDIAP smart meeting room [9]. The recording code is IDI_20051213-1422. The objective of the experiment was threefold. First, we are interested in the accuracy of the CRF in detecting the correct number of speakers for each time slice. Second, we wanted to see how well the generative approach described in section 2 can handle the parts that multiple speakers vocalize. Thirdly, we want to see how much this improves the speaker diarization results in comparison with approaches that follow the typical assumptions of a single-speaker per time slice, or a single-speaker after removing the silence parts.

Initially, in section 6.1, we present the results on detection of the number of speakers. In section 6.2, we present the results in the task of speaker diarization on our data. The proposed method of speaker diarization is very generic since any voice model or feature space can be used. We perform speaker diarization under three different experimental settings, in order to see how efficiently we cope with multiple simultaneous speakers. In the first setup, our proposed model is applied, multi-speaker system states are detected, and results acquired through this model are labeled as *full*. We then lowered the dimensionality of our hidden states space, to that including only states implying a single speaker or silence. We label this experiment as *low*. Finally, we excluded the audio windows labeled from our CRF as silence in preprocessing step, and used a model containing only the single speaker states. This experiments are denoted as *pre*. In the *low* experiments, we did not use the distribution over the number of speakers but instead modeled silence as a fifth speaker. In the *pre* experiments, the distribution over the number of speakers would not make any difference since all states correspond to a single speakers. Finally, in section 6.3 the results on classification of multiple speaker parts are detected.

6.1   Accuracy in Detection of Number of Speakers

The results of speaker diarization using the speaker independent data can be seen in table 2. As we can see, the CRF exhibits similar behavior with that in table 1, where it manages to distinguish the different number of speakers reliably. Furthermore, it distinguishes very well between silence and single speaker windows, which is very important since these are the dominant classes of a meeting recording. The CRF is not a Bayesian model. Therefore, the conditional probability $p\left(n_{1:T}|A_{1:T}\right)$ that we maximize, is not a posterior but a conditional likelihood function. In order to focus the classification accuracy on silence and single speaker data, we had to train our model with a dataset containing more data from the specific classes.

The overall Diarization Error (DER) in determining the correct number of speakers was 44%. A task commonly tackled in diarization systems is distinguishing between speech and non-speech parts. In this case, the proposed CRF has a 14% DER. In the work of [5], the baseline system applied in similar recordings has a 16.8% error in the distinguishing speech from non-speech parts, while the improved version exhibits a DER of 4.3%. Since our system was not specifically trained to distinguish between speech and non-speech parts the 14% DER in this task is satisfactory. The CRFs can provide a useful tool for separation of speech and non-speech parts.

Table 2. Number of speakers detection accuracy on the audio recording coming from the IDIAP smart meeting room data

Number of Speakers Accuracy	0	1	2	3	4
0	**0.52**	0.43	0	0.02	0.01
1	0.018	**0.96**	0.0	0.01	0.01
2	0.01	0.75	**0.19**	0.03	0.01
3	0	0.74	0.11	**0.14**	0
4	0	0.17	0	0	**0.82**

Table 3. Speaker diarization results

Pre	0	1	2	3	4	Low	0	1	2	3	4	Full	0	1	2	3	4
0	0.00	0.67	0.13	0.12	0.07	0	**0.79**	0.07	0.05	0.05	0.03	0	**0.72**	0.14	0.02	0.08	0.03
1	0.00	**0.40**	0.21	0.18	0.20	1	0.11	**0.35**	0.18	0.15	0.18	1	0.10	**0.41**	0.15	0.13	0.18
2	0.00	0.23	**0.46**	0.14	0.14	2	0.14	0.17	**0.44**	0.12	0.13	2	0.17	0.13	**0.48**	0.12	0.08
3	0.00	0.19	0.13	**0.48**	0.18	3	0.14	0.11	0.15	**0.44**	0.16	3	0.12	0.09	0.10	**0.54**	0.14
4	0.00	0.11	0.08	0.13	**0.66**	4	0.09	0.07	0.06	0.11	**0.64**	4	0.09	0.07	0.06	0.11	**0.63**

6.2 Accuracy in Speaker Diarization

In table 3 we can see the results achieved under the three different assumptions. In *pre*, we assume that each window was created by a sinsgle speaker. As a consequence, the silence parts are also assigned to a speaker. The segments belonging to a single speaker have high classification accuracy, since there are no multi-speaker or silent system state labels available to the model. The random classification accuracy here would be 25%. In *low*, only silence and single speaker states compete. We achieve here high accuracy results in silence detection, but lower on the speaker diarization. When a single person is speaking there are silent parts, and therefore segments belonging to a single speaker are classified as silence. In *full*, we can see the results of our proposed framework. Silence detection has slightly lower precision, since silence is not modeled as an independent speaker, but rather detected through the preprocessing step. On the other hand, the speaker diarization has much higher accuracy, and this difference can prove essential in ASR or automatic transcription tasks.

The overall DER of our system is 40% which lacks behind DER between 16.5% and 25% presented in [5]. We believe that by using features more suitables for this dataset and more elaborate speaker models, this accuracy can increase. What is really interesting to notice is that systems which lower the dimensionality of the hidden state space perform a DER of 60% which is very near the baseline system presented in [5]. However, full probabilistic treatment of all the possible multi-speakers situations, which is the contribution of this work, improves significantly the results. If we combine this treatment with state of the art voice models it can produce optimal output.

6.3 Multiple Speaker Parts

Finally, we would like to investigate is how well our model classifies the multi-speaker parts. The results are visible in table 4 and follow the pre-processing results presented in table 2. Thus, the parts with two or three speakers are detected with low accuracy, while the four person parts are detected very accurately. The reason is that most of the two person speaking results correspond to audio feedback given from one person when another person speaks. Thus, they are short in duration and harder to detect.

In the third column of table 4, *speakers detected*, we see how many of the correctly detected multi-speaker windows were assigned to the correct persons. In the case of two speakers there are 6 difference system states combinations to choose from, in the case of three speakers there are 4 states, while in the case that four speakers are detected there is only one corresponding system state. This is an indication of the difficulty of

Table 4. Accuracy in multiple speaker parts

Number of speakers in a window	Total windows in data	Windows detected	Speakers detected
2	5300	0.28	0.54
3	1472	0.22	0.92
4	2693	0.65	1.00

selecting the correct speakers and it is depicted in the *speakers detected* results, where the accuracy increases as the number of states to choose from decreases.

7   Discussion and Conclusions

The results in section 6 present the potential of a hybrid approach to speaker diarization. We do not claim that our model and parameter choices for each sub-task are optimal, but it is our strong belief that the proposed method consists a sound probabilistic approach to the task of speaker diarization. The experimental results of section 6.1 show that a discriminative approach can detect the number of active speakers reliably. Multi-speaker parts, although rear in the stream, can be detected without jeopardizing high accuracy in single-speaker and silence detections. The CRF framework allows much space for tuning, and the use of more training data, coming straight from meeting audio in combination with the use of problem-specific features can further improve the results.

The results in section 6.2 show that the proposed hybrid model can rest the assumptions about a single speaker (and silence) at each time of the stream. These two classes are detected with extremely high accuracy, while the multi-speaker parts are treated in a uniform manner. Once more, more elaborate voice-models or voice-synthesis methods can improve the results further. Finally in section 6.3, we present the results on the detected multi-speaker parts. We see that the audio modality is partially able to distinguish the active speakers. In order to improve results here, either the video modality or a different voice-synthesis model should be used.

References

1. Anguera, X., Wooters, C., Hernando, J.: Automatic cluster complexity and quantity selection: Towards robust speaker diarization. In: Renals, S., Bengio, S., Fiscus, J.G. (eds.) MLMI 2006. LNCS, vol. 4299, pp. 248–256. Springer, Heidelberg (2006)
2. Bertsekas, D.P.: Nonlinear Programming, 2nd edn. Athena Scientific, Belmont (1999)
3. Bilmes, J.: A gentle tutorial on the em algorithm and its application to parameter estimation for gaussian mixture and hidden markov models (1997)
4. Dines, J., Doss, M.M.: A study of phoneme and grapheme based context-dependent asr systems. IDIAP-RR 12, IDIAP (2007)
5. Huang, E.M.J., Visweswariah, K., Potamianos, G.: The ibm rt07 evaluation systems for speaker diarization on lecture meetings. In: Proc. Rich Transcription Evaluation Work, pp. 282–289. Morgan Kaufmann Publishers Inc, San Francisco (2007)

6. Karafia't, M., Gre'zl, F., Schwarz, P., Burget, L., Cernocky', J.: Robust heteroscedastic linear discriminant analysis and lcrc posterior features in meeting data recognition. In: Renals, S., Bengio, S., Fiscus, J.G. (eds.) MLMI 2006. LNCS, vol. 4299, pp. 275–284. Springer, Heidelberg (2006)
7. Lafferty, J.D., McCallum, A., Pereira, F.C.N.: Conditional random fields: Probabilistic models for segmenting and labeling sequence data. In: ICML 2001: Proceedings of the Eighteenth International Conference on Machine Learning, pp. 282–289. Morgan Kaufmann Publishers Inc., San Francisco (2001)
8. Laskowski, K., Schultz, T.: Modeling vocal interaction for segmentation in meeting recognition. In: Popescu-Belis, A., Renals, S., Bourlard, H. (eds.) MLMI 2007. LNCS, vol. 4892, pp. 259–270. Springer, Heidelberg (2008)
9. Moore, D.: The IDIAP Smart Meeting Room (2002)
10. Moore, D., Dines, J., Doss, M.M., Vepa, J., Cheng, O., Hain, T.: Juicer: A weighted finite-state transducer speech decoder. In: Renals, S., Bengio, S., Fiscus, J.G. (eds.) MLMI 2006. LNCS, vol. 4299. Springer, Heidelberg (2006)
11. Rabiner, L.R.: A tutorial on hidden markov models and selected applications in speech recognition, pp. 267–296 (1990)
12. Reynolds, D., Torres-Carrasquillo, P.: Approaches and applications of audio diarization. In: IEEE ICASSP, pp. 953–956 (2005)
13. Cuendet, D.H.-T.S., Shriberg, E.: Automatic labeling inconsistencies detection and correction for sentence unit segmentation in conversational speech. In: Popescu-Belis, A., Renals, S., Bourlard, H. (eds.) MLMI 2007. LNCS, vol. 4892, pp. 144–155. Springer, Heidelberg (2008)
14. Sutton, C., McCallum, A.: An introduction to Conditional Random Fields for Relational Learning. In: Introduction to Statistical Relational Learning, ch. 1. MIT Press, Cambridge (2006)

A Neural Network Based Regression Approach for Recognizing Simultaneous Speech

Weifeng Li, Kenichi Kumatani, John Dines, Mathew Magimai-Doss, and Hervé Bourlard

IDIAP Research Institute, CH-1920 Martigny, Switzerland
{wli,mathew,dines,Kenichi.Kumatani,bourlard}@idiap.ch

Abstract. This paper presents our approach for automatic speech recognition (ASR) of overlapping speech. Our system consists of two principal components: a speech separation component and a feature estmation component. In the speech separation phase, we first estimated the speaker's position, and then the speaker location information is used in a GSC-configured beamformer with a minimum mutual information (MMI) criterion, followed by a Zelinski and binary-masking post-filter, to separate the speech of different speakers. In the feature estimation phase, the neural networks are trained to learn the mapping from the features extracted from the pre-separated speech to those extracted from the close-talking microphone speech signal. The outputs of the neural networks are then used to generate acoustic features, which are subsequently used in acoustic model adaptation and system evaluation. The proposed approach is evaluated through ASR experiments on the *PASCAL Speech Separation Challenge II* (SSC2) corpus. We demonstrate that our system provides large improvements in recognition accuracy compared with a single distant microphone case and the performance of ASR system can be significantly improved both through the use of MMI beamforming and feature mapping approaches.

Keywords: neural network, speech separation, speech recognition, microphone arrays.

1 Introduction

A recent thrust of ASR research has focused on techniques to efficiently integrate inputs from multiple distant microphones (multi-channel) for multiparty meetings (where more than one speakers can be active at the same time). There are two common approaches to the separation of overlapping speech: blind source separation (BSS) [1] and beamforming techniques. BSS exploits the assumption of statistical independence or de-correlated components between the overlapped signals in order to separate them, while beamforming provides an enhanced version of the input speech based on the location of the speakers. The most fundamental and important multi-channel method is the microphone array beamforming method, which consists of enhancing signals coming from a particular location by filtering and combining the individual microphone signals. The simplest technique is *delay-sum* (DS)

A. Popescu-Belis and R. Stiefelhagen (Eds.): MLMI 2008, LNCS 5237, pp. 110–118, 2008.

beamforming, which performs a summation of delayed microphone inputs, where the delays are calculated to compensate for the differing time of arrival of the the desired sound source at each of the microphones in the array.

Other sophisticated beamforming techniques, such as those proposed by Frost [2] or the *Generalized Sidelobe Canceller* (GSC) [3], optimize the beamformer to produce a spatial pattern with a dominant response for the location of interest. The main limitation of these schemes is the issue of signal cancellation. In [4] a superdirective beamformer and a further post-filtering have also been proposed to suppress interfering speech. However, in the case of overlapping speech (with coherent noise), the estimation of coherence matrix is far from trivial, and inaccurate estimations may consequently introduce artifacts into the reconstructed signal. Such disadvantages to conventional beamforming have spurred the development of approaches such as the MMI beamforming criterion for beamforming [13] which alleviates the signal cancellation problem by ensuring the orthogonality of desired and interfering signals.

It is important to note that the motivation behind the microphone array techniques such as delay-sum beamforming is to enhance or separate the speech signals, and as such they are not designed directly in the context of ASR. In practice, it is common for meeting ASR that a well trained acoustic model is first obtained using clean speech data (conversational telephone speech, broadcast news), which is then adapted by using the meeting speech both from close talking microphone (nearfield) as well as distant microphone speech after enhancing the speech by delay-sum beamforming [5] or superdirective beamforming [7]. This approach has been shown to perform well. However, if one looks closely at the ASR errors, a considerable amount of errors occur at the places where speakers overlap (multiple speakers are active) [6]. Thus, improving the signal-to-noise ratio (SNR) of the signal captured through distant microphones may not necessarily be the best means of extracting features for robust ASR on distant microphone data, particularly during periods of speaker overlap.

In our previous work [8], we have proposed to estimate the log spectral energies or Mel-frequency cepstral coefficients (MFCC) of clean speech based on a mapping of delay-and-sum beamformed speech using neural networks. The mapping method could be viewed as a non-linear processing technique that aims to approximate the clean speech through the fusion of the target speech and interfering speech. If the qualities of the estimated target speech and interfering speech are improved, then it is highly possible that the clean speech can be approximated with greater precision. Therefore, we propose to first separate the target speech and the interfering speech using MMI beamforming techniques, followed by a Zelinski and binary-masking based postfilter, and then to perform the mapping method for estimating the MFCCs of the clean speech. Our studies on the PASCAL SSC2 corpus [11] show the effectiveness of the proposed methods.

Although non-linear feature mapping using neural networks has been studied for robust distant microphone ASR in the cepstral domain [17][18][19], the inputs used for the estimation of the clean features in their algorithms are the noisy features obtained from a single input from either distant microphone speech [17][18] or microphone array beamformed speech [19]. We distinguish our approach by exploiting additional sources of information to improve the effectiveness of the mapping. More specifically, we perform a mapping of features of target and interfering sound sources, that have been firstly separated using state of the art beamforming techniques.

This paper is organised as follows. Section 2 presents the system configuration as a whole. Section 3 and Section 4 give a detailed description of speech separation algorithms and non-linear feature estimation using neural networks, respectively. Section 5 then presents and discusses experimental results, and Section 6 gives conclusions and further work which may improve the performance of the system.

2   System Configuration

The system consists of two principal components as shown in Figure 1: speech separation followed by feature estimation. Initially we estimate the speaker's position with the speaker localization system. The speaker location information is used in a GSC-configured beamformer with a minimum mutual information (MMI) criterion to separate the speech of the two speakers, and the non-correlated noise and the competing speech are canceled by means of a Zelinski and binary-masking post-filter applied to the beamformer output. Then the features of the pre-separated speech are extracted and the features of the clean speech are estimated based on a non-linear regression. Finally the estimated features are recognised by the ASR system for evaluation. In the following two sections, the speech separation and feature estimation algorithms are described in details.

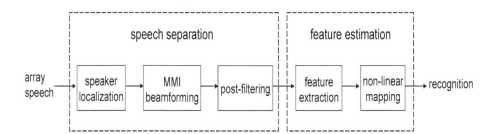

Fig. 1. Diagram of system configuration

3   Speech Separation Algorithms

3.1   Speaker Localization

The speaker tracking system we employed was based on [12]. New observations are associated with an active target or with the clutter model through the calculation of posterior probabilities. After the association step, the position of each speaker can be updated through the modified Kalman filter. In addition to the speeaker's position, the system is also capable of determining when each speaker is active.

3.2   MMI Beamforming

The speaker location information is used in a GSC-configured beamformer with a minimum mutual information (MMI) criterion [13] to separate the speech of different speakers. Assuming there are two such beamformers aimed at different sources as shown in Figure 2, the output of the i-th beamformer for a given subband can be expressed as,

$$Y_i = (\mathbf{w}_{q,i} - \mathbf{B}_i \mathbf{w}_{a,i})^H \mathbf{X} \tag{1}$$

where $\mathbf{w}_{q,i}$ is the *quiescent weight vector* for the i-th source, $\mathbf{B}_i$ is the *blocking matrix*, $\mathbf{w}_{a,i}$ is the *active weight vector*, and $\mathbf{X}$ is the input subband *snapshot vector*. In keeping with the GSC formalism, $\mathbf{w}_{q,i}$ is chosen to preserve a signal from the *look direction* and, at the same time, to suppress an interference [15, §6.3]. $\mathbf{B}_i$ is chosen such that $\mathbf{B}_i^H \mathbf{w}_{q,i} = \mathbf{0}$. $\mathbf{w}_{a,i}$ can be optimized by minimizing the mutual information $I(Y_1, Y_2)$ where Y_1 and Y_2 are the outputs of the two beamformers. The optimization procedure of finding that $\mathbf{w}_{a,i}$ under a minimum mutual information (MMI) criterion is described in Kumatani et al. [13].

Minimizing a mutual information criterion yields a weight vector $\mathbf{w}_{a,i}$ capable of canceling interference that leaks through the sidelobes without the signal cancellation problems encountered in conventional beamforming. The GSC constraint solves the problems with source permutation and scaling ambiguity typically encountered in conventional blind source separation algorithms [14].

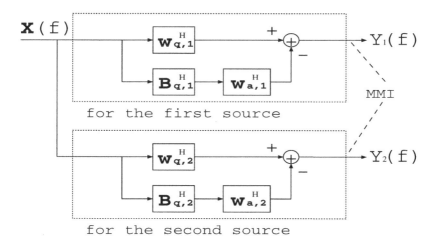

Fig. 2. An MMI beamformer in GSC configuration

3.3   Post-filtering

In order to further alleviate the non-correlated noise on different channels, a fequency-domain Zelinski post-filter [20] is applied to the MMI-beamformed speech, which can be estimated by

$$\hat{g}_i(f) = \frac{\frac{2}{M(M-1)} \Re\{\sum_i^{M-1} \sum_{j=i+1}^{M} \phi_{x_i x_j}(f)\}}{\frac{1}{M} \sum_i^{M} \phi_{x_i x_i}(f)}, \tag{2}$$

Here $\Re\{\cdot\}$ and M denote the real operator and the number of channels, respectively. $\phi_{x_i x_i}$ and $\phi_{x_i x_j}$ represent the auto- and cross-spectral densities of the time-aligned inputs, respectively. Furthermore, a frequency-domain binary-masking filter [21]

$$\hat{h}_i(f) = \begin{cases} 1 & \text{if } i = \text{argmax}_{i'} |b_{i'}(f)|, i' = 1, ..., I \\ 0 & \text{otherwise} \end{cases} \tag{3}$$

where $b_i(f)$ is Zelinsky filtered output (in this work $I = 2$), is used to eliminate the signal from competing speakers. Finally the frequency-domain post-filtered output $Z_i(f)$ is obtained by

$$Z_i(f) = \hat{g}_i(f)\hat{h}_i(f)Y_i(f). \tag{4}$$

4   Feature Estimation

4.1   Feature Extraction

The frequency-domain outputs are reconstructed into time-domain speech signals. The speech signals are extracted with a 25-millisecond window and a 10-millisecond frame shift. 26-channel Mel-filterbank analysis followed by the log operation is subsequently applied. Finally 12 Mel-frequency cepstral coefficients (MFCC) are obtained through the discrete cosine transformation (DCT) [9].

4.2   Non-linear Mapping

The idea of the mapping method is to approximate the MFCC extracted from the speech signals captured by close-talking microphones through the non-linear combination of the MFCC from pre-separated speech signals, as shown in Figure 3. Let $\mathbf{s}_1(n)$ and $\mathbf{s}_2(n)$ denote the MFCC vectors extracted from the two pre-separated speech signals z_1 and z_2 at frame n, respectively. At the n-th frame the feature vector of the clean speech from the first speaker, $c_1(n)$, can be estimated using the neural network with one hidden layer:

$$\hat{\mathbf{c}}_1(n) = f(\mathbf{s}_1(n), \mathbf{s}_2(n))$$
$$= \sum_{p=1}^{P} \left(w_p \cdot g \left(b_p + \mathbf{w}_{p1}^T \mathbf{s}_1(n) + \mathbf{w}_{p2}^T \mathbf{s}_2(n) \right) \right) + b \tag{5}$$

Neural network training (90 utterances from the development data set)

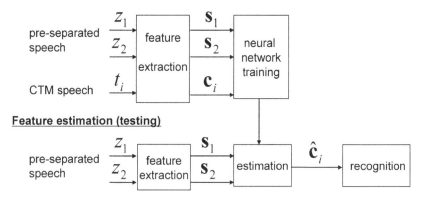

Feature estimation (testing)

Fig. 3. Diagram of the mapping-based speech recognition. CTM: close-talking microphone.

where $g(\cdot)$ and P are the sigmoidal activation function and number of the neurons employed in the hidden layer. The clean speech from the second speaker can be estimated by swapping the inputs to the MLP, ie. $\hat{c}_2(n) = f(s_2(n), s_1(n))$.

The parameters $\Theta = \{w_p, b_p, \mathbf{w}_{p1}, \mathbf{w}_{p2}, b\}$ are obtained by minimizing the mean squared error:

$$\mathcal{E}_i = \sum_{n=1}^{N} [\mathbf{c}_i(n) - \hat{\mathbf{c}}_i(n)]^2, \tag{6}$$

over the training examples. Here $\mathbf{c}_i(n), i \in \{1, \ldots, I\}$ denotes the MFCC vector from the ith close talking microphone where in this work $I = 2$. We denote the sample index as n coming from a total of N training examples. The optimal parameters can be found through the error back-propagaton algorithm [16].

Note that the clean speech is required for finding the optimal parameters in the neural network training, while in the test phase the clean speech is no longer required, i.e., it is predicted from the input feature vectors from the enhanced target speech and the interfering speech.

Note that before being fed into MLP, the two pre-separated speech inputs must be kept in a consistent order. We firstly normalize both the pre-separated speech and close-talking microphone speech, and then find each of the pre-separated speech near to the corresponding close-talking microphone speech based on the minimum distance between their spectral envelopes. In our mapping method, the inputs of neural networks s_1 and s_2 are 21-dimensional MFCC vectors, while the dimensionality of the output $\mathbf{c}_i$ is 13. These settings are based on our previous studies [10].

5   Experiments and Results

We performed far-field automatic speech recognition experiments on the *PASCAL Speech Separation Challenge 2* (SSC2) [11] corpus. The data contain recordings

Table 1. Recognition accuracies (as percentages) on the development data set

	without adaptation	with adaptation
Close-talking microphone	80.6	88.0
Lapel microphone	38.5	67.5
Single distant microphone	0.7	9.4
Separated speech	10.6	35.8
Mapping of separated speech	46.9	58.9
Mapping of lapel microphone speech	70.1	78.8

Table 2. Recognition accuracies (as percentages) on the evaluation data set

	without adaptation	with adaptation
Close-talking microphone	82.0	83.1
Lapel microphone	42.1	53.7
Single distant microphone	0.2	1.4
Separated speech	27.9	34.9
Mapping of separated speech	46.7	49.5
Mapping of lapel microphone speech	63.4	68.9

of two speakers simultaneously and the uttrances is from the 5,000 word vocabulary Wall Street Journal (WSJ) task. The data were recorded with two circular, eight-channel microphone arrays. The diameter of each array was 20 cm, and the sampling rate of the recordings was 16 kHz. The database also contains speech recorded with close talking microphones (CTM). This is a challenging task for source separation algorithms given that the room is reverberant and some recordings include significant amounts of background noise.

Prior to beamforming, we first estimated the speaker's position with the speaker localization system described in [12]. In our beamforming system, the Gaussian pdf is used. The active weights for each subband were nitialized to zero. The system uses an HTK recognizer [9] with acoustic models trained on the WSJCAM0 database from close talking microphones. MLLR based transform is used to adapt the baseline acoustic models.

The corpus is divided into develop data set (178 utterances) and evaluation data set (143 utterances). For the development data set, a leave-one-out cross-validation approach is employed for the adaptation. For the evaluation data set, the development data is used for the adaptation. In our feature mapping method, 104 utterances from the development dataset are used for the neural networking training. The total number of training examples (frames) is 63,826.

Tables 1 and 2 show recognition accuracies (as percentages) for the development and evaluation data sets for a number of different conditions. We can draw following observations from the results:

– ASR performance drops significantly when going from close-talking microphone, lapel microphone, and a single distant microphone. We also observe

the expected results, which have also been earlier observed in the literature [23][5], that model level adaptation improves performance.
- The speech separation system gives much higher recognition accuracies than single distant microphone. However, these results are still much lower than those of the lapel and close-talking microphones.
- By the mapping the MFCCs to those of close-talking microphone, the recognition performance is further significantly increased. Note that without adaptation, the mapping system yields better recognition performance than the lapel microphones, which clearly demonstrates the effectiveness of the feature mapping process. With the mapping of separated speech, the recognition accuracies are higher on the development dataset than on the evaluation data set partly because the training data of neural networks is from one part of development data set.
- When the feature mapping method is applied to the lapel microphones, the recognition performance could also be increased.

6   Conclusions

We have presented our approach to automatically recognize simultaneous speech. Our system consisted of two principal components: a speech separation component which returns the separated speech as well as the locations of simultaneous speakers, and a feature estimation component in which we proposed to further enhance the feature vectors used for speech recognition. The technique achieves better performance to the lapel microphones without acoustic model adaptation, and shows large improvements in recognition accuracy compared with a single distant microphone case. In this work, the mapping was learned between distant microphones signal and clean speech signal. The future work in this direction is to detect speaker overlap and non-overlap regions in multiparty meetings and train/adapt the MLP directly using close-talking microphone speech as target speech. Another issue is to address the scenarios where there are more than two speakers speaking simultaneously.

Acknowledgments. This work was supported by the European Union 6th FWP IST Integrated Project AMIDA (Augmented Multi-party Interaction with Distant Access, FP6-033812) and the Swiss National Science Foundation through the Swiss National Center of Competence in Research (NCCR) on Interactive Multimodal Information Management (IM2). The authors would like to thank Ivan Himawan, Dr. Iain McCowan, and Dr. Mike Lincoln for the helpful discussions.

References

1. Haykin, S.: Unsupervised adaptive filtering. Blind source seperation, vol. 1. Wiley, New York (2000)
2. Frost, O.L.: An algorithm for linearly constrained adaptive array processing. Proc. IEEE 60(8), 926–935 (1972)

3. Griffiths, L.J., Jim, C.W.: An Alternative Approach to Linearly Constrained Adaptive Beamforming. IEEE Trans. on Antennas and Propagation AP-30(1), 27–34 (1982)
4. Moore, D., McCowan, I.: Microphone array speech recognition: Experiments on overlapping speech in meetings. In: Proc. ICASSP, pp. 497–500 (2003)
5. Stolcke, A., et al.: The SRI-ICSI Spring 2007 Meeting and Lecture Recognition System. LNCS. Springer, Heidelberg (2007)
6. Cetin, O., Shriberg, E.: Speaker overlaps and ASR errors in meetings: Effects before, during, and after the overlap. In: Proc. ICASSP, vol. 1, pp. 357–360 (2006)
7. Hain, T., Burget, L., Dines, J., Garau, G., Wan, V., Karafiat, M., Vepa, J., Lincoln, M.: The AMI system for the transcription of speech in meetings. In: Proc. ICASSP, Honolulu, Hawaii (2007)
8. Li, W., Magimai.-Doss, M., Dines, J., Bourlard, H.: MLP-based log spectral energy mapping for robust overlapping speech recognition, IDIAP Technical Report, 07-54 (2007)
9. Young, S., et al.: The HTK Book, Version 3.4., http://htk.eng.cam.ac.uk/docs/docs.shtml
10. Li, W., Dines, J., Magimai.-Doss, M., Bourlard, H.: Neural Network based Regression for Robust Overlapping Speech Recognition using Microphone Arrays, IDIAP Technical Report 08-09 (2008)
11. Lincoln, M., McCowan, I., Vepa, I., Maganti, H.K.: The multichannel Wall Street Journal audio visual corpus (mc-wsj-av): Specification and initial experiments. In: Proc. ASRU, pp. 357–362 (2005)
12. Gehrig, T., McDonough, J.: Tracking and far-field speech recognition for multiple simultaneous speakers. In: Proc. the Workshop on Machine Learning and Multimodal Interaction (September 2006)
13. Kumatani, K., Gehrig, T., Mayer, U., Stoimenov, E., McDonough, J., Wölfel, M.: Adaptive beamforming with a minimum mutual information criterion. IEEE Transactions on Audio, Speech and Language Processing 15, 2527–2541 (2007)
14. Buchner, H., Aichner, R., Kellermann, W.: Blind source seperation for convolutive mixtures: A unified treatment. In: Audio Signal Processing for Next-Generation Multimedia Communication Systems, pp. 255–289. Kluwer Academic, Boston (2004)
15. Van Trees, H.L.: Optimum Array Processing. Wiley-Interscience, New York (2002)
16. Werbos, P.J.: Beyond Regression: New Tools for Prediction and Analysis in the Behavioral Sciences, PhD Thesis. Harvard University, Cambridge, MA (1974)
17. Sorensen, H.B.D.: A cepstral noise reductionmulti-layer neural network. In: Proc. ICASSP, vol. 2, pp. 933–936 (1991)
18. Yuk, D., Flanagan, J.: Telephone speech recognition using neural networks and hiddenMarkov models. In: Proc. ICASSP, vol. 1, pp. 157–160 (1999)
19. Che, C., Lin, Q., Pearson, J., de Vries, B., Flanagan, J.: Microphone arrays and neural networks for robust speech recognition. In: Proc. the workshop on Human Language Technology, pp. 342–347 (1994)
20. Uwe Simmer, K., Bitzer, J., Marro, C.: Post-filtering techniques. In: Brandstein, M., Ward, D. (eds.) Microphone Arrays, ch. 3, pp. 39–60. Springer, Heidelberg (2001)
21. McCowan, I., Hari-Krishna, M., Gatica-Perez, D., Moore, D., Ba, S.: Speech Acquisition in Meetings with an Audio-Visual Sensor Array. In: Proc. the IEEE International Conference on Multimedia and Expo (ICME) (July 2005)
22. Rabiner, L.R., Juang, B.H.: Fundamentals of Speech Recognition. Prentice-Hall, Englewood Cliffs (1993)
23. Lin, Q., Che, C., Yuk, D.-S., Jin, L., de Vries, B., Pearson, J., Flanagan, J.: Robust distant-talking speech recognition. In: Proc. ICASSP, vol. 1, pp. 21–24 (1996)

Hilbert Envelope Based Features for Far-Field Speech Recognition

Samuel Thomas, Sriram Ganapathy, and Hynek Hermansky*

IDIAP Research Institute, Martigny, Switzerland
Ecole Polytechnique Fédérale de Lausanne (EPFL), Switzerland
{tsamuel,ganapathy,hynek}@idiap.ch
http://www.idiap.ch

Abstract. Automatic speech recognition (ASR) systems, trained on speech signals from close-talking microphones, generally fail in recognizing far-field speech. In this paper, we present a Hilbert Envelope based feature extraction technique to alleviate the artifacts introduced by room reverberations. The proposed technique is based on modeling temporal envelopes of the speech signal in narrow sub-bands using Frequency Domain Linear Prediction (FDLP). ASR experiments on far-field speech using the proposed FDLP features show significant performance improvements when compared to other robust feature extraction techniques (average relative improvement of 43% in word error rate).

Keywords: Hilbert Envelopes, Frequency Domain Linear Prediction, Far-field Speech, Automatic Speech Recognition.

1 Introduction

When speech is recorded in rooms using far-field microphones, the speech signal that reaches the microphone is superimposed with multiple reflected versions of the original speech signal. These superpositions can be modeled by the convolution of the room impulse response, that accounts for individual reflection delays, with the original speech signal, i.e.,

$$r(t) = s(t) * h(t), \tag{1}$$

where $s(t)$, $h(t)$ and $r(t)$ denote the original speech signal, the room impulse response and the reverberant speech respectively. The effect of reverberation on the short-time Fourier transform (STFT) of the speech signal $s(t)$ can be represented as

$$R(t, \omega_k) = S(t, \omega_k) H(t, \omega_k), \tag{2}$$

---

* This work was supported by the European Commission 6th Framework DIRAC Integrated Project and the Swiss National Center of Competence in Research (NCCR) on Interactive Multi-modal Information Management IM2, managed by the IDIAP Research Institute on behalf of the Swiss Federal Authorities.

A. Popescu-Belis and R. Stiefelhagen (Eds.): MLMI 2008, LNCS 5237, pp. 119–124, 2008.

where $S(t, \omega_k)$ and $R(t, \omega_k)$ are the STFT's of the clean speech signal $s(t)$ and reverberant speech $r(t)$ respectively and $H(t, \omega_k)$ denotes the STFT of the room impulse response $h(t)$. For long analysis windows, this effect of reverberation can be approximated as multiplicative in the frequency domain [1], i.e., $H(t, \omega_k)$ is not a function of time and Eq. (2) becomes

$$R(t, \omega_k) \simeq S(t, \omega_k) H(\omega_k). \tag{3}$$

In the techniques reported in [2,3], the effect of reverberation is compensated by subtracting from $\log\left(R(t, \omega_k)\right)$, its mean.

In this paper, we propose a technique that uses gain normalized temporal trajectories of sub-band energies to compensate for the room reverberation artifacts. Hilbert envelopes of sub-band signals are estimated by applying linear prediction in the frequency domain [4] (Sec. 2). Unlike conventional approaches that use mean compensation for reverberant speech recognition [2,3], the proposed technique alleviates the reverberation artifacts present in long temporal envelopes of narrow frequency sub-bands(Sec. 3). The application of the proposed compensation technique to the FDLP features significantly improves the recognition accuracies for reverberant speech recorded using far-field microphones (Sec. 4).

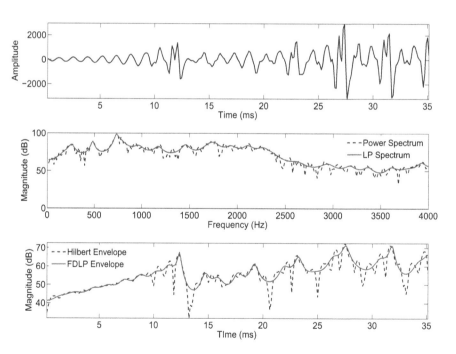

Fig. 1. Linear Prediction in time and frequency domains for a portion of speech signal

2   Frequency Domain Linear Prediction

Typically, Auto-Regressive (AR) models have been used in speech/audio applications for representing the envelope of the power spectrum of the signal (Time Domain Linear Prediction (TDLP) [5]). This paper utilizes AR models for obtaining smoothed, minimum phase, parametric models for temporal rather than spectral envelopes (Fig. 1). Since we apply the LP technique to exploit the redundancies in the frequency domain, this approach is called Frequency Domain Linear Prediction (FDLP) [4], [6]. For the FDLP technique, the squared magnitude response of the all-pole filter approximates the Hilbert envelope of the signal (in a manner similar to the approximation of the power spectrum of the signal using TDLP [5]).

When speech is analyzed in narrow sub-bands using such long analysis windows, each sub-band signal can be modeled in terms of the product of a slowly varying, positive, envelope function and an instantaneous phase function [7]. In the case of far-field speech, each of these sub-band signals gets modified by the room impulse response and can be approximated as the convolution of the Hilbert envelope of the clean speech signal in that sub-band with that of the room impulse function [7]. Since the Hilbert envelope and the spectral auto-correlation function form Fourier transform pairs [4], normalizing the gain of the sub-band FDLP envelopes suppresses the multiplicative effect present in the spectral autocorrelation function of the reverberant speech.

3   Features Based on Frequency Domain Linear Prediction

For the purpose of feature extraction, segments of the input speech signal (of the order of 1000 ms) are decomposed into sub-bands, where FDLP is applied to obtain a parametric model of the temporal envelope. The whole set of sub-band temporal envelopes forms a two dimensional (time-frequency) representation of the input signal energy. Each of these temporal envelopes is gain normalized to suppress the reverberation artifacts. This two-dimensional representation is convolved with a rectangular window of duration 25 ms and resampled at a rate of 100 Hz (10 ms intervals, similar to the estimation of short term power spectrum in conventional feature extraction techniques). These sub-sampled short-term

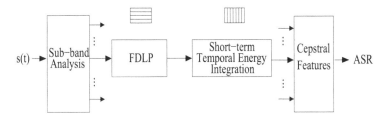

Fig. 2. FDLP feature extraction for ASR

spectral energies are converted to short-term cepstral features similar to the PLP feature extraction technique [8]. In our experiments, we use 39 dimensional cepstral features containing 13 cepstral coefficients along with the delta and double-delta features. The block schematic for the FDLP feature extraction technique is shown in Fig. 2.

4   Experiments and Results

We apply the proposed features and techniques to a connected word recognition task on a digits corpus using the Aurora evaluation system [9] along with the "complex" version of the back end proposed in [10]. We train models using a training dataset used in [3] which contains of 8400 clean speech utterances, consisting of 4200 male and 4200 female utterances downsampled to 8 kHz. In order to study the effect of finer spectral resolution for the proposed compensation technique, we first perform experiments using a test set of 3003 clean utterances also used in [3]. We also create a test set for artificially reverberated speech by convolving the clean test set with a room impulse response (with RT60 of 0.5 seconds and a direct-to-reverberant energy ratio of 0 dB [12]).

The first set of experiments compare the performance of FDLP based features with the conventional features for clean and artificially reverberated speech. We also study the effect of finer spectral resolution for the proposed compensation technique by increasing the number of frequency sub-bands. Table 1 shows the word accuracies for PLP features (PLP) and FDLP features when the number of sub-bands is varied from 24 (FDLP-24) to 120 (FDLP-120). This is accomplished by increasing the duration of the temporal analysis (from 1000 ms to 2400 ms) for a constant width and overlap of the DCT windows. For all these experiments we employ gain normalized temporal envelopes along with rectangular windows in the DCT domain.

The next set of experiments are performed on the digits corpus recorded using far-field microphones as part of the ICSI Meeting task [11]. The corpus consists of four sets of 2790 utterances each. Each of these sets correspond to speech recorded simultaneously using four different far-field microphones [11]. Each of

Table 1. Word Accuracies (%) for PLP and FDLP features for clean and reverberant speech

Feature Set	Clean Speech	Revb. Speech
PLP	99.68	80.12
FDLP-24	99.18	89.49
FDLP-33	99.13	91.86
FDLP-67	99.09	92.93
FDLP-76	99.16	93.60
FDLP-96	99.07	94.79
FDLP-108	99.03	94.63
FDLP-120	98.91	94.55

Table 2. Word Accuracies (%) using different feature extraction techniques on far-field microphone speech

Channel	PLP	CMS	LDMN	LTLSS	FDLP
Channel E	68.1	71.2	73.2	74.0	85.2
Channel F	75.5	77.4	80.4	81.0	88.1
Channel 6	74.1	78.3	80.9	81.1	89.6
Channel 7	58.6	67.6	70.5	71.0	84.9

these sets contain 9169 digits similar to those found in TIDIGITS corpus. The number of sub-bands for the FDLP features is fixed at 96 along with a temporal analysis window of duration 2000 ms. We use the HMM models trained with the clean speech from earlier experiments. The results for the proposed FDLP technique are compared with those obtained for several other robust feature extraction techniques proposed for reverberant ASR namely Cepstral Mean Subtraction (CMS) [13], Long Term Log Spectral Subtraction (LTLSS) [3] and Log-DFT Mean Normalization (LDMN) [2]. In our LTLSS experiments, we calculated the means independently for each individual utterance (which differs from the approach of grouping multiple utterances for the same speaker described in [3]) using a shorter analysis window of 32 ms, with a shift of 8 ms. Table 2 shows the word accuracies for the different feature extraction techniques using the far-field test data, where we obtain a relative error improvement of about 43% over the best other feature extraction technique.

5   Conclusions

Unlike many single microphone based far-field speech recognition approaches, the proposed technique does not normalize speech signals using long term mean subtraction in spectral domain. We show that the effect of reverberation is reduced when features are extracted from gain normalized temporal envelopes of long duration in narrow sub-bands. FDLP provides an efficient way to suppress the reverberation artifacts and hence, FDLP features extracted in reverberant environments provide significant improvements over other robust feature extraction techniques.

References

1. Avendano, C.: Temporal Processing of Speech in a Time-Feature Space. Ph.D. thesis, Oregon Graduate Institute (1997)
2. Avendano, C., Hermansky, H.: On the Effects of Short-Term Spectrum Smoothing in Channel Normalization. IEEE Trans. Speech and Audio Proc. 5(4), 372–374 (1997)
3. Gelbart, D., Morgan, N.: Double the trouble: handling noise and reverberation in far-field automatic speech recognition. In: Proc. ICSLP, Colorado, USA, pp. 2185–2188 (2002)

4. Herre, J., Johnston, J.D.: Enhancing the Performance of Perceptual Audio Coders by using Temporal Noise Shaping (TNS). In: Proc. 101st AES Conv., Los. Angeles, USA, pp. 1–24 (1996)
5. Makhoul, J.: Linear Prediction: A Tutorial Review. Proc. of the IEEE 63(4), 561–580 (1975)
6. Athineos, M., Hermansky, H., Ellis, D.P.W.: LP-TRAPS: Linear Predictive Temporal Patterns. In: Proc. INTERSPEECH, Jeju Island, Korea, pp. 1154–1157 (2004)
7. Mourjopoulos, J., Hammond, J.K.: Modelling and Enhancement of Reverberant Speech using an Envelope Convolution Method. In: Proc. ICA, Boston, USA, pp. 1144–1147 (1983)
8. Hermansky, H.: Perceptual Linear Predictive (PLP) Analysis of Speech. J. Acoust. Soc. Am. 87(4), 1738–1752 (1990)
9. Hirsch, H.G., Pearce, D.: The AURORA Experimental Framework for the Performance Evaluations of Speech Recognition Systems under Noisy Conditions. In: Proc. ISCA ITRW ASR 2000, Paris, France, pp. 18–20 (2000)
10. Pierce, D., Gunawardana, A.: Aurora 2.0 speech recognition in noise: Update 2. In: Colorado, U.S.A. (ed.) Proc. ICSLP Session on Noise Robust Rec, Colorado, USA (2002)
11. The ICSI Meeting Recorder Project, http://www.icsi.berkeley.edu/Speech/mr
12. ICSI Room Responses, http://www.icsi.berkeley.edu/speech/papers/asru01-meansub-corr.html
13. Rosenberg, A.E., Lee, C., Soong, F.K.: Cepstral Channel Normalization Techniques for HMM-Based Speaker Verification. In: Proc. ICSLP, Yokohama, Japan, pp. 1835–1838 (1994)

Multimodal Unit Selection for 2D Audiovisual Text-to-Speech Synthesis

Wesley Mattheyses, Lukas Latacz, Werner Verhelst, and Hichem Sahli

Vrije Universiteit Brussel, Dept. ETRO, Pleinlaan 2, B-1050 Brussels, Belgium

Abstract. Audiovisual text-to-speech systems convert a written text into an audiovisual speech signal. Lately much interest goes out to data-driven 2D photorealistic synthesis, where the system uses a database of pre-recorded auditory and visual speech data to construct the target output signal. In this paper we propose a synthesis technique that creates both the target auditory and the target visual speech by using a same audiovisual database. To achieve this, the well-known unit selection synthesis technique is extended to work with multimodal segments containing original combinations of audio and video. This strategy results in a multimodal output signal that displays a high level of audiovisual correlation, which is crucial to achieve a natural perception of the synthetic speech signal.

1 Introduction

1.1 Text-to-Speech Synthesis

A classical text-to-speech (TTS) system is an application that converts a written text into an auditory speech signal. In general, the TTS synthesis procedure can be split-up in two main parts. In a first stage the target text is analyzed by a linguistic front-end which converts it into a sequence of phonetic tokens and the accompanying prosodic information like timing, pitch and stress parameters. Then, in a second step, this information is used by the synthesis module of the TTS system to construct the actual physical waveform. In the early years, model based synthesis was the common technique to create the target speech. This means that the properties of the output waveform are calculated by using pre-defined rules based on measurements on natural speech. For instance, formant-based synthesizers create the synthetic speech by designing a time-varying spectral envelope that mimics the formants found in natural speech. Although these model-based synthesizers are able to produce an intelligible speech signal, their output signals lack a natural timbre to successfully mimic human speech. This led to the development of a different synthesis methodology: data driven synthesizers. These systems construct the target speech by selecting and concatenating appropriate segments from a database with natural pre-recorded speech. If the system can select a good set of segments, the output speech will be perceived as (more or less) natural and it will display a realistic timbre. Currently this data-driven technique is the most common strategy used by high-end TTS systems, where

A. Popescu-Belis and R. Stiefelhagen (Eds.): MLMI 2008, LNCS 5237, pp. 125–136, 2008.

the segments are selected from a large database containing continuous natural speech signals [12].

1.2 Audiovisual Text-to-Speech Synthesis

In human to human speech communication, not only the audio but also the visual mode of speech is important. Accordingly, when thinking of a program that converts a written text into a speech signal, ideally this system should create together with the audio a synthetic visual track containing a person that speaks the target text. Such systems are referred to as audiovisual TTS systems. To construct this visual speech signal, the same two major approaches found in classical auditory TTS synthesis exist: model-based and data-based synthesis [1]. Model-based visual speech synthesizers create the visual signal by rendering a 3D model of a human head. To simulate the articulator movements, pre-defined rules are used to alter the polygons of the model in accordance with the target phonetic sequence. Unfortunately, 3D visual speech synthesis systems are unable to produce a completely photorealistic visual speech signal, even when sophisticated models and texture-mapping techniques are used. Similar to the evolution in auditory TTS systems, in recent years more and more interest goes out to data-driven approaches to create a synthetic visual speech signal that is - in the most ideal case - indistinguishable from a natural speech signal. Data-driven audiovisual TTS systems construct the target photorealistic video signal using visual speech data selected from a database containing recordings of natural visual speech. The major downside of data-driven synthesis, both in the audio and in the visual domain, is the fact that the freedom of output generation is limited by the nature and the amount of the pre-recorded data in the database. For instance, the large majority of 2D photorealistic visual speech synthesis systems will only produce a frontal image of the talking head, since their databases consist of frontal recordings only. This means that the system can not be used in, for example, 3D scenery creation in an animated movie. Nevertheless, a 2D frontal synthesis can be applied in numerous practical cases due to its similarity with regular 2D television and video. Research has shown that humans tend to better comprehend a speech signal if they can actually see the talking person's face and mouth movements [18]. Furthermore, people feel more positive and confident if they can see the person that is talking to them. This is an important issue when we think about creating synthetic speech in the scope of machine-user communication. When a TTS system is used to make a computer system pronounce a certain text toward a user, the addition of a visual signal displaying a person speaking this text will indeed increase both the intelligibility and the naturalness of the communication. 2D audiovisual TTS systems are also very useful for educational applications. For instance, small children need a visual stimulus on top of the auditory speech even more than adults do, as it will make them feel more connected with the machine and helps in drawing their attention. Other possible applications can be found in the infotainment sector, where these photorealistic speech synthesizers can be used to create a synthetic news anchor or a virtual reporter which can, for instance, be employed to create up-to-date audiovisual reports to broadcast via the Internet.

In the remainder of this paper we will focus on data-driven 2D audiovisual TTS synthesis. In the next section we give a general description of this data-driven approach, together with a short overview of the previous work found in the literature. Next, in section 3 we introduce our technique for tackling the synthesis question and we describe our audiovisual text-to-speech system. Our results are discussed in section 4 and section 5 describes how this research can be extended in the future.

2   2D Photorealistic Audiovisual Speech Synthesis

2.1   Database Preparation

Audiovisual data-driven speech synthesis is performed by gathering and combining data from a database. In a first step, an offline recording of the audiovisual database is needed. Note that from the recordings of one single speaker, only one synthetic speaker can be created. This implies that for every virtual speaker we want to create, a new database has to be recorded. In addition, the positioning of the camera determines the possible views of the synthetic head that can be created during synthesis. Another point that needs to be considered is the fact that every head movement of the recorded speaker causes his/her facial parts like the nose, the eyes and the lips to move from their location (when seen from the fixed camera position). So, if we record data including head movements, later on processing will be needed to cope with these displacements. In general, it is not necessary that the audio data is recorded together with the video database, even more: it is not obliged that the same speaker is used. Nevertheless, since the audio and the video mode of an audiovisual speech signal show a great deal of correlation, recording both modes together can have a lot of benefits as will be explained in more detail later. After recording, the database must be analyzed to construct meta-data that can be applied during synthesis. Since this is still an offline step, much effort should be spent on an accurate examination of the speech data because the quality of the synthesis will be for a great deal determined by the nature and the quality of this meta-data. First of all, the speech must be phonetically annotated: the audio signal is segmented in series of consecutive phonemes and the visual signal is segmented in consecutive visemes. In addition, extra properties in both modes are annotated to ensure that the most appropriate segments can be selected during synthesis. Examples of such properties are given in section 3.3.

2.2   Speech Synthesis

To create a new audiovisual speech signal, the synthesizer must select and apply the appropriate data from the database. To create the synthetic audio track, concatenative auditory speech synthesis is the most commonly applied technique. A general description of this strategy is given in section 3.3 and can be found for instance in [12]. In order to create the synthetic video track, the system has to cope with several requirements. First of all, the synthetic mouth and face movements have to represent the correct phonetic sequence. Note that there is no one-on-one mapping between phonemes and their visual counterpart (visemes): different phonemes can be represented by the same viseme (so-called viseme-classes [2]). On the other hand, due to a strong visual co-articulation effect, several possible visual representations for a same phoneme exist. A second requirement is that the synthetic visual articulators (e.g.: lips, tongue, jaw) should move in a natural manner. Finally, the system must assure that there is a good coherence between the output audio and video mode. In the following section we will briefly describe some techniques that are mentioned in the literature for tackling this synthesis question.

2.3   Previous Work

A first important remark that should be made when we inspect the literature on 2D photorealistic speech synthesis is that most of these systems synthesize the audio and the video mode separately from each other. They first acquire the target audio from an external auditory text-to-speech system or from a recording of natural speech and then, afterwards, this audio track and its phonetic transcript are used as input to create the visual mode of the synthetic speech. A second observation is that the systems found in the literature only focus on creating the appropriate mouth movements, after which they complete the synthesis by merging this mouth together with a background face. In the remainder of this paper, although sometimes not explicitly mentioned, we discuss techniques used to synthesize only the mouth-area of the visual speech signal.

In an early system designed by *Bregler et al.* [3], the visual database is first segmented in triphones using the phonetic annotation of the audio track. The system creates a series of output frames by selecting the most appropriate triphones from the database based on two criteria. The first one expresses how well the phonemes of the triphone chunk match the target phonemes: two phonemes from a same viseme-class contribute zero penalty. The second criterion expresses how closely the mouth contours in the boundary frames of the triphone chunk match those in adjacent output frames. Other systems described by *Ezzat et al.* [7] and *Goyal et al.* [10] are based on the idea that the relation between phonemes and visemes can be simplified as a many-to-one relation. First they create a database of still images, one for each viseme-class. For each phoneme in the output audio, its representative still image is added to the output video track. To accomplish a smooth transition between these keyframes, image warping is used to create the appropriate intermediate frames. Much research on 2D speech synthesis was conducted by *Cosatto et al.* [4][5][6]. In the first versions of their system, a map of different mouth occurrences is defined. The different entries of this map are determined by visual properties like the width and the height of the mouth-opening. For each entry, several frames are pre-selected from the database. To synthesize a new visual speech sequence, a trajectory through the map can be calculated by first training the system with some sample speech data. Then these trajectories are sampled, where the system selects from the target map entries those frames that are most suitable for concatenation. Over the years, their synthesis method evolved more and more towards a real unit selection synthesis, similar to the unit selection techniques used in auditory text-to-speech synthesis. In their approach, the new video track is constructed by selecting and concatenating segments consisting of a variable amount of original frames. This selection is based on how well the fragment matches the ideal target segment and how good it can be concatenated with the other selected chunks.

Ezzat et al. [8] and *Theobald et al.* [19] worked on model-based 2D photorealistic synthesis. Their systems first define a model that represents the frames of the visual speech corpus based on shape parameters (e.g.: optical flows or landmarks) and appearance parameters (e.g.: principal components analysis (PCA) coefficients). Such a model can be an analysis tool, since every new frame can be represented as a combination of these shape and appearance parameters. By using such models, the system can generate new unseen frames as every new set of parameters defines a new image. To create the target visual speech signal, trajectories through the parameter space are calculated in accordance with the target phoneme sequence. Based on these trajectories, the system is then able to create a new series of appropriate video frames.

3   The Proposed Audiovisual Speech Synthesis System

3.1   General Approach

By developing a Dutch (Flemish) audiovisual speech synthesizer, we wish to investigate how the naturalness of 2D audiovisual TTS synthesis can be further optimized. As explained in section 2.2, the goal in audiovisual speech synthesis is not only to create a visual speech signal that looks fluent and natural, it is also important to reach a high level of multimodal coherence in the output. Since humans are trained to capture and process inputs from both modes of an audiovisual speech input simultaneously, they are sensitive to unnatural combinations of auditory and visual speech. Consequently, the major drawback of the systems described in section 2.3 resides in the fact that they only produce a video signal. Afterwards this signal is merged with an audio track coming from a completely different source (from a different speaker) in order to create the final multimodal output. Although this new video track can appear very natural and smooth, users tend to observe that the auditory speech they hear actually could not have been produced by the facial animation they see. This is often caused by the fact that the visual synthesizer creates a 'safe' representation of the viseme sequence, based on the most common visual representation(s) of the input phoneme sequence. In practice, however, the output audio speech track does include some more extreme phoneme instances (e.g.: badly pronounced ones), which do need a corresponding visual counterpart in the accompanying video track.

In this study, our main goal is to synthesize the output by concatenating audiovisual chunks, selected from an audiovisual database. This means that from the continuous speech in the database, the system will select an appropriate set of multimodal segments from which both the audio and the video track will be used to construct the output speech. This strategy has the advantage that the final output will consist of original combinations of auditory and visual speech fragments, which will maximize the audiovisual correlation in this synthetic signal. This will lead to a more natural perception of the combination of synthetic auditory and synthetic visual speech and it will obviously minimize quality degradations caused by audiovisual co-articulation effects (e.g.: the McGurk effect [16]). In addition, a careful selection and concatenation of the selected audiovisual segments will result in a new multimodal speech signal that exhibits smoothness and naturalness in both its audio and its video mode.

3.2   Database Preparation

We recorded a preliminary small audiovisual speech corpus containing 53 sentences from weather forecasts. It is obvious that this limited amount of data will have a negative influence on the overall synthesis quality. Nevertheless, by synthesizing sentences from this limited domain, significant observations are possible. Also, a valorization of the synthesis techniques for the open domain can be attained by expanding the database. The audiovisual speech was recorded with the video sampled at 25 frames per second and the audio sampled at 44100 Hz. We assured that the asynchrony between both modes is negligible small. After recording, the data was analyzed off-line to create the meta-data for synthesis. For the audio track, we computed energy, pitch and spectral properties, together with pitch mark information. The video track was processed to obtain for each frame a set of landmark points, which indicate the location of the facial parts (see figure 1). Additionally, we subtracted from each frame the mouth region and calculated its PCA coefficients. Finally the frames were further processed to detect the amount of visible teeth and the dark area inside the open mouth.

3.3   Segment Selection

Our audiovisual synthesis system is designed as an extension of our unit selection auditory TTS system [14], which uses a Viterbi search on cost functions to select the appropriate segments from the database. The total cost (C_{total}) of selecting a particular audiovisual segment includes target cost functions (C_{target}) that indicate how well this segment matches the target speech, and join cost functions (C_{join}) which indicate how well two consecutive segments can be concatenated without the creation of disturbing artifacts. To use with our multimodal unit selection technique, these cost functions are needed for the audio track as well as for the video track, since the selection of a particular audiovisual unit will depend on the properties of both these modes. As primary target cost we used the phonetic correctness of the segment. Note that, contrary to the systems described in section 2.3, no viseme-classes are used since the auditory synthesis requires an exact phonetic match. Since the co-articulation effect - the fact that the visual properties of a certain phoneme strongly depend on the nature of the surrounding phonemes and visemes - is very pronounced for the visual mode, looking for those segments that have a phonetic context matching as well as possible the target speech is crucial. For this reason, the target cost function is further refined to reward a match in the extended phonetic context (see also [14]). To calculate the join cost between two segments, both auditory (CA_{join}) and visual (CV_{join}) properties are used. For the audio mode, we measure the difference in energy, pitch and mel-scale cepstra. For the visual domain we define an essential cost function that is calculated after aligning the two segments, by measuring the differences between the landmark positions in frames at the border of selected neighboring segments. By using this cost we ensure smooth concatenations in the video mode, since it rewards the selection of mouth instances that are similar in shape. Furthermore, other visual cost functions are needed to select mouths with similar appearances in order to avoid the creation of artifacts at the join positions. This is achieved by comparing properties like the amount of visible teeth and the amount of mouth opening present in the frames. Finally, we implemented a cost function based on the PCA coefficients of the mouth regions, which can be used to measure shape as well as appearance differences.

$$C_{total} = \sum_i w^i_{target} C^i_{target} + \sum_j w^j_{join} C^j_{join} \qquad with:$$

$$\begin{cases} \sum_i w^i_{target} C^i_{target} = w_{phoneme} C_{phoneme} + w_{phoneme-context} C_{phoneme-context} \\ \sum_j w^j_{join} C^j_{join} = \sum_m w^m CA^m_{join} + \sum_n w^n CV^n_{join} \\ \sum_m w^m CA^m_{join} = w_{energy} C_{energy} + w_{pitch} C_{pitch} + w_{mel-scale} C_{mel-scale} \\ \sum_n w^n CV^n_{join} = w_{landmarks} C_{landmarks} + w_{teeth} C_{teeth} + w_{mopen} C_{mopen} + w_{PCA} C_{PCA} \end{cases}$$

By adjusting the weights w, an optimal trade-off between all the different contributions to the total cost can be found. At this point in time, the weights in our system are experimentally optimized, although in a later stage of this research, an automatic training of these parameters might be used to further optimize the selection procedure.

3.4   Concatenation and Synthesis

The selected audiovisual segments have to be joined together to create the final output signal. The joining of two fragments that both contain an original combination of audio and video requires two concatenation actions - one for the audio and one for the video track. The two segments that have to be joined are overlapped by an extend that optimizes the concatenation. This join position is first roughly determined by the phonetic transcript of the audio track: former research on auditory speech synthesis has shown that the most optimal join position is the most stable part of the boundary phonemes of the two segments. Each join can be further optimized by fine-tuning this point until the total join cost for this particular join is minimal. In order to successfully transfer the inherent audiovisual coherence from the two audiovisual segments to the joined speech fragment, the location of the join in the video track is kept as close as possible to the location of the join in the audio track (see also further in this section). Joining the two multimodal segments with a certain overlap implies the need for some sort of advanced crossfade technique for both the audio and the video track, as will be explained next.

Audio Concatenation. When two voiced speech waveforms are joined, we have to make sure that the resulting signal shows a continuous periodicity. Therefore, we designed a join technique based on pitch mark information that tackles the problem by a pitch-synchronous window/overlap technique. For more details the reader is referred to [15].

Video Concatenation. When the video tracks of the two audiovisual segments are played consecutively, we will have to cope with the fact that the transition from the last frame(s) of the first video sequence to the first frame(s) of the second sequence can be too abrupt and unnatural. Therefore, to smooth the visual concatenation, we replace the frames at the end and at the beginning of the first and second video segment, respectively, by a sequence of new intermediate frames. Image morphing is a widely used technique for creating a transformation between two digital images. It consists of a combination of a stepwise image warp and a stepwise cross-dissolve. To perform an image morph, the correspondence between the two input images has to be established by means of pairs of feature primitives. A common approach is to define a mesh as feature primitive for both inputs - so-called mesh warping [20]. A careful definition of these meshes results in a high quality metamorphosis, however, this is not always straightforward and often very time-consuming. Fortunately, when we apply this morphing technique to smooth the visual concatenations in our speech synthesizer, every image given as input to the morph algorithm will be a frame from the speech database and will thus be quite similar to other morph inputs. This means that we only need a strategy to construct the appropriate mesh for a typical frame in the database. To achieve this, we define for each frame a morph-mesh based on the landmarks determined by tracking the facial parts through the database. By using this data as input for the image metamorphosis algorithm, we managed to generate for every concatenation the appropriate new frames that realize the transition of the mouth region from the first video fragment toward the second one. An example of a morph input and the resulting output frames are showed in figure 1.

To construct a full-face output signal, the same technique that can be found in the literature is used (see section 2.3): we first construct the appropriate mouth region signal, which is afterwards merged with a background video showing the other facial parts. Note that some little head movements in the background video have to be allowed, since a completely static head lacks any naturalness. Currently, we only cope with small translations of the background face which we mimic by carefully aligning the new mouth sequence with the background video.

Audiovisual Synchronization. To successfully transfer the original multimodal coherence from the two selected segments to the concatenated speech, it is important to retain the audiovisual synchronization. In [11], it is concluded

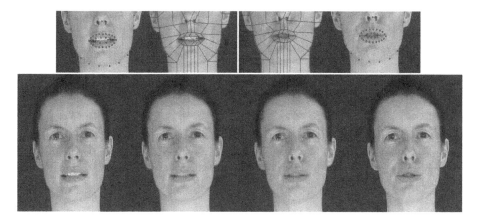

Fig. 1. Example of the smoothing technique. The two newly created frames shown in the middle of the lower panel will replace the segments' original boundary frames in order ensure the continuity during the transition from the left frame to the right one. A detail of the landmark data and morph inputs is shown on top.

that humans are very sensitive to a lead of the audio track in front of the video track in audiovisual speech perception. On the other hand, there is quite a tolerance on the lead of the video signal. In our audiovisual synthesis we exploit this property to cope with the fact that the audio sample rate (44100 Hz) is much higher than the video sample rate (25 Hz). Consequently, the audio component of the selected segments can be joined at exactly the optimal join position (see above), but not so in the video mode whose accuracy is much lower. Therefore, in order to optimize the audiovisual synchrony in the multimodal output signal, at each concatenation, we ensure that the original combinations of auditory and visual speech are desynchronized by maximum half of a frame (20 ms), where a video lead is preferred.

Our system uses the Nextens [13] Dutch linguistic front-end to convert the input text into its phonetic transcript and accompanying prosody information. After concatenation, the sequence of joined segments does not necessarily contain this target prosody. Although we use pitch levels as one of the selection criteria, the concatenated speech will sometimes need extra tweaking to attain the desired output prosody. Therefore, the audio track is processed by a PSOLA algorithm [17] to alter the pitch and the timing of the speech waveform. In order to do so, a warping path that defines how the timing of the original concatenated signal is mapped on the target timing is constructed. This path is then used to also time-scale the video signal. This visual time-scaling is accomplished by removing or duplicating appropriate frames in such a way that the audiovisual asynchrony remains within the above-mentioned constraints. [1]

---

[1] We also experimented with more advanced visual time-scaling techniques (e.g.: interpolation by image warping algorithms). However, testing showed that this extra computational workload delivers only very little or even zero gain in signal quality.

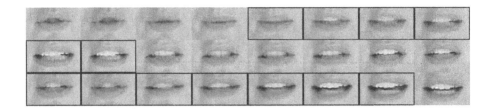

Fig. 2. From left to right, top to bottom the synthesized mouth sequence for the Dutch phoneme sequence '...*O p n e r s l A x s t Ei...*' (coming from the sentence '*De kans op neerslag stijgt*') is shown. Edged frames are newly created ones to smooth the concatenations; the other ones are copied directly from the database.

4   General Discussion

Our audiovisual text-to-speech system aims to improve current state-of-the-art audiovisual speech synthesis techniques by increasing the multimodal coherence in the output speech. To achieve this, we apply original combinations of sound/video for concatenation. To select these multimodal fragments, the unit selection paradigm is well-suited since it has been shown to be the most suitable current technique for auditory speech synthesis. Moreover, in [3] as well as in [6] this strategy was successfully applied for the synthesis of the video mode. In contrast with [9], we spent much effort in sophisticating the selection and concatenation process of the synthesizer. Unfortunately, our current speech database is too small to systematically compare and evaluate the overall performance of the system. Nevertheless, preliminary synthesized results from within the limited domain of the database show that an experimentally optimized combination of auditory and visual costs does result in the selection of suitable audiovisual fragments. Furthermore, the two modes of these segments are successfully joined by the proposed multimodal concatenation procedure. An even more important conclusion that can be drawn from the obtained results is that the concatenation of original combinations of audio and video does result in a very high audiovisual coherence in the output signal. This is for instance very noticeable at synthesis points where the selected segments are not optimal. When this results in some irregularity (non-typical output) in the audio track, the same behavior is noticed in the video track (and vice-versa). More importantly, also at regular synthesis instances the resulting high audiovisual coherence improves the perception of the synthetic multimodal speech, since observers truly believe that the person displayed in the visual mode could indeed have been the source of the presented auditory speech signal. Examples of synthesized sentences can be found at   `http://www.etro.vub.ac.be/Research/DSSP/Projects/AVTTS/demo_AVTTS.htm`. Note that, in order to obtain these results, no manual corrections on the analysis nor on the synthesis were performed.

5 Future Work

To further enhance the output quality, the audiovisual database will be enlarged. As found in previous studies on classical auditory text-to-speech systems, providing more initial data to the selection algorithms results in the selection of more optimal units, at the expense of a larger data footprint and a higher computing load. Since audiovisual speech recordings require a lot of data, we expect to find an optimum in this trade-off at about two hours of speech recordings[2]. We will experimentally search for this optimum by conducting listening-tests using databases of variable sizes. Future research will also have to point out new techniques to further optimize the segment selection strategy itself. A first possible enhancement is to tweak the influences of the different cost functions on the total selection cost (e.g.: the importance of visual costs over auditory costs). Another option is to introduce a certain amount of audiovisual asynchrony in order to optimize the concatenations of the segments. Indeed, for each selected audiovisual fragment we could vary the audio and the video join positions independently in such a way that the concatenation can be optimized in both modes separately. Further, aside from the selection of the appropriate mouth segments, a more natural output can be achieved by also altering the movements of the other facial parts in accordance with the input text. Hurdles that will have to be taken to successfully achieve this are the definition of the rules to generate a target visual prosody and the search for a strategy to merge all the different synthesized facial parts into one final, realistic representation of the face.

Acknowledgments

The research described in this paper was partly sponsored by the IWT project SPACE (SBO/040102) and by the IWOIB project EOS. We would also like to thank Barry-John Theobald for his assistance in landmarking the video in the database.

References

1. Bailly, G., Brar, M., Elisei, F., Odisio, M.: Audiovisual speech synthesis. International Journal of Speech Technology 6, 331–346 (2003)
2. Breen, A.P., Bowers, E., Welsh, W.: An Investigation into the Generation of Mouth Shapes for a Talking Head. In: International Conference on Spoken Language Processing, vol. 4, pp. 2159–2162 (1996)
3. Bregler, C., Covell, M., Slaney, M.: Video Rewrite: Driving Visual Speech with Audio. In: Association for Computing Machinery's Special Interest Group on Graphics and Interactive Techniques, pp. 353–360 (1997)
4. Cosatto, E., Graf, H.P.: Sample-Based Synthesis of Photo-Realistic Talking Heads. Computer Animation, 103–110 (1998)

---

[2] Using a limited-domain approach will always increase the synthesis quality, although this might not be necessary at this database size.

5. Cosatto, E., Graf, H.P.: Photo-realistic talking-heads from image samples. IEEE Transactions on multimedia 2, 152–163 (2000)
6. Cosatto, E., Potamianos, G., Graf, H.P.: Audio-Visual Unit Selection for the Synthesis of Photo-Realistic Talking-Heads. International Conference on Multimedia and Expo, pp. 619–622 (2000)
7. Ezzat, T., Poggio, T.: Visual Speech Synthesis by Morphing Visemes (MikeTalk). MIT AI Lab, A.I Memo 1658 (1999)
8. Ezzat, T., Geiger, G., Poggio, T.: Trainable videorealistic speech animation. Association for Computing Machinery's Special Interest Group on Graphics and Interactive Techniques 21, 388–398 (2002)
9. Fagel, S.: Joint Audio-Visual Units Selection - The Javus Speech Synthesizer. In: International Conference on Speech and Computer (2006)
10. Goyal, U.K., Kapoor, A., Kalra, P.: Text-to-Audio Visual Speech Synthesizer. Virtual Worlds, 256–269 (2000)
11. Grant, K.W., Greenberg, S.: Speech Intelligibility Derived From Asynchrounous Processing of Auditory-Visual Information. In: Workshop on Audio-Visual Speech Processing, pp. 132–137 (2001)
12. Hunt, A., Black, A.: Unit selection in a concatenative speech synthesis system using a large speech database. In: International Conference on Acoustics, Speech and Signal Processing, pp. 373–376 (1996)
13. Kerkhoff, J., Marsi, E.: NeXTeNS: a New Open Source Text-to-speech System for Dutch. In: 13th meeting of Computational Linguistics in the Netherlands (2002)
14. Latacz, L., Kong, Y., Verhelst, W.: Unit Selection Synthesis Using Long Non-Uniform Units and Phoneme Identity Matching. In: 6th ISCA Workshop on Speech Synthesis, pp. 270–275 (2007)
15. Mattheyses, W., Latacz, L., Kong, Y.O., Verhelst, W.: Flemish Voice for the Nextens Text-To-Speech System. In: Fifth Slovenian and First International Language Technologies Conference (2006)
16. McGurk, H., MacDonald, J.: Hearing lips and seeing voices. Nature 264, 746–748 (1976)
17. Moulines, E., Charpentier, F.: Pitch-synchronous waveform processing techniques for text-to-speech synthesis using diphones. Speech Communication 9, 453–467 (1990)
18. Pandzic, I., Ostermann, J., Millen, D.: Users Evaluation: Synthetic talking faces for interactive services. The Visual Computer 15, 2330–2340 (1999)
19. Theobald, B.J., Bangham, J.A., Matthews, I.A., Cawley, G.C.: Near-videorealistic synthetic talking faces: implementation and evaluation. Speech Communication 44, 127–140 (2004)
20. Wolberg, G.: Digital image warping. IEEE Computer Society Press, Los Alamitos (1990)

Decision-Level Fusion for Audio-Visual Laughter Detection

Boris Reuderink[1], Mannes Poel[1], Khiet Truong[1,2],
Ronald Poppe[1], and Maja Pantic[1,3]

[1] University of Twente, P.O. Box 217, 7500 AE Enschede, The Netherlands
{reuderin,m.poel,truongkp,poppe,panticm}@ewi.utwente.nl
[2] TNO Defence, Sec. and Safety, P.O. Box 23, 3769 ZG Soesterberg, The Netherlands
[3] Imperial College, Dept. of Computing, 180 Queen's Gate, London SW7 2AZ, UK

Abstract. Laughter is a highly variable signal, which can be caused by a spectrum of emotions. This makes the automatic detection of laughter a challenging, but interesting task. We perform automatic laughter detection using audio-visual data from the AMI Meeting Corpus. Audio-visual laughter detection is performed by fusing the results of separate audio and video classifiers on the decision level. This results in laughter detection with a significantly higher AUC-ROC[1] than single-modality classification.

1 Introduction

Laughter is omnipresent in human vocal communication, and conveys cues for emotional states. This makes automatic laughter detection an interesting research subject. Earlier work on laughter detection has mainly focused on laughter detection in audio. In this work, we will add the video modality, and perform audio-visual laughter detection. We will construct classifiers for the audio and video modalities independently, and test if fusion of these modalities can improve the performance of automatic laughter detection.

In the next section we will describe some previous research on laughter detection and fusion of audio-visual data. Then we will outline the experiment, present our results and end with conclusions and suggestions for future work.

2 Previous Work

2.1 Laughter Detection in Audio

Automatic laughter detection has been studied several times in the context of meetings, for audio indexing and to detect affective states. We will describe a number of studies on automatic laughter detection in audio, and summarize some characteristics of these studies.

---

[1] Area under curve - receiver operating characteristic.

A. Popescu-Belis and R. Stiefelhagen (Eds.): MLMI 2008, LNCS 5237, pp. 137–148, 2008.
© Springer-Verlag Berlin Heidelberg 2008

Campbell et al. developed a system to classify a laugh in different categories [3]. They constructed a corpus from daily speech containing four affective classes of laughter: a hearty laugh, an amused laugh, a satirical laugh and a social laugh. A training set of 3000 hand-labeled laughs was used to train Hidden Markov Models (HMMs). The HMMs recognized the affective class correctly in 75% of the test cases. Automatic laughter detection is frequently studied in the context of meetings. Kennedy and Ellis [13] detected multiple laughing participants in the ICSI Meeting Corpus. Using a Support Vector Machine (SVM) on one second windows of Mel-Frequency Cepstrum Coefficients (MFCCs) features, an equal error rate (EER) of 13% was obtained. Truong and Van Leeuwen [21] used a clean subset of the ICSI Meeting Corpus to train Gaussian Mixture Model (GMM) and SVM classifiers. Instances containing speech and inaudible laughs were removed to form the clean subset. The classifiers were trained on spectral features, pitch & energy, pitch & voicing features and modulation-spectrum features. Usually, the SVM classifiers performed better than the GMM classifiers. Fusion based on the output of the GMM and SVM classifiers increases the discriminative power, as does fusion between classifiers based on spectral features and classifiers based on prosodic information.

When we compare the results of these studies, GMMs and SVMs seem to be used most for automatic laughter recognition. Spectral features seem to outperform prosodic features, and although different corpora are used, an EER of 12–13% seems to be usual.

2.2   Audio-Visual Fusion

Most work on audio-visual fusion has focused on the detection of emotions [2, 9, 10, 25, 27]. Some other studies perform cry detection [15], movie classification [24], tracking [1], speech recognition [6] and laughter detection [12]. These studies all try to exploit the complementary nature of audio-visual data. Decision-level fusion is usually performed using the product, or a (weighted) sum of the predictions of single-modality classifiers. As an alternative to decision-level fusion, sometimes feature-level fusion is used where the features are merged before classification. An overview of relevant work on audio-visual fusion can be found in Table 1.

Audio-visual laughter detection has already been performed by Ito et al. [12] on a database with Japanese, English and Chinese subjects. The lip lengths, the lip angles and the mean intensities of the cheek areas were used as features for the video modality. Frame level classification of the video features was performed using a perceptron, resulting in a recall of 71%, and a precision of 52%. Laughter sound detection was performed on MFCC and delta-MFCC features, using two GMMs, one for laughter, and one for other sounds. A recall of 96% and a precision of 60% was obtained using 16 Gaussian mixtures. Decision-level fusion was performed with manually designed rules, resulting in a recall of 71% and a precision of 74%. Ito et al. do not report if this increase is statistically significant.

Recently, Petridis and Pantic performed audio-visual discrimination between laughter and speech [17]. The AMI Meeting database was used to create a corpus

Table 1. Audio-visual fusion. The last column contains the performance using different modalities and fusion techniques; A indicates audio, V indicates video, FF indicates feature-level fusion, and DF indicates decision-level fusion. The performance is measured in classification accuracy, except for [12, 17, 18] for which we present the F_1 measure instead of recall - precision pairs.

Study	Dataset	Performance
Petridis and Pantic [17] (2008)	AMI, spontaneous, laughter	A: $F_1 = 0.64$, V: $F_1 = 0.80$, DF: $F_1 = 0.82$, FF: $F_1 = 0.81$
Petridis and Pantic [18] (2008)	AMI, spontaneous, laughter	A: $F_1 = 0.69$, V: $F_1 = 0.80$, DF: $F_1 = 0.88$
Zeng et al. [26] (2007)	AAI, spontanous, 2 emotions	A: 70%, V: 86% DF: 90%
Hoch et al. [10] (2005)	Posed, 3 emotions	A: 82%, V: 67%, DF: 87%
Ito et al. [12] (2005)	Spontaneous, laughter	A: $F_1 = 0.72$, V: $F_1 = 0.60$, DF: $F_1 = 0.72$
Wang and Guan [23] (2005)	Posed, 6 emotions	A: 66%, V: 49%, FF: 82%
Busso et al. [2] (2004)	Posed, 4 emotions	A: 71%, V: 85%, FF: 89%, DF: 89%
Go et al. [8] (2003)	Unknown, 6 emotions	A: 93, V: 93%, DF: 97%
Dupont and Luettin [6] (2000)	M2VTS, spontaneous, 10 words	A: 52% V: 60%, FF: 70%, MF: 80%, DF: 82%

with 40 laughter segments and 56 speech segments. These laughter segments contain a clearly audible harmonic laugh, and do not contain speech. Video features were extracted by tracking 20 facial points, and transformed to uncorrelated features using a PCA similar to our approach in [19]. A few relevant principal components were used to calculate distance based features. Perceptual Linear Prediction coding (PLP) was used to obtain audio-features. For classification, AdaBoost was used to select a feature-subset, on which an Artificial Neural Network classifier was trained. Both decision-level and feature-level fusion of the audio and video modality seem to improve on the performance of the video-classifier slightly (see Table 1) but it remains to be seen on which level fusion works best. In a follow-up study Petridis and Pantic use the same dataset to perform decision-level fusion based on different configurations of single-modality classifiers, such as spectral and pitch & energy based audio-classifiers, and face-component and head-component based video-classifiers [18]. The best combination was formed by the combination of the spectral audio-classifier and both the head and face modality for video.

From Table 1 it appears that fusion of the audio and video modality boosts the classification performance generally with a few percent. However, most work does not report the significance of this gain in performance. The fusion of audio and video modalities seems to work best when the individual modalities both have a low performance, for example due to noise in the audio-visual speech recognition of Dupont [6]. When single classifiers have a high performance, the performance gain obtained by fusion of the modalities is low, and sometimes fusion even degrades the performance, as observed in the work of Gunes and Piccardi [9].

3 Methodology

We perform fusion on the decision-level where the audio and video modalities are classified separately. When the classifiers for both modalities have classified the instance, their results are used to make a final multi-modal prediction. We have chosen to evaluate decision-level fusion because it allows us to use different classifiers for each of the two modalities.

3.1 Dataset

Previous work on laughter detection often used the ICSI Meeting Corpus. Because this corpus does not provide video recordings, we have created a dataset based on the AMI Meeting Corpus. The AMI Meeting Corpus consists of 100 hours of meeting recordings, stored in different signals that are synchronized to a common time line. The meetings are recorded in English, mostly spoken by non-native speakers. For each meeting, there are multiple audio and video recordings. We used seven unscripted meetings recorded in the IDIAP-room (IB4001, IB4002, IB4003, IB4004, IB4005, IB4010, IB4011) as these meetings contain a fair amount of spontaneous laughter. We removed two of the twelve subjects; one displayed extremely asymmetrical facial expressions (IB4005.2), the other displayed a strong nervous tick in the muscles around the mouth (IB4003.3, IB4003.4). We used the close-up video recording (DivX AVI codec 5.2.1, 2300 Kbps, 720×576 pixels, 25 frames per second) and the headset audio recording (16 KHz WAV file) of each participant for our corpus.

We were unable to use the laughter-annotations provided with the AMI-Corpus as these are often not correctly aligned. Therefore the seven meetings we selected from the AMI Meeting Corpus were segmented into laughter by the first author. Due to the spontaneous nature of these meetings, speech, chewing and occlusions sometimes co-occur with the laughter and non-laughter segments.

The final corpus is built from the segmented data. The laughter instances are created by padding each laughter segment with 3 seconds on each side to capture the visual onset and offset of a laughter event. Laughter segments that overlapped after padding are merged into a single laughter instance. A preliminary experiment indicated that including these 3 seconds improved the classification performance significantly. The non-laughter instances are created from the audio-visual data that remains after removing all the laughter segments. The length of the non-laughter instances is taken from a random Gaussian distribution with a mean and standard deviation equal to the mean and standard deviation of the laughter segments.

We have based our corpus on 60 randomly selected laughter and 120 randomly selected non-laughter instances, in which 20 facial points needed for tracking are

Fig. 1. Example laughter segments for the subjects

visible. We included some barely audible laughs and laughter overlapping with speech, in contrast to [17, 18] where no speech was included in the laughter segments. Some examples of laughter segments are displayed in Fig. 1. We made sure no smiles occurred in the non-laughter instances. To test the validity of the class-labels, two other annotators annotated the corpus. One annotator rated 4 laughter-instances as non-laughter, the other annotator agreed completely, resulting in a agreement of 97.7%. Of all the 180 instances, 59% contains speech of the visible participant. Almost all instances contain background speech. Together these instances form 25 minutes of audio-visual data. The dataset is available at http://hmi.ewi.utwente.nl/ami-laughter.

3.2 Features

Audio Features. We use RASTA-PLP features to encode the audio-signal. RASTA-PLP adds filtering capabilities for channel distortions to PLP features, and yields significantly better results for speech recognition tasks in noisy environments than PLP [6]. We used the same settings as were used by Truong and Van Leeuwen for PLP features [21]. The 13 cepstral coefficients (12 model order, 1 gain) are calculated over a window of 32 ms with a step-size of 16 ms. Combined with the temporal derivative (calculated by convolving with a simple linear-slope filter over 5 audio frames) this resulted in a 26 dimensional feature vector per audio frame. We normalized these 26-dimensional feature vectors to a mean $\mu = 0$ and a standard deviation $\sigma = 1$ using z-normalization.

Video Features. The video channel is transformed into sequences of 20 two-dimensional facial points located on key features of the human face. These point sequences are subsequently transformed into orthogonal features using a Principal Component Analysis (PCA).

The points are tracked as follows. The points are manually assigned at the first frame of an instance movie and tracked using a tracking scheme based on particle filtering with factorized likelihoods [16]. We track the brows (2 points each), the eyes (4 points each), the nose (3 points), the mouth (4 points) and chin (1 point). This results in a compact representation of the facial movement in a movie using 20 (x, y)-tuples per frame. This tracking configuration has been used successfully for the detection of the atomic action units of the Facial Action Coding System (FACS) [22].

After tracking, we performed a PCA on the 20 points per video-frame without reducing the number of dimensions; the principal components now serve as a parametric model, similar to the Active Shape Model of Cootes et al. [5]. No label information was used to create this model. An analysis of the eigenvectors revealed that the first five principal components encode the head pose, including translation, rotation and scale. The other components encode interpersonal differences, facial expressions and corrections for the linear approximations of movements (see Figure 3.5 of [19]).

In order to capture temporal aspects of this model, the first order derivative for each component is added to each frame. The derivative is calculated with $\Delta t = 4$ frames on a moving average of the principal components with a window length of 2 frames. Again, we normalized this 80-dimensional feature vector to a mean $\mu = 0$ and a standard deviation $\sigma = 1$ using z-normalization.

3.3 Classification

We evaluate Gaussian Mixture Models (GMMs), Hidden Markov Models (HMMs) and Support Vector Machines (SVMs) for classification. GMMs and HMMs model the distribution for both classes and classify by estimating the probability that an instance was produced by the model for a specific class. GMMs and HMMs are frequently used in speech recognition and speaker identification, and have been used before for laughter recognition [3, 12, 14, 21]. SVMs are discriminatory classifiers, and have been used for laughter detection in [13, 21]. We used HMMs and GMMs for the audio-modality and SVMs for the video-modality as this resulted in the best performance [19].

The HMMs we use model the generated output using a mixture of Gaussian distributions. We used two different topologies; the left-right HMMs that are frequently used in speech recognition, and ergodic HMMs that allow transitions from all states to all states. For the SVMs we use a sliding window of 1.20 seconds to create fixed-length features from the video segments. During classification, a probability estimate for the different windows of an instance is calculated. The final prediction of an instance is the mean of its window-predictions. We use Radial Basis Function (RBF) kernel SVMs, which are trained using LIBSVM [4].

To estimate the generalization performance of the classifiers, we perform two times 15-fold cross-validation. Inside each fold, we use $1/28$ of the training data as a validation set to select model parameters such as the HMM configuration, the number of Gaussians and the C and γ parameter of the SVMs, the rest of the training data is used to train classifiers. To find well-performing model parameters we use a multi-resolution grid search [11]. Note that we extracted the PCA-model outside of the cross-validation loop to focus on the generalization performance of the classification. However, we do not expect that this has a big influence on the measured performance.

Fusion. Fusion is performed on the decision-level, which means that the output of an audio and a video classifier is used as input for the final fused prediction. For each instance we classify, probability estimates are generated for the audio and video modalities. Fusion SVMs are trained on the z-scores of the estimates using the same training, validation and test sets as used for the single modality classifiers. The output of these SVMs is a multi-modal prediction based on high-level fusion. As an alternative to this learned fusion, we tested fusion using a weighted-sum of the single-modality predictions:

$$f_{\text{fused}}(x) = \alpha * f_{\text{video}}(x) + (1 - \alpha) * f_{\text{audio}}(x). \tag{1}$$

Evaluation. We have chosen to use the Area Under Curve of the Receiver Operating Characteristic (AUC-ROC) as performance measure because it does not depend on the bias of the classifier, and is class-skew invariant [7]. The AUC-ROC of a classifier is equivalent to the probability that the classifier will rank a randomly chosen positive instance higher than a randomly chosen negative instance. In addition to the AUC-ROC performance, we will report the EER for a classifier. The EER is the point on the ROC where the false-positive rate equals the false-negative rate. A paired two-tailed t-test is used to compare the AUC-ROCs of the different classifiers.

4   Results

For audio, the GMM classifiers performed better than the HMM classifiers, resulting in a mean AUC-ROC of 0.825. On average 16.9 Gaussian mixtures were used to model laughter, non-laughter was modeled using 35.6 Gaussian mixtures. The HMM performed slightly worse with an AUC-ROC of 0.822. The HMMs used 11.6 fully connected states to model laughter, and 21.3 fully connected states to model non-laughter. Surprisingly, no left-right HMMs were selected in

Table 2. The performance of the audio and video classifiers. The standard deviation of the AUC-ROCs is displayed between parenthesis.

Classifier	Params	AUC-ROC	EER
RASTA-GMM	16.9 (3.2) pos. mix., 35.6 (5.9) neg. mix.	0.825 (0.143)	0.258
RASTA-HMM	11.6 (1.9) pos. states, 21.3 (1.9) neg. states	0.822 (0.135)	0.242
Video-SVM	$C = 2.46$, $\gamma = 3.8 \times 10^{-6}$	0.916 (0.114)	0.133

Table 3. Results of the decision-level fusion. The t-test is a paired samples t-test on the AUC-ROCs of the video-SVM (V-SVM) classifier and the specified fusion classifiers. The mean value of the AUC-ROCs is displayed with the standard deviation displayed between parenthesis.

Fusion	Features	T-test	AUC-ROC	EER
RBF-SVM	V-SVM + R-GMM	$t(29) = 2.45, p < 0.05$	0.928 (0.107)	0.142
RBF-SVM	V-SVM + R-HMM	$t(29) = 1.93, p = 0.06$	0.928 (0.104)	0.142
W-sum, $\alpha = 0.57$	V-SVM + R-GMM	$t(29) = 2.69, p < 0.05$	0.928 (0.107)	0.142
W-sum, $\alpha = 0.55$	V-SVM + R-HMM	$t(29) = 2.38, p < 0.05$	0.930 (0.101)	0.142

the model selection procedure. This indicates that there was no strict sequential pattern for laughter that could be exploited for recognition, which seems to support the claim that laughter is a group of sounds [20].

The SVM video-classifier outperformed the audio-classifiers with an AUC-ROC of 0.916, using a mean $C = 2.46$ and a mean $\gamma = 3.8 \times 10^{-6}$. See Table 2 for the performance of the different single-modality classifiers. Note that these performances are measured on normalized datasets, and we do not test the generalization performance over subjects.

We used these classifiers to perform decision-level fusion. The performance of the different fusion configurations is displayed in Table 3. The fused classifiers have a higher mean AUC-ROC than the single-modality classifiers. In the case of SVM-fusion, the combination of the video-SVM classifier and the RASTA-GMM classifiers outperforms the best single-modality classifier slightly, but significantly. Inspection of the trained (RBF) SVM-classifiers reveals that the separating hyperplane is nearly linear.

In addition to fusion using a SVM, we used a weighted-sum rule (1) to combine the output of the audio and video classifiers. The weight of both modalities is determined using the α parameter. The highest mean AUC-ROC values are obtained in the region with a more dominant audio-classifier. However, for a significant improvement over the video-SVM classifier $\alpha = 0.57$ and $\alpha = 0.55$ are needed for the RASTA-GMM and the RASTA-HMM classifier respectively (see Table 3).

When we compare the ROC of the linear fusion classifiers with the ROC of the video-SVM classifiers, we can see that the EER of the fused classifiers is higher than the EER of the video-SVM classifiers (see Fig. 2). Most of the performance-gain is obtained in the direct vicinity of the EER point, where the error-rates are not equal. This trend is also visible with the SVM-fusion. This can

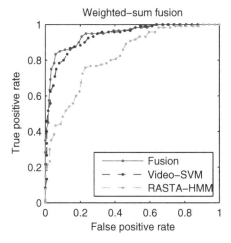

Fig. 2. ROCs for the video-SVM, RASTA-HMM and weighted sum ($\alpha = 0.55$) fusion

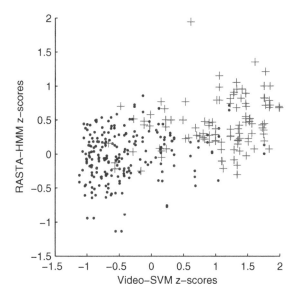

Fig. 3. The normalized output of the audio and video classifiers on the test-sets. Laughter instances are marked with an plus, non-laughter instances are marked with a dot.

be explained by the observation that for unequal error rates the fusion classifier can exploit the complementary nature of both modalities, which it cannot do for the threshold with an equal error rate, where the hyperplane needs to separate instances for which both modalities are uncertain (see Fig. 3).

5   Conclusion and Future Work

Our goal was to perform automatic laughter detection by fusing audio and video signals on the decision level. We have built audio and video-classifiers, and demonstrated that the fused classifiers significantly outperformed the best single-modality classifiers. The best audio-visual classifiers are constructed using a weighted sum of the RASTA-HMM and video-SVM classifiers, resulting in a AUC-ROC performance of 0.930. While fusion on the decision-level improves the performance of the laughter-classifier significantly, fusion seems only beneficial for classification with unequal false-negative and false-positive rates. With equal error rates, the decision-boundary has to separate instances for which both modalities are uncertain. For unequal error rates, these instances fall on one side of the decision-boundary, and now instances with only one uncertain modality can be classified more reliably, resulting in a better performance.

For future work we recommend an investigation of fusion on the feature-level. We have demonstrated that decision-level fusion can improve the performance, but it is not yet clear how this relates to other fusion techniques, such as feature-level fusion. Previous work on audio-visual laughter detection is inconclusive on this subject. A limitation of this experiment is that we removed smiles from our corpus. Adding a smile class to the corpus would most likely decrease the performance of the video-classifier. A follow-up experiment could show if fusion would increase the performance in this setting. In addition to these technical challenges, focussing on the context in which laughter and smiles occur would form an interesting subject. During segmentation we observed interaction between laughter and smiles of different participants in a meeting. It is likely that laughter detection can be improved by explicit use of interactions and semantic information.

References

[1] Beal, M.J., Jojic, N., Attias, H.: A graphical model for audiovisual object tracking. IEEE Transactions on Pattern Analysis and Machine Intelligence (PAMI) 25(7), 828–836 (2003)

[2] Busso, C., Deng, Z., Yildirim, S., Bulut, M., Lee, C.M., Kazemzadeh, A., Lee, S., Neumann, U., Narayanan, S.: Analysis of emotion recognition using facial expressions, speech and multimodal information. In: Proceedings of the International Conference on Multimodal Interfaces (ICME 2004), State College, PA, October 2004, pp. 205–211 (2004)

[3] Campbell, N., Kashioka, H., Ohara, R.: No laughing matter. In: Proceedings of the Interspeech, Lisbon, Portugal, September 2005, pp. 465–468 (2005)

[4] Chang, C.C., Lin, C.J.: LIBSVM: a library for support vector machines (2001), http://www.csie.ntu.edu.tw/~cjlin/libsvm/

[5] Cootes, T.F., Taylor, C.J., Cooper, D.H., Graham, J.: Active shape models - their training and application. Computer Vision and Image Understanding (CVIU) 61(1), 38–59 (1995)

[6] Dupont, S., Luettin, J.: Audio-visual speech modeling for continuous speech recognition. IEEE Transactions on Multimedia 2(3), 141–151 (2000)

[7] Fawcett, T.: An introduction to ROC analysis. Pattern Recognition Letters 27(8), 861–874 (2006)

[8] Go, H.-J., Kwak, K.-C., Lee, D.-J., Chun, M.-G.: Emotion recognition from the facial image and speech signal. In: Proceedings of the SICE Annual Conference, Fukui, Japan, August 2003, vol. 3, pp. 2890–2895 (2003)

[9] Gunes, H., Piccardi, M.: Fusing face and body display for bi-modal emotion recognition: Single frame analysis and multi-frame post integration. In: Tao, J., Tan, T., Picard, R.W. (eds.) ACII 2005. LNCS, vol. 3784, pp. 102–111. Springer, Heidelberg (2005)

[10] Hoch, S., Althoff, F., McGlaun, G., Rigoll, G.: Bimodal fusion of emotional data in an automotive environment. In: Proceedings of the IEEE Conference on Acoustics, Speech and Signal Processing (ICASSP 2005), Philadelphia, PA, vol. 2, pp. 1085–1088 (2005)

[11] Hsu, C.-W., Chang, C.-C., Lin, C.-J.: A practical guide to support vector classification. Technical report, National Taiwan University, Taipei, Taiwan (July 2003)

[12] Ito, A., Wang, X., Suzuki, M., Makino, S.: Smile and laughter recognition using speech processing and face recognition from conversation video. In: Proceedings of the International Conference on Cyberworlds (CW 2005), Singapore, November 2005, pp. 437–444 (2005)

[13] Kennedy, L.S., Ellis, D.P.W.: Laughter detection in meetings. In: Proceedings of the NIST Meeting Recognition Workshop at the IEEE Conference on Acoustics, Speech and Signal Processing (ICASSP 2004), Montreal, Canada (May 2004)

[14] Lockerd, A., Mueller, F.L.: Leveraging affective feedback camcorder. In: Extended abstracts of the Conference on Human Factors in Computing Systems (CHI 2002), Minneapolis, MN, April 2002, pp. 574–575 (2002)

[15] Pal, P., Iyer, A.N., Yantorno, R.E.: Emotion detection from infant facial expressions and cries. In: Proceedings of the IEEE Conference on Acoustics, Speech and Signal Processing (ICASSP 2006), Toulouse, France, May 2006, vol. 2, pp. 721–724 (2006)

[16] Patras, I., Pantic, M.: Particle filtering with factorized likelihoods for tracking facial features. In: Proceedings of the IEEE International Conference on Automatic Face and Gesture Recognition (FG 2004), Seoul, Korea, pp. 97–102 (2004)

[17] Petridis, S., Pantic, M.: Audiovisual discrimination between laughter and speech. In: Proceedings of the IEEE Conference on Acoustics, Speech and Signal Processing (ICASSP 2008), Las Vegas, NV, pp. 5117–5120 (2008)

[18] Petridis, S., Pantic, M.: Fusion of audio and visual cues for laughter detection. In: Proceedings of the ACM International Conference on Image and Video Retrieval (CIVR 2008), Niagara Falls, Canada (to appear, 2008)

[19] Reuderink, B.: Fusion for audio-visual laughter detection. Technical report, University of Twente (2007)

[20] Trouvain, J.: Segmenting phonetic units in laughter. In: Proceedings of the International Conference of the Phonetic Sciences, Barcelona, Spain, August 2003, pp. 2793–2796 (2003)

[21] Truong, K.P., van Leeuwen, D.A.: Automatic discrimination between laughter and speech. Speech Communication 49(2), 144–158 (2007)

[22] Valstar, M.F., Pantic, M., Ambadar, Z., Cohn, J.F.: Spontaneous vs. posed facial behavior: automatic analysis of brow actions. In: Proceedings of the International Conference on Multimodal Interfaces (ICME 2006), Banff, Canada, November 2006, pp. 162–170 (2006)

[23] Wang, Y., Guan, L.: Recognizing human emotion from audiovisual information. In: Proceedings of the IEEE Conference on Acoustics, Speech and Signal Processing (ICASSP 2005), Philadelphia, PA, vol. 2, pp. 1125–1128 (2005)

[24] Xu, M., Chia, L.-T., Jin, J.S.: Affective content analysis in comedy and horror videos by audio emotional event detection. In: Proceedings of the International Conference on Multimodal Interfaces (ICME 2005), Amsterdam, The Netherlands, July 2005, pp. 622–625 (2005)

[25] Zajdel, W., Krijnders, J., Andringa, T., Gavrila, D.: CASSANDRA: Audio-video sensor fusion for aggression detection. In: Proceedings of the IEEE Conference on Advanced Video and Signal Based Surveillance (AVSS 2007), London, United Kingdom, September 2007, pp. 200–205 (2007)

[26] Zeng, Z., Hu, Y., Roisman, G.I., Wen, Z., Fu, Y., Huang, T.S.: Audio-visual spontaneous emotion recognition. Artifical Intelligence for Human Computing, 72–90 (2007)

[27] Zeng, Z., Tu, J., Liu, M., Huang, T.S., Pianfetti, B., Roth, D., Levinson, S.: Audio-visual affect recognition. IEEE Transactions on Multimedia 9(2), 424–428 (2007)

Detection of Laughter-in-Interaction in Multichannel Close-Talk Microphone Recordings of Meetings

Kornel Laskowski and Tanja Schultz

Cognitive Systems Lab, Universität Karlsruhe, Karlsruhe, Germany
Language Technologies Institute, Carnegie Mellon University, Pittsburgh PA, USA

Abstract. Laughter is a key element of human-human interaction, occurring surprisingly frequently in multi-party conversation. In meetings, laughter accounts for almost 10% of vocalization effort by time, and is known to be relevant for topic segmentation and the automatic characterization of affect. We present a system for the detection of laughter, and its attribution to specific participants, which relies on simultaneously decoding the vocal activity of all participants given multi-channel recordings. The proposed framework allows us to disambiguate laughter and speech not only acoustically, but also by constraining the number of simultaneous speakers and the number of simultaneous laughers independently, since participants tend to take turns speaking but laugh together. We present experiments on 57 hours of meeting data, containing almost 11000 unique instances of laughter.

1 Introduction

Laughter is a key element of human-human interaction, occurring surprisingly frequently in multi-party conversation. In meetings, laughter accounts for almost 10% of vocalization effort by time [1]. It has been identified as potentially relevant to discourse segmentation [2], to inference of humorous intent and detection of interlocutor-specific emotional expression [3], and to classification of perceived emotional valence [4]; several of these tasks call for not only the detection of laughter, but also its correct attribution to specific participants. Laughter is known to lead to the temporary abandonment of turn-taking policy, making its detection relevant in topic change detection [5], important for meeting browsing [6], and potentially instrumental to the identification of conversational hotspots, of which an overwhelming majority is associated with amusement [7].

Laughter detection in meetings has received some attention, beginning with [2] in which farfield group laughter was detected automatically, but not attributed to specific participants. Subsequent research has focused on laughter/speech classification [8, 9] and laughter/non-laughter segmentation [10, 11]. However, in both cases, only a subset of all laughter instances, those not occurring in the temporal proximity of the laugher's speech, was considered. Furthermore, in segmentation work, some form of pre-segmentation was assumed to have eliminated long stretches of channel inactivity [10, 11]. These measures have led to

A. Popescu-Belis and R. Stiefelhagen (Eds.): MLMI 2008, LNCS 5237, pp. 149–160, 2008.
© Springer-Verlag Berlin Heidelberg 2008

significantly higher recall and precision rates than would be obtained by a fully automatic segmenter with no a priori channel activity knowledge.

The aim of the current paper is to provide a first fully automatic baseline system for the detection and participant attribution of laughter as it occurs naturally in multiparticipant conversation. While in single-participant recordings laughter can be detected using a speech recognizer augmented with laughter models, in multiparticipant contexts audio must first be segmented and crosstalk from background participants to each channel suppressed. The latter represents a significant challenge for vocal activity detectors in meetings [12]. In constructing the proposed baseline system, we rely on several contrastive aspects of laughter and speech, including acoustics, duration, and the degree of vocalization overlap.

This work begins with a description of the meeting data used in our experiments (Section 2), which was selected to be exactly the same as in previous work [2, 8, 9, 10, 11]. However, our aim is to detect all *laughter-in-interaction*, including laughter which is interspersed among lexical items produced by each participant. We describe our multiparticipant vocal activity model in Section 3 and quantify the performance of its implementation in Section 4. Contrastive experiments are presented in Section 5, leading to a discussion of various aspects of the proposed task. Finally, we compare our findings and observations with those of other authors in Section 6, before concluding in Section 7.

2   Data

As in other work on laughter in naturally occurring meetings [2, 8, 9, 10, 11], we use the ICSI Meeting Corpus [13]. 67 of the 75 meetings in the corpus are of one of three types, `Bed`, `Bmr`, and `Bro`, representing longitudinal recordings of three groups at ICSI. The total number of distinct participants in these three subsets is 23; there are 3 participants who attend both `Bmr` and `Bro` meetings, and only 1 participant who attends both `Bmr` and `Bed` meetings. Importantly, none of the meeting types have a fixed number of participants per meeting, allowing us to demonstrate the applicability of our methods to arbitrary group sizes.

We rely on two reference segmentations of the ICSI corpus, one for speech and one for laughter. The speech segmentation was constructed using the word start and end times from automatic forced alignment, available in the ICSI MRDA Corpus [14]. Inter-word gaps shorter than 0.3 s have been bridged to yield *talkspurts* [15], consisting of one or more words (and/or word fragments); this process, as well as the 0.3 s threshold, has been used extensively in NIST Rich Transcription Meeting Recognition evaluations [16]. The corresponding segmentation of *laugh bouts* [17] has recently been built for this data [1, 18] using the available mark-up in the orthographic transcription and a combination of automatic and manual alignment methods. Intervals during which a participant both laughs and speaks (a phenomenon referred to as "speech-laughs" [19]) have been mapped to speech only, such that the categories of silence $\mathcal{N}$, speech $\mathcal{S}$, and laughter $\mathcal{L}$ are mutually exclusive.

The majority of experiments we present are performed using one type of meeting in the corpus, the `Bmr` meetings. In [2, 8, 9, 10, 11], the first 26 `Bmr` meetings were designated as training data, and the last 3 held out for testing. We retain that division in the current work.

3   Multiparticipant 3-State Vocal Activity Recognition

3.1   Model Topology

Detection in the proposed system consists of Viterbi decoding in a hidden Markov model (HMM) state space which simultaneously describes the state of all K participants to a particular conversation C. Each participant k, $1 \leq k \leq K$, can occupy one of three acoustically distinct (AD) states: speech $\mathcal{S}$, laughter $\mathcal{L}$, and non-vocalization $\mathcal{N}$; where convenient, we will also refer to vocalization $\mathcal{V} \equiv \neg \mathcal{N} \equiv \mathcal{S} \cup \mathcal{L}$. Furthermore, each AD state is implemented by a left-to-right state sequence, enforcing a minimum duration constraint on AD state occupation. A projection of the complete K-participant HMM topology onto the state subspace of any single participant is shown in Figure 1. Each minimum duration constraint T^{Υ}_{min}, $\Upsilon \in \{\mathcal{S}, \mathcal{L}, \mathcal{N}\}$, yields the corresponding number of

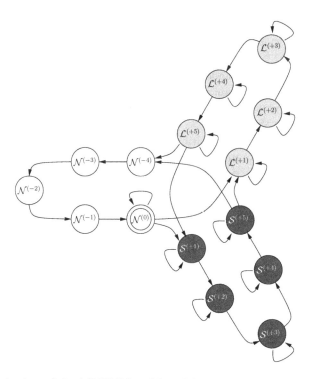

Fig. 1. A projection of the full HMM multiparticipant state space onto the state subspace of a single participant. Shown are three acoustically distinct (AD) states, each duplicated 5 times to illustrate how minimum AD state occupation is enforced. $\mathcal{N}^{(0)}$ represents the default long-time inactive state.

single-participant topology states per AD state, $N_{min}^{\Upsilon} \equiv \lceil T_{min}^{\Upsilon}/T_{step} \rceil$, where T_{step} is the frame step or shift. As a result, the single-participant state subspace consists of $N = \sum_{\Upsilon} N_{min}^{\Upsilon}$ states.

A consequence of the above is that a multiparticipant conversation C, of K participants, can be in one of N^K states. To render search computationally tractable, we admit only a fraction of these states during decoding, via three constraints: (1) the number of simultaneously speaking participants can be no greater than $K_{max}^{\mathcal{S}}$; (2) the number of simultaneously laughing participants can be no greater than $K_{max}^{\mathcal{L}}$; and (3) the number of participants not in the "default" state $\mathcal{N}^{(0)}$ can be no greater than $K_{max}^{\neg\mathcal{N}}$. The resulting space consists of N_{eff} states, $\{\mathbf{S}_i\}$, with $1 \leq i \leq N_{eff}$. Each state $\mathbf{S}_i$ emits a multi-channel observation with time-independent emission probability b_i.

Transition from state $\mathbf{S}_i$ to state $\mathbf{S}_j$, $\mathbf{S}_i \rightarrow \mathbf{S}_j$, with $1 \leq i \leq N_{eff}$ and $1 \leq j \leq N_{eff}$, is possible provided that for each speaker k, the single-participant transition $\mathbf{S}_i[k] \rightarrow \mathbf{S}_j[k]$ is licensed by Figure 1. An allowed transition $\mathbf{S}_i \rightarrow \mathbf{S}_j$ is taken with time-independent probability $a_{ij} = P(\mathbf{q}_{t+1} = \mathbf{S}_j \mid \mathbf{q}_t = \mathbf{S}_i)$, where $\mathbf{q}_t$ is the multiparticipant state of the meeting at time t.

3.2   Acoustic Model

We seek to define the probability density that a particular *multi-channel* observation $\mathbf{X}_t \in \Re^{K \times F}$, where F is the number of features drawn from a single channel in an observation window of T_{size} in duration, is emitted from a *multi-participant* state $\mathbf{S}_i$. The main difficulty is that K, the number of participants, may vary from conversation to conversation, and we wish to avoid having to train variable-length observation models. We address this difficulty as in [20], by introducing the factorial decomposition $P(\mathbf{X}_t \mid \mathbf{S}_i) = \prod_{k=1}^{K} P(\mathbf{X}_t[k] \mid \zeta(\mathbf{S}_i, k))$. Each factor is a Gaussian mixture model (GMM) likelihood

$$P(\mathbf{X}[k] \mid \zeta(\mathbf{S}_i, k)) = \sum_{m=1}^{M} p_{\zeta(i,k),m} P\left(\mathbf{X}[k] \mid \mathbf{N}\left(\mu_{\zeta(i,k),m}, \sigma_{\zeta(i,k),m}^2\right)\right), \quad (1)$$

where M is the number of GMM components, $\sum_{m=1}^{M} p_{\zeta(i,k),m} = 1$ and $\mathbf{N}(\mu, \sigma^2)$ is a multivariate, diagonal-covariance Gaussian distribution. The number of dimensions is equal to F, the number of single-channel features computed. $\zeta(i,k)$ represents the state of the kth close-talk microphone, as explained below.

Although modeling each microphone as being in one of three states is the most natural approach to $\mathcal{N}/\mathcal{S}/\mathcal{L}$ segmentation, efforts in single-participant $\mathcal{N}/\mathcal{S}$ segmentation have extended this model to farfield activity states (ie. [21]). In [22], three states were considered: $\mathcal{S}$, $\mathcal{N}$, and $\mathcal{V}_F$, the latter corresponding to only farfield speech. We make the corresponding extension here, whereby

$$\zeta(i,k) \equiv \begin{cases} \mathcal{S}, & \text{if } \mathbf{S}_i[k] = \mathcal{S} \\ \mathcal{L}, & \text{if } \mathbf{S}_i[k] = \mathcal{L} \\ \mathcal{V}_F, & \text{if } \mathbf{S}_i[k] = \mathcal{N} \text{ and } \exists j \text{ such that } \mathbf{S}_i[j] \neq \mathcal{N} \\ \mathcal{N}, & \text{if } \mathbf{S}_i[j] = \mathcal{N} \ \forall j \ . \end{cases} \quad (2)$$

As a result, there are 4^K multimicrophone states; however, only 3^K of them correspond to valid conversation states (e.g., all participants cannot be in $\mathcal{V}_F$).

All 4 single-microphone acoustic models are defined over a feature space of $F = 41$ features: log-energy, 13 Mel-frequency cepstral coefficients (MFCCs; excluding $\mathbf{C}_0$), their first- and second-order derivatives, as well as the minimum and maximum normalized log-energy differences (NLEDs). The latter two features were designed for differentiating between nearfield and farfield vocal activity [23]. Using the reference speech and laughter segmentation of all 26 Bmr meetings, one Gaussian mixture with $M = 64$ components was trained per model to maximize the class-conditional likelihood of the training data.

3.3 Transition Model

We seek to define a time-independent probability that conversation C will transition out of a multiparticipant state $\mathbf{S}_i$ into a multiparticipant state $\mathbf{S}_j$. As with emission probabilities, the fundamental difficulty is the potential for K to not be known, or ever seen in the training material.

Although a full exposition of our transition model considerably exceeds the current space limitations, we mention that the model probabilities are independent both of the identities of all participants and of their assignment to particular channels k, namely that

$$
\begin{aligned}
a_{ij} &= P\left(\mathbf{q}_{t+1} = \mathbf{S}_j \mid \mathbf{q}_t = \mathbf{S}_i\right) \\
&= P\left(\mathbf{R}\cdot\mathbf{q}_{t+1} = \mathbf{R}\cdot\mathbf{S}_j \mid \mathbf{R}\cdot\mathbf{q}_t = \mathbf{R}\cdot\mathbf{S}_i\right) \quad .
\end{aligned}
\tag{3}
$$

where $\mathbf{R}$ is an arbitrary $K\times K$ row rotation operator. We refer the reader to [24] for full details of the model, its general training algorithm, and its application.

Here, the transition model probabilities a_{ij} were trained using forced-alignment of the reference 3-way $\mathcal{N}/\mathcal{S}/\mathcal{L}$ multiparticipant segmentation. To achieve this, each frame $\mathbf{q}_t$ was assigned a pseudo-likelihood $P\left(\mathbf{q}_t|\mathbf{S}_i\right) = \alpha^d$, where d is the number of mismatched participant states between $\mathbf{q}_t$ and $\mathbf{S}_i$, and α is a small number (10^{-4}). The Viterbi pass was performed with all allowed transitions a_{ij} having a probability of unity (leading to $\sum_i a_{ij} \geq 1$), to not disfavor self-transitions at high fan-out states.

4 Performance of Proposed System

The HMM topology described in Subsection 3.1 was constructed with frame step and size of $T_{step} = T_{size} = 0.1$ seconds, as in our work on $\mathcal{V}/\neg\mathcal{V}$ segmentation [25]. The minimum duration constraints $\mathbf{T}_{min} \equiv \left(T_{min}^{\mathcal{S}}, T_{min}^{\mathcal{L}}, T_{min}^{\mathcal{N}}\right)$ were set to $(0.2, 0.4, 0.3)$ seconds, leveraging our findings in [25] and [1]. The latter work, in which it was shown that overlap rates are higher for laughter than for speech, has also led us to impose the overlap constraints $\mathbf{K}_{max} \equiv \left(K_{max}^{\mathcal{S}}, K_{max}^{\mathcal{L}}, K_{max}^{\neg\mathcal{N}}\right) = (2, 3, 3)$. System sensitivity to these settings is explored in Section 5.

With emission and transition probabilities inferred as described in Subsections 3.2 & 3.3, the system was applied to the 3 Bmr meetings in the testset.

Table 1. Confusion matrix for 3-way $\mathcal{N}/\mathcal{S}/\mathcal{L}$ participant-state recognition for the system described in Section 3. Reference (Ref) class membership is shown in rows, hypothesized membership in columns. Time is shown in minutes; the total duration of the analyzed audio is 827 minutes. Total reference and hypothesized state occupation (*total*), per state, is given in italics in the last column and row, respectively.

Ref	Hypothesized as			
	$\mathcal{N}$	$\mathcal{S}$	$\mathcal{L}$	*total*
$\mathcal{N}$	685.4	7.8	22.9	*716.2*
$\mathcal{S}$	11.0	79.0	4.5	*94.4*
$\mathcal{L}$	6.5	1.0	9.2	*16.6*
total	*702.9*	*87.8*	*36.6*	

The resulting confusion matrix is shown in Table 1. As can be seen, the prior distribution over the three classes $\mathcal{N}$, $\mathcal{S}$, and $\mathcal{L}$ (column 5), is significantly unbalanced. Laughter is hypothesized for 9.2 minutes out of the total 16.6 present, yielding a recall of 55.2%. However, laughter is also hypothesized for 22.9 minutes of nearfield silence, pulling precision down to 25.1%. In fact, the largest confusions in the matrix are seen between laughter and nearfield silence. Preliminary analysis suggests that this is due to laughter models capturing participants' breathing. Unvoiced laughter in particular is perceptually similar to exhalation. This suggests that, in future work, voiced and unvoiced laughter should be modeled separately, especially given that unvoiced laughter is overlapped with other unvoiced laughter only infrequently; the same is not true for voiced laughter [18].

5 Contrastive Experiments

In this section, we would like to answer the following questions:

1. *What role do minimum duration constraints play in detecting laughter?*
2. *What role do vocalization overlap constraints play in detecting laughter?*
3. *How does detection performance generalize to unseen datasets?*

We train alternate systems to answer each question, and contrast performance with that of the system from Section 4. Recall, precision, and F-scores of both speech and laughter $\mathcal{V} \equiv \mathcal{S} \cup \mathcal{L}$, of speech alone $\mathcal{S}$, and of laughter alone $\mathcal{L}$, are shown over the full 13.8 hours of test audio.

5.1 Minimum Duration Constraints

To determine the impact of duration modeling on system performance, we train two alternate transition models, differing in the minimum duration constraints $\mathbf{T}_{min} \equiv \left(T_{min}^{\mathcal{S}}, T_{min}^{\mathcal{L}}, T_{min}^{\mathcal{N}}\right)$ from the system described in Section 4. The first of these systems involves a fully-connected (ergodic) HMM topology, on which no minimum duration constraints are imposed (ie. $\mathbf{T}_{min} = (0.1, 0.1, 0.1)$ seconds, given our analysis frame step $T_{step} = 0.1$ s). The second system enforces equal minimum duration constraints of 0.3 s on each of the three AD states, $\mathcal{N}$, $\mathcal{S}$, and

Table 2. Recall (R), precision (P) and F-score (F) as a function of minimum duration constraints $\mathbf{T}_{min} \equiv \left(T_{min}^{S}, T_{min}^{L}, T_{min}^{N}\right)$. The frame step and frame size are identically 100ms, and the maximum simultaneous vocalization constraints $\mathbf{K}_{max} \equiv \left(K_{max}^{S}, K_{max}^{L}, K_{max}^{\neg N}\right)$ are $(2, 3, 3)$ for all systems shown. Performance is shown for vocalization $V = S \cup L$ (versus N) in columns 2-4, for S (versus $\neg S = N \cup L$) in columns 5-7, and for L (versus $\neg L = N \cup S$) in columns 8-10. The system from Section 4 is identified with "§4"; best performance on each metric, across systems, is in bold.

$\mathbf{T}_{min}$ (s)	$V \equiv S \cup L$			S			L		
	R	P	F	R	P	F	R	P	F
$(0.1, 0.1, 0.1)$	84.1	72.8	78.1	82.3	89.9	86.0	**55.9**	22.1	31.7
$(0.3, 0.3, 0.3)$	**84.5**	75.1	**79.5**	**83.7**	**90.4**	**86.9**	54.7	24.2	33.6
§4 $(0.2, 0.4, 0.3)$	84.3	**75.3**	**79.5**	83.6	90.0	86.7	55.2	**25.1**	**34.5**

L; its $\mathbf{T}_{min}$ is $(0.3, 0.3, 0.3)$ seconds. In every other respect, these two systems are identical to that in Section 4; performance of all three is shown in Table 2.

As the table shows, the system with equal minimum duration constraints of 300 ms on the occupation of each of N, S, and L outperforms the ergodic system on all measures except recall of laughter, which is lower by 1.2%. In particular, we note a 2.3% increase in V precision and a 2.1% increase in L precision. This variation is expected since the non-ergodic system cannot hypothesize spurious single-frame segments, which are unlikely to be vocal productions for physiological reasons. For assessing whether minimum duration constraints discriminate between speech and laughter, the $\mathbf{T}_{min} = (0.3, 0.3, 0.3)$ system is most appropriate because both it and the system in Section 4 allow each participant to be in one of 9 states; in the ergodic system, that number of states is 3. Table 2 shows that both the recall and precision of laughter are higher in the $(0.2, 0.4, 0.3)$ system than in the $(0.3, 0.3, 0.3)$ system, and suggests that minimum duration constraints can be used to advantage when detecting laughter-in-interaction in multi-channel audio.

5.2 Maximum Simultaneous Vocalization Constraints

Second, we assess the impact of limiting the maximum number of participants allowed to simultaneously vocalize by modifying the maximum simultaneous vocalization constraints $\mathbf{K}_{max} \equiv \left(K_{max}^{S}, K_{max}^{L}, K_{max}^{\neg N}\right)$. For this purpose, we construct 3 alternate systems. The first, whose $\mathbf{K}_{max} = (2, 2, 2)$, allows up to two participants to be in single-participant states other than $N^{(0)}$, and up to two participants to be simultaneously speaking or laughing. This is a standard extension of our meeting recognition $V/\neg V$ segmenter [25]. The second alternate system, whose $\mathbf{K}_{max} = (2, 2, 3)$, adds two additional cases: (1) only two participants speaking and only one participant laughing; and (2) only two participants laughing and one participant speaking. Finally, the third alternate system ($\mathbf{K}_{max} = (3, 2, 3)$) adds the case of only three participants speaking and none laughing. In contrast, the system desribed in Section 4, allows for only three participants laughing and none speaking. The $\mathbf{K}_{max} = (3, 2, 3)$ could be expected

Table 3. Recall (R), precision (P), and F-score (F) as a function of maximum simultaneous vocalization constraints $\mathbf{K}_{max} \equiv \left(K_{max}^{\mathcal{S}}, K_{max}^{\mathcal{L}}, K_{max}^{\neg\mathcal{N}}\right)$. The frame step and frame size are identically 100ms, and the minimum duration constraints $\mathbf{T}_{min} \equiv \left(T_{min}^{\mathcal{S}}, T_{min}^{\mathcal{L}}, T_{min}^{\mathcal{N}}\right)$ are $(0.2, 0.4, 0.3)$ seconds for all systems shown. Symbols as in Table 2.

$\mathbf{K}_{max}$	$\mathcal{V} \equiv \mathcal{S} \cup \mathcal{L}$			$\mathcal{S}$			$\mathcal{L}$		
	R	P	F	R	P	F	R	P	F
$(2,2,2)$	80.5	**82.1**	**81.3**	83.3	**90.6**	**86.8**	36.9	**27.8**	31.7
$(2,2,3)$	84.0	76.1	79.9	84.0	89.0	86.4	48.8	24.3	32.4
$(3,2,3)$	84.1	76.1	79.9	**84.2**	88.6	86.4	49.1	24.6	32.8
§4 $(2,3,3)$	**84.3**	75.3	79.5	83.6	90.0	86.7	**55.2**	25.1	**34.5**

to outperform the $\mathbf{K}_{max} = (2,3,3)$ system if speech exhibited higher rates of overlap than does laughter. All 4 systems are shown in Table 3.

As Table 3 shows, increasing $K_{max}^{\neg\mathcal{N}}$ from 2 to 3 increases recall but reduces precision; the effect is more dramatic for $\mathcal{L}$ than for $\mathcal{S}$ because more of laughter than of speech occurs in overlap. Allowing a third simultaneous speaker decreases $\mathcal{S}$ precision by 0.4% and increases $\mathcal{S}$ recall by 0.2%. In contrast, allowing a third simultaneous laugher increases $\mathcal{L}$ precision by 0.8%, and at the same time increases $\mathcal{L}$ recall by 6.4%.

5.3   Generalization to Other Data

To close this section, we explore the performance of the system described in Section 4 on several other datasets drawn from the ICSI Meeting Corpus. In Table 4, we show the performance of our system on the Bro meetings, of which there are 23, and on the Bed meetings, of which there are 15. Both of these sets were completely unseen during development, and consist of 116 and 81 total hours of single-channel audio, respectively.

We note first of all that although $\mathcal{V}$ recall and precision are lower on Bmr(test) than on Bmr(train) by 0.8% and 0.4%, respectively, the differences are small. This suggests that model complexity is low and the system not particularly prone to

Table 4. Recall (R), precision (P), and F-score (F) of the system described in Section 4 on different subsets of the ICSI Meeting Corpus. $p_{\mathcal{V}}(\mathcal{L})$ is the proportion of vocalization time spent in laughter. Symbols as in Table 2.

Test data	$p_{\mathcal{V}}(\mathcal{L})$	$\mathcal{V} \equiv \mathcal{S} \cup \mathcal{L}$			$\mathcal{S}$			$\mathcal{L}$		
		R	P	F	R	P	F	R	P	F
Bmr train	10.91	85.1	**75.7**	**80.1**	83.4	89.8	86.5	53.0	19.4	28.4
Bmr test	14.94	84.3	75.3	79.5	83.6	90.0	**86.7**	55.2	**25.1**	**34.5**
Bro (all)	5.94	83.7	73.2	78.1	81.1	**90.6**	85.6	57.8	11.4	19.0
Bed (all)	7.53	**88.5**	65.2	75.1	**84.6**	85.7	85.2	**58.7**	10.0	17.0

overfitting. It is more surprising that $\mathcal{V}$ performance on the training data is not higher, and may be indicative of the difficulty of the task.

As can be seen, laughter detection for Bmr(test) is better than for Bmr(train), and much better in both Bmr subsets than for either the Bed or Bro meetings. It appears that $\mathcal{L}$ precision is strongly correlated ($r = 0.943$) with the proportion of vocalization time spent in laughter ($p_{\mathcal{V}}(\mathcal{L})$ in column 3). Although $p_{\mathcal{V}}(\mathcal{L})$ is higher for Bed meetings than for Bro meetings, F-scores are higher for the latter for all three of $\mathcal{V}$, $\mathcal{S}$, and $\mathcal{L}$. This is likely attributable to the fact that fewer of the Bed meeting participants than of the Bro meeting participants are present in the Bmr training data (cf. Section 2).

The above findings indicate that the proposed data split [2, 8, 9, 10, 11] is not particularly helpful in predicting laughter detection performance on unseen data. This is because the Bmr test meetings contain an atypically high proportion of transcribed laughter, even within the Bmr subset, rendering the distribution of vocal activity types more balanced than elsewhere in the corpus, and therefore detection results more optimistic. Further analysis is required to assess the correlation between detectability and factors such as participant identity, laughter quality, and the degree of laughter overlap by time.

6   Qualitative Comparison with Related Work

As mentioned in the Introduction, aspects of laughter detection in meetings have been treated in [2, 8, 9, 10, 11]. Although the goal of each of the aforementioned publications was different from ours, we present several common and differentiating aspects in Table 5.

In the earliest work, [2], the authors dealt with multiple farfield microphones, in an effort to identify simultaneous laughter from the majority of participants

Table 5. Overview of previous research on laughter/speech ($\mathcal{L}/\mathcal{S}$) classification and laughter/non-laughter ($\mathcal{L}/\neg\mathcal{L}$) segmentation, and of the current work, in terms of several differentiating aspects

Aspect	$\mathcal{L}/\mathcal{S}$ class. [8]	$\mathcal{L}/\mathcal{S}$ class. [9]	$\mathcal{L}/\neg\mathcal{L}$ segm. [11]	$\mathcal{L}/\neg\mathcal{L}$ segm. [10]	$\mathcal{L}/\neg\mathcal{L}$ segm. [2]	this work
close-talk microphones	✓	✓	✓	✓		✓
farfield microphones					✓	
single channel at-a-time	✓	✓	✓	✓		
multi-channel at-a-time					✓	✓
participant attribution	✓	✓	✓	✓		✓
only group laughter					✓	
only isolated laughter	✓		✓	✓		
only clear laughter		✓				
rely on pre-segmentation	✓	✓	?			
rely on prior rebalancing	✓	✓	?			
rely on channel exclusion			?	✓		

present, with no intention of attributing laughter to specific participants. These three aspects make [2] the most dissimilar from among the work cited in Table 5.

Research on laughter/speech classification [8, 9] has assumed the presence of manual pre-segmentation into intervals of approximately 2 s in duration and anticipates balanced priors in the testset. Furthermore, it treats only 47% of the transcribed laugh bouts, namely those which have been assigned their own utterances by the original ICSI transcription team. Although these conditions are different from the ones faced in the current work, [9] has shown that focusing on only 28% of the transcribed laugh bouts, those considered clearly perceptible, decreases EERs by 4%. This suggests that $\mathcal{N}/\mathcal{S}/\mathcal{L}$ segmentation may benefit by treating different types of laughter differently, especially if applications distinguish among laughter types.

Research in laughter/non-laughter segmentation [10, 11] is more relevant to the current work. This is not least because, as we have shown, nearfield laughter tends to be confused much more with nearfield silence than with nearfield speech. In spite of this, and despite identical training and testing data, a direct performance comparison with the current work is not possible. [10] assumes the presence of a preliminary (perfect) vocal activity detector which justifies the exclusion of nearfield channels exhibiting prolonged silence during testing. This is effectively a form of pre-segmentation which also achieves prior rebalancing, and the extent to which [10] relies on such exclusion is not documented. Furthermore, contrary to our own unpublished observations, the experiments in [10] recommend a framing policy with a small frame step but a large frame size; in conjunction with the current work, a potential emerging strategy is multipass segmentation in which frame step and frame size decrease and increase, respectively, from one pass to the next.

For completion, it should be noted that low precision continues to be a challenging problem [12] in speech/non-speech segmentation [21, 22, 26], and automatic speech recognition word error rates are currently 2-3% absolute higher with automatically produced segments than with manual segmentation [23, 25, 27]. As our confusion matrix in Section 4 shows, the separation between speech and silence appears to be easier than that between laughter and silence, and laughter segmenters exposed to the full duration of meeting audio are likely to incur more insertions than those exposed only to pre-segmented portions.

7 Conclusions

We have proposed a simultaneous multiparticipant architecture for the detection of laughter in multi-channel close-talk microphone recordings of meetings. The implemented system does not rely on any form of manual pre-segmentation, and achieves laughter recall and precision rates of 55.2% and 25.1%, respectively, on a commonly used 14-hour dataset in which laughter accounts for 2% of time. These figures represent the first baseline results for this task, and the findings indicate that discrimination between nearfield laughter and nearfield silence, rather than between nearfield laughter and nearfield speech, presents the biggest difficulties.

Our experiments suggest that laughter segmentation stands to benefit from contrastive constraints placed on the maximum allowed degree of simultaneous vocalization as well as on minimum allowed state duration. Finally, we have shown that laughter precision throughout the ICSI Meeting Corpus is most strongly a function of the proportion of laughter present, and only second a function of participant novelty.

Acknowledgments

We would like to thank Liz Shriberg for access to the ICSI MRDA Corpus.

References

1. Laskowski, K., Burger, S.: Analysis of the occurrence of laughter in meetings. In: Proc. INTERSPEECH, Antwerpen, Belgium, pp. 1258–1261 (2007)
2. Kennedy, L., Ellis, D.: Laughter detection in meetings. In: Proc. ICASSP Meeting Recognition Workshop, Montreal, Canada, NIST, pp. 118–121 (2004)
3. Russell, J., Bachorowski, J.A., Fernandez-Dols, J.M.: Facial and vocal expressions of emotion. Annual Review of Psychology 54, 329–349 (2003)
4. Laskowski, K., Burger, S.: Annotation and analysis of emotionally relevant behavior in the ISL Meeting Corpus. In: Proc. LREC, Genoa, Italy (2006)
5. Galley, M., McKeown, K., Fosler-Lussier, E., Jing, H.: Discourse segmentation of multi-party conversation. In: Dignum, F.P.M. (ed.) ACL 2003. LNCS (LNAI), vol. 2922, pp. 562–569. Springer, Heidelberg (2004)
6. Banerjee, S., Rose, C., Rudnicky, A.: The necessity of a meeting recording and playback system, and the benefit of topic-level annotations to meeting browsing. In: Costabile, M.F., Paternó, F. (eds.) INTERACT 2005. LNCS, vol. 3585, pp. 643–656. Springer, Heidelberg (2005)
7. Wrede, B., Shriberg, E.: Spotting "hotspots" in meetings: Human judgments and prosodic cues. In: Proc. EUROSPEECH, Geneva, Switzerland, pp. 2805–2808 (2003)
8. Truong, K., van Leeuwen, D.: Automatic detection of laughter. In: Proc. INTERSPEECH, Lisbon, Portugal, pp. 485–488 (2005)
9. Truong, K., van Leeuwen, D.: Automatic discrimination between laughter and speech. Speech Communication 49(2), 144–158 (2007)
10. Knox, M., Mirghafori, N.: Automatic laughter detection using neural networks. In: Proc. INTERSPEECH, Antwerpen, Belgium, pp. 2973–2976 (2007)
11. Truong, K., van Leeuwen, D.: Evaluating automatic laughter segmentation in meetings using acoustic and acoustics-phonetic features. In: Proc. ICPhS Workshop on The Phonetics of Laughter, Saarbrücken, Germany, pp. 49–53 (2007)
12. Pfau, T., Ellis, D., Stolcke, A.: Multispeaker speech activity detection for the ICSI Meeting Recorder. In: Proc. ASRU, Madonna di Campiglio, Italy, pp. 107–110 (2001)
13. Janin, A., et al.: The ICSI Meeting Corpus. In: Proc. ICASSP, Hong Kong, China, pp. 364–367 (2003)
14. Shriberg, E., Dhillon, R., Bhagat, S., Ang, J., Carvey, H.: The ICSI Meeting Recorder Dialog Act (MRDA) Corpus. In: Proc. SIGdial, Cambridge MA, USA, pp. 97–100 (2004)

15. Norwine, A.C., Murphy, O.J.: Characteristic time intervals in telephonic conversation. Bell System Technical Journal 17, 281–291 (1938)
16. Fiscus, J., Ajot, J., Michel, M., Garofolo, J.: The Rich Transcription 2006 Spring Meeting Recognition Evaluation. In: Renals, S., Bengio, S., Fiscus, J.G. (eds.) MLMI 2006. LNCS, vol. 4299, pp. 309–322. Springer, Heidelberg (2006)
17. Bachorowski, J.-A., Smoski, M., Owren, M.: The acoustic features of human laughter. J. of Acoustical Society of America 110(3), 1581–1597 (2001)
18. Laskowski, K., Burger, S.: On the correlation between perceptual and contextual aspects of laughter in meetings. In: Proc. ICPhS Workshop on the Phonetics of Laughter, Saarbrücken, Germany (2007)
19. Nwokah, E., Hsu, H.-C., Davies, P., Fogel, A.: The integration of laughter and speech in vocal communication: A dynamic systems perspective. J. of Speech, Language & Hearing Research 42, 880–894 (1999)
20. Laskowski, K., Schultz, T.: A supervised factorial acoustic model for simultaneous multiparticipant vocal activity detection in close-talk microphone recordings of meetings. Technical Report CMU-LTI-07-017, Carnegie Mellon University, Pittsburgh PA, USA (December 2007)
21. Wrigley, S., Brown, G., Wan, V., Renals, S.: Speech and crosstalk detection in multichannel audio. IEEE Trans. Speech and Audio Proc. 13(1), 84–91 (2005)
22. Huang, Z., Harper, M.: Speech activity detection on multichannels of meetings recordings. In: Renals, S., Bengio, S. (eds.) MLMI 2005. LNCS, vol. 3869, pp. 415–427. Springer, Heidelberg (2006)
23. Boakye, K., Stolcke, A.: Improved speech activity detection using cross-channel features for recognition of multiparty meetings. In: Proc. INTERSPEECH, Pittsburgh PA, USA, pp. 1962–1965 (2006)
24. Laskowski, K., Schultz, T.: Modeling duration contraints for simultaneous multiparticipant vocal activity detection in meetings. Technical report, Carnegie Mellon University, Pittsburgh PA, USA, (February 2008)
25. Laskowski, K., Fügen, C., Schultz, T.: Simultaneous multispeaker segmentation for automatic meeting recognition. In: Proc. EUSIPCO, Poznań, Poland, pp. 1294–1298 (2007)
26. Wrigley, S., Brown, G., Wan, V., Renals, S.: Feature selection for the classification of crosstalk in multi-channel audio. In: Proc. EUROSPEECH, Geneva, Switzerland, pp. 469–472 (2003)
27. Dines, J., Vepa, J., Hain, T.: The segmentation of multi-channel meeting recordings for automatic speech recognition. In: Proc. INTERSPEECH, Pittsburgh PA, USA, pp. 1213–1216 (2006)

Automatic Recognition of Spontaneous Emotions in Speech Using Acoustic and Lexical Features

Khiet P. Truong[1] and Stephan Raaijmakers[2]

[1] TNO Defence, Security and Safety, Soesterberg, The Netherlands
khiet.truong@tno.nl
[2] TNO Information and Communication Technology, Delft, The Netherlands
stephan.raaijmakers@tno.nl

Abstract. We developed acoustic and lexical classifiers, based on a boosting algorithm, to assess the separability on arousal and valence dimensions in spontaneous emotional speech. The spontaneous emotional speech data was acquired by inviting subjects to play a first-person shooter video game. Our acoustic classifiers performed significantly better than the lexical classifiers on the arousal dimension. On the valence dimension, our lexical classifiers usually outperformed the acoustic classifiers. Finally, fusion between acoustic and lexical features on feature level did not always significantly improve classification performance.

1   Introduction

There is a vast amount of literature available about the acoustic correlates of emotional speech. One of the goals of finding acoustic voice profiles for specific emotions is to provide discriminative speech features for automatic emotion recognition. For example, low values of pitch, intensity and speech rate are characteristic for sad speech [5]. Increased levels of pitch, intensity and speech rate are characteristic for angry speech, but also for happy speech [5]. Thus it appears that some emotions share similar acoustic characteristics which makes it difficult for learning algorithms to discriminate between these emotions. This is one of the reasons why acoustic discriminability on the valence dimension (i.e., positive vs. negative) is still problematic: there are no strong discriminative speech features available to discriminate between 'positive' speech (e.g., happiness) and 'negative' speech (e.g., anger). On the other hand, studies have found some acoustic features that correlate with arousal (i.e., active vs. passive): researchers agree that some acoustic features are discriminative between 'active' speech (e.g., anger) and 'passive' speech (e.g., sadness). Since it remains a challenge to find acoustic profiles for emotions, other modalities through which emotions can be expressed are increasingly being combined with the acoustic one.

In this paper, we focus on the use of *acoustic* and *lexical* features for emotion recognition in spontaneous speech. Previous studies have already succesfully combined acoustic and lexical information (e.g., [2,3,4]) for emotion recognition. However, few have examined the relation between the type of information used, acoustic or lexical, and the type of emotion dimension that is being modelled,

A. Popescu-Belis and R. Stiefelhagen (Eds.): MLMI 2008, LNCS 5237, pp. 161–172, 2008.

arousal or valence. For example, are lexical features more discriminative than acoustic ones on the valence dimension? This is one of the research questions that we address in our classification experiments.

In order to perform these classification experiments, we collected spontaneous emotional speech data by letting participants play a first-person shooter video game against each other. After playing the video game, the participants were asked to rate their own emotions in categories and arousal and valence scales. Boosting was used as a learning algorithm for our acoustic and lexical features. The features were combined on feature level into one large feature vector. Finally, the performances of the classifiers were compared to each other. We have defined three hypotheses that we will test in this paper:

1. The arousal dimension is better modelled by acoustic than lexical classifiers
2. The valence dimension is better modelled by lexical than acoustic classifiers
3. A fusion between acoustic and lexical information always improves classification performance

In assessing the performances of the classifiers, we are thus more interested in the *relative* performance rather than the *absolute* performance of the classifiers.

This paper is structured as follows. In Section 2, we describe the data collection and annotation procedure. The boosting algorithm and the acoustic and lexical features are presented in Section 3. Section 4 explains how the classifiers were evaluated. The results are presented in Section 5 and discussed in Section 6.

2   Data

2.1   Collecting Data

We collected spontaneous multimodal emotion data that contains recordings from participants (all were native speakers of Dutch) who are playing a first-person shooter video game (i.e., Unreal Tournament by Epic Games). In total, we invited 28 participants (17 males and 11 females) to play the video game. Each team consisting of 2 participants played against another team. The recruited participant was asked to bring a friend as a teammate. The participants had an average age of 22.1 years (2.8 standard deviation). A compensation fee was paid to all participants and bonusses were granted to the winning team and the team with 'best collaboration'. The latter bonus was provided to encourage the participants to be vocally expressive.

The game mode selected was 'Capture the flag' in which the goal was to capture the other teams' flag as many times as possible. In order to elicit more emotional events, the experimenter generated 'surprising' game events with the game engine during the course of the game at an approximate rate of one 'surprising event' per minute. For example, the experimenter issued sudden deaths or sudden appearances of monsters, and also hampered the keyboard or mouse controls during the game. The participants played two game sessions, each of 20 minutes long. Prior to each game session, they were allowed to 'try' the game for 10 minutes to get acquainted with the controls and the game. Furthermore, they received instructions and a training session (40 minutes) involving the annotation tasks (see Section 2.3) that were carried out by the players themselves (50 minutes) after each gaming session.

2.2   Recordings

High quality speech recordings were made with microphones that were attached near the mouth to minimize the effect of crosstalk (overlapping speech from other speakers) and background noise. The recorded speech was manually transcribed (by the first author) after pre-processing the speech signal by a relatively simple silence detection algorithm in Praat [7]. Furthermore, frontal views of the face were recorded with webcams that were placed at eye-level height. Finally, the video stream of the game content itself was captured as well.

2.3   Emotion Annotation: Self-reported Emotion Ratings

After a game session, each participant annotated his/her own emotions based on the 3 types of information that were recorded during the game session and that was made available to them: the audiovisual content containing (1) vocal and (2) facial expressions in frontal view, and (3) the game content that was captured. The participants watched the video content twice and performed two different annotation tasks based on two approaches: 1) a discrete category-based approach, and 2) a (semi-)continuous dimensional-based approach.

A category-based approach: 'event-based'. In the category-based annotation task, participants were asked to select and de-select emotion labels (see Table 1) whenever they felt the emotion that they experienced at that moment in the game, i.e., click to select an emotion label to mark the beginning of the corresponding emotion and click again on the same label to de-select and to mark the ending of that emotional event. The twelve emotion labels from which the participants could choose were based on the 'Big Six' emotions and typically game-related emotions that were investigated in a study described in [8]. We expected that these labels (Table 1) would cover a large part of the range of emotions that could occur during video gaming. Participants also had the possibility to say aloud an emotion label if they felt the appropriate emotion label was missing. The selection of multiple emotion labels at the same time was possible, enabling the possibility to have 'mixed' emotions.

In a perception experiment, 18 subjects (we will refer to them as *observers* or *raters*) rated a small subset of the data in exactly the same way as the players themselves (we will refer to them as *self-raters*) had rated the data. We calculated Krippendorff's α [6] pair-wisely between the self-rater and an observer to assess their agreement. We can observe in Table 2(a) that the averaged agreement is relatively low (α ranges from -1 to 1) which is not entirely unexpected given the highly subjective nature of the data.

Table 1. The emotion labels used in the category-based annotation task (with the Dutch labels in brackets)

Happiness (Blijdschap)	Fear (Angst)
Boredom (Verveling)	Anger (Boosheid)
Amusement (Amusering)	Relief (Opluchting)
Surprise (Verbazing)	Frustration (Frustratie)
Malicious Delight (Leedvermaak)	Wonderment (Verwondering)
Excitement (Opgewondenheid)	Disgust (Walging)

Table 2. Pair-wise agreement (Krippendorff's α) between the self-rater and the observers

Emotion category	mean	min	max
Frustration	0.36	0.15	0.69
Happiness	0.22	-0.11	0.56
Relief	0.14	-0.11	0.65
Excitement	0.13	-0.11	0.74
Amusement	0.09	-0.21	0.29

(a) Category-based annotation

	Arousal			Valence		
	mean	min	max	mean	min	max
raw	0.16	-0.27	0.51	-0.09	-0.45	0.34
scaled	0.34	-0.07	0.70	0.30	-0.21	0.62

(b) Dimensional-based annotation

A dimensional-based approach: '(semi-)continuous-based'. In the dimensional-based approach, the participants were asked to rate their own emotions on two emotion scales namely arousal (active vs. passive) and valence (positive vs. negative). As opposed to the category-based approach where the participants had to mark the beginning and ending of an emotional event, the participants now had to give ratings each 10 seconds on arousal and valence scales (running from 0 to 100, with 50 being neutral) separately (thus *not* simultaneously as is the case in Feeltrace [9]). To adjust for individual differences, we also re-scaled all the ratings per rater such that each rater has a range of [0,1]. The non-scaled ratings will be referred to as 'raw' and the re-scaled ratings will be referred to as 'scaled'.

Similar to the category-based approach, we assessed the agreement between the self-rater and a number of observers (Table 2(b)). The agreement seems to be comparable with the agreement in the category-based annotation task.

2.4   Selection of Data Used in Classification Experiments

Since the participants were provided audiovisual data during the self-annotation process, and participants were asked to rate what they felt, not all annotated data is useful when we want to train acoustic models: not all emotional expressions need to be expressed via speech. Therefore, a selection of data had to be made: for each emotional event or rating, we needed to know whether speech was involved and if that was the case, we extracted this segment of speech and labeled it as a certain emotion. Furthermore, a transcription at word level was needed to train lexical models. To facilitate the transcription process, a relatively

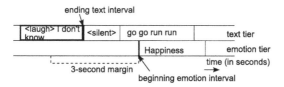

Fig. 1. Selection of speech segments that can be associated with an emotional event

simple silence detection algorithm (Praat [7]) was applied to the data. This detection algorithm also determined the size of the *units* (we will also refer to these units as *segments*) that were used for training and testing. The data was manually transcribed at word level (by the first author) and some punctuation marks, exclamation and question marks, were transcribed as well.

In the category-based approach, participants marked the beginning and ending of an emotional event. We assumed that the marker of the beginning is more reliable than the ending marker since we noticed that some emotional events were extremely long; we suspect that participants might have forgotten to deselect the emotion label to mark the ending. Also, we assume that there is a delay between the real occurence of an emotional event and the moment that an emotion label is selected. Figure 1 shows how we associated emotional events with speech segments: check for a maximum of 5 segments prior to the moment that the label was selected if 1) the segment ends within a margin of 3 seconds before the label was selected, and 2) the segment contains speech. For the dimensional-based approach, a similar selection procedure was applied. Each 10 seconds, an arrow appeared on the screen to signal the participants to give an arousal and valence rating. We assume that there is a delay between the moment that the arrow appeared and the moment that participants gave their ratings:

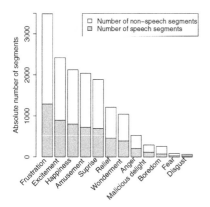

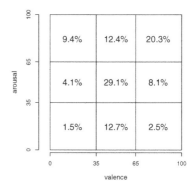

Fig. 2. Frequency of emotion category labels: the grey areas indicate the amount of speech segments that could be associated with an emotion 'click'

Fig. 3. Amount of speech segments that could be associated with arousal and valence ratings, divided in 9 regions of the arousal-valence space

Table 3. Amount of emotional speech data used in classification experiments

| | # segments | | | | in minutes | # unique |
	pos	neu	neg	tot	(μ, σ in seconds)	words
Category-based	1372		1458	2830	78.6 (1.67s, 1.26s)	1322
Dimension-based	pos 2308 act 3145	neu 4047 neu 3083	neg 1118 pas 1245	7473	186.2 (1.50s, 1.12s)	1963

for a maximum of 5 segments, check if 1) the segment starts within a margin of 3 seconds from the moment that the arrow appeared, and 2) the segment contains speech. Figures 2 and 3 visualize the amount of speech data that could be associated with a category emotion or an arousal or valence rating.

The total amount of emotional speech data consists of approximately 78 minutes (2830 segments) and 186 minutes (7473 segments) for the category-based and dimensional-based annotation approach respectively (see Table 3). In due time, we hope to release the dataset publicly for research purposes.

3   Method

3.1   Learning Algorithm

We used boosting, i.e., Boostexter [1] as a learning algorithm for our acoustic and lexical features. Boosting is an iterative algorithm that is based on the principle of combining many simple and moderately inaccurate rules into a single, highly accurate rule. These simple rules are also called *weak hypotheses*. The boosting algorithm finds a set of weak hypotheses by calling the weak learner repeatedly in a series of *rounds*. The weak hypotheses have the same basic form as that of a one-level decision tree. As the boosting process progresses, importance weights increase for training examples that are hard to predict and decrease for training examples that are easy to classify. In this way, the weak learner can be forced to concentrate on those examples which are hardest to classify. Boostexter is an implementation of boosting that focusses on text categorization tasks. An advantage of Boostexter is that it can deal with both continuous-valued input (e.g., age) and textual input (e.g., a text string).

3.2   Acoustic Features

For the extraction of the acoustic features, we used the program Praat [7]. The features were extracted over the whole segment. Based on previous studies that have investigated acoustic correlates of emotion, we extracted mean, standard deviation, the range (max−min) and the averaged slope of pitch and intensity. Furthermore, information about the distribution of energy in the spectrum was also employed (the more vocal effort, the more energy there is in the higher frequencies of the long-term spectrum [11]): we computed the slope of the long-term averaged spectrum, the centre of gravity (a measure that indicates how high the frequencies in a spectrum are on average) and skewness (a measure for how much the shape of the spectrum below the centre of gravity is different from the shape above the mean frequency), and the so-called Hammarberg index that measures the difference between the energy in the low-frequency area and the energy in the high-frequency area. These acoustic features were normalized to $\mu = 0$ and $\sigma = 1$ (where μ and σ were calculated over a development set).

In Boostexter, many simple rules are constructed by a sequence of rounds. Each rule consists of a simple binary test, and predictions for each outcome of this test. For continuous input, this test consists of determining whether a continuous value is below or above a certain threshold. The outcome of this test is associated with weights over the possible labels.

3.3   Lexical Features

As lexical features, we used relatively simple statistical language models that model the sequences of words, i.e., an 'N-gram' model. For textual input, Boostexter makes rules that ask whether a sequence of N words is present or not in the given text. Each outcome of a rule is described by a set of weights over the possible labels that describe the strength of the prediction if the ngram is present or not. In addition, speech rate was also extracted. Speech rate is usually considered a prosodic feature but since we based its calculation on lexical features, i.e., the number of words per seconds, we consider it in this particular case lexical. These features were extracted on the manual or automatic transcription. The automatic transcription was obtained by an automatic speech recognition (ASR) system that performed free recognition. The TNO ASR system (Speech-Mill, based on SONIC [10]) was trained on clean, grammatically correct read aloud Dutch speech which forms a mismatch with our spontaneous speech data. As a consequence, word error rate was extremely high.

3.4   Fusion

An advantage of Boostexter is that it can handle continuous and textual input simultaneously which made fusion relatively easy and convenient. The lexical and acoustic features were combined on feature level into one large feature vector by simply concatenating the features.

4   Evaluation Procedure

In order to test our hypotheses, we defined three tasks and three conditions. Task 1 investigates the separability on the valence dimension; it deals with Positive vs. Negative emotions that were defined by the *category-based* annotation. Unfortunately, a similar *category-based* arousal discrimination task could not be defined because the category-based annotation did not provide us a sufficient amount of Passive speech data. Tasks 2 and 3 investigate separability on

Table 4. Task definitions

	Task description	Type of annotation
Task 1	Positive vs. Negative	Category
Task 2	Positive vs. Neutral vs. Negative	Dimensional
Task 3	Active vs. Neutral vs. Passive	Dimensional

valence (Positive vs. Neutral vs. Negative) and arousal (Active vs. Neutral vs. Passive) dimensions respectively where the annotated data is acquired by the semi-continuous *dimensional-based* annotation. Each task (see Table 4) is carried out in 2 conditions that vary in the type of transcriptions:

1. Condi (MAN): word-level manual transcription made by first author
2. Condii (ASR): word-level automatic transcription obtained with ASR

Note that the same segments were used in Task 2 and 3 with the difference that the distribution of the segments over the classes is different: this will make a sound comparison between Task 2 and 3 possible. A 10-fold cross validation was applied. In each fold, the data was divided in 3 exclusive sets: a training ($\sim$ 80%), development ($\sim$ 10%) and testing set ($\sim$ 10%). The proportions of the classes were maintained in all sets. The development set was mainly used to perform a parameter search. The following parameters of Boostexter were tuned: 1) number of rounds (100 . . . 1500), 2) the window length for creating word-grams (1 . . . 5), and 3) the type of word-grams (sparse word-grams up to a maximal length|full word-grams up to a maximal length|full word-grams of maximal length only). The criterion was to maximize the macro averaged F-measure (as the number of categories is larger than two, we take the average of the per- categories results). As performance measures, we report the macro averaged F-measure and accuracy (number of correct classification divided by total number of classifications). In addition, we report the accuracy of a baseline classifier that always chooses the majority class.

5   Results

5.1   Task 1: Positive vs. Negative (Category-Based)

For Task 1, we achieved F-measures that lie within the range of $0.56 - 0.68$ which are better than the baseline classifier (see Table 5). Since this is a binary classification problem, we can also readily visualize the performance in ROC and DET curves using the assigned weights of the test segments as decision scores, see Figure 4(a) and 4(b). We can observe in Table 5 that the acoustic classifier performs worse than the lexical one, and that fusion slightly improves performance. McNemar tests confirmed that the lexical classifier is significantly better than the acoustic one and that the fused classifier is not significantly better than the best performing separate classifier ($p < 0.05$), i.e., the lexical one. Condii ASR, based on the ASR transcription, expectedly performed worst.

Table 5. F-measure (F) and accuracy (A) of classifiers in Task 1 in two conditions: MAN and ASR. Base refers to the baseline classifier that always chooses the majority class.

	Acoustic		Lexical		Fusion		Base
	F	A	F	A	F	A	A
MAN	0.57	0.60	0.65	0.68	0.67	0.69	0.52
ASR	0.57	0.60	0.56	0.56	0.59	0.60	

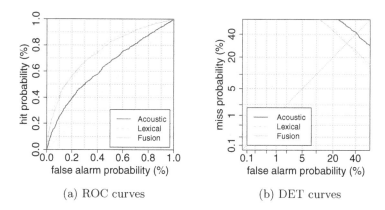

(a) ROC curves   (b) DET curves

Fig. 4. Results of binary classification Task 1, MAN condition: Positive vs. Negative

Table 6. Examples of sequences of words that were found in the weak hypotheses during training in Task 1, condi MAN. 'Pos weight' refers to the weight that is assigned to the Positive class when the word-gram is present in a text.

	Unigram			Bigram		
	Dutch	English	Pos Weight	Dutch	English	Pos Weight
Top5 Positive	geplaatst	placed	1.179	goed zo	well done	1.279
	geluk	lucky	1.074	over heen	thereover	1.188
	zijkant	sideway	1.074	punt ik	point I	1.173
	geweldig	great	1.060	pak ik	get I	1.121
	jah	yeah	1.057	oh <lach>	<laughter>	1.119
Top5 Negative	damn	damn	-1.286	geen punt	no point	-1.429
	dacht	thought	-1.224	elke keer	each time	-1.297
	elke	each	-1.218	ik nou	I well	-1.258
	geeft	gives	-1.211	eh ik	uh I	-1.251
	pakt	gets	-1.205	vlag niet	flag not	-1.249
Misc.	dankjewel	thank you	1.020	yes gelukt	yes done	0.908
	<lach>	<laughter>	0.971	oke ja	OK yes	1.071
	monster	monster	-1.182	dood shit	dead shit	-1.026
	frustrerend	frustrating	-1.182	heel irritant	very irritating	-0.993

Finally, in Table 6, we present a selection of sequences of words that were found in the boosting progress in the weak hypotheses. Some word grams that have an obvious inherent emotional connotation indeed received heavy weights, e.g., '<laughter>', 'frustrating', 'very irritating', while other seemingly neutral word grams are receiving high weights as well, e.g., 'sideway', 'get I' etc.

5.2   Task 2: Positive vs. Neutral vs. Negative (Dimensional-Based)

The results achieved in Task 2 are less encouraging; we can observe in Table 7 that the classifiers barely perform above the baseline. However, when we compare the results of the acoustic, lexical and fused classifier to each other, we can find some support for the hypothesis that the lexical classifier significantly performs better than the acoustic one (see Table 8(a)). Re-scaling the annotated data or fusing acoustic and lexical features did not always improve performance: the fused classifier did not perform significantly better than the best individual one (i.e., the lexical one, see Table 8(a)).

5.3   Task 3: Active vs. Neutral vs. Passive (Dimensional-Based)

The arousal dimension seems to be better modelled than the valence dimension (see Table 9); the classifiers perform better than the baseline classifier. We also found strong evidence for the hypothesis that acoustic classifiers can model arousal better than lexical classifiers (see Table 8(b)): the acoustic classifiers perform significantly better than the lexical classifiers. Furthermore, fused classifiers perform significantly better than single classifiers on the arousal scale (Table 8).

Table 7. Results Task 2: F-measure (F) and accuracy (A) in two conditions: MAN and ASR. Base refers to a baseline classifier that always chooses the majority class.

	'raw'						'scaled'						
	Acoustic		Lexical		Fusion		Acoustic		Lexical		Fusion		Base
	F	A	F	A	F	A	F	A	F	A	F	A	A
MAN	0.37	0.55	0.38	0.54	0.40	0.55	0.37	0.47	0.38	0.47	0.41	0.48	0.54
ASR	0.37	0.55	0.33	0.51	0.38	0.54	0.37	0.47	0.32	0.51	0.38	0.47	

Table 8. Significance of Task 2 and 3: '**A**'=acoustic, '**L**' =lexical. The underscore indicates which single-modality classifier had the higher performance.

cond	Hypothesis	$p < 0.05$ raw scaled
MAN	**L > A**	no yes
ASR	**A > L**	yes yes
MAN	Fuse > max(**A**,**L**)	no yes
ASR	Fuse > max(**A**,**L**)	no no

(a) Task 2

cond	Hypothesis	$p < 0.05$ raw scaled
MAN	**A > L**	yes yes
ASR	**A > L**	yes yes
MAN	Fuse > max(**A**,**L**)	yes yes
ASR	Fuse > max(**A**,**L**)	no no

(b) Task 3

Table 9. Results Task 3: F-measure (F) and accuracy (A) in two conditions: MAN and ASR. Base refers to a baseline classifier that always chooses the majority class.

	'raw'						'scaled'						
	Acoustic		Lexical		Fusion		Acoustic		Lexical		Fusion		Base
	F	A	F	A	F	A	F	A	F	A	F	A	A
MAN	0.39	0.49	0.38	0.46	0.42	0.51	0.41	0.43	0.38	0.41	0.44	0.45	0.42
ASR	0.39	0.49	0.34	0.44	0.40	0.48	0.41	0.43	0.33	0.38	0.41	0.43	

6   Discussion and Conclusions

We have investigated automatic emotion recognition in spontaneous speech using multimodal information. Although the *absolute* performances are relatively low, in our analyses we mainly assessed the *differences* between performances to investigate what type of classifier works better in what emotion dimension. The three types of classifiers were based on acoustic, lexical or acoustic plus lexical information. These classifiers were trained to assess separability on the arousal and valence dimensions. To that end, three tasks were defined: Task 1 and Task 2 investigated separability on the valence dimension and Task 3 investigated separability on the arousal dimension. We tested 3 hypotheses against the performances of the classifiers. The first hypothesis stated that discriminability on the valence dimension is better modelled by lexical classifiers than acoustic classifiers (Task 1, Task 2). We found strong evidence for this hypothesis: in the majority of conditions that we have tested, we found that lexical classifiers indeed performed significantly ($p < 0.05$) better than acoustic ones on the valence dimension (see Table 8). The second hypothesis tested whether acoustic classifiers modelled the arousal dimension better than the lexical classifiers (Task 3). We can accept this hypothesis since we found that all acoustic classifiers performed significantly better than the lexical classifiers on the arousal dimension (Table 8(b)). The third hypothesis tested whether fusion always improves performance over the individual classifier. We did not find conclusive evidence for this hypothesis. However, other ways of fusing multimodal information might be more succesful, for example, fusion on decision level (i.e., combining the output of the individual acoustic and lexical classifiers) rather than feature level (i.e., concatenating features into one large feature vector) could improve performance.

An issue that needs to be further discussed and investigated is to what extent the performance is dependent on the annotation quality. In the current study, we used the self-annotations of the players themselves who rated their own emotions. As such, the classifiers presumably learned 'felt' emotions rather than 'expressed' emotions. The relative low averaged agreement between the self- rater and the observers might indicate that the players did not always display felt emotions. A re-annotation of the complete data by observers might be useful for classifiers to learn expressed emotions. In future research, we also plan on improving the absolute performance of the classifiers discussed in the current study.

Furthermore, for the lexical classifier we used relatively simple language models. The lexical features can be enhanced by incorperating information from affective lexical resources that list words and their corresponding affective ratings. In addition, we can transform the textual input to a continuous representation of the textual input by using *normalized term frequencies* (tf-idf). These continuous-valued vectors can be used as input to other learning algorithms such as Support Vector Machines.

Acknowledgements

This study was supported by the Dutch BSIK project MultimediaN.

References

1. Schapire, R.E., Singer, Y.: A Boosting-based system for text categorization. Machine Learning 39, 135–168 (2000)
2. Schuller, B., Muller, R., Lang, M., Rigoll, G.: Speaker independent emotion recognition by early fusion of acoustic and linguistic features within ensembles. In: Proceedings of Interspeech, pp. 805–808 (2005)
3. Litman, D.J., Forbed-Riley, K.: Predicting student emotions in computer-human tutoring dialogues. In: Proceedings of ACL, pp. 351–358 (2004)
4. Lee, C.H., Narayanan, S.S., Pieraccini, R.: Combining acoustic and language information for emotion recognition. In: Proceedings of ICSLP, pp. 873–876 (2002)
5. Ververidis, D., Kotropoulos, C.: Emotional speech recognition: Resources, features, and methods. Speech Communication 48, 1162–1181 (2006)
6. Krippendorff, K.: Computing Krippendorff's Alpha-Reliability (Accessed, 29/03/08), http://www.asc.upenn.edu/usr/krippendorff/webreliability.doc
7. Boersma, P., Weenink, D.: Praat: doing phonetics by computer (Version 5.0.19) [Computer program] Retrieved April 4 (2008), from http://www.praat.org/
8. Lazarro, N.: Why whe play games: 4 keys to more emotion without story. In: Game Developers Conference (2004)
9. Cowie, R., Douglas-Cowie, E., Savvidou, S., McMahon, E., Sawey, M., Schröder, M.: Feeltrace: An instrument for recording perceived emotion in real time. In: Proceedings of the ISCA Workshop on Speech and Emotion, pp. 19–24 (2000)
10. Pellom, B.: SONIC: The university of Colorado Continuous Speech Recognizer. Technical Report TRCSLR-2001-01, University of Colorado, Boulder (2001)
11. Pittam, J., Gallois, C., Callan, V.: The long-term spectrum and perceived emotion. Speech Communication 9, 177–187 (1990)

Daily Routine Classification from Mobile Phone Data

Katayoun Farrahi and Daniel Gatica-Perez

IDIAP Research Institute, Martigny, Switzerland
Ecole Polytechnique Fédérale de Lausanne (EPFL), Lausanne, Switzerland
{kfarrahi,gatica}@idiap.ch

Abstract. The automatic analysis of real-life, long-term behavior and dynamics of individuals and groups from mobile sensor data constitutes an emerging and challenging domain. We present a framework to classify people's daily routines (defined by day type, and by group affiliation type) from real-life data collected with mobile phones, which include physical location information (derived from cell tower connectivity), and social context (given by person proximity information derived from Bluetooth). We propose and compare single- and multi-modal routine representations at multiple time scales, each capable of highlighting different features from the data, to determine which best characterized the underlying structure of the daily routines. Using a massive data set of 87000+ hours spanning four months of the life of 30 university students, we show that the integration of location and social context and the use of multiple time-scales used in our method is effective, producing accuracies of over 80% for the two daily routine classification tasks investigated, with significant performance differences with respect to the single-modal cues.

1 Introduction

Human activity modeling from large-scale sensor data is an emerging domain relevant to many applications, such as determining the behaviour and habits of individuals and the structure and dynamics of organizations [1,2,3]. This could be useful for social science research and self-awareness tools. Given the massive amount of data captured by ubiquitous sensors over long periods of time and involving many people, fundamental questions to address through automatic analysis include: Do people follow similar routines? Do certain people not follow other's routines? Are routines useful in group discovery?

Recent research has attempted to analyze complex, real-life activities from indoor sensors such as cameras, microphones, proximity, or motion sensors [3,4,5,6]. The limitations with indoor spaces are that the sensors are often fixed and only those activities that occur in the (local) physical space covered by the sensors can be recognized. Other recent approaches use wearable devices carried by people, which collect various types of evidence of their activities, including motion in dynamic environments [7] and audio in face-to-face conversations [1,8]. However, these wearable devices are not always practical for multiple users over long

A. Popescu-Belis and R. Stiefelhagen (Eds.): MLMI 2008, LNCS 5237, pp. 173–184, 2008.

periods of time. In this paper, we study human routines from sensors that have become an integral part of our daily lives, mobile phones. The functionality of this ubiquitous infrastructure of mobile devices is dramatically increasing [2,9], not requiring users to modify their daily behavior for data collection.

We define routines to be temporal regularities in people's lives. A routine often involves patterns of locations (e.g. being at work or at home, or going from work to home) and human interactions (e.g. as reflected by proximity information) over time, possibly over different time scales. Automatic routine classification and discovery are in general challenging tasks as people's locations and interactions often vary from day to day and from individual to individual, and data from sensors can frequently be incomplete or noisy.

The problems addressed in this work are as follows: given a day in someone's life, measured solely in terms of the noisy location and proximity information obtainable from a mobile phone, would this day more closely resemble a weekend or a weekday? If the person analyzed was a student, would a day in her life reveal potential group affiliations? More concretely, looking at the visualizations of location and proximity days in Figure 1, does a given day (a row in each of the visualizations) more closely resemble a weekend or a weekday? And do the day's routines appear more like an engineering or a business student's typical rituals? Answering such questions is difficult as users often work on weekends and the similarity in routines over days is often high. We would like to know how well we can automate these tasks. Using real-life data from the Reality Mining dataset [2], involving a large group of people over thousands of hours of activity, our work provides answers to these questions. This domain of research has been reviewed as a very promising technology [10].

The first contribution of this work is the novel investigation of a set of discriminant representations of location (measured from cell tower connection information) and proximity (measured from Bluetooth information) within a supervised learning framework. We investigated various representations characterizing proximity and location features in a day, such as multiple time-scales, proximity identity, quantity of proximate people, and representations with and without time considerations, to determine which best represented the underlying structure of the daily routines. The second contribution is the investigation of location-driven and proximity-driven day-type classification from a single day in the life of a user. The third contribution is the investigation of location-driven and proximity-driven group-type classification from single users' days. The fourth contribution is the comparison of single-modal versus multi-modal (i.e. multiple information sources) representations for location and proximity data for the two activity recognition tasks at hand.

Overall, we found that integrating information at multiple time-scales is useful, that fusing proximity and location information is beneficial compared with individual cues, and that the targeted daily routines (day-type and student-type) can be recognized with good accuracy (80.3% and 89.6%, respectively) even though the sensor data is partly incomplete.

There are many difficulties inherent to the activity recognition tasks at hand, complicating the already challenging dataset we used. Issues with mobile phone sensor data include poor indoor reception, incorrect data entries (due to the phone being left behind) and Bluetooth errors, to name a few. Further, proximity data is not always available, leaving many days without any information. Besides difficulties with the dataset itself, other challenges include the facts that students do not follow strict schedules, for example, they work on weekends regularly complicating the day type classification and that students might work or take classes in different buildings or offices, share offices or other spaces infrequently, etc and none of this is known a priori. Further, the dataset contains various types of students (undergraduate, graduate), which may follow different routines.

The paper is organized as follows. Section 2 presents the data set and highlights its inherent challenges. Section 3 describes our approach. Experiments and results are discussed in Section 4. Conclusions are given in Section 5.

2   Sensing Activity with Mobile Phones

The most widely deployed and used mobile computing device today is the mobile phone [11]. Current mobile phones can capture data related to the daily routines of large numbers of people over a large period of time. More specifically, their locations, such as being at work or home, can be captured from cell tower connections. Interactions can be captured by Bluetooth, which detects other Bluetooth devices within a small radius. Phone call and SMS activities can further be recorded. Phone application usage can be saved including the camera, calendar, games, and web browser usage [2]. Finally, content, including photos and video, can also be collected [9]. From the potential options, in this paper we examine both location and Bluetooth data.

Recent work has been done using coarse-grained Global System for Mobile communications (GSM) data from mobile phones to recognize high-level properties of user mobility (walking versus driving), as well as daily step count for a very small number (3) of users over the course of one month [11]. Both coarse and fine-grained location systems have been used to perform location-driven activity inference [11,12]. In work by Eagle and Pentland [13], which is the closest to ours, student type affiliations are determined by clustering location information aggregated over a period of nine months. All of the works described used location-driven activity inference. In this work, we investigate the student-type task considering proximity-driven inference, in addition to location-driven inference. Further, we investigate an additional task of day type classification. In addition, we evaluate several representations for the dataset, inferring class types from *single days* of data, as opposed to aggregated intervals of data.

There are many challenges and sources of noise inherent in mobile phone data. They can be forgotten, turned off, or out of battery. There are also issues with cell tower connections such as poor indoor reception and fluctuating connections. Bluetooth errors include detection between certain types of walls, recording people who are not physically proximate. There is also a small probability Bluetooth will not discover other proximate devices [2]. Further, ground truth collection is a difficult task especially over long periods of time. Users labeling is often incomplete, unclear and often unavailable, sometimes due to privacy concerns. All these issues lead to noisy, partly incomplete and partly inaccurate data with very little ground truth to rely on.

We use the Reality Mining dataset [2], collected by N. Eagle at MIT. The activities of 100 subjects were recorded by Nokia 6600 smart phones over the 2004-2005 academic year. This comprises over 800 000 hours of data on human activity; if we take into account the location, proximity, and phone call information, this corresponds to over 2 million hours of collected data. This dataset has been built respecting the privacy concerns of individuals in the study. The subjects in the study are students and staff of MIT that live in a large geographical area covered by over 32000 cell towers. They work in offices with computers that have Bluetooth devices which can sense in a 5-10m radius [2]. The public location information available for all subjects in the study includes the cell tower ID, as well as the date and duration of connection. All of the subjects labeled the cell tower ID's which correspond to their homes. We obtained a list of MIT work cell towers which correspond to the Media Lab and the Sloan Business school. The Bluetooth proximity data collected contains the IDs of two proximate devices as well as the date and duration of interaction. The list of work cell tower IDs obtained from MIT was incomplete as many students never connected to any of the cell towers in this list and thus were never considered to be at work. To resolve this issue, additional work labels were inferred from being in proximity to each person's computer; we did not consider being in proximity to one's laptop as being at work due to the mobile nature of the device. We assign a location label of HOME(H), WORK(W), or OTHER(O) to the 32000 cell towers. Towers which are not labeled as H or W are categorized as O. We have a fourth location label, NO RECEPTION(N), when there is no tower connection recorded for a person for a given time (eg. no battery, phone off or no reception).

3   Classifying Daily Routines

We address two classification tasks for daily routines: weekday vs. weekend routines, and engineering student-like vs. business student-like routines. In both cases, the input data is one day of location and/or proximity information.

3.1   Data Representation

The goal is to represent a day using location and proximity information that is discriminant to daily pattern classification. A day can be represented at multiple time scales, and people's routines usually follow block-type schedules. In this paper, we quantify location and proximity information at two levels (one fine-grain at 30 minutes and one coarse-grain at 3-4 hours). These two time scales provide a simple model of time management that is appropriate, in our opinion, to characterize many people's lives. For location data, keeping in mind the H, W, O, N

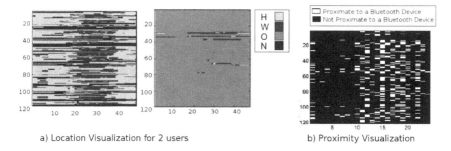

a) Location Visualization for 2 users   b) Proximity Visualization

Fig. 1. a) Visualization of location patterns using the fine-grain location representation, L_a, for 2 users over 121 days. Each row in the graph represents a day in the life of the individual. The labels H, W, O, N represent home, work, other, and no reception respectively. The day is divided into 48 fine-grain (30 minute) timeslots, each with a location label. The user on the left has a rich set of routines visible in the location patterns, whereas the user on the right is mostly incomplete due to lack of celltower labels. b) The proximity representation, P_b, is visualized for a user. Only proximity with users in the group are considered. Each row in the graph represents a day in the life of the user. The day is divided into 8 timeslots, each with 3 elements indicating the quantity of proximate users for that timeslot. For this user, most proximity activity occurs later in the day for most days.

labels, in addition to time considerations, useful information may be contained in the quantity of these locations present in a day, or the dynamics in which they occur (for example, work often follows home). Further, for proximity data, sources of useful data include the identity of the person with whom a user was proximate, the number of proximate people (quantity of proximity disregarding the user's identities), as well as time considerations. These features motivated the various location-driven and proximity-driven representations presented next.

Location Representation

L_a *Fine-Grain Location.* For the fine-grain location representation, visualized in Figure 1 and 2 a), a day is divided into 30 minute non-overlapping time intervals, resulting in 48 blocks per day. We assign a location label of W, H, O, or N to each 30 minute block. For classification purposes, this 48 element vector was transformed to binary format. Note that over a 30 minute interval, typically several cell tower connections are made, often with continuous fluctuations between a few. To address this source of noise we select the cell tower with the maximum connection time over each 30 minute interval.

L_b *Bag of Location Transitions.* This representation was built from the fine-grain location representation considering 8 coarse-grain timeslots in a day. A location word contains 3 consecutive location labels presented for the fine-grain representation corresponding to 1.5 hour intervals followed by one of the 8 timeslots in which it occurred. Thus a location word has 4 components, 3 location labels followed by a timeslot. We take overlapping 1.5 hour sets

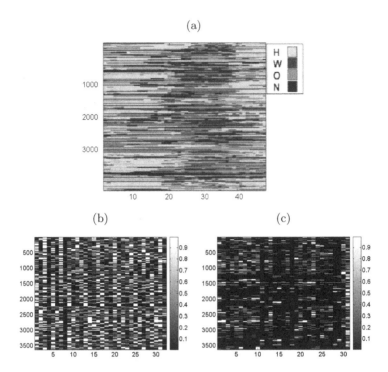

Fig. 2. a) Fine-grain location representation, L_a, visualized over the entire set of days and users in the study. The x axis corresponds to the 48 half hour time intervals in a day. The y axis corresponds to a given day of a user in the dataset. b) Coarse-grain location representation, L_c, visualized over all days and users. c) UserID proximity, P_a, displayed over all users and days.

of labels to make a location word, so that if we had a pattern HHHOW in timeslot 1, we would have the following location words: HHH1, HHO1, and HOW1. The bag of location transitions is the histogram of the present location words in the day.

L_c *Coarse-Grain Location.* For this representation, visualized in Figure 2 b), a day is also divided into 8 coarse timeslots. For each timeslot, there is a binary element representing the four location labels (H, W, O, N). If one of these labels was present within the given timeslot, it is counted as one, if this location was not present, it is counted as zero. This is a simplification of the bag of location transitions, in which the dimensionality was reduced to be comparable to some of the proximity representations described in the next subsection.

L_d *Two-Feature Location.* This representation is the simplest, in which the number of 30-minute H and W labels are counted without taking into account when exactly they occur in a day.

Proximity Representation

P_a *UserID Proximity.* The userID proximity representation is also illustrated in Figure 2 c). There are 31 binary components for a given day, reflecting the 30 people considered in this study (see Section 4.1), and the last component for the case when no one is in proximity. If the person was in proximity with one of the 30 individuals, the value for that component will be one; for days when the person is not in proximity with anyone, the last component will be one. Thus, we only consider proximity within the set of 30 people. We do not consider a person to be in proximity with oneself.

P_b *Coarse-Grain Proximity.* The coarse-grain proximity representation, visualized in Figure 1 b), contains again the same 8 timeslots in a day. In this description of proximity, the identities of people are disregarded and only the quantity of proximate people for a timeslot is considered. In the first timeslot, the first element is one if 1 to 2 people are in proximity, the second if 3 to 4 people are, and the last if 5 or more people are in proximity. The resulting representation contains 8 timeslots, each with 3 elements. This idea of binary quantization is repeated over the 8 timeslots giving a quantification of interaction within the total set of people over different times in the day.

P_c *One-Feature Proximity.* This is the simplest representation for proximity. We count the number of proximate people for a person within a day, and use this value.

Combined Representation. For the combined representation, we concatenate one of the location representations with one of the proximity representations. In this paper, we only consider cases with comparable location and proximity dimensionality. Feature extraction techniques (e.g. PCA) could have been applied on the joint representations but were not explored here.

3.2   Classification

The classification was performed using a support vector machine (SVM) with a Gaussian kernel. For both daily routine classification tasks (days as weekends or weekdays, or days as belonging to business students or engineering students), the training strategy was leave-one-user-out, specifically testing on all the days for one unseen person while training on the data for all other people (note: proximity features are by definition relational involving pairs of people); we tested on each of the people and averaged the results. We optimized the kernel parameter on one data split for a randomly chosen person.

4   Experiments and Results

4.1   Data Set

From the Reality Mining data set, we experimented with 30 people and 121 consecutive days, resulting in approximately 3600 data points. Our choice was guided by the goal of analyzing people and days for which data was reasonably available. The exact dates in the experiment were August 26, 2004 to December 24, 2004. The people selected had the most number of days with at least one W or H label. We removed days which were entirely N (no reception) labels since these had no useful information, which resulted in approximately 2800 data points. To select the interval of 121 days, we found the time interval with the most number of useful days (i.e., days with W, H, or O labels) over all 30 people. The resulting subset is still massive, amounting to over 87 000 hours, or about 10 years of data, and remains quite challenging in terms of noise, incompleteness, and complexity. This is illustrated in Figure 2 where it might be very difficult for a human to differentiate days as weekends/weekdays, or whether the day corresponds to a business student or engineering student.

For the student-type daily routine classification task, a subset of 23 of these 30 people were considered based on their student type labels. There were 6 business school students, and 17 engineering students. The engineering students covered a broader scope, including both undergraduate and graduate levels.

4.2 Weekday/Weekend Routine Classification

The weekend/weekday classification results are presented in Table 1 and reveal the difficulty of the task solely based on location or proximity information. In each table, the classification accuracy averaged over all people is presented first, and the average accuracy for each class is presented later. Generally, weekdays are more easily identified with location as input, and weekends are characterised better by proximity data. We can understand this by identifying weekdays with WORK cell towers, and weekends by not being in proximity with colleagues. However, in this dataset, students appearing to be in W locations on

Table 1. Weekend (WE) and Weekday (WD) daily routine classification accuracy. The top table shows the difficulty in determining weekends based on location information alone. Proximity data is more deterministic of weekend routines. Classification obtained by combining location and proximity results in the best performance. Significance values are shown for the most significant results.

Location Accuracy (%)				Proximity Accuracy (%)			
Method	Overall	WE	WD	Method	Overall	WE	WD
L_a	74.2	19.3	95.3	P_a	74.3	70.7	75.8
L_b	76.8	44.1	89.1	P_b	72	54.2	78.7
L_c	76	36.6	90.8	P_c	74.6	67.9	77.1
L_d	75.7	30	93.1				

Combined Accuracy (%)		
Method	Overall	Eng	Bus
(L_d,P_c)	76.9	47.35	88.1
(L_c,P_a)	80.3	65.8	85.8
(L_c,P_b)	79	53.4	89.3
(L_a,P_a)	76.5	60.2	82.8

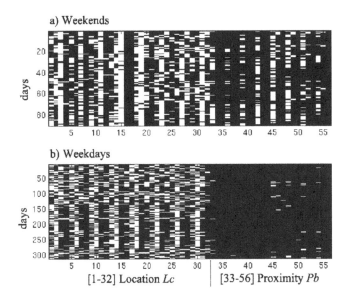

a) Weekends

b) Weekdays

[1-32] Location Lc [33-56] Proximity Pb

Fig. 3. Advantages of the joint location-proximity representation (L_c, P_b). Visualization of a) weekends and b) weekdays for which the proximity-only data was misclassified, but for which the location-only data and the combined proximity-location data were correctly classified. The sparsity of the weekday proximity-only data (columns 33-56 in b)), resulted in incorrect classification since sparsity in interaction is typical weekend behavior. However, when we added the location information, the resulting combined representation was correctly classified. The opposite phenomena can be observed in plot a), for which weekends have abundant proximity data, typical of weekday behavior.

weekends complicate the classification task, resulting in at best 44.1% weekend classification accuracy by the bag of location transitions (L_b), which performs overall better than the others, also having the highest dimensionality. The coarse-grain approach L_c (fused bag of location words) performs slightly worse for weekends with a significantly smaller dimension. The fine-grain location representation, L_a, performs the worst for WE, the best for WD, and slightly better than the two-feature location case. All methods perform better than a 'naive' guess that assumes all days are weekdays, which results in $5/7 = 71.4\%$ accuracy.

Proximity information alone is useful in characterizing weekends, but does not perform as well as location data for identifying weekdays. There are many weekdays with little group interaction, resulting in higher confusion with weekdays. The userID proximity and one-feature cases $(P_a$ and $P_c)$ reveal about 2% difference between their weekend and weekday performances, overall resulting in the highest performance of approximately 74%.

The lower panel in Table 1 shows the improvement in classification with the combination of proximity and location data. Note that in all cases the overall performance of the joint representations improved over that of the singleton case. We achieved over 80% accuracy with the combined representation (L_c, P_a)

trading-off 2-3% weekday accuracy for improved weekend classification. In Figure 3, we visualize the days for which the proximity-alone data (columns 33-56) was misclassified, however when we added the location data (columns 1-32), the resulting 56-component vectors were correctly classified. In both figures, the first 32 columns visualize the location representation L_c and the last 24 columns illustrate the proximity representation P_b, so each row displays a day of the combination (L_c, P_b). Figure 3a) are weekends which performed incorrectly for proximity-alone data due to the abundance of proximity interactions, which are not typical of weekends. In contrast, Figure 3b) shows weekdays which were mistaken for weekends due to the sparsity in interactions, not typical of weekdays. The addition of the location information in both cases resulted in correct classification, thus illustrating cases for which the combination of information improved classification performance.

The performance difference between the best location only method (L_b) and the best combined method (L_c, P_a) is statistically significant at the 1% level. The same is true for the performance difference between the best proximity only method (P_c) and the best combined method (L_c, P_a).

4.3   Business/Engineering Student Routine Classification

Effectively classifying daily routines as belonging to business students or engineering students based on proximity-only observations was representation-dependent. Proximity representation P_c, the one-feature case, was inadequate in differentiating between student types, suggesting that the overall quantity of proximity within each group is on average the same. If the business students had much more proximity within the total set of people, or vice versa, we could expect the one-feature case to have higher accuracy. The coarse-grain proximity representation P_b improved the accuracy of business student classification, however, the userID proximity representation proved to be the best, with almost 99% accuracy in engineering student classification and 61% for business students. The knowledge of identity from proximity is the key for discriminating student disciplines.

Location knowledge was inadequate in student type determination for the most part. This is likely due to the simplified representation used where the 32 000 cell tower IDs have been reduced to four location classes. It is expected that a representation more precisely identifying the location of a student would perform better. However, the representation used here is useful in understanding whether student types differ in the amount of time spent at school, home, or out and about. The two-feature location case, L_d, having low accuracy, indicates that the amount of time spent at school and home is not indicative of student type. The most effective characteristics in differentiating, which can be observed by the highest performance with the bag of location transitions representation, might be patterns of "going to work" in a timeslot, or "coming home" in a timeslot, or other similar routines which are captured by this representation.

Table 2. Engineering (Eng) vs. Business (Bus) student daily routine classification results. Proximity within the specific group is most representative of student type, especially when student identity is retained. The joint location and proximity data improves classification performance for the (L_c, P_a) combination. However, the other combinations generally perform as well as the singleton cases. Significance values are shown for the most relevent results.

Location Accuracy (%)				Proximity Accuracy (%)			
Method	Overall	Eng	Bus	Method	Overall	Eng	Bus
L_a	66.8	90.4	0	P_a	89.1	98.9	61.2
L_b	74.54	94.3	19	P_b	78.1	96	28.1
L_c	74.5	94.8	17.1	P_c	50.2	95.3	0
L_d	74.8	99.6	4.5				

Combined Accuracy (%)			
Method	Overall	Eng	Bus
(L_d, P_c)	73.3	97.6	4.5
(L_c, P_a)	89.6	99	62.9
(L_c, P_b)	78.76	93.4	37.4
(L_a, P_a)	84.5	95	54.7

The performance difference between the best location only method (L_d) and the best combined method (L_c, P_a) is statistically significant at the 1% level. The performance difference between the best proximity only method (P_a) and the best combined method (L_c, P_a) is not statistically significant.

5   Conclusion

We presented a method to classify daily life routines from massive, complex data collected with mobile phones. Using over 87 000 hours of data, we achieved over 80% accuracy in identifying whether a given day more closely resembles a weekend or weekday. This is not an easy task as students spend many weekends in work locations and have many weekdays with few group interactions. We showed that the integration of location and proximity data performed significantly better than the single observation sources, and that using representations that consider multiple time scales was beneficial. We further succeeded in identifying whether a user is an engineering or business student with over 89% accuracy based on a single day pattern of activity. The identity of individuals, measured by proximity, was key in this case, which confirms that social context is very helpful to identify people's routines. We plan to further exploit this concept for other daily routines relevant for the analysis of mobile social networks.

Acknowledgments. This research has been supported by the Swiss National Science Foundation through the MULTI project. We thank Nathan Eagle (MIT) for sharing the data and helping with various aspects of the collection structure.

References

1. Choudhury, T., Pentland, A.: Sensing and Modeling Human Networks using the Sociometer. In: Fensel, D., Sycara, K.P., Mylopoulos, J. (eds.) ISWC 2003. LNCS, vol. 2870. Springer, Heidelberg (2003)
2. Eagle, N., Pentland, A.: Reality mining: Sensing complex social systems. Personal and Ubiquitous Computing 10(4), 255–268 (2006)
3. Wren, C., Ivanov, Y., Kaur, I., Leigh, D., Westhues, J.: SocialMotion: Measuring the Hidden Social Life of a Building. In: Hightower, J., Schiele, B., Strang, T. (eds.) LoCA 2007. LNCS, vol. 4718, pp. 85–102. Springer, Heidelberg (2007)
4. McCowan, I., Gatica-Perez, D., Bengio, S., Lathoud, G.: Automatic Analysis of Multimodal Group Actions in Meetings. IEEE Transactions on Pattern Analysis and Machine Intelligence (T-PAMI) 27(3), 305–317 (2005)
5. Stiefelhagen, R., Bernardin, K., Ekenel, H.K., McDonough, J., Nickel, K., Voit, M., Woelfel, M.: Audio-Visual Perception of a Lecturer in a Smart Seminar Room. In: Signal Processing - Special Issue on Multimodal Interfaces, vol. 86 (12). Elsevier, Amsterdam (2006)
6. Oliver, N., Horvitz, E., Garg, A.: Layered Representations for Learning and Inferring Office Activity from Multiple Sensory Channels. In: Proceedings of Int. Conf. on Multimodal Interfaces (ICMI), Pittsburgh, PA (2002)
7. Munguia Tapia, E., Intille, S.S., Haskell, W., Larson, K., Wright, J., King, A., Friedman, R.: Real-time recognition of physical activities and their intensities using wireless accelerometers and a heart monitor. In: Proc. Int. Symp. on Wearable Comp., Boston (2007)
8. Wyatt, D., Choudhury, T., Kautz, H.: Capturing Spontaneous Conversation and Social Dynamics: A Privacy-Sensitive Data Collection Effort. In: Proceedings of International Conference on Acoustics, Speech, and Signal Processing (ICASSP), Honolulu (2007)
9. Davis, M., House, N.V., Towle, J., King, S., Ahern, S., Burgener, C., Perkel, D., Finn, M., Viswanathan, V., Rothenberg, M.: MMM2: Mobile media metadata for media sharing. In: Proceedings of ACM CHI, Portland (2005)
10. Technology Review, http://www.technologyreview.com/specialreports/specialreport.aspx?id=25
11. Sohn, T., Varshavsky, A., LaMarca, A., Chen, M., Choudhury, T., Smith, I., Consolvo, S., Hightower, J., Griswold, W.G., Lara, E.: Mobility Detection Using Everyday GSM Traces. In: Dourish, P., Friday, A. (eds.) UbiComp 2006. LNCS, vol. 4206, pp. 212–224. Springer, Heidelberg (2006)
12. Hariharan, R., Krumm, J., Horvitz, E.: Web-Enhanced GPS. In: Strang, T., Linnhoff-Popien, C. (eds.) LoCA 2005. LNCS, vol. 3479. Springer, Heidelberg (2005)
13. Eagle, N., Pentland, A.: Eigenbehaviors: Identifying structure in routine. Behavioral Ecology and Sociobiology (in submission, 2007)

Hybrid Multi-step Disfluency Detection

Sebastian Germesin, Tilman Becker, and Peter Poller

Deutsches Forschungszentrum für Künstliche Intelligenz GmbH
Stuhlsatzenhausweg 3, 66123 Saarbrücken, Germany
sebastian.germesin@dfki.de
tilman.becker@dfki.de
peter.poller@dfki.de

Abstract. Previous research has shown that speech disfluencies - speech errors that occur in spoken language - affect NLP systems and hence need to be repaired or at least marked. This study presents a hybrid approach that uses different detection techniques for this task where each of these techniques is specialized within its own disfluency domain. A thorough investigation of the used disfluency scheme, which was developed by [1], led us to a detection design where basic rule-matching techniques are combined with machine learning approaches. The aim was both to reduce computational overhead and processing time and also to increase the detection performance. In fact, our system works with an accuracy of 92.9% and an F-Score of 90.6% while working faster than real-time.

1 Introduction

One major problem in natural language processing (NLP) systems is that they get confused when processing spoken language. This is because of **speech disfluencies** - speech phenomena that are based on the incrementality of human speech production [2]. In fact, 5% - 15% of our speech is disfluent in the form of corrections (1), filled pauses (2), disruptions (3) or even uncorrected sentences (4).

(1) I want to go **to Alex, no,** to Joe.
(2) **Uh,** I want to go to Joe.
(3) **I want to.**
(4) I want to **gone** to Joe.

These disfluencies decrease the performance of ASP systems. [3] quantified the influence of disfluencies on data-driven parsing of spoken language and his experiment showed that "the parsing performance is increased when disfluencies are removed prior to parsing". [4] observed the effect of uncleaned speech disfluencies on N-gram models and described an increased perplexity of the N-gram models which were built on the uncleaned speech material. For cost and time reasons, disfluency detection and correction could be done via an automatic system that is placed right behind a speech-to-text (STT) system (see figure 1).

The scheme of the disfluency types this study is based on was developed by [1] as part of the AMI project and is explained in detail in section 2. AMI

A. Popescu-Belis and R. Stiefelhagen (Eds.): MLMI 2008, LNCS 5237, pp. 185–195, 2008.
© Springer-Verlag Berlin Heidelberg 2008

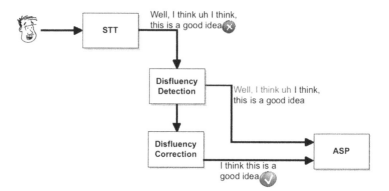

Fig. 1. Speech to ASP with Disfluency Detection

stands for *Augmented Multi-party Interaction* and is a multi-disciplinary research project to "develop technology to support human interaction in meetings and to provide better structure in the way meetings are run and documented" [5]. The meeting scenario is focused on business meetings with four participants whose task is to design a remote television control. All meetings are held in English and the uncontrolled and natural-like environment produce very good reflections of what happens in real meetings (including speech disfluencies). More details of the corpus possessed by the project and the available disfluency annotations is given in section 3.

1.1   Related Work

A number of researchers published different techniques to detect disfluencies. [6] developed a TAG-based approach (TAG - Tree Adjoining Grammar) combined with a noisy channel model and yielded results of 79.7% F-Score on the Penn 3 disfluency-tagged Switchboard corpus. Later on, [7] extended this approach with a maximum-entropy reranker and manually written deterministic rules and outperformed all state-of-the-art systems in the RT-04F evaluation task. The idea of writing lexical rules for the detection of disfluencies was also followed by [8] who gained competitive results. Additionally, many studies trained machine learning algorithms to recognize disfluencies on lexical [9] as well as on prosodic features [10] and gained equally good results. [10] claimed that combining lexical and prosodic features would result in a system that would outperform both.

1.2   Hybrid Approach

The present work continues these studies in the way that our invented system copes with a broader set of disfluency types. The observed heterogeneity of the disfluencies led us to the assumption that such a system should be designed in a hybrid way which means that each disfluency should be detected by a special detection technique that was fine-tuned for this disfluency domain. These individual techniques should be combined, resulting in a system that is able to cope with more disfluency types than the individual systems. Additionally, this design leads to a reduced computational overhead and an improved detection performance. Both implementations of the individual techniques as well as of the hybrid system are presented in section 4. The results of the detection systems are contrasted and discussed in the sections 5 and 6.

2   Disfluency Scheme

Disfluencies are "syntactical and grammatical [speech] errors" [1] that occur in spoken language and are present in nearly every conversation. This is based on the incremental speech building process in human articulation [11] and the impossibility to take back already uttered words [12]. [10] found out that between 5% - 10% of our speech is disfluent and, in fact, our corpus contains about 15% erroneous speech material which can be justified by our broader annotation scheme, invented by [1].

The common structure of a disfluency consists of three regions: The **Reparandum** which contains the erroneous speech material, an optional medial region which is called **Interregnum** and the repairing part called the **Reparans**. [1] states that not all disfluencies fit into that scheme and hence splits up her classification scheme into what she calls **simple** and **complex** disfluencies. Simple disfluencies consist only of erroneous speech material while complex disfluencies fit into the common structure. Furthermore, she considers types of disfluencies where the annotator (or the system) has to insert new speech material to gain the speakers intended utterance. She calls them *Uncorrected* disfluencies as they are grammatical errors which were left uncorrected by the speaker.

Table 1. Overview of all Disfluencies used in this study

class	abbrev.	example
Hesitation	hesit	This **uh** is an example.
Stuttering	stutter	This is an **exa** example.
Disruption	disrupt	This is an example **and I**
Slip Of the Tongue	sot	This is an **y** example.
Discourse Marker	dm	**Well,** this is an example.
Explicit Editing Term	eet	This is **uh this** is an example.
Deletion	delete	**This really is** this is an example.
Insertion	insert	**This an** this is an example.
Repetition	repeat	**This is** this is an example.
Replacement	replace	**This was** this is an example.
Restart	restart	**We should,** this is an example.
Mistake	mistake	This **be** an example.
Order	order	This **an is** example.
Omission	omiss	This is **[ ]** example.
Other	other	

Finally, she created a finely granulated classification scheme including 15 different classes which are listed in table 1. It shows the abbreviations of these classes and examples that help in the understanding of the particular meaning of the disfluency types. The disfluencies whose name is written in italics are of the simple structure and the rest are complex disfluencies. The disfluency types *Mistake*, *Order* and *Omission* are in fact the previously mentioned *Uncorrected* disfluencies.

3   AMI Corpus

The aims of the AMI (Augmented Multi-party Interaction) project are to develop technology to support human interaction in meetings and to provide better structure in the way meetings are run and documented [5]. To fulfill these, the project possesses a speech corpus with more than 100 hours of four person project meetings. These meetings are all held in English and the task of the particular participants is to design a television remote control. Next to the transcribed speech of the participants, the corpus offers different *annotation layers* that contain a variety of information (e.g., dialog acts, extractive summaries, ASR output, topics, ...).

28 out of the 135 meetings are annotated with our disfluency scheme. The detailed distribution of all classes and the separation in training set and evaluation set are shown in table 2. It is noticeable that the top five disfluencies cover 75% of all appearing disfluencies, which makes them important in the detection task. We split the disfluency corpus into an 80% training set and 20% evaluation set which corresponds to an amount of 10.19 and 2.79 hours meeting time. Despite this, our investigation of the disfluency annotated corpus showed that nearly 15%

Table 2. Distribution of disfluency classes in the corpus

	TRAIN	EVAL	SUM	%	kumul. %
hesit	3472	1038	4510	28.67	28.67
repeat	2038	360	2398	15.24	43.92
dm	1981	256	2237	14.22	58.14
disrupt	1389	203	1601	10.18	68.32
sot	928	214	1142	7.26	75.58
omiss	871	82	953	6.06	81.63
mistake	703	61	764	4.86	86.49
stutter	537	123	660	4.20	90.69
restart	502	97	599	3.81	94.49
replace	319	50	369	2.35	96.84
eet	141	19	160	1.02	97.86
insert	117	25	142	0.90	98.76
other	107	6	113	0.72	99.48
order	67	7	74	0.47	99.95
delete	6	2	8	0.05	100.0

Table 3. N-gram Corpus Statistics

N	OOV	PP
1	3.47%	1181.85
2	27.13%	2674.26
3	80.17%	33310.79
4	95.35%	86872.62

of all words are disfluent and 40.5% of all dialog acts contain at least one disfluency. Taking into account that these disfluencies would confuse an NLP system, this is quite a huge amount and we will see that our system is able to decrease this. The structure of the disfluencies allow the embedding of other disfluencies but we found out that most of them have either no parent disfluency or just one. The deepest layered disfluency has five parents. Furthermore, we analyzed the length of the disfluencies and about 95% of all simple disfluencies consist of one or two words and the most complex disfluencies have an average length of two to ten words. The longest disfluency - a *Disruption* - contains 24 words.

Additionally, some features for the machine learning approach need N-grams which had to be build on fluent speech material. Therefore, we calculated these N-grams out of the disfluency annotated - and cleaned - training part of the corpus which contains 3760 unique words. As this is a relatively small corpus for the estimation of statistical word probabilities, we were not able to gain the best out-of-vocabulary and perplexity results (see table 3). Therefore, a corpus with more material is definitely preferable and would lead to better performances.

4   Hybrid Detection System

The disfluency detection system is composed of different individual classification methods. Each method is responsible for a subset of disfluency classes and is fine-tuned based on this. In fact, we have two different subsets and hence two different detection approaches.

4.1   Rule-Matching Approach

The rule-matching based approach detects disfluencies of the types *Hesitation*, *Stuttering* and *Repetitions* and uses regular expressions as well as simple word matching techniques. We will see that these techniques are very strong and lead to no performance loss while transferring them from the development environment into the hybrid system.

4.2   Machine Learning Approach

The machine learning approach is implemented with the help of the freely available WEKA toolkit [13] which contains many state-of-the-art machine learning algorithms and a variety of evaluation metrics. Furthermore, it allows for the adaption of other algorithms due to its simple interface. Disfluencies of the classes *Discourse Marker, Slip of the Tongue, Explicit Editing Term, Restart, Replacement, Insertion, Deletion* and *Other* are detected by a machine learning approach that performs a word-by-word detection. In general, we have four different types of features: **lexical, prosodic, speaker-related** and **dynamic**.

Lexical features are estimated on the word-layer and consider also the POS tags of the particular words. Next to the absolute words, we use some relative lexical features that describe the lexical parallelism between the current word and its neighbors. As [10] describes, prosodic features are well suited for the disfluency detection task and hence we use them as well. The term **prosodic** means, in this context, features that describe the *duration, energy, pitch pauses* and *velocity* of the words. The *duration* and *pauses* features are calculated directly from the word-boundaries as annotated in the corpus. The *velocity* of a single word is defined by its duration divided by the number of syllables. For the *energy-* and *pitch*-based features, we have 10 ms frames available for each channel of a meeting. As these raw values cannot be used directly, we first had to normalize them globally, based on each channel to eliminate the influence of the microphones. After that, we computed the features on a word and a sub-word level. The **speaker-related** features describe the speakers *role, gender, age* and *native-language* as we found a correlation between these characteristics and the rate of disfluent words. The last type of features are the **dynamic** features that are generated during the process of the classification and describe the relationship between the disfluency type of the ongoing word to its neighbors.

4.3 Hybrid Design

Figure 2 shows the schematic drawing of the architecture that has been developed. There we can see that both the rule matching subsystem and the machine learning approach work on the data for itself instead of a combined solution where both approaches process the data in parallel. In the first step, the rule-matching system processes the speech material until no more disfluencies can be found. After that, the system's state advances to the machine learning approach where the remaining types of the disfluencies are marked. If this subsystem found any disfluencies, the speech material gets directly re-inserted into the rule-matching system. If not, the labeled stream or the cleaned speech material is made available for a possible subsequent NLP system.

When developing the hybrid system, the first step after the implementation of the particular subsystems was to decide how to arrange both approaches. The presented architecture emerged from a set of different design ideas that were all evaluated on the evaluation part of the corpus. The particular ideas differed in the way both subsystems were placed and in the way the speech was carried through them. In all design steps, we focussed our attention on keeping the precision as high as possible, because wrongly disfluent marked words have more of a bad influence on the meaning of the sentence than wrongly fluent marked ones.

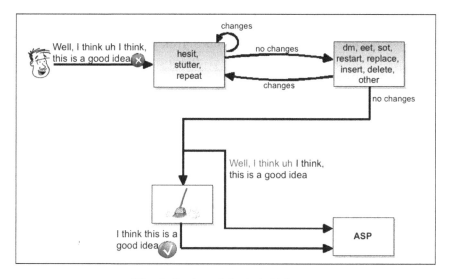

Fig. 2. Design of the hybrid System

5   Experimental Results

This section first describes the evaluation of our experimental results for the individual classification systems with the results that were gained in the development setting and after that the results for the hybrid system where all individual classification methods are combined to create the final architecture as shown in figure 2. The metrics are estimated on a per-word matching of the classified and the corpus-based labeling. As we do not want to present Precision, Recall and F-Scores for all different classes, we combined the results for all classes by a weighted mean for each metric where the weight is the probability of the particular disfluency type. This has the advantage that numerous disfluencies, which are hence more important for the detection approach, get a higher rank than the less frequent ones.

5.1   Individual Results

The evaluation results of the rule-matching based approach is shown in table 4 where both the baseline and the particular results are presented. We can see that the system works very fast (6 seconds detection time for about 10,000 seconds of speech material) and yields a very good outcome with an accuracy of 98.75% and an F-Score of 98.78%.

For the machine learning approach, which detects disfluencies of type *Discourse Marker, Slip of the Tongue, Explicit Editing Term, Restart, Replacement, Insertion, Deletion, Disruption* and *Other*, we tried several machine learning algorithms to gain the best suited one for this task and, in fact, the **Decision Tree** implementation from the WEKA toolkit outperformed all others. We can

Table 4. Results of Rule Matching

	Baseline	RuleMatcher
Evalinstances	25449	
Evaltime	–	6 sec
Accuracy [%]	93.29	98.75
avg. Precision [%]	87.09	98.78
avg. Recall [%]	93.29	98.75
avg. F-Score [%]	90.08	98.76

Table 5. Results for the Machine Learning Approach

	Baseline	DecisionTree
Traininstances	98562	
Evalinstances	24728	
Traintime	–	20:41 h
Evaltime	–	7 sec
Accuracy [%]	96.09	97.34
avg. Precision [%]	92.34	97.15
avg. Recall [%]	96.09	97.34
avg. F-Score [%]	94.17	97.24

see in table 5 that it also works very fast with good performance but needs an immense amount of training time.

5.2 Hybrid Approach

Since we combined the two previously mentioned individual approaches, the hybrid approach is able to detect all their disfluency types. In addition to the word-based evaluation metrics, we decided to calculate the amount of disfluent dialog acts (see table 6) where a disfluent dialog act is a dialog act that contains at least one disfluency. In our evaluation set, 64% of the dialog acts contained disfluencies with 12.5% of disfluent words. These are the baselines for the particular evaluation metrics which are listed in table 6. There, you can see that our

Table 6. Performance of hybrid Detection and Correction System

	Word Level			DA Level	
	Baseline [%]	Result [%]		uncleaned [%]	cleaned [%]
Accuracy	87.5	92.9	fluent	64.3	77.3
Precision	78.4	90.6	disfluent	35.9	22.7
Recall	89.6	90.5			
F-Score	83.6	90.6			
Real Time	2:47 h				
Processing Time	1:10 h				

hybrid approach is able to label 92.9% of all words correct which means that it detects more than 56% of all disfluencies. Furthermore, after cleaning the dialog acts of the found disfluencies, the amount of fluent dialog acts increased to more than 77%.

The processing time increased to 1:10 h which is justified by the multi-step design where the transformation of the words to the instances requires a huge amount of time for each of the steps. This could be reduced by omitting the POS tagging by accepting a little degradation of the performance. Nevertheless, the current system still works faster than real-time.

5.3   Detection of the Remaining Disfluency Types

So far, we excluded the detection of disfluencies with type *Disruptions, Mistake, Order* and *Omission* from the hybrid design. Nevertheless, we tried to implement two systems that could deal with the detection of these disfluencies and we want to present them here as well.

The approach that should detect *Disruptions* was also implemented with machine learning based techniques and - for the development setting - produced very good results. The **Decision Tree** outperformed all other algorithms and the particular results with the corresponding baselines are presented in table 7. Unfortunately, by transferring this approach from the development setting into the final system, it's performance crashed and did not yield any detection improvements.

The detection of the remaining disfluencies, which are *Omission, Mistake* and *Order*, was the most difficult task because the speaker did not produce explicit editing terms or any other information about his/her error. A statistical approach like the N-gram technique seemed to be a good way to gain information about the correctness of a word-order or a possible missing/superuous word. Unfortunately, the N-gram approach did not yield any detection improvements which is most likely due to the small size of the available corpus. The N-gram statistics have to be estimated on a huge text that must be fluent and from the same context as the evaluation text. Both properties are fulfilled by the training set but it was too small to gain useful N-gram probabilities as seen in the perplexity and out-of-vocabulary values presented in table 3.

Table 7. Results for the Disruption Detection

	Baseline	Decision Tree
Traininstances	76666	
Evalinstances	19653	
Traintime	–	10:14 h
Testtime	–	4 sec
Accuracy [%]	98.99	99.23
avg. Precision [%]	98.64	99.13
avg. Recall [%]	98.99	99.23
avg. F-Score [%]	98.81	99.18

6   Conclusions

We have described the implementation and evaluation of a hybrid multi-step system for the detection and correction of disfluencies. We used machine learning techniques as well as rule-based approaches. For the machine learning approach, we estimated a variety of lexical, prosodic, speaker-related and dynamic features. Unfortunately, we had to be aware that the detection of disfluencies with type *Disruption*, *Mistake*, *Order* and *Omission* was not successful and therefore not included in the final system. Despite this, we have shown that the system works and detects and corrects the remaining disfluencies. We reached an Accuracy of 92.9% with an F-Score of 90.6%. Evaluating on the dialog act level, we were able to clean more than 56% of all disfluent dialog acts which resulted in 77.3% clean dialog acts.

6.1   Future Work

The next planned steps are to increase the stability of the machine learning based approaches to ensure their performance in the multi-step hybrid environment. Additionally, we will use a larger text source for the calculation of the N-gram statistics to give the approach for the detection of disfluencies of class *Uncorrected* a better basis for the probability calculation of the correctness of an ongoing utterance. Furthermore, another design of the hybrid approach is thinkable where the different classification methods are used in parallel with a particular weighting to detect whether a word is disfluent or not.

Acknowledgment

This work is supported by the European IST Programme Project FP6-0033812 (AMIDA), Publication ID - AMIDA-26. This paper only reflects the authors views and funding agencies are not liable for any use that may be made of the information contained herein. The used POS tags were estimated with the help of the freely available Stanford POS-Tagger and, hence, we want to thank the persons from the Stanford NLP group.
(http://nlp.stanford.edu/software/tagger.shtml)

References

1. Besser, J.: A Corpus-Based Approach to the Classification and Correction of Disfluencies in Spontaneous Speech. Master's thesis, Saarbrücken (2006)
2. Ferreira, F., Lau, E., Bailey, K.: Disfluencies, Language Comprehension and Tree Adjoining Grammars. Cognitive Science, 28, 721–749 (2004)
3. Jorgensen, F.: The Effects of Disfluency Detection in Parsing Spoken Language. In: NODALIDA-2007, pp. 240–244 (2007)
4. Stolcke, A., Shriberg, E.: Statistical Language Modeling for Speech Disfluencies. In: Proc. ICASSP 1996, pp. 405–408 (1996)

5. Carletta, Jean, Ashby, S., Bourban, S., Flynn, M., et al.: The AMI Meeting Corpus. In: Proceedings of the Measuring Behavior 2005 symposium on "Annotating and measuring Meeting Behaviour" (2005)
6. Charniak, E., Johnson, M.: A TAG-based noisy channel model of speech repairs. In: Annual Meeting of the Association for Computational Linguistics (2004)
7. Lease, M., Johnson, M., Charniak, E.: Recognizing disfluencies in conversational speech. In: IEEE Transactions on Audio, Speech and Language Processing, pp. 1566–1573 (September 2006)
8. Snover, M., Dorr, B., Schwartz, R.: A lexically-driven algorithm for disfluency detection. In: Human Language Technology Conference (2004)
9. Moreno, I., Pineda, L.: Speech Repairs in the DIME Corpus (2006)
10. Shriberg, E., Bates, R., Stolcke, A.: A Prosody-Only Decision-Tree Model for Disfluency Detection. In: Proc. Eurospeech 1997, pp. 2383–2386 (1997)
11. Finkler, W.: Automatische Selbstkorrektur bei der inkrementellen Generierung gesprochener Sprache unter Realzeitbedinungen, Dissertation, Universität des Saarlandes, 165, DISKI (1997)
12. Eklund, R.: Disfluency in Swedish human-human and human-machine travel booking dialogues (2004)
13. Witten, I., Frank, E.: Data Mining: Practical Machine Learning Tools and Techniques, vol. 2. Morgan Kaufmann, San Francisco (2005)

Exploring Features and Classifiers for Dialogue Act Segmentation

Harm op den Akker[1] and Christian Schulz[2]

[1] Twente University, Enschede, The Netherlands
[2] Deutsche Forschungszentrum für Künstliche Intelligenz (DFKI),
Saarbrücken, Germany

Abstract. This paper takes a classical machine learning approach to the task of Dialogue Act segmentation. A thorough empirical evaluation of features, both used in other studies as well as new ones, is performed. An explorative study to the effectiveness of different classification methods is done by looking at 29 different classifiers implemented in WEKA. The output of the developed classifier is examined closely and points of possible improvement are given.

1 Introduction

Current research in the AMIDA project is focussed on a deeper understanding of meeting discourse semantics. An important first step towards this goal is the structuring of utterances into meaningful parts, like sentences or Dialogue Acts. A Dialogue Act is a sequence of subsequent words from a single speaker that form a single statement, an intention or an expression. Segmenting spoken or written text into Dialogue Acts contributes to a better understanding of the utterances; is the speaker for example asking something, or is he conveying a meaning? A lot of work on DA and linguistic segmentation and DA classification (or tagging) has already been done, on the AMI Corpus: [1], but also on other corpora [2], [3], [4], [5] and [6]. However, this is not a closed topic yet and many techniques still need to be explored.

The following is a Dialogue Act annotated example taken from the AMI corpus, using its 15 tag tagset:

You know. (**Elicit-Assessment**) *Yep.* (**Assess**) *Mm-hmm.* (**Backchannel**) *I think one factor would be production cost.* (**Inform**)

This is an example of a segmentend and tagged series of words. This paper looks at the task of segmentation alone, where the input is the sequence of words (without interpunction or capitalization), and the goal is to tag each word as either a segment **S**tart or an **I**nternal:

you/**S** *know*/**I** *yep*/**S** *mm-hmm*/**S** *i*/**S** *think*/**I** *one*/**I** *factor*/**I** *would*/**I** *be*/**I** *production*/**I** *cost*/**I**

The Dialogue Acts as used within the AMI project are defined to be uttered by a single speaker only (no single Dialogue Act can span multiple speakers).

A. Popescu-Belis and R. Stiefelhagen (Eds.): MLMI 2008, LNCS 5237, pp. 196–207, 2008.

For this reason, the input for the classifier is the sequence of words sequentially uttered per speaker.

This paper looks into stand-alone segmentation using a two-class classification approach. It can also be seen as a sequence-based machine learning problem in which case techniques like Hidden Markov Models, Conditional Random Fields (CRFs) or Memory-Based Tagging can be used.

For every machine learning task there are four major aspects that can and should be looked into. These are: features, classification method, classifier parameters and data. This article will focus on the evaluation of features using a Bayesian Network classifier, and takes a quick look at other classification methods.

For this project the AMI Corpus is used, which will be described first. Next, a list of features that have been derived from the data is defined. All these features need to be evaluated to see how useful they are. Simply using all available information to train classifiers is not efficient. The amount of training data needed for the classifier to automatically learn that some features, for example, contain little or no information can become extremely large. Therefore a thorough feature selection is conducted, which is described in Section 4. Experiments to explore the influence of different classification techniques are described 5. Then, a thorough evaluation of the final results (for Bayesian Networks) will be done, which gives insight in the types of errors made by the classifier. This evaluation also shows that using standard performance measures like precision and accuracy should not be taken too strict because of the large amount of non-harmful errors that are made.

2   The AMI Corpus

All the data that is used in this project comes from the AMI Corpus [7]. The largest part of the corpus (72 hours in total) are scenario-based meetings which are covered by 35 series, totalling 138 meetings. The following split into training-, test,- and evaluation sets has been made:

Training set: ES2002, ES2005-2010, ES2012, ES2013, ES2015, ES2016, IS1000-1007, TS3005, TS3008-3012 (98 meetings)
Evaluation set: ES2003, ES2011, IS1008, TS3004, TS3006 (20 meetings)
Development set: ES2004, ES2014, IS1009, TS3003, TS3007 (20 meetings)

The training set contains 465.478 words, the evaluation set 106.742 words and the development set contains 99.372 words [1]. For all the words, begin- and endtime information is available as well as the person who uttered the word and his/her role in the meeting (either Project Manager, Industrial Designer, Marketing Expert or User Interface designer). Also the wave signals of all the meetings and for every participant are available, which will be used for prosodic feature extraction. All annotations are hand transcribed.

---

[1] For this research, the evaluation-, and development sets are switched around from the standard AMI configuration.

3   Definition of Features

The input for the classifier is a feature-vector for each word in the corpus. Features are derived from the word itself, timing and prosodic information. The types of features that have been used in other work on DA segmentation will be used, as well as some features that are introduced here.

Next follows a list of all the features used in this project. The number $(\#x)$ is used throughout the article to identify the feature.

3.1   Time Related Features

Features derived from the start- and end times of the words in the corpus:

- **#1. Pause between the words:** The duration between the starttime of the current word and the endtime of the last word by the same speaker.
- **#2. Pause nominal:** A 'boolean feature', *pause* or *no pause*. Note that due to forced time alignment in the AMI corpus, all small pauses between words have been truncated to zero.
- **#3. Duration of word:** Self-explanatory.
- **#4. Mean duration of word:** The average duration of this word in the whole training set.
- **#5. Relative duration of word:** The duration of the word minus the mean duration of the word.

3.2   Word Related Features

Features derived from the words themselves.

- **#6. Current word:** The word itself. Because most classifiers cannot handle String input, the feature is converted into a nominal feature for each word in the corpus (e.g. 'current_word_hello' {Yes,No}). Only words that occur more than 100 times are considered (452 in total)[2].
- **#7. Next word:** The next word from the same speaker (with frequency of 100 or more).
- **#8. Previous word:** The previous word from the same speaker (with frequency of 100 or more).
- **#9. Part-of-Speech Current word:** A part of speech tag given to the current word. The word is tagged by the Stanford Part-Of-Speech Tagger[3], where the input to the tagger is the current word and the surrounding 6 words. This window of 7 words is also used in e.g. [8]. The tagger uses the Penn Treebank English tagset, which is a commonly used tagset consisting of 37 tags [9].
- **#10. PoS Previous word:** The Part-Of-Speech tag for the word preceding the current word (Penn Treebank Tagset).

---

[2] Experiments have shown that less frequently occuring words contain no information on segment boundaries.

[3] http://nlp.stanford.edu/software/tagger.shtml

- **#11. PoS Next word:** The Part-Of-Speech tag for the word following the current word (Penn Treebank Tagset).
- **#12. #13. #14. PoS Reduced Tagset:** Intuitively, a 37-tag tagset is too fine grained for the DA segmentation task. The Penn Treebank set has been mapped to a 6 tag set: *Verbs, Nouns, Adjectives, Adverbs, WH-words* and *Other*. Feature #12 is the current PoS tag using this reduced tagset, feature #13 the PoS of the previous word and feature #14 that of the next word.
- **#15. #16. #17. PoS with keywords:** These three features, for the current word, previous word and next word respectively, use the reduced tagset but extended with certain important keywords. This approach is analogous to [3], where some words get their own tag. Preliminary experiments show that the most important cue words for a segment border are: '*yeah*', '*so*', '*okay*', '*but*' and '*and*', so these get their own tag.
- **#18. Word repeat:** True, if the current word is the same as the next word, false otherwise.
- **#19. Word repeat 2:** True, if the current word is the same as the previous word, false otherwise.

3.3 Prosodic Features

Features derived from the word pitch and energy information[4]. All values have been normalized to the microphones.

- **#20. #21. #22. Pitch Features:** The minimum-, maximum- and mean pitch respectively.
- **#23. #24. #25. Energy Features:** The minimum,- maximum- and mean energy respectively.
- **#26. Speechflow Past:** This feature defines a 'talking speed' over the current word W_0 and the words W_{-1}, W_{-2} and W_{-3}. The feature is the total time of those 4 words (including pauses in between them), divided by the total number of syllables in the words.
- **#27. Speechflow Future:** The talking speed over the future 3 words: the time of words $W_0 - W_3$ divided by the total number of syllables in those words.
- **#28. Speechflow Change:** Substract feature #27 from feature #26.

3.4 Online Features

The following four features must be calculated during the classification because their value depends on previously assigned borders.

- **#29. Number of words in previous segment:** Self-explanatory.
- **#30. Distance (number of words) to the last segment:** A counter that keeps track how far this word is away from the last assigned border.

---

[4] Thanks to Gabriel Murray for supplying the scripts and to Sebastian Germesin for the word-alignment.

- **#31. Relative position of word inside segment:** Analogous to feature #30 only now the counter counts blocks of 5 words, see [10].
- **#32. Time interval of current word to last segment:** The total time between the end of the last segment border and the beginning of the current word.

4   Feature Selection Results

The goal of the feature selection phase is to see what the influence of individual features is, as well as to see how certain combinations of features influence the classifier performance. There are 32 different features, three of which (the word features) are expanded to one feature for every frequently occuring word. This makes the total feature vector 1309-dimensional. To find an optimal feature subset within this space is computationally impossible (2^{1309} possibilities), so the first step is to filter out those features that contain little information. To do this, the InfoGain Attribute Evaluator from WEKA[5] is used. This method calculates the probability of an instance being a segment border (prior probability) and compares this to the probability of a segment border given that a feature has a certain value. The higher the change in probability, the more useful this feature is. The results of the InfoGain ranking top 30 can be seen in Table 1.

In the second step of the feature selection phase, a BayesNet classifier has been repeatedly trained and evaluated with different feature subsets, taken from the best 30 features (Table 1). Because an exhaustive subset evaluation is still impossible to do, feature subsets are manually chosen and expanded upon, until all options that are likely to improve the results have been tried. A total of 528

Table 1. Result of the Information Gain ranking algorithm on all features

Rank	Feature	Infogain	Rank	Feature	Infogain
1	#1	0.2462	16	#8 (yeah)	0.0260
2	#2	0.2399	17	#11	0.0213
3	#4	0.2191	18	#27	0.0190
4	#5	0.1373	19	#6 (so)	0.0152
5	#26	0.1311	20	#30	0.0152
6	#32	0.1066	21	#6 (okay)	0.0139
7	#15	0.0818	22	#8 (okay)	0.0114
8	#16	0.0664	23	#25	0.0107
9	#9	0.0517	24	#17	0.0106
10	#10	0.0490	25	#6 (but)	0.0102
11	#28	0.0461	26	#6 (and)	0.0088
12	#13	0.0424	27	#12	0.0086
13	#6 (yeah)	0.0347	28	#21	0.0084
14	#29	0.0323	29	#6 (mm-hmm)	0.0084
15	#23	0.0308	30	#6 (mm)	0.0078

---

[5] http://www.cs.waikato.ac.nz/ml/weka/

Table 2. Best Performing Feature Subset for Bayesian Network Classifier

ID	Feature
#1	Pause between the words
#2	Pause nominal
#4	Mean duration of word
#6	Current word (mm-hmm, but, yeah, so, okay, and)
#8	Previous word (okay)
#10	PoS Previous word
#11	Pos Next word
#16	Pos Previous word (with keywords)
#23	Minimum Energy
#25	Mean Energy
#28	Speechflow change
#32	Time interval of current word to last segment

experiments have been done, and the resulting best performing subset is seen in Table 2.

This feature set achieved an F-measure of **0.75** with **0.79** precision and **0.72** recall. There are a few interesting things about this set. First, the *pause* and the *nominal pause* (#1 and #2) seem to contribute both, even though they are obviously correlated. Leaving one of them out lowers the performance of the classifier. Second, the Part-of-Speech tags of the previous and next word (#10 and #11) are selected, but not that of the current word (this doesn't seem intuitive). Third, in contrast to the literature, the words of the Part-of-Speech tagset enhanced with keywords (#15, #16 and #17) are better added as individual features, instead of incorporating it in a PoS-feature like in [3].

5   Classifier Experiments

Bayesian Networks are just one of many possible techniques for building a machine classifier. To get a quick overview of how other classifiers handle the task of DA segmentation, a number of different classifiers have been trained and tested. An exhaustive search in the feature - classifier - parameter space is extremely time consuming, therefore we save time by a) using default classifier parameters and b) use only 50.000 training instances[6]. Note that different classifiers may be affected differently by size of training set, parameter optimization and feature sets, so optimally these should all be varied [11]. In these experiments, the 97 best performing feature sets[7] have been fed to the different classifiers. The results are reported for the best feature vector (F-measure) for every classifier (see Table 3). The names of the classifiers in Table 3 refer to the names of the WEKA classes that implement them.

---

[6] Experiments showed that after 50.000 instances, no significant improvements in results could be noticed with a Bayesian Network classifier.

[7] All scoring better than pause feature alone.

Table 3. Classifier experiment results

Classifier	F-measure		Classifier	F-measure
LMT	0.76		DecisionTable	0.73
J48	0.75		VotedPerceptron	0.73
NBTree	0.75		SimpleLogistic	0.73
ADTree	0.75		SMO (Poly)	0.73
SimpleCart	0.75		SMO (RBF)	0.73
PART	0.75		Ridor	0.73
BayesNet	0.75		RBFNetwork	0.73
REPTree	0.75		NNge	0.70
...	...		...	...
Logistic	0.73		HyperPipes	0.27

Many of these classifers perform in line with the Bayesian Network classifier, whereas the variance in results is much larger when changing the feature set. This shows that changing the classification method is far less significant than optimizing features. It is unclear whether any of the classifiers score significantly better than the BayesNet classifier, but because this is only an exploratory experiment we don't worry about that now and continue the experiments using Bayesian Networks.

6   Evaluation

In order to determine how good the results are, they are compared to a baseline and a theorized top score, both based on the intrinsic properties of the task. The baseline is defined by a least-effort method. The 'maximum achievable score' is based on the intrinsic vagueness of the Dialogue Act problem by looking at the inter-annotator confusion analysis of Dialogue Act segmentation in [1]. The least effort, or baseline classifier consists of a single rule: *if there is a pause between two words, the second word is the start of a new Dialogue Act.* See Table 4 for a summary of the results [8].

To answer the question how good a 0.05 improvement on the baseline is, we must hypothesize a roof for the results. The best score we can expect from an

Table 4. Result overview for evaluation- and test set, including baseline, using BayesNet classifier

Set	Instances	Acc.	Prec.	Recall	F	NIST-SU
Development	99372	0.93	0.79	0.72	0.75	0.47
Evaluation	106742	0.92	0.79	0.72	0.76	0.47
Baseline	106742	0.92	0.97	0.55	0.70	0.47

---

[8] The added "NIST Sentence-like Units" error metric is used in many other publications. It is the total number of false positives and false negatives, divided by the total number of boundaries in the reference data.

Table 5. Recall/Precision and average F-score values for inter-annotator segmentation

	dha	dha-c	mar	s95	s95-c	vka	**Avg. F-score**
dha	–	0.91	0.93	0.84	0.92	0.91	**0.86**
dha-c	0.93	–	0.94	0.84	0.92	0.91	**0.87**
mar	0.77	0.79	–	0.76	0.80	0.86	**0.85**
s95	0.81	0.83	0.89	–	0.85	0.87	**0.82**
s95-c	0.89	0.91	0.94	0.85	–	0.92	**0.87**
vka	0.72	0.74	0.83	0.72	0.75	–	**0.82**
Total average F-score:							**0.85**

automatic Dialogue Act segmenter depends on how "vague" a segment boundary is defined, or what the intrinsic difficulty of the task is. As a best possible score we take the results from [1] on inter-annotator confusion analysis. Table 5 shows the recall/precision values between two different annotators if one is taken as the gold-standard and the other as the "classifier output". The table is based on the IS1003d meeting which has been annotated by four different annotators.

The last column for each row contains the average F-measure for the annotator on that row with all the other annotators. The total average F-score for all annotator pairs is 0.85. This can be seen as a maximum achievable score. Note that the argument that a classifier is capable of learning through noise, and thus perform better may be true, but this is not reflected in F-score. Most importantly, this puts our results of around 0.76 into perspective: on a scale from 0.70 to 0.85, we're achieving only one third of what is possible!

6.1 Detailed Error Analysis

To pinpoint where we can improve the performance of our classifier, and see how representative the F-score measure is for this taks, we take a look at the output it produces. Because the definition of a Dialogue Act is not perfectly defined, some of the output may mismatch that of the gold standard, but could still be considered correct. Table 6 lists the words that are most frequently incorrectly classified.

It is interesting to see that the words 'yeah', 'so', 'okay', 'but' and 'and' that have previously been proved to be useful features, now all occur in the top 6 of most frequently occuring errors. They all have word-error percentages between 20% and 35% and the six words make up 42% of the total amount of errors made by the classifier. The first 20 words cover 70% of the total errors, while the other 30% is covered by 507 other words. This shows that a large improvement can be gained by looking at a small number of words. Therefore, we take a closer look at the 6 words that cause 42% of the errors. We distinguish between errors that are not actually harmful, like not splitting up an *"um - yeah"* into two segments, and *real errors* like not to make the split in *"...we'll discuss that - and then I just wanna mention some new project requirements..."*. For the following 6 words, the results of 100 false positive, and 100 false negative error cases were

Table 6. Word error distribution (evaluation set)

word	occurence	total errors	error percentage	false positives	false negatives	true positives	true negatives
and	2160	761	35%	531 (24%)	230 (11%)	719	680
yeah	3437	675	20%	629 (19%)	46 (1%)	2640	122
i	2471	552	22%	82 (3%)	470 (19%)	472	1447
so	1667	470	28%	395 (24%)	75 (4%)	1003	194
okay	1303	410	31%	393 (30%)	17 (1%)	823	70
but	975	322	33%	274 (28%)	48 (5%)	603	50
um	1205	290	24%	126 (10%)	164 (14%)	375	540
uh	2980	268	9%	42 (1%)	226 (8%)	333	2379
you	2359	219	9%	18 (0%)	201 (9%)	118	2022
we	1677	196	12%	9 (1%)	187 (11%)	72	1409
it's	1076	177	16%	29 (2%)	148 (14%)	166	733
that's	727	163	22%	42 (5%)	121 (17%)	112	452
the	4753	145	3%	13 (0%)	132 (3%)	121	4487
or	681	137	20%	17 (2%)	120 (18%)	57	487
it	2157	117	5%	1 (0%)	116 (5%)	85	1955

closely examined. For every word, some basic cases or rules are identified that could help in improving the segmenter.

The 'and' case: For the false positives, 29% of the errors were not considered harmful. All non-harmful cases can be described as belonging to the following class:

- **Disfluency class:** cases were the word is preceded by a disfluency ("um", false start, etc...). The classifier and gold standard segmentation often do not agree on whether the disfluency is part of the previous or the next segment (or is a segment in itself). For example: "...I mean fr - and from the point of view ...", where the classifier seperates the false start, but the annotator did not.

The remaining real errors largely corresponded to one of the following two classes:

- **'And such and so' class:** cases of "... and such", "... and so on", "... and stuff". In these cases, there probably should not be a boundary.
- **'Fruit and Vegetables' class:** most of the false positives are related to splitting a summation of items into two segments, like: "[research] and [development]", "[my brother] and [my dad]", "[up] and [down]". But some of the examples are a bit more complex, like: "[the actual lcd] and [maybe to a certain extent the joystick]".

The 'yeah' case: Looking at the examples for 'yeah' is unfortunately quite uninformative most of the times.

The 'I' case: Approximately one third of the FP's can be seen as non-harmful and can be categorized in the same "disfluency class" as for the 'and' cases. For the real errors, about 55% of the errors belong to this class:

- **'Yeah I class':** an 'I' following a 'yeah' or sometimes an 'okay', as in "...yeah I think so". There is no pause between the 'yeah' and the 'i', so the 'yeah' is not just a short backchannel, but part of the statement. In this case the 'I' should not be tagged as boundary.

The 'so' case: The FN's can sometimes be considered non-harmful because they are close to "um's". For the FP's, 47% of the errors can be seen as non-harmful and can be attributed to the "disfluency class". For the actual errors, there are a few cases that could be handled differently:

- **non-Consequently class:** The word 'so' is often used as a conjunction, like: "...so a small speaker you mean...". These cases are likely DA segment boundary candidates. But the word 'so' can also be used in other cases like "...so far so good...", "...i think so...", or "...that's so great...". In these cases it is far less likely to be a segment boundary.

The 'okay' case: Half of the FP's can be subcategorized in the following two classes:

- **Double-positive class:** 24% of the FP's are examples where the classifier splits a double-backchannel or "positive expression" into two, like: "...yeah okay...", "...right okay..." or "...okay okay...".
- **Uhm-okay class:** 18% of the false positives are cases where a sort of 'uhm' preceding an 'okay' is split in two; for example: "...oh okay...', "...uh okay ..." or ""...hmm okay". These are considered non-harmful errors.

The 'but' case: For the FN's, 9 out of the 48 errors can not really be considered harmful, because the 'but' has no real meaning. It is used as a filler/disfluency, where sometimes it is considered as a seperate segment, and sometimes it is part of the previous or next segment. For the FP's, 27% can be seen as "disfluency class", while 21% can be categorized as follows:

- **Yeah but class:** For example a false split between "...yeah - but...", "...no - but..." or "...okay - but...". In these cases there should generally be no boundary.

The detailed analysis of these error cases could be used to create a rule-based pre- or post processing system to aid the automatic segmentation methods. A lot of errors are produced by disfluency, so a preprocessing step to remove disfluency could also help increase performance (see [12]).

7   Conclusion

The experiments done on DA segmentation on the AMI corpus show that reasonable results can be achieved using a variety of word related, time related, online-, and prosodic features. More importantly it is shown that there are still quite a lot of things to be done that can possibly increase performance. The classifier experiments in Section 5 indicate that a lot of different classifiers already perform well with default settings. Solving the search problem of a combined optimization of feature subsets and classifier parameters could possible lead to a significant improvement in results, as [11] points out.

Further improvements could be achieved by optimizing the feature representation. The Part-of-Speech feature, for example, has proven to be useful, even though the tag-set has not been changed for the specific task of segmentation. A detailed analysis of the Part-of-Speech of words near segment boundary could lead to a better tag-set, and could possibly improve the overall classifier performance. The same goes for all the numeric features like pause, "speechflow" and the prosodic features, where optimal binning configurations can be found using simple brute-force techniques, such as in [13].

The detailed analysis of frequently occuring errors in Section 6.1 could provide a basis for a rule-based pre-processing of the data. Because the six words mentioned in this section make up such a large amount of the errors produced by the classifier, more attention should definitely be put into handling these cases. Since the words occur so frequently, there is enough data to train classifiers specifically for these words. In combination with rules covering the identified error classes, some improvement of the overall results can be expected.

Another important conclusion that can be drawn from the error analysis is that disfluency in the spontaneous speech in the AMI corpus causes a lot of gold-standard errors. These errors are not always expected to be very harmful, but it is worth looking into a way of avoiding them. A preprocessing step to correct disfluency errors might be very helpful for these types of errors.

Besides the abovementioned points that still need to be addressed, future work on Dialogue Act segmentation should include features that look at the interaction between speakers, as well as multimodal features like gaze, gestures and movement.

Acknowledgement

This work is supported by the European IST Programme Project FP6-0033812. The main author's contributions where done while on a traineeship at DFKI, Saarbrücken, Germany. Thanks to Peter Poller, Tilman Becker, Sebastian Germesin, Rieks op den Akker, Dirk Heylen and Dennis Reidsma.

References

[1] AMIDA: Augmented Multiparty Interaction with Distance Acces Deliverable D5.2: Report on multimodal content abstraction. Technical report, Brno University of Technology, DFKI, ICSI, IDIAP, TNO, University of Edinburgh, University of Twente and University of Sheffield (2007)

[2] Zimmermann, M., Liu, Y., Shriberg, E., Stolcke, A.: Toward joint segmentation and classification of dialog acts in multiparty meetings. In: Renals, S., Bengio, S. (eds.) MLMI 2005. LNCS, vol. 3869, pp. 187–193. Springer, Heidelberg (2006)

[3] Stolcke, A., Shriberg, E.: Automatic linguistic segmentation of conversational speech. In: Proc. ICSLP 1996, Philadelphia, PA, vol. 2, pp. 1005–1008 (1996)

[4] Kolář, J., Liu, Y., Shriberg, E.: Speaker adaptation of language models for automatic dialog act segmentation of meetings (2007)

[5] Zimmermann, M., Stolcke, A., Shriberg, E.: Joint segmentation and classification of dialog acts in multiparty meetings. In: Proc. IEEE ICASSP, Toulouse, France, vol. 1, pp. 581–584 (2006)

[6] Cuendet, S., Shriberg, E., Favre, B., Fung, J., Hakkani-Tur, D.: An analysis of sentence segmentation features for broadcast news, broadcast conversations, and meetings. In: Proceedings SIGIR Workshop on Searching Conversational Spontaneous Speech, Amsterdam, Netherlands, pp. 37–43 (2007)

[7] McCowan, I., et al.: The AMI meeting corpus. In: Proceedings of the 5th International Conference on Methods and Techniques in Behavioral Research (2005)

[8] Poel, M., Stegeman, L., den op Akker, R.: A Support Vector Machine Approach to Dutch Part-of-Speech Tagging. In: R. Berthold, M., Shawe-Taylor, J., Lavrač, N. (eds.) IDA 2007. LNCS, vol. 4723, pp. 274–283. Springer, Heidelberg (2007)

[9] Marcus, M.P., Santorini, B., Marcinkiewicz, M.A.: Building a large annotated corpus of english: The penn treebank. Computational Linguistics 19(2), 313–330 (1994)

[10] Dielmann, A., Renals, S.: DBN based joint dialogue act recognition of multiparty meetings. In: Proc. IEEE ICASSP, vol. 4, pp. 133–136 (2007)

[11] Daelemans, W., Hoste, V., De Meulder, F., Naudts, B.: Combined optimization of feature selection and algorithm parameter interaction in machine learning of language. In: Lavrač, N., Gamberger, D., Todorovski, L., Blockeel, H. (eds.) ECML 2003. LNCS (LNAI), vol. 2837, pp. 84–95. Springer, Heidelberg (2003)

[12] Germesin, S., Becker, T., Poller, P.: Hybrid multi-step disfluency detection. In: MLMI 2008 (2008)

[13] Webb, N., Hepple, M., Wilks, Y.: Empirical determination of thresholds for optimal dialogue act classification (2005)

Detecting Action Items in Meetings

Gabriel Murray[1] and Steve Renals[2]

[1] University of British Columbia, Vancouver, Canada
gabrielm@cs.ubc.ca
[2] University of Edinburgh, Edinburgh, Scotland
s.renals@ed.ac.uk

Abstract. We present a method for detecting action items in spontaneous meeting speech. Using a supervised approach incorporating prosodic, lexical and structural features, we can classify such items with a high degree of accuracy. We also examine how well various feature subclasses can perform this task on their own.

1 Introduction

Meetings tend to occur in series with regular intervals. While some meetings will be one-off occasions, many others occur weekly or bi-weekly with more or less the same group of participants. As a consequence, the discussion within a given meeting might reference the discussion from a previous meeting, or describe what will happen between the current and upcoming meetings. It is this latter phenomenon of stated *action items* that we are interested in detecting in the current research. Providing a meeting participant with such action items from a previous meeting would be very useful for reminding the individual of what needs to be accomplished before the upcoming meeting.

In this paper we describe a supervised method for detecting these action items, presenting results on a corpus of spontaneous meeting speech. We analyze how well prosodic, lexical, structural and speaker-related features aid this particular task.

2 Experimental Setup

In this section we describe the meeting corpus used, the relevant action item annotations, and the classifier used for these experiments.

2.1 Corpora

For these experiments, we use the AMI meetings corpus [1]. The corpus consists of about 100 hours of recorded and annotated meetings, divided into *scenario* and *non-scenario* meetings. In the scenario portion, groups of four participants role-play in a series of four meetings. Here we use only the scenario meetings from the AMI corpus, numbering 138 in total, with 20 meetings used for our test set. The participants consist of both native and non-native English speakers.

The corpus contains both hand-authored and automatic speech recognition (ASR) transcripts. The ASR system employs the standard framework of context-dependent HMM/GMM acoustic modelling and trigram language models, and features a word error rate (WER) of 38.9%.

A. Popescu-Belis and R. Stiefelhagen (Eds.): MLMI 2008, LNCS 5237, pp. 208–213, 2008.

2.2 Annotation

For each meeting in the corpus, multiple human annotators are asked to write abstractive summaries of the meeting discussion. The abstract summary consists of a general abstract section in addition to abstract subsections describing *decisions*, *actions* and *problems* from the meeting. The annotators then go through the meeting transcript and link meeting dialogue acts (DAs) to sentences within the abstract, creating a many-to-many mapping of sentences and DAs. We can then determine which DAs represent action items by whether or not they are linked to sentences in the *actions* portion of the transcript. The instruction given to the annotators for writing the *actions* subsection was to "name the next steps that each member of the group will take until the next meeting." There is an average of just under three action item DAs per meeting, but the number depends greatly on which meeting in the series it is – for example, the final meetings in each series contain few action items.

Two examples of action item DAs are given below, taken from meeting IS1003c:

- Speaker A: So you will have Baba and David Jordan you will have to work together on the prototype
- Speaker A: and you will have next time to show us modelling a clay remote control

In these experiments we employed a manual DA segmentation, although automatic approaches are available [3].

2.3 Classifier

The classifier used is the *liblinear* logistic regression classifier[1]. The *liblinear* toolkit incorporates simple feature subset selection based on calculating the f statistic for each feature and performing cross-validation with subsets of various sizes, comparing the resultant balanced accuracy scores. The f statistic for each feature is first calculated [2], and then feature subsets of size n are tried, where n equals 19, 17, 15, 13, 11, 9, 7, 5, and 3, with the n best features included at each step based on the f statistic. The feature subset size with the highest balanced accuracy during cross-validation is selected as the feature set for training. The logistic regression model is then trained on the training data using that subset.

3 Features Description

Table 1 lists and briefly describes the set of the features used. The prosodic features consist of energy , F0, pause, duration and a rate-of-speech measure. We calculate both the duration of the complete DA, as well as of the uninterrupted portion. The structural features include the DA's position in the meeting and position within the speaker's turn (which may contain multiple DAs). There are two measures of speaker dominance: the dominance of the speaker in terms of meeting DAs and in terms of total speaking time. There are two term-weighting metrics, *tf.idf* an d *su.idf*, the former favoring words that

---

[1] http://www.csie.ntu.edu.tw/ cjlin/liblinear/

Table 1. Features Key

Feature ID	Description
Prosodic Features	
ENMN	mean energy
F0MN	mean F0
ENMX	max energy
F0MX	max F0
F0SD	F0 stdev.
PPAU	precedent pause
SPAU	subsequent pause
ROS	rate of speech
Structural Features	
MPOS	meeting position
TPOS	turn position
Speaker Features	
DOMD	speaker dominance (DAs)
DOMT	speaker dominance (seconds)
Length Features	
DDUR	DA duration
UINT	uninterrupted length
WCNT	number of words
Lexical Features	
SUI	su.idf sum
TFI	tf.idf sum
ACUE	abstractive cuewords
FPAU	filled pauses

are frequent in the given document but rare across all documents, and the latter favoring words that are used with varying frequency by the different speakers [9]. We also include the number of filled pauses in the dialogue act, and the number of abstractive cuewords. These abstractive cuewords are automatically derived from the training data. We examine terms that occur often in the abstracts of meetings but less often in the *extracts* of meetings. We score each word according to the ratio of these two frequencies,

$$TF(t, j)/TF(t, k)$$

where $TF(t, j)$ is the frequency of term t in the set of abstracts j from the training set meetings and $TF(t, k)$ is the frequency of term t in the set of extracts k from the training set meetings. These scores are used to rank the words from most abstractive to least abstractive, and we keep the top 50 words as our list of meta cuewords. The top 5 abstractive cuewords are "team", "group", "specialist", "member", and "manager." For both the manual and ASR feature databases, each DA then has a feature indicating how many of these high-level terms it contains.

4   Results

Figure 1 depicts the f statistics for the features used. The most interesting result is that the abstractive cuewords feature is by far the best single feature according to this measure. The position of the DA in the meeting is also a very useful feature for this task.

Using manual transcripts, the optimal feature set as determined by feature subset selection is comprised of only three features: abstractive cuewords, DA position in meeting, and DA duration. However, with ASR there is a total of nine features selected: abstractive cuewords, DA position in meeting, uninterrupted length, word count, duration, *tf.idf* score, *su.idf* score, and both measures of speaker dominance.

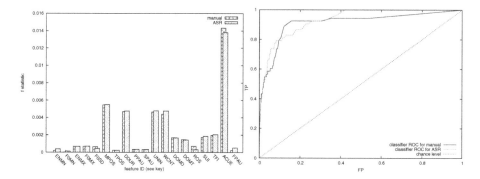

Fig. 1. f statistics for AMI database features   **Fig. 2.** Classifier ROC Curves, Manual/ASR

The action item DAs tend to have higher mean and max energy, and higher max F0 and F0 standard deviation than in the negative class. They tend to occur very late in the meeting and also later in a given speaker's turn. They have a much longer duration, higher word count, longer precedent pause, and shorter subsequent pause. They tend to be spoken by the meeting participants who are more dominant in the meeting overall. The rate-of-speech is higher, as are both term-weight scores. The number of abstractive cuewords is dramatically higher, and there tend to be more filled pauses.

Figure 2 shows the ROC curves for both manual and ASR transcripts. The area under the ROC curve (AUROC) is very high in each case: 0.91 for manual transcripts and 0.93 for ASR transcripts, with 0.50 equal to chance performance. This shows that action items can be detected with a high degree of accuracy, and that the classification is robust to ASR errors. This resilience to ASR errors is similar to the finding in automatic speech summarization that summarization results do not greatly deteriorate on speech recognition output [10,13].

4.1 Feature Subsets

Though the f statistics provide us with interesting information about the usefulness of individual features, we would also like to analyze how particular feature *classes* aid the detection of action items. We therefore separate the features into five classes: prosodic, structural, speaker, length and lexical features. Note that we do not consider DA duration and uninterrupted duration to be prosodic features, but rather length features along with DA word count. We then build logistic regression classifiers for each feature class and run the classifiers over the test data. Figure 3 shows the ROC curves and the AUROCs for the feature classes using manual transcripts. The structural class performs the best, with an AUROC of 0.93. This is somewhat surprising, as the structural class contains only two features: DA position in the meeting and DA position in the turn. The length and lexical classes are comparable to each other, with AUROCs of 0.80, while prosodic and speaker features are less useful on their own.

The story is much the same with ASR transcripts. Structural features again are the best performing feature class, and all of the feature classes are robust to ASR errors. Figure 4 shows the ROC curves and AUROCs for ASR transcripts.

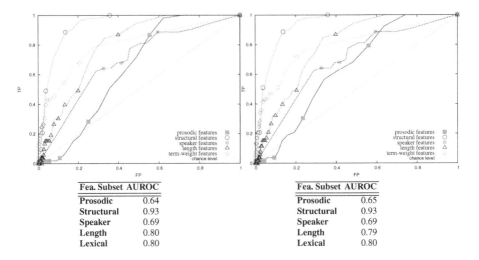

Fea. Subset	AUROC
Prosodic	0.64
Structural	0.93
Speaker	0.69
Length	0.80
Lexical	0.80

Fea. Subset	AUROC
Prosodic	0.65
Structural	0.93
Speaker	0.69
Length	0.79
Lexical	0.80

Fig. 3. AUROC Values, Manual Transcripts   **Fig. 4.** AUROC Values, ASR Transcripts

5   Discussion

It is encouraging to find that action items can be detected with a high degree of accuracy with the given features. Even a small set of lexical and structural features can yield very good performance. It is interesting to note that while abstractive cuewords are the best single feature according to the f statistic, the best feature class is the structural class. Using only information about DA position in the meeting and in the speaker's turn is still enough to detect the action items. Prosodic features are less useful for this task than for speech summarization work [7,8]. While none of the prosodic features are selected for either manual or ASR transcripts, we do however show that they perform well above chance level when used on their own.

Related work has been carried out by Purver et al. [11,12] as part of the CALO project, using ICSI meeting data [6]. In that research, the authors used a variety of lexical, structural and prosodic features to detect not just action items in general, but subclasses of action items such as explicit mentions of the action item timeframe and the action item "owner." Like automatic decision detection [5], this work can also be considered a type of focused extractive summarization [4,10]. By extracting DAs based on more meaningful criteria than simply informativeness/uninformativeness distinctions, we can create structured or hierarchical summaries.

6   Conclusion

We have shown that action items can be detected with high accuracy using structural and lexical cues. We have also described how these action items are realized in terms of structural, lexical, prosodic, and speaker features. Breaking the features into several classes, we have assessed the performance of each class on its own.

Acknowledgements. This work is supported by the European IST Programme Project AMIDA (FP6-0033812). Thanks to the AMI-ASR team for providing the ASR.

References

1. Carletta, J., Ashby, S., Bourban, S., Flynn, M., Guillemot, M., Hain, T., Kadlec, J., Karaiskos, V., Kraaij, W., Kronenthal, M., Lathoud, G., Lincoln, M., Lisowska, A., McCowan, I., Post, W., Reidsma, D., Wellner, P.: The AMI meeting corpus: A pre-announcement. In: Renals, S., Bengio, S. (eds.) MLMI 2005. LNCS, vol. 3869, pp. 28–39. Springer, Heidelberg (2006)
2. Chen, Y.-W., Lin, C.-J.: Combining SVMs with various feature selection strategies. In: Guyon, I., Gunn, S., Nikravesh, M., Zadeh, L. (eds.) Feature extraction, foundations and applications. Springer, Heidelberg (2006)
3. Dielmann, A., Renals, S.: DBN based joint dialogue act recognition of multiparty meetings. In: Proc. of ICASSP 2007, Honolulu, USA, pp. 133–136 (2007)
4. Galley, M.: A skip-chain conditional random field for ranking meeting utterances by importance. In: Proc. of EMNLP 2006, Sydney, Australia, pp. 364–372 (2006)
5. Hsueh, P.-Y., Kilgour, J., Carletta, J., Moore, J., Renals, S.: Automatic decision detection in meeting speech. In: Popescu-Belis, A., Renals, S., Bourlard, H. (eds.) MLMI 2007. LNCS, vol. 4892. Springer, Heidelberg (2008)
6. Janin, A., Baron, D., Edwards, J., Ellis, D., Gelbart, D., Morgan, N., Peskin, B., Pfau, T., Shriberg, E., Stolcke, A., Wooters, C.: The ICSI meeting corpus. In: Proc. of IEEE ICASSP 2003, Hong Kong, China, pp. 364–367 (2003)
7. Maskey, S., Hirschberg, J.: Comparing lexial, acoustic/prosodic, discourse and structural features for speech summarization. In: Proc. of Interspeech 2005, Lisbon, Portugal, pp. 621–624 (2005)
8. Murray, G.: Using Speech-Specific Features for Automatic Speech Summarization. PhD thesis, University of Edinburgh (2007)
9. Murray, G., Renals, S.: Term-weighting for summarization of multi-party spoken dialogues. In: Popescu-Belis, A., Renals, S., Bourlard, H. (eds.) MLMI 2007. LNCS, vol. 4892, pp. 155–166. Springer, Heidelberg (2008)
10. Murray, G., Renals, S., Carletta, J.: Extractive summarization of meeting recordings. In: Proc. of Interspeech 2005, Lisbon, Portugal, pp. 593–596 (2005)
11. Purver, M., Dowding, J., Niekrasz, J., Ehlen, P., Noorbaloochi, S.: Detecting and summarizing action items in multi-party dialogue. In: Proc. of the 9th SIGdial Workshop on Discourse and Dialogue, Antwerp, Belgium (2007)
12. Purver, M., Ehlen, P., Niekrasz, J.: Detecting action items in multi-party meetings: Annotation and initial experiments. In: Renals, S., Bengio, S., Fiscus, J.G. (eds.) MLMI 2006. LNCS, vol. 4299, pp. 200–211. Springer, Heidelberg (2006)
13. Valenza, R., Robinson, T., Hickey, M., Tucker, R.: Summarization of spoken audio through information extraction. In: Proc. of the ESCA Workshop on Accessing Information in Spoken Audio, Cambridge, UK, pp. 111–116 (1999)

Modeling Topic and Role Information in Meetings Using the Hierarchical Dirichlet Process

Songfang Huang and Steve Renals

The Centre for Speech Technology Research
University of Edinburgh, Edinburgh, EH8 9LW, UK
{s.f.huang,s.renals}@ed.ac.uk

Abstract. In this paper, we address the modeling of topic and role information in multiparty meetings, via a nonparametric Bayesian model called the hierarchical Dirichlet process. This model provides a powerful solution to topic modeling and a flexible framework for the incorporation of other cues such as speaker role information. We present our modeling framework for topic and role on the AMI Meeting Corpus, and illustrate the effectiveness of the approach in the context of adapting a baseline language model in a large-vocabulary automatic speech recognition system for multiparty meetings. The adapted LM produces significant improvements in terms of both perplexity and word error rate.

1 Introduction

A language model (LM) aims to provide a predictive probability distribution for the next word based on a history of previously observed words. The n-gram model, which forms the conventional approach to language modeling in state-of-the-art automatic speech recognition (ASR) systems, simply approximates the history as the immediately preceding $n - 1$ words. Although this has been demonstrated to be a simple but effective model, the struggle to improve over it continues. Broadly speaking, such attempts focus on the improved modeling of word sequences, or on the incorporation of richer knowledge. Approaches which aim to improve on maximum likelihood n-gram models of word sequences include neural network-based models [1], latent variable models [2], and a Bayesian framework [3,4]. The exploitation of richer knowledge has included the use of morphological information in factored LMs [5], syntactic knowledge using structured LMs [6], and semantic knowledge such as topic information using Bayesian models [7].

In this paper, we investigate language modeling for ASR in multiparty meetings through the inclusion of richer knowledge in a conventional n-gram language model. We have used the AMI Meeting Corpus[1] [8], which consists of 100 hours of multimodal meeting recordings with comprehensive annotations at a number

---

[1] http://corpus.amiproject.org

A. Popescu-Belis and R. Stiefelhagen (Eds.): MLMI 2008, LNCS 5237, pp. 214–225, 2008.

of different levels. About 70% of the corpus was elicited using a design scenario, in which the four participants play the roles of project manager (PM), marketing expert (ME), user interface designer (UI), and industrial designer (ID), in an electronics company that decides to develop a new type of television remote control. Our work in this paper is motivated by the fact that the AMI Meeting Corpus has a wealth of multimodal information such as audio, video, lexical, and other high-level knowledge. From the viewpoint of language modeling, the question for us is whether there are cues beyond lexical information which can help to improve an n-gram LM. If so, then what are those cues, and how can we incorporate them into an n-gram LM? To address this question, we here focus on the modeling of topic and role information using a hierarchical Dirichlet process [9].

Consider an augmented n-gram model for ASR, with its context enriched by the inclusion of two cues from meetings: the *topic* and the speaker *role*. Unlike role, which could be seen as deterministic information available in the corpus, topic refers to the semantic context, which is typically extracted by an unsupervised approach. One popular topic model is latent Dirichlet allocation (LDA) [10], which can successfully find latent topics based on the co-occurrences of words in a 'document'. However, there are two difficulties arising from the application of LDA to language modeling of multiparty conversational speech. First, it is important to define the notion of document to which the LDA model can be applied: conversational speech consists of sequences of utterances, which do not comprise well-defined documents. Second, it is not easy to decide the number of topics in advance, a requirement for LDA.

The hierarchical Dirichlet process (HDP) [9] is a nonparametric generalization of LDA which extends the standard LDA model in two ways. First, the HDP uses a Dirichlet process prior for the topic distribution, rather than the Dirichlet distribution used in LDA. This enables the HDP to determine the number of topics required. Second, the hierarchical tree structure enables the HDP to share mixture components (topics) between groups of data. In this paper we exploit the HDP as our modeling approach for automatic topic learning. Moreover, we also find it easier to incorporate roles together with topics by expressing them as an additional level of variables into the HDP hierarchy.

Some previous work has been done in the area of combining n-gram models and topic models such as LDA and probabilistic latent semantic analysis (pLSA) for ASR on different data, for example, broadcast news [11,12], lecture recordings [13], and Japanese meetings [14]. The new ideas we exploit in this work cover the following aspects. First, we use the nonparametric HDP for topic modeling to adapt n-gram LMs. Second, we consider sequential topic modeling, and define documents for the HDP by placing a moving window over the sequences of short sentences. Third, we incorporate the role information with topic models in a hierarchical Bayesian framework. In the rest of this paper, we will review topic models, and introduce our framework for modeling topic and role information using the HDP, followed by a set of perplexity and word error rate (WER) experiments.

2   Probabilistic Topic Model

Topic models, which have received a growing interest in the machine learning community, are used in document modeling to find a latent representation connecting documents and words — the topic. In a topic model, words in a document exchangeably co-occur with each other according to their semantics, following the "bag-of-words" assumption.

Suppose there are D documents in the corpus, and W words in the vocabulary. Each document $d = 1, \ldots, D$ in the corpus is represented as a mixture of latent topics, with the mixing proportions over topics denoted by $\boldsymbol{\theta}_d$. Each topic $k = 1, \ldots, K$ in turn is a multinomial distribution over words in the vocabulary, with the vector of probabilities for words in topic k denoted by $\boldsymbol{\phi}_k$.

In this section, we review two "bag-of-word" models, LDA and the HDP, following Teh et al. [9,15,16].

2.1   Latent Dirichlet Allocation

Latent Dirichlet allocation [10] is a three-level hierarchical Bayesian model, which pioneered the use of the Dirichlet distribution for latent topics. That is, the

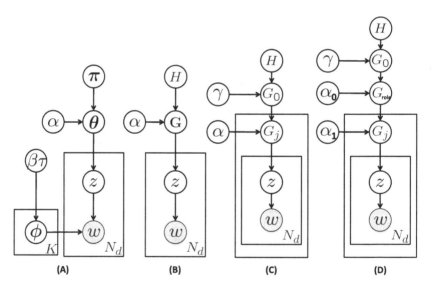

Fig. 1. Graphical model depictions for (A) latent Dirichlet allocation (finite mixture model), (B) Dirichlet process mixture model (infinite mixture model), (C) 2-level hierarchical Dirichlet process model, and (D) the role-HDP where G_{role} denotes the DP for one of the four roles (PM, ME, UI, and ID) in the AMI Meeting Corpus. Each node in the graph represents a random variable, where shading denotes an observed variable. Arrows denote dependencies among variables. Rectangles represent plates, or repeated sub-structures in the model.

topic mixture weights $\boldsymbol{\theta}_d$ for the dth document are drawn from a prior Dirichlet distribution with parameters $\alpha, \boldsymbol{\pi}$:

$$P(\boldsymbol{\theta}_d | \alpha \boldsymbol{\pi}) = \frac{\Gamma(\sum_{i=1}^{K} \alpha \pi_i)}{\prod_{i=1}^{K} \Gamma(\alpha \pi_i)} \theta_1^{\alpha \pi_1 - 1} \dots \theta_K^{\alpha \pi_K - 1} \tag{1}$$

where K is the predefined number of topics in LDA, Γ is the Gamma function, $\alpha \boldsymbol{\pi} = \{\alpha \pi_1, \dots, \alpha \pi_K\}$ represents the prior observation counts of the K latent topics with $\alpha \pi_i > 0$: $\boldsymbol{\pi}$ is the corpus-wide distribution over topics, and α is called the concentration parameter which controls the amount of variability from $\boldsymbol{\theta}_d$ to their prior mean $\boldsymbol{\pi}$.

Similarly, Dirichlet priors are placed over the parameters $\boldsymbol{\phi}_k$ with the parameters $\beta \boldsymbol{\tau}$. We write:

$$\boldsymbol{\theta}_d | \boldsymbol{\pi} \sim \mathrm{Dir}(\alpha \boldsymbol{\pi}) \qquad \boldsymbol{\phi}_k | \boldsymbol{\tau} \sim \mathrm{Dir}(\beta \boldsymbol{\tau}) \tag{2}$$

Fig. 1.(A) depicts the graphical model representation for LDA. The generative process for words in each document is as follows: first draw a topic k with probability θ_{dk}, then draw a word w with probability ϕ_{kw}. Let w_{id} be the ith word token in document d, and z_{id} the corresponding drawn topic, then we have the following multinomial distributions:

$$z_{id} | \boldsymbol{\theta}_d \sim \mathrm{Mult}(\boldsymbol{\theta}_d) \qquad w_{id} | z_{id}, \boldsymbol{\phi}_{z_{id}} \sim \mathrm{Mult}(\boldsymbol{\phi}_{z_{id}}) \tag{3}$$

2.2   Hierarchical Dirichlet Process

LDA uses Dirichlet distributed latent variables to represent shades of memberships to different cluster or topics. In the HDP nonparametric models are used to avoid the need for model selection [16]. Two extensions are made in the HDP: first the Dirichlet distributions in LDA are replaced by Dirichlet processes in the HDP as priors for topic proportions; second, the priors are arranged in a tree structure.

Dirichlet Process. The Dirichlet process (DP) is a stochastic process, first formalised in [17] for general Bayesian modeling, which has become an important prior for nonparametric models. Nonparametric models are characterised by allowing the number of model parameters to grow with the amount of training data. This helps to alleviate over- or under-fitting problems, and provides an alternative approach to parametric model selection or averaging.

A random distribution G over a space Θ is called a Dirichlet process distributed with base distribution H and concentration parameter α, if

$$(G(A_1), \dots, G(A_r)) \sim \mathrm{Dir}(\alpha H(A_1), \dots, \alpha H(A_r)) \tag{4}$$

for every finite measurable partition $A_1, \dots, A_r$ of Θ. We write this as $G \sim \mathrm{DP}(\alpha, H)$. The parameter H, a measure over Θ, is intuitively the mean of the DP. The parameter α, on the other hand, can be regarded as an inverse variance of its mass around the mean H, with larger values of α for smaller variances. More importantly in infinite mixture models, α controls the expected number of mixture components in a direct manner, with larger α implying a larger number of mixture components a priori.

Draws from a DP are composed as a weighted sum of point masses located at the previous draws $\theta_1, \ldots, \theta_n$. This leads to a constructive definition of the DP called the stick-breaking construction [18]:

$$\beta_k \sim \text{Beta}(1, \alpha) \qquad \pi_k = \beta_k \prod_{l=1}^{k-1} (1 - \beta_k) \qquad \theta_k^* \sim H \qquad G = \sum_{k=1}^{\infty} \pi_k \delta_{\theta_k^*} \qquad (5)$$

Then $G \sim \text{DP}(\alpha, H)$. θ_k^* is a unique value among $\theta_1, \ldots, \theta_n$, and $\delta_{\theta_k^*}$ denotes a point mass at θ_k^*. The construction of π can be understood as follows [15]. Starting with a stick of length 1, first break it at β_1, assign π_1 to be the length of stick just broken off. Then recursively break the other portion to obtain π_2, π_3 and so forth. The stick-breaking distribution over π is sometimes written as $\pi \sim \text{GEM}(\alpha)^2$, and satisfies $\sum_{k=1}^{\infty} \pi_k = 1$ with probability one. This definition is important for the inference for the DP.

Recall in Equation 2 for LDA, a finite-dimensional Dirichlet distribution (i.e., in which π is a K-dimensional vector) is used as prior for distribution of topic proportions. LDA, in this sense, is a finite mixture model. If we use a DP instead as prior for mixing topic proportions, that is, $\theta_d \sim \text{DP}(\alpha, H)$ where $\phi_k | H \sim \text{Dir}(\beta \tau)$, then the stick-breaking construction for $\pi \sim \text{GEM}(\alpha)$ will produce a countably infinite dimensional vector π. In this way, the number of topics in this DP-enhanced LDA model is potentially infinite, the number of topics increasing with the available data.

This model, as shown in Fig. 1.(B), is called the Dirichlet process mixture model (also known as an infinite mixture model).

Hierarchical Framework. Besides the nonparametric extension of LDA from Dirichlet distribution to Dirichlet process, Teh et al. [9] further extended the Dirichlet process mixture model from a flat structure to a hierarchical structure, called a hierarchical Dirichlet process mixture model. This extended model uses the hierarchical Dirichlet process as priors. Similar to the DP, the HDP is a prior for nonparametric Bayesian modeling. The difference is that in the HDP, it is assumed that there are groups of data, and that the infinite mixture components are shared among these groups.

Considering a simple 2-level HDP as an example, as shown is Fig. 1.(C), the HDP defines a set of random probability measure G_j, one for each group of data, and a global random probability measure G_0. The global measure G_0 is distributed as a DP with concentration parameter γ and base probability measure H, and the random measure G_j, assuming conditionally independent given G_0, are in turn distributed as a DP with concentration parameter α and base probability measure G_0:

$$G_0 | \gamma, H \sim \text{DP}(\gamma, H) \qquad G_j | \alpha, G_0 \sim \text{DP}(\alpha, G_0) \qquad (6)$$

---

[2] GEM stands for Griffiths, Engen, and McCloskey.

This results in a hierarchy of DPs, in which their dependencies are specified by arranging them in a tree structure. Although this is a 2-level example, the HDP can readily be extended to as many levels as required.

An HDP-enhanced LDA model, therefore, will have a potentially infinite number of topics, and these topics will be shared among groups of data. If an HDP is used as a prior for topic modeling, then the baseline distribution H provides the prior distribution for words in the vocabulary, i.e., $\phi_k | H \sim \text{Dir}(\beta\boldsymbol{\tau})$. The distribution G_0 varies around the prior H with the amount of variability controlled by γ, i.e., $G_0 \sim \text{DP}(\gamma, \text{Dir}(\beta\boldsymbol{\tau}))$. The actual distribution G_d for dth group of data (words in dth document in topic models) deviates from G_0, with the amount of variability controlled by α, i.e., $G_d \sim \text{DP}(\alpha, G_0)$. Together with (3), this completes the definition of an HDP-enhanced LDA topic model.

3   Modeling Topic and Role Using HDP

In this section we discuss three key questions concerning the modeling of topic and role using the HDP. First, how should a document be defined in a multiparty meeting? Second, how do we introduce role into the HDP framework? Third, how can the local estimates from an HDP be used to adapt a baseline n-gram LM for an ASR system?

Document Definition. The target application of the HDP in this paper is the adaptation of LMs for a multiparty conversational ASR system. For each sentence in the testing data, we need to find a corresponding document for the HDP, based on which topics are extracted, and then the LM is dynamically adapted according to the topic information. Documents also include information about speaker role. In the AMI Meeting Corpus, meetings are manually annotated with word transcription (in `*.words.xml`), with time information being further obtained via forced alignment. Also available in the corpus are the segment annotations (in `*.segments.xml`). Role information can be easily determined from the annotations in the corpus. We used the following procedure,

```
foreach meeting m in the corpus
    retrieve words with time and role info for m;
    align all words in m to a common timeline;
    foreach segment s in m
        st = starttime(s); et = endtime(s);
        if et-st < winlen L: st = et-L;
        foreach w in words[st:et]
            if not stopword(w): doc(s) += w;
        end
        role(s) = role assigned to most words;
    end
end
```

Fig. 2. The procedure used to define documents for the HDP/rHDP

as shown in Fig. 2, to obtain documents: for each scenario meeting, first align all the words in it along a common timeline; then for each sentence/segment, collect those non-stop words belonging to a window of length L, by backtracing from the end time of the sentence/segment, as the document. The role that has been assigned to the most of words in the window is selected as the role for that document.

By collecting all documents for meetings belonging to the training and testing data respectively, we can obtain the training data for HDP model and the testing data for perplexity evaluation. A similar idea applies to finding documents dynamically for ASR experiments. The difference is that we do not have the segment annotations in this case. Instead speech segments, obtained by either automatic or manual approaches, are used as units for finding documents as well as for ASR. In the ASR case we use an online unsupervised method: ASR hypotheses (with errors and time information) from previous segments are used to define documents for HDP inference for the current segment. In both cases above, we simply ignore those segments without corresponding documents.

Incorporation of Role Information. As a preliminary attempt, we consider the problem of introducing role into the HDP hierarchy to enable better topic modeling. In the scenario meetings of the AMI Meeting Corpus, each of the four participants in a meeting series was assigned a different role (PM, ME, UI, or ID). Since different participants have different roles to play, there may be a different topic distribution, and in turn different dominant words, specific to each role. However, we still expect topic models to work as a whole on the corpus rather than having four separate topic models. The HDP is thus an appropriate model, because it has a flexible framework to express DP dependencies using a tree structure.

Documents were defined as described above for those scenario meetings with role information, a one-to-one mapping. We grouped the documents for each of the four roles, and assigned a DP G_{role} for each role, which then served as the parent DP in the HDP hierarchy (the base probability measure) for all DPs corresponding to documents belonging to that role. To share the topics among four roles, a global DP G_0 was used as the common base probability measure for the four role DPs G_{role}. See the graphical model shown in Fig. 1.(D) for the HDP hierarchy. Formally speaking, we used a 3-level HDP, referred to as rHDP, to model topic and role information in the AMI Meeting Corpus:

$$G_0|\gamma, H \sim \mathrm{DP}(\gamma, H), G_{\mathrm{role}}|\alpha_0, G_0 \sim \mathrm{DP}(\alpha_0, G_0), G_j|\alpha_1, G_{\mathrm{role}} \sim \mathrm{DP}(\alpha_1, G_{\mathrm{role}}) \quad (7)$$

Combination with n-grams. A topic in an HDP is a multinomial distribution over words in the vocabulary (denoted as ϕ_k), which can be considered as a unigram model. To be precise, we use $P_{\mathrm{hdp}}(w|d)$ to denote the unigram probabilities obtained by the HDP based on the jth document d. The HDP probability $P_{\mathrm{hdp}}(w|d)$ is approximated as a sum over all the latent topics ϕ_k for that document, supposing there are K topics in total in the HDP at the current time:

$$P_{\mathrm{hdp}}(w|d) \approx \sum_{k=1}^{K} \phi_{kw} \cdot \theta_{dk} \qquad (8)$$

where the probability vector ϕ_k is estimated during training and remains fixed in testing, while the topic weights $\theta_d|G_0 \sim \mathrm{DP}(\alpha_0, G_0)$ are document-dependent and thus are calculated dynamically for each document. For rHDP, the difference is that the topic weights are derived from role DPs, i.e., $\theta_d|G_{\mathrm{role}} \sim \mathrm{DP}(\alpha_1, G_{\mathrm{role}})$.

As in [19], we treat $P_{\mathrm{hdp}}(w|d)$ as a dynamic marginal and use the following equation to adapt the baseline n-gram model $P_{\mathrm{back}}(w|h)$ to get an adapted n-gram $P_{\mathrm{adapt}}(w|h)$, where $z(h)$ is a normalisation factor:

$$P_{\mathrm{adapt}}(w|h) = \frac{\alpha(w)}{z(h)} \cdot P_{\mathrm{back}}(w|h) \qquad \alpha(w) \approx \left(\frac{P_{\mathrm{hdp}}(w|d)}{P_{\mathrm{back}}(w)} \right)^{\mu} \qquad (9)$$

4   Experiment and Result

We report some experimental results in this section. The HDP was implemented as an extension to the SRILM toolkit[3]. All baseline LMs used here were trained using SRILM, and the N-best generation and rescoring were based on a modified tool from SRILM.

Since we considered the role information, which is only available in scenario AMI meetings, we used part of the AMI Meeting Corpus for our experiments. There are 138 scenario meetings in total, of which 118 were used for training and the other 20 for testing (about 11 hours). We used the algorithm introduced in Section 3 to extract the corresponding document for each utterance. The average number of words in the resulting documents for window lengths of 10 and 20 seconds was 10 and 14 respectively. Data for n-gram LMs were obtained as usual for training and testing.

We initialized both HDP and rHDP models with 50 topics, and $\beta = 0.5$ for Equation 2. HDP/rHDP models were trained on documents of 10 seconds window length from the scenario AMI meetings with a fixed size vocabulary of 7,910 words, using a Markov Chain Monte Carlo (MCMC) sampling method. The concentration parameters were sampled using the auxiliary variable sample scheme in [9]. We used 3,000 iterations to 'burn-in' the HDP/rHDP models.

4.1   Perplexity Experiment for LMs

In order to see the effect of the adapted LMs on perplexity, we trained three baseline LMs: the first one used the AMI n-gram training data, the second used the Fisher conversational telephone speech data (fisher-03-p1+p2), and the third used the Hub-4 broadcast news data (hub4-lm96). A fourth LM was trained using all three datasets. All the four LMs were trained with standard parameters using SRILM: trigrams, cut-off value of 2 for trigram counts, modified Kneser-Ney smoothing, interpolated model. A common vocabulary with 56,168 words

---

[3] http://www.speech.sri.com/projects/srilm

Table 1. The perplexity results of HDP/rHDP-adapted LMs

LMs	Baseline	HDP-adapted	rHDP-adapted
AMI	107.1	100.7	100.7
Fisher	228.3	176.5	176.4
Hub-4	316.4	248.9	248.8
AMI+Fisher+Hub-4	172.9	144.1	143.9

was used for the four LMs, which has 568 out-of-vocabulary (OOV) words for the AMI test data.

The trained HDP and rHDP models were used to adapt the above four baseline n-gram models respectively, using Equation 9 with $\mu = 0.5$. Different vocabularies were used by the HDP/rHDP models compared with the baseline n-gram models. Only those words occurring in both the HDP/rHDP vocabulary and the n-gram vocabulary were scaled using Equation 9. Table 4.1 shows the perplexity results for the adapted n-gram models. We can see both HDP- and rHDP-adapted LMs produced significant reduction in perplexity, however there was no significant difference between using the HDP or rHDP as the dynamic marginal in the adaptation.

4.2 ASR Experiment

Finally, we investigated the effectiveness of the adapted LMs based on topic and role information from meetings on a practical large vocabulary ASR system. The AMIASR system [20] was used as the baseline system.

We began from the lattices for the whole AMI Meeting Corpus, generated by the AMIASR system using a trigram LM trained on a large set of data coming from Fisher, Hub4, Switchboard, webdata, and various meeting sources including AMI. We then generated 500-best lists from the lattices for each utterance. The reason why we used N-best rescoring instead of lattice rescoring is because the baseline lattices were generated using a trigram LM.

We adapted two LMs (Fisher, and AMI+Fisher+Hub4) trained in Section 4.1 according to the topic information extracted by HDP/rHDP models based on the previous ASR outputs, using a moving document window with a length of 10 seconds. The adapted LM was destroyed after it was used to rescore the current N-best lists. Two adapted LMs together with the baseline LM were then used to rescore the N-best lists with a common language model weight of 14 (the same as for lattice generation) and no word insertion penalty.

Table 4.2 shows the WER results. LMs adapted by HDP/rHDP both yield an absolute reduction of about 0.7% in WER. This reduction is significant using a matched-pair significance[4] test with $p < 10^{-15}$. However, again there was no significant difference between the HDP and the rHDP.

To further investigate the power of HDP/rHDP-adapted LMs, we trained a standard unigram, AMI-1g, on the AMI training data, which is the same data

---

[4] http://www.icsi.berkeley.edu/speech/faq/signiftest.html

Table 2. The %WER results of HDP/rHDP-adapted LMs

LMs	SUB	DEL	INS	WER
Fisher	22.7	11.4	5.8	39.9
AMI-1g-adapted	22.4	11.3	5.7	39.4
HDP-adapted	22.2	11.3	5.6	39.1
rHDP-adapted	22.3	11.3	5.6	39.2
AMI+Fisher+Hub4	21.6	11.1	5.4	38.2
AMI-1g-adapted	21.3	11.0	5.4	37.8
HDP-adapted	21.2	11.1	5.3	37.6
rHDP-adapted	21.2	11.1	5.3	37.5

used for HDP/rHDP training. This unigram was trained using the same vocabulary of 7,910 words as that for HDP/rHDP training. We then used this unigram as dynamic marginal to adapt the baseline LMs, also using the formula in Equation 9. The "AMI-1g-adapted" lines in Table 4.2 shows the WER results. We see, although AMI-1g-adapted LMs have lower WERs than that of the baseline LMs, HDP/rHDP-adapted LMs still have better WER performances (with 0.2–0.3% absolute reduction) than AMI-1g-adapted. Significant testing indicates that both improvements for the HDP/rHDP are significant, with $p < 10^{-6}$.

5   Discussion and Future Work

In this paper, we successfully demonstrated the effectiveness of using the topic (and partly role) information to adapt LMs for ASR in meetings. The topics were automatically extracted using the nonparametric HDP model, which provides an efficient and flexible Bayesian framework for topic modeling. By defining the appropriate 'documents' for HDP models, we achieved a significant reduction in both perplexity and WER for a test set comprising about 11 hours of AMI meeting data.

To our understanding, the reasons for the significant improvements by adapted LMs based on the topic and role information via the HDP come from the following sources. First, the meeting corpus we worked on is a domain-specific corpus with limited vocabulary, especially for scenario meetings, with some words quite dominant during the meeting. So by roughly estimating the 'topic', and scaling those dominant words correctly, it is possible to improve LM accuracy. Second, HDP models can extract topics well, particularly on the domain-specific AMI Meeting Corpus. One interesting result we found is that different HDP/rHDP models, though trained using various different parameters, did not result in significant differences in either perplexity or WER. By closely looking at the resulting topics, we found that some topics have very high probability regardless of the different training parameters. One characteristic of those topics is that the top words normally have very high frequency. Third, the sentence-by-sentence style LM adaption provides further improvements, to those obtained using the AMI-1g-adapted LMs in Table 4.2. Language models are dynamically adapted according to the changes of topics detected based on the previous recognized results. This can be intuitively understood as a situation where there are K unigram LMs, and we dynamically select one unigram to adapt the baseline LMs according to the context (topic). In this paper, however, both the number of unigram models K and the unigram selected for a particular time are automatically determined by the HDP/rHDP. Although this is unsupervised adaptation, it performs better than LM adaptation using static LMs trained on reference data.

One the other hand, the rHDP had a similar accuracy to the HDP in terms of both perplexity and WER. Our interpretation for this is that we did not explicitly use the role information for adapting LMs, only using it as an additional DP level for sharing topics among different roles. As mentioned above, based on the AMI Meeting Corpus, which has a limited domain and consequently limited vocabulary words, this will not cause much difference in the resulting topics, no matter whether HDP or rHDP is used for topic modeling. Despite this, including the role information in the HDP framework can give us some additional information, such as the topics proportion specified to each role. This implies some scope to further incorporate role information into the hierarchical Bayesian framework for language modeling, for example by sampling the role randomly for each document, empirically analysing the differences between HDP and rHDP, and explicitly using the role for language modeling. Another possibility for further investigation is about the prior parameter for Dirichlet distribution: can prior knowledge from language be used to set this parameter? Finally, more ASR experiments to verify the consistence and significance of this framework on more meeting data, e.g., a 5-fold cross-validation on the AMI Meeting Corpus, would be informative.

Acknowledgement

We thank the AMI-ASR team for providing the baseline ASR system for experiments. This work is jointly supported by the Wolfson Microelectronics Scholarship and the European IST Programme Project FP6-033812 (AMIDA). This paper only reflects the authors' views and funding agencies are not liable for any use that may be made of the information contained herein.

References

1. Bengio, Y., Ducharme, R., Vincent, P., Jauvin, C.: A neural probabilistic language model. Journal of Machine Learning Research 3, 1137–1155 (2003)
2. Blitzer, J., Globerson, A., Pereira, F.: Distributed latent variable models of lexical co-occurrences. In: Proceedings of the 10th International Workshop on Artificial Intelligence and Statistics (2005)
3. Teh, Y.W.: A hierarchical Bayesian language model based on Pitman-Yor processes. In: Proc. of the Annual Meeting of the ACL, vol. 44 (2006)
4. Huang, S., Renals, S.: Hierarchical Pitman-Yor language models for ASR in meetings. In: Proc. IEEE Workshop on Automatic Speech Recognition and Understanding (ASRU 2007) (2007)

5. Bilmes, J.A., Kirchhoff, K.: Factored language models and generalized parallel backoff. In: Proceedings of HLT/NACCL, pp. 4–6 (2003)
6. Xu, P., Emami, A., Jelinek, F.: Training connectionist models for the structured language model. In: Empirical Methods in Natural Language Processing, EMNLP 2003 (2003)
7. Wallach, H.M.: Topic modeling: Beyond bag-of-words. In: Proceedings of the 23rd International Conference on Machine Learning, Pittsburgh, PA (2006)
8. Carletta, J.: Unleashing the killer corpus: experiences in creating the multi-everything AMI Meeting Corpus. Language Resources and Evaluation Journal 41(2), 181–190 (2007)
9. Teh, Y., Jordan, M., Beal, M., Blei, D.: Hierarchical Dirichlet processes. Journal of the American Statistical Association 101(476), 1566–1581 (2006)
10. Blei, D.M., Ng, A.Y., Jordan, M.I.: Latent Dirichlet allocation. Journal of Machine Learning Research 3 (2003)
11. Mrva, D., Woodland, P.C.: Unsupervised language model adaptation for Mandarin broadcast conversation transcription. In: Proc. of Interspeech (2006)
12. Tam, Y.C., Schultz, T.: Unsupervised LM adaptation using latent semantic marginals. In: Proc. of Interspeech (2006)
13. Hsu, B.J., Glass, J.: Style and topic language model adaptation using HMM-LDA. In: Proc. of EMNLP (2006)
14. Akita, Y., Nemoto, Y., Kawahara, T.: PLSA-based topic detection in meetings for adaptation of lexicon and language model. In: Proc. of Interspeech (2007)
15. Teh, Y.W.: Dirichlet processes. Encyclopedia of Machine Learning (Submitted, 2007)
16. Teh, Y.W., Kurihara, K., Welling, M.: Collapsed variational inference for HDP. Advances in Neural Information Processing Systems 20 (2008)
17. Ferguson, T.S.: A Bayesian analysis of some nonparametric problems. Annals of Statistics 1(2), 209–230 (1973)
18. Sethuraman, J.: A constructive definition of Dirichlet priors. Statistica Sinica 4, 639–650 (1994)
19. Kneser, R., Peters, J., Klakow, D.: Language model adaptation using dynamic marginals. In: Proc. of Eurospeech, Rhodes (1997)
20. Hain, T., et al.: The AMI system for the transcription of speech in meetings. In: Proc. of ICASSP 2007 (2007)

Time-Compressing Speech: ASR Transcripts Are an Effective Way to Support Gist Extraction

Simon Tucker, Nicos Kyprianou, and Steve Whittaker

Department of Information Studies, University of Sheffield, Sheffield, UK
{s.tucker,s.whittaker}@shef.ac.uk

Abstract. A major problem for users exploiting speech archives is the laborious nature of speech access. Prior work has developed methods that allow users to efficiently identify and access the gist of an archive using textual transcripts of the conversational recording. Text processing techniques are applied to these transcripts to identify unimportant parts of the recording and to excise these, reducing the time taken to identify the main points of the recording. However our prior work has relied on human-generated as opposed to automatically generated transcripts. Our study compares excision methods applied to human-generated and automatically generated transcripts with state of the art word error rates (38%). We show that both excision techniques provide equivalent support for gist extraction. Furthermore, both techniques perform better than the standard speedup techniques used in current applications. This suggests that excision is a viable technique for gist extraction in many practical situations.

1 Introduction

Large archives of speech recordings are becoming more common, as the cost of storage continues to decrease. Such speech archives include: meeting records [9], news [3] and voicemail [18]. Recent tools for accessing these archives either assist users in locating recordings of interest [3] or on supporting the listening process by providing complex visual browsers for access [16]. However people are increasingly using simple, mobile devices (phones or PDAs), where rich displays are not available. In previous work we have developed and evaluated a number of *temporal compression* techniques which do not rely on complex visual displays. They aim to reduce the time taken to listen to a speech recording while still allowing users to extract the most important information. Such techniques are designed to support *gist extraction*, i.e. general understanding of a recording rather than providing access to specific facts.

There are two main ways to reduce the amount of time required to listen to a recording. We can either excise unimportant portions to reduce its length, or alter the playback rate, i.e. speed it up. *Speedup* is used in many commercial applications, e.g. voicemail. With speedup, playback rate is altered so as to not

A. Popescu-Belis and R. Stiefelhagen (Eds.): MLMI 2008, LNCS 5237, pp. 226–235, 2008.

affect speaker pitch, and the speedup can be non-linear, reflecting the way in which humans naturally increase their speech rate [2, 6]. Whilst speed up ensures that listeners hear the complete recording, *excision* compresses it by removing parts - using semantic or acoustic cues to identify unimportant information for subsequent removal.

In previous experiments [14, 15] we evaluated various novel temporal compression techniques, including speedup, excision and hybrid methods that combined speedup and excision techniques. In [14] we used a measure of gist extraction to compare excision and non-linear speed up against an uncompressed control. Our findings show that excision leads to objectively better listener performance than speedup, and excision is also preferred to speedup. Both excision and speedup compression methods lead to more efficient gist extraction than uncompressed speech. Whilst there is evidence that using ASR as opposed to a manual transcript has only a small effect on textual summarization [12] an outstanding question is what effect transcript accuracy has on the ability of listeners to *extract useful information* from temporally compressed audio. This paper examines this question and determine whether listeners are able to extract gist from temporally compressed recordings when the underlying transcripts contain ASR errors.

We therefore compare excision performance for human generated transcripts, with ASR transcripts containing a word error rate (WER) of 38%. This error rate represents state of the art recognition quality for meetings corpora [4]. We compare these with standard speedup techniques for different levels of temporal compression. We also investigate the effects of compression under two sets of conditions: passive exposure to speech excerpts where users listen to speech clips without being able to stop or replay what they hear; and more active exploration of clips using a simple browsing interface. We first describe the evaluation procedure, following which we outline and discuss the results of the study.

2   Assessment Procedure

The assessment procedure aims to objectively and efficiently measure users' ability extract gist from spoken materials. Typical measures of understanding used in this domain focus on recall of specific facts [17]. However our techniques are intended to support *gist extraction* rather than factual knowledge making these techniques inappropriate. An alternative way to measure gist extraction asks users to summarize what they have heard, which is then scored against a gold standard summary [1]. However summarization and evaluation are time-consuming for subjects. More importantly, there is no consensus about metrics or methods for the effective evaluation of summaries [13]. We assume that effective gist extraction requires users to distinguish the importance of different utterances, being able to say which utterances are central to the meeting and which are peripheral. We therefore devised a hybrid evaluation method which employs judges to produce an initial gold standard importance ranking of representative utterances from the recording. In the evaluation stage, we ask experimental subjects to rank the same utterances after they have listened to different types of

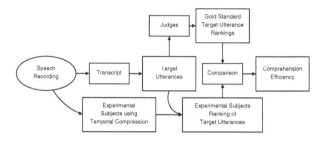

Fig. 1. Overview of assessment procedure. Judges examine the transcript ranking selected target utterances.

temporally compressed recordings. The objective measure of gist extraction is then the correlation between gold standard rankings and those obtained under temporal compression. Our measure of the quality of temporal compression is the extent to which subjects listening using temporal compression are able to replicate the judges gold standard rankings. A high correlation between subject rankings and the gold standard indicates the temporal compression technique provides good support for gist extraction. The evaluation process is described in detail below.

2.1   Algorithms

We used 33 transcripts altogether; 27 four-minute and 6 thirty-minute meeting excerpts from the ICSI meeting corpus [10], using the human generated transcripts supplied with the corpus. The automatically produced (ASR) transcripts were generated using a six pass architecture using 16 component Gaussian HMMs as acoustic models [4]; the WER for the ASR transcripts was 38%. This error rate is state of the art for meetings data.

From both of these transcript sets we first identified stop words (such as 'the', 'and', them', etc.). We then separately determined the importance of non-stop words using measures of term frequency * inverse document frequency (TF*IDF)[7]:

$$imp_{td} = \frac{log(count_{td} + 1)}{log(length_d)} \times log(\frac{N}{N_t}), \tag{1}$$

where imp_{td} is the importance of a term t in a document d, $count_{td}$ is the frequency with which term t appears in transcript d, $length_d$ is the number of unique terms in transcript d, N is the number of transcripts in the corpus and N_t is the number of transcripts in the corpus which contain the term t.

2.2   Gold Standard Measurements

We then computed the importance of each *utterance* in the transcripts as the mean importance of the non-stop words which appear in the utterance. These importance scores were then used to select a subset of utterances which we presented to the judges for gold standard ranking. We did this for long and short extracts. The short excerpts five *target utterances* were manually chosen from the full range of importance levels. Thus both highly important and unimportant utterances were chosen, as well as utterances distributed across the intermediate levels of importance. Utterances were manually selected to ensure that the selected utterances were meaningful and non-repetitive. For the longer excerpts twenty utterances were chosen using the same criteria. Target utterances were chosen to be less than a minute long and represented speech from a single speaker and were a mean of 16 words in length.

We built a small web-based application to collect judges' target utterance rankings. Each judge was assigned a selection of either short or long excerpts and at least three independent rankings were collected for each meeting excerpt.

The judges ranked the five selected utterances for the short excerpts and twenty utterances for the long excerpts. They were given an unlimited amount of time to perform their rankings. To determine reliability we measured Kendall's coefficient of concordance for these rankings. The coefficient in all cases was greater than 0.6 with a mean concordance of 0.75, indicating a good level of agreement ($p < 0.05$). We then constructed the gold-standard rankings by computing the mean ranking for each target utterance across judges, with the assumption that the rankings can be evenly spread on a linear scale. Note that this means that target utterances can be assigned non-integral rankings.

2.3 Compression Techniques

We evaluated two different temporal compression algorithms, one that used excision and the other that used a standard speedup technique [2]. The excision technique removed unimportant utterances, and was applied to both ASR and human generated transcripts.

Insignificant Utterance Excision. Our excision approach relies purely on the words in the transcript and does not require complex natural language or acoustic processing. We first compute utterance importance scores using TF*IDF ([7]) using the method described above, to rank the utterances contained within the transcript in order of their importance. The compressed clip is constructed by adding utterances to an empty file in order of their importance until the file reaches the length required by the specified compression level. Utterances are presented in the order in which they occurred in the original recording. We apply the approach to both ASR and human generated transcripts to generate two insignificant utterance excision files - one generated from ASR transcripts and the other from the human generated transcripts.

Non-Linear Speech Rate Alteration. We used the Mach1 speedup algorithm [2] which aims to replicate the phonetic variations which occur when humans naturally modify their speech rate. We first compute a measure of the relative speed rate for each part of the recording. We then linearly transform this relative speed contour so that the entire excerpt duration meets the desired

Fig. 2. The interface used in the active condition

level of compression. This transformed contour is then used to dynamically alter the speed rate using a standard SOLA algorithm [6].

2.4   Compression Levels

In addition to modifying the *type* of compression we also alter the compression level. We also investigate the effects of compression under two sets of conditions: *passive exposure* to short speech excerpts where users cannot stop or replay what they are hearing; and more *active exploration* of longer clips using a simple browsing interface. This simple interface shown in Fig.2 allows users to turn the compression on/off, pause or re-listen to a recent portion of the recording when processing became difficult or they feel they have missed something important.

For the short excerpts we applied three levels of compression (66, 50 and 40% of the original duration, which corresponds to 1.5, 2 and 2.5 times normal speed) and for the longer excerpts two levels of compression were applied (66 and 50% of the original length). These levels of compression are consistent with accepted comfortable listening levels [5].

2.5   Subjects

Eleven subjects were selected from university staff and students. They were aged between 20 and 40. None reported any hearing difficulties and each received a confectionery reward for taking part.

2.6   Experimental Procedure

All experiments took place in a noise-reduced acoustic booth; excerpts were presented diotically over Sennheiser HD250 Linear II headphones. A Java program was used to present the excerpts and to collect the results.

Subjects attended experiments over three days and were presented with a single compression technique for each day. Each day consisted of two phases, a passive phase and an active phase.

In the first (passive) phase, users heard nine different compressed excerpts (three repetitions of each of the three compression levels). After hearing each complete excerpt they were presented with the set of target utterances for that excerpt and asked to rank the importance of each of the utterances in the context of the whole excerpt. Subjects performed their rankings by choosing labels from a five point Likert scale ('important' to 'unimportant') from drop down menus next to the target utterances. The ordering of the target utterances was randomized for each user.

Before carrying out the active exposure using the simple browser, subjects were given a short tutorial that explained the various functions of the browser interface. They then briefly experimented wit the browser on a short speech excerpt until they felt there were comfortable using it. In the active phase subjects had thirty minutes to explore each excerpt using the browser. The experiment was time limited and either ended after thirty minutes, or when the subjects had listened to the excerpt in its entirety. Typically, subjects finished before the thirty minute deadline. The interface indicated how much time was remaining and it was made clear to subjects that they should attempt to use the interface controls for replaying or decompressing sparingly to ensure that they have enough time to listen to the full recording. When they had finished listening they were presented with the twenty target utterances and the same five ranking levels were used to judge (rather than rank) the importance level of each of the target utterances. In both phases subjects were given an unlimited amount of time to perform their rankings or judgments.

2.7   Performance Measures and Data Collected

We used Kendall's tau to measure the level of agreement between the gold standard rankings and the subject ranking and judgments. The performance score was computed using the following equation:

$$\tau = 1 - 2i/p, \tag{2}$$

where i is the number of inversions between ranking pairs and p is the total number of ranking pairs. Thus we compute the proportion of target utterance pairs which users have ranked in a different order from the ordering present in the gold standard. By computing Kendall's tau in this way we overcome any problems associated with the non-integral rankings (since we focus on the direction of the pairwise orderings). The same scoring technique is used for both the long and short meeting excerpts. We additionally normalize the scores by the mean τ across subjects and conditions for clarity.

This simple measure of agreement, however, does not capture a key aim of temporal compression - which is to reduce the time taken to effectively process a recording. We therefore normalize the success scores to take account of listening time as a function of the original recording length. We call this normalized measure Comprehension Efficiency (C_e):

$$C_e = \frac{\tau/\hat{\tau}}{t_{listening}/t_{original}}, \tag{3}$$

where, $\hat{\tau}$ is the mean tau across all subjects and conditions, $t_{listening}$ is the total listening time and $t_{original}$ is the uncompressed length of the recording.

In addition to Comprehension Efficiency measure, we collected users' subjective reactions to the various compression techniques, asking them to compare and contrast their listening experiences. We also logged their use of the browser, specifically different browser actions such as stopping playback, replaying speech or removing compression to determine how this was used in the different compression conditions.

2.8   Hypotheses

We made separate predictions for the passive and active listening conditions.

Passive Condition. We did not expect ASR to affect comprehension efficiency. We expected subjects to be able to extract gist equally efficiently with both the ASR and human transcript based excision methods. As in [14], we expect excision to be superior to speedup, regardless of the type of transcript. We also expect that increased compression levels will lead to greater levels of comprehension efficiency since subjects will be able to extract gist more rapidly, given that our comprehension measure is normalized according to clip length.

Active Condition. In the active condition, because the user is able to recover from listening errors using the browser, we do not expect the compression technique to affect comprehension efficiency. Our previous experiment found that comprehension efficiency increased with the compression level and we expect this to be the same here. Again, we expect that users will make more active use of the browsing interface when processing sped up speech since this condition requires the listener to clarify key points uncompressed.

3   Results

3.1   Passive Condition

To assess the objective results for the passive condition we conducted a 3 (compression level) X 3 (compression type) ANOVA with comprehension efficiency as the dependent variable. The results are shown in the two left hand graphs in Fig.3.

As predicted, we found an overall main effect of compression type on comprehension efficiency ($F_{(2,288)} = 3.386, p < 0.05$). Planned comparisons confirmed that there was no significant difference between comprehension efficiency in the two excision conditions regardless of whether the transcript was human or ASR generated ($p > 0.3$). However, as predicted, comprehension efficiency in the speed up condition was worse than in the two excision conditions combined ($p < 0.02$).

The ANOVA confirmed the effect of compression level on comprehension efficiency ($F_{(2,288)} = 7.005, p < 0.05$), with planned comparisons confirming that there was greater comprehension efficiency at the two higher compression levels compared with 1.5 times compression ($p < 0.05$).

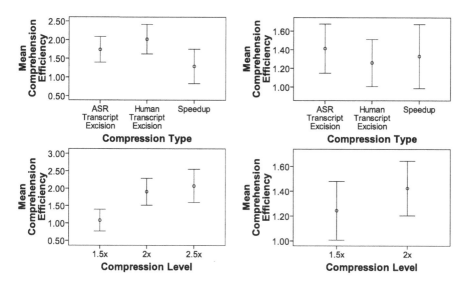

Fig. 3. Error bar graphs showing comprehension efficiency against compression type (bottom) and compression level (top) for the short (left) and long (right) conditions

3.2 Active Condition

To assess the objective results for the long condition we conducted a 2 (compression level) X 3 (compression type) MANOVA with comprehension efficiency and interface actions as the dependent variables.

Consistent with our predictions, there was no effect of compression technique on comprehension efficiency ($F_{(2,60)} = 0.302, p > 0.7$). As in our previous study it seems that the use of the interface allows subjects to extract gist efficiently, independently of the interface condition by stopping, uncompressing the speech and by replaying elements they failed to understand.

We found no effect of compression level on the comprehension efficiency in the long condition ($F_{(1,60)} = 1.254, p > 0.25$). We think that this could be an effect of the interface controls causing any potential processing gains afforded by the shorter playing time to be dampened.

As in our previous study we found that there was an effect of compression technique on the number of interface actions performed ($F_{(2,60)} = 9.593, p < 0.01$). Planned comparisons indicated that more actions were used in the speed up condition ($p < 0.01$) but there was no significant difference between the actions used in the excision conditions ($p > 0.7$). There was no indication therefore, that subjects had to make more adjustments with ASR than human-transcript excision.

3.3 Qualitative Results

An analysis of the questionnaire results for the passive condition shows a main effect of condition on the subject answers ($F_{(2,30)} = 5.117, p < 0.01$). Tukey planned comparisons indicate that this was a result of the differences in the answers for the excision and speed up (each $p < 0.05$); there was no difference between the answers given for the excision conditions (each $p > 0.08$). In the active condition listeners felt that the "speech was too fast" in the speed up case compared with excision($p < 0.03$) and that they "repeatedly had to go back in the speech" ($p < 0.05$) in speedup compared with excision conditions. We found no subjective difference between the excision conditions ($p > 0.08$).

4   Discussion

This paper examines the effects of using ASR transcripts to construct compressed meeting recordings to support gist extraction. We found no differences in gist extraction performance between human generated and ASR transcripts for state of the art ASR error levels (38% WER). ASR also had no effect on the interaction strategies employed by listeners when processing temporally compressed speech nor on the subjective assessment of the techniques. However ASR methods were superior to state of the art techniques currently used for speedup [2]. Other findings are consistent with our previous work [14].

Our results extend our previous work on temporal compression and add to the body of literature which shows that errorful transcripts can be highly useful in a variety of other tasks, e.g. speech retrieval or speech browsing ([3, 18]). Given that these experiments were carried out using informal multi-participant conversational speech the approach taken here could also be promising when applied to other speech domains such as news domains or recorded presentations.

Whilst our compression algorithms work well in this domain there are several ways they might be improved. Firstly, we rely exclusively on lexical techniques to compute importance; more sophisticated measures of utterance importance (using syntactic or prosodic information [8] or even information about speaker role [11]) could lead to improvements in comprehension efficiency. Secondly, we could also exploit other sources or metadata to refine our importance scores - for example using visual cues to participant attention [19], or slide usage to indicate regions of high interest to meeting participants.

Future work will examine the use of these techniques for accessing other types of information - for example we have shown that they work well for extracting gist, but it is an open question as to how effective they are when used to answer more specific, factual, styles of questions.

Acknowledgments

This work is supported by the European IST Programme Project FP6-0033812.

References

1. Baeza-Yates, R., Maki, J.E.: Modern Information Retrieval. Addison-Wesley, Reading (1999)
2. Covell, M., Withgott, M., Slaney, M.: Mach1 for nonuniform time-scale modification of speech. In: Proceedings of ICASSP 1998 (1998)

3. Garofolo, J.S., Auzanne, C.G.P., Voorhees, E.M.: The TREC spoken document retrieval track: A success story. In: RIAO 2000: Content-Based Multimedia Information Access, vol. 1, pp. 1–20 (2000)
4. Hain, T., Burget, L., Dines, J., Garau, G., Karafiat, M., Lincoln, M., McCowan, I., Moore, D., Wan, V., Orderland, R., Renals, S.: The 2005 AMI system for the transcription of speech in meetings. In: Proceedings of the Measuring Behavior 2005 symposium on Annotating and Measuring Meeting Behavior (2005)
5. He, L., Gupta, A.: User benefits of non-linear time compression. Technical Report MSR-TR-2000-96, Microsoft Research (September 2000)
6. Hejna, D.J.: Real-time time-scale modification of speech via the synchronized overlap-add algorithm. Master's thesis, MIT (1990)
7. Jones, K.S.: A statistical interpretation of term specificity and its application in retrieval. Journal of Documentation 28, 11–21 (1972)
8. Koumpis, K., Renals, S.: Automatic summarization of voicemail messages using lexical and prosodic features. ACM Transactions on Speech and Language Processing 2 (2005)
9. McCowan, I., Carletta, J., Kraaij, W., Ashby, S., Bourban, S., Flynn, M., Guillemot, M., Hain, T., Kadlec, J., Karaiskos, V., Kronenthal, M., Lathoud, G., Lincoln, M., Lisowska, A., Post, W., Reidsma, D., Wellner, P.: The AMI meeting corpus. In: Proceedings of the Measuring Behavior 2005 symposium on Annotating and Measuring Meeting Behavior (2005)
10. Morgan, N., Baron, D., Edwards, J., Ellis, D., Gelbert, D., Janin, A., Pfau, T., Shriberg, E., Stolcke, A.: The meeting project at ICSI. In: Human Language Technologies Conference (March 2001)
11. Murray, G., Hsueh, P., Tucker, S., Kilgour, J., Carletta, J., Moore, J.D., Renals, S.: Automatic segmentation and summarization of meeting speech. In: Proceedings of NAACL-HLT (2007)
12. Murray, G., Renals, S.: Term-weighting for summarization of multi-party spoken dialogues. In: Popescu-Belis, A., Renals, S., Bourlard, H. (eds.) MLMI 2007. LNCS, vol. 4892, pp. 155–166. Springer, Heidelberg (2008)
13. Nenkova, A., Passonneau, R., McKeown, K.: The pyramid method: incorporating human content selection variation in summarization evaluation. ACM Transactions on Speech and Language Processing 4(2) (2007)
14. Tucker, S., Whittaker, S.: Time is of the essence: An evaluation of temporal compression algorithms. In: Proceedings of CHI 2006, pp. 71–80 (April 2006)
15. Tucker, S., Whittaker, S.: Temporal compression of speech: An evaluation. In: IEEE Transactions on Audio, Speech and Language Processing (in press, 2008)
16. Wellner, P., Flynn, M., Guillemot, M.: Browsing recording of multi-party interactions in ambient intelligent environments. In: Proceedings of Conference on Human Factors in Computing Systems (CHI) (April 2004)
17. Wellner, P., Flynn, M., Tucker, S., Whittaker, S.: A meeting browser evaluation test. In: Proceedings of Conference on Human Factors in Computing Systems (CHI) (April 2005)
18. Whittaker, S., Hirschberg, J., Amento, B., Stark, L., Bacchiani, M., Isenhour, P., Stead, L., Zamchick, G., Rosenberg, A.: SCANMail: A voicemail interface that makes speech browsable, readable and searchable. In: Proceedings of Conference on Human Factors in Computing Systems (CHI) (April 2002)
19. You, J., Liu, G., Sun, L., Li, H.: A multiple visual models based perceptive analysis framework for multilevel video summarization. IEEE Transactions on Circuits and Systems for Video Technology 17(3), 273–285 (2007)

Meta Comments for Summarizing Meeting Speech

Gabriel Murray[1] and Steve Renals[2]

[1] University of British Columbia, Vancouver, Canada
gabrielm@cs.ubc.ca
[2] University of Edinburgh, Edinburgh, Scotland
s.renals@ed.ac.uk

Abstract. This paper is about the extractive summarization of meeting speech, using the ICSI and AMI corpora. In the first set of experiments we use prosodic, lexical, structural and speaker-related features to select the most informative dialogue acts from each meeting, with the hypothesis being that such a rich mixture of features will yield the best results. In the second part, we present an approach in which the identification of "meta-comments" is used to create more informative summaries that provide an increased level of abstraction. We find that the inclusion of these meta comments improves summarization performance according to several evaluation metrics.

1 Introduction

Speech summarization has attracted increasing interest in the past few years. There has been a variety of work concerned with the summarization of broadcast news [3, 8, 14, 19], voicemail messages [11], lectures [9, 21] and spontaneous conversations [18, 22]. In this paper we are concerned with the summarization of multiparty meetings. Small group meetings provide a compelling setting for spoken language processing, since they feature considerable interaction (up to 30% of utterances are overlapped), and informal conversational speech. Previous work in the summarization of meeting speech [6, 16, 20] has been largely based on the extraction of informative sentences or dialogue acts (DAs) from the source transcript. The extracted portions are then concatenated to form a summary of the meeting, with informativeness gauged by various lexical and prosodic criteria, among others.

In this work we first present a set of experiments that aim to identify the most useful features for the detection of informative DAs in multiparty meetings. We have applied this extractive summarization framework to the ICSI and AMI meeting corpora, described below. Extractive summaries of multiparty meetings often lack coherence, and may not be judged to be particularly informative by a user. In the second part of the paper, we aim to produce summaries with a greater degree of abstraction through the automatic extraction of "meta" DAs: DAs in which the speaker refers to the meeting itself. Through the inclusion of such DAs in our summaries, we hypothesize that the summaries will be more coherent and more obviously informative to an end user. Much as human abstracts tend to be created in a high-level fashion from a third-party perspective, we aim to automatically create extracts with similar attributes, harnessing the self-referential quality of meeting speech. Using an expanded feature set, we report results on the AMI corpus and compare with our previously generated extractive summaries.

A. Popescu-Belis and R. Stiefelhagen (Eds.): MLMI 2008, LNCS 5237, pp. 236–247, 2008.

2   Experimental Setup

We have used the the AMI and ICSI meeting corpora. The AMI corpus [1] consists of about 100 hours of recorded and annotated meetings, divided into *scenario* and *non-scenario* meetings. In the scenario portion, groups of four participants take part in a series of four meetings and play roles within a fictitious company. While the scenario given to them is artificial, the speech and the actions are completely spontaneous and natural. There are 138 meetings of this type in total. The length of an individual meeting ranges from 15 to 45 minutes, depending on which meeting in the series it is and how quickly the group is working. For these experiments, we use only the scenario meetings from the AMI corpus.

The second corpus used herein is the ICSI meeting corpus [10], a corpus of 75 naturally occurring meetings of research groups, approximately one hour each in length. Unlike the AMI scenario meetings and similar to the AMI non-scenario meetings, there are varying numbers of participants across meetings in the ICSI corpus, ranging from three to ten, with an average of six participants per meeting.

Both corpora feature a mixture of native and non-native English speakers and have been transcribed both manually and using automatic speech recognition(ASR) [7]. The resultant word error rates were 29.5% for the ICSI corpus, and 38.9% for the AMI corpus.

2.1   Summary Annotation

For both the AMI and ICSI corpora, annotators were asked to write abstractive summaries of each meeting and to extract the DAs in the meeting that best conveyed or supported the information in the abstractive summary. A many-to-many mapping between transcript DAs and sentences from the human abstract was obtained for each annotator. It is also possible for a DA to be extractive but unlinked. The human-authored abstracts each contain a general abstract summary and three subsections for "decisions," "actions" and "problems" from the meeting.

Kappa values were used to measure inter-annotator agreement. The ICSI test set has a lower kappa value (0.35) compared with the AMI test set (0.48), reflecting the difficulty in summarizing the much less structured (and more technical) ICSI meetings.

2.2   Summary Evaluation

To evaluate automatically produced extractive summaries we have extended the weighted precision measure [17] to weighted precision, recall and F-measure. This evaluation scheme relies on the multiple human annotated summary links described in the previous section. Both weighted precision and recall share the same numerator

$$num = \sum_{i=1}^{M} \sum_{j=1}^{N} L(s_i, a_j)$$

where $L(s_i, a_j)$ is the number of links for a DA s_i in the machine extractive summary according to annotator a_i, M is the number of DAs in the machine summary, and N is the number of annotators. Weighted precision is defined as:

$$precision = \frac{num}{N \cdot M}$$

and weighted recall is given by

$$recall = \frac{num}{\sum_{i=1}^{O} \sum_{j=1}^{N} L(s_i, a_j)}$$

where O is the total number of DAs in the meeting, N is the number of annotators, and the denominator represents the total number of links made between DAs and abstract sentences by all annotators. The weighted F-measure is calculated as the harmonic mean of weighted precision and recall.

We have also used the ROUGE evaluation framework [13] for the second set of experiments, in particular ROUGE-2 and ROUGE-SU4. We believe that ROUGE is particularly relevant for evaluation in that case, as we are trying to create extracts that are more abstract-like, and ROUGE compares machine summaries to gold-standard human abstracts.

3   Features for Meeting Summarization

In this section we outline the features and classifiers used for extractive summarization of meetings, presenting results using the AMI and ICSI corpora.

Table 1 lists and briefly describes the set of the features used. The prosodic features consist of energy, F0, pause, duration and a rate-of-speech measure. We calculate both the duration of the complete DA, as well as of the uninterrupted portion. The structural features include the DA's position in the meeting and position within the speaker's turn (which may contain multiple DAs). There are two measures of speaker dominance: the dominance of the speaker in terms of meeting DAs and in terms of total speaking time. There are two term-weighting metrics, *tf.idf* and *su.idf*, the former favoring words that are frequent in the given document but rare across all documents, and the latter favoring words that are used with varying frequency by the different speakers [15]. The prosodic and term-weight features are calculated at the word level and averaged over the DA. In these experiments we employed a manual DA segmentation, although automatic approaches are available [5].

For each corpus, a logistic regression classifier is trained on the seen data as follows, using the *liblinear* toolkit[1]. Feature subset selection is carried out using a method based on the f statistic:

$$F(i) = \frac{(\bar{x}_i^{(+)} - \bar{x}_i)^2 + (\bar{x}_i^{(-)} - \bar{x}_i)^2}{D^{(+)} + D^{(-)}}$$

$$D^{(\pm)} = \frac{1}{n_\pm - 1} \sum_{k=1}^{n_\pm} (x_{k,i}^{(\pm)} - \bar{x}_i^{(\pm)})^2$$

where n_+ and n_- are the number of positive instances and negative instances, respectively, $\bar{x}_i$, $\bar{x}_i^{(+)}$, and $\bar{x}_i^{(-)}$ are the means of the ith feature for the whole, positive and

---

[1] http://www.csie.ntu.edu.tw/~cjlin/liblinear/

Table 1. Features Key

Feature ID	Description
Prosodic Features	
ENMN	mean energy
F0MN	mean F0
ENMX	max energy
F0MX	max F0
F0SD	F0 stdev.
PPAU	precedent pause
SPAU	subsequent pause
ROS	rate of speech
Structural Features	
MPOS	meeting position
TPOS	turn position
Speaker Features	
DOMD	speaker dominance (DAs)
DOMT	speaker dominance (seconds)
Length Features	
DDUR	DA duration
UINT	uninterrupted length
WCNT	number of words
Lexical Features	
SUI	su.idf sum
TFI	tf.idf sum
ACUE (experiment 2)	abstractive cuewords
FPAU (experiment 2)	filled pauses

negative data instances, respectively, and $x_{k,i}^{(+)}$ and $x_{k,i}^{(-)}$ are the ith features of the kth positive and negative instances [2]. The f statistic for each feature was first calculated, and then feature subsets of size $n = 3, 5, 7, 9, 11, 13, 15, 17$ were tried, with the n best features included at each step based on the f statistic. The feature subset size with the highest balanced accuracy during cross-validation was selected as the feature set for training the logistic regression model.

The classifier was then run on the unseen test data, and the class probabilities were used to rank the candidate DAs for each meeting and create extracts of 700 words. This length was chosen so that the summaries would be short enough to be read by a time-constrained user, much as a short human abstract might be quickly consulted, but long enough to index the most important points of the meeting. This short summary length also necessitates a high level of precision since we extract relatively few DAs.

3.1 AMI Results

For the AMI data the best feature subset according to the feature selection method includes all 17 features, for both manual and ASR transcriptions. For both transcription types, the best five features (in order) were DA word count, *su.idf* score, DA duration, uninterrupted length of the DA, and *tf.idf* score. Figure 1 shows the histograms of the feature f statistics using both the manual and ASR transcriptions.

We calculated the ROC curves and areas under the curve (AUROC) for the classifiers that identified the extractive DAs, using both manual and ASR transcriptions. For the manual transcripts AUROC = 0.855, for the ASR transcripts AUROC= 0.850, with chance level classification at 0.5.

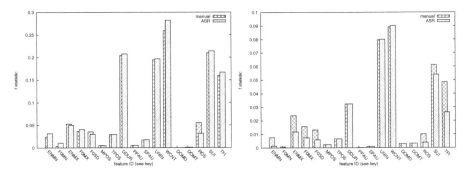

Fig. 1. f statistics for AMI database features   **Fig. 2.** f statistics for ICSI database features

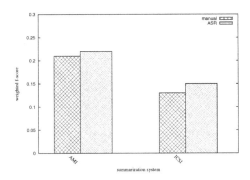

Fig. 3. Weighted F-Measures for AMI and ICSI Corpora, Manual and ASR Transcripts

Figure 3 illustrates the weighted F-measures for the 700-word summaries on manual and ASR transcripts using the feature-based approach. There is no significant difference between the manual and ASR F-measures according to paired t-test, and the ASR scores are on average slightly higher.

3.2   ICSI Results

For the ICSI corpus using manual transcripts, the optimal feature subset consisted of 15 features according to balanced accuracy, excluding mean F0 and precedent pause. The best 5 features according to the f statistic were DA word count, uninterrupted length, *su.idf* score, *tf.idf* score and DA duration. The optimal subset for ASR transcripts consisted of the same 15 features. Figure 2 shows the histograms for the feature f statistics using both the manual and ASR databases.

We calculated the ROC and AUROC for each classifier applied to the 6 test set meetings. For manual transcripts AUROC = 0.818, and for ASR transcripts AUROC = 0.824.

Figure 3 shows the weighted F-measures for the 700-word summaries for both manual and ASR transcripts. As with the AMI corpus, there is no significant difference between manual and ASR results and the ASR average is again slightly higher.

3.3   Discussion

In this first experiment we have shown that a rich mixture of features yields good re-sults, based on feature subset selection with the f statistic. We have also compared the AMI and ICSI corpora in terms of feature selection. For both corpora, summarization is slightly better on ASR than on manual transcripts, in terms of weighted F-measure. It is worth pointing out, however, that the weighted F-measure only evaluates whether the correct DAs have been extracted and does not penalize misrecognized words within an extracted DA. Such ASR errors create a problem for textual summaries, but are less im-portant for multimodal summaries (e.g. those produced by concatenating audio and/or video segments).

In the next section we provide a more detailed analysis of the effectiveness of various feature subsets for an altered summarization task.

4   Meta Comments in Meeting Speech

In the second experiment we aim to improve our results through the identification of meta DAs to be included in machine summaries. These are DAs in which the speaker refers to the meeting itself. We first describe scheme we used to annotate meta DAs, then present an expanded feature set, and compare summarization results with the first experiment.

The AMI corpus contains *reflexivity* annotations: a DA is considered to be reflexive if it refers to the meeting or discussion itself. Reflexive DAs are related to the idea of meta comments, but the reflexivity annotation alone is not sufficient. Many of the DAs deemed to be reflexive consist of statements like "Next slide, please." and "Can I ask a question?" in addition to many short feedback statements such as "Yeah" and "Okay." Although such DAs do indeed refer to the flow of discussion at a high level, they are not particularly informative. We are not interested in identifying DAs that are *purely* about the flow of discussion, but rather we would like to detect those DAs that refer to low-level issues in a high-level way. For example, we would find the DA "We decided on a red remote control" more interesting than the DA "Let's move on".

In light of these considerations, we created an annotation scheme for meta DAs, that combined several existing annotations in order to form a new binary meta/non-meta annotation for the corpus. The ideal condition would be to consider DAs as meta only if they are labelled as both extractive and reflexive. However, there are relatively few such DAs in each meeting. For that reason, we also consider DAs to be meta if they are linked to the "decisions," "actions" or "problems" subsections of the abstract. The intuition behind using the DA links to those three abstract subsections is that areas of a discussion that relate to these categories will tend to indicate where the discussion moves from a lower level to a higher level. For example, the group might discuss technical issues in some detail and then make a decision regarding those issues, or set out a course of action for the next meetings.

For this second experiment, we trained the classifier to extract only these newly-labelled meta DAs rather than all generally extract-worthy DAs as in the first exper-iment. We analyze which individual features and feature subsets are most effective for this novel extraction task. We then evaluate our brief summaries using weighted

F-measure and ROUGE and make an explicit comparison with the previously generated summaries. This work focuses solely on the AMI data, for two reasons: the ICSI data does not contain the reflexivity annotation, and the ICSI abstracts have slightly different subsections than the AMI abstracts.

4.1   Filled Pause and Cueword Features

In these experiments we have two additional lexical features to the feature set used in the previous section, which we hypothesise to be relevant to the meta DA identification task. The first new feature is the number of filled pauses in each DA. This is included because the fluency of speech might change at areas of conversational transition, perhaps including more filled pauses than on average. These filled pauses consist of terms such as "uh", "um", "erm", "mm," and "hmm."

The second new feature is the presence of abstractive or meta cuewords, as automatically derived from the training data. Since we are trying to create summaries that are somehow more abstract-like, we examine terms that occur often in the abstracts of meetings but less often in the *extracts* of meetings. We score each word according to the ratio of these two frequencies,

$$TF(t, j)/TF(t, k)$$

where $TF(t, j)$ is the frequency of term t in the set of abstracts j from the training set meetings and $TF(t, k)$ is the frequency of term t in the set of extracts k from the training set meetings. These scores are used to rank the words from most abstractive to least abstractive, and we keep the top 50 words as our list of meta cuewords. The top 5 abstractive cuewords are "team", "group", "specialist", "member", and "manager." For both the manual and ASR feature databases, each DA then has a feature indicating how many of these high-level terms it contains.

4.2   Evaluation of Meta DA Extraction

We evaluated the resulting 700-word summaries using three metrics: weighted F-measures using the new extractive labels, weighted F-measures using the old extractive labels, and ROUGE. For the second of those evaluations, it is not expected that the summaries derived from meta DAs will fare as well as using the original extractive summaries, since the vast majority of previously extractive DAs are now considered members of the negative class and the evaluation metric is based on the previous extractive/non-extractive labels; the results are included out of interest nonetheless.

We experimented using the AMI corpus. With manual transcripts, the feature subset that was selected consisted of 13 features, which excluded mean F0, position in the speaker's turn, precedent pause, both dominance features, and filled pauses. The best five features in order were *su.idf*, DA word-count, *tf.idf*, DA duration, and uninterrupted duration. In the case of ASR transcription, all 19 features were selected and the best five features were the same as for the manual transcripts.

We calculated the ROC and AUROC for the meta DA classifiers applied to the 20 test set meetings using both manual and ASR transcription. For manual, AUROC =

0.843 and for ASR, AUROC = 0.842. This result is very encouraging, as it shows that it is possible to discriminate the meta DAs from other DAs (including some marked as extractive). Given that we created a new positive class based on a DA satisfying one of four criteria, and that we consider everything else as negative, this result shows that DAs that meet at least one of these extraction criteria do have characteristics in common with one another and can be discerned as a separate group from the remainder.

4.3   Feature Analysis

The previous sections have reported a brief features analysis according to each feature's f statistic for the extractive/non-extractive classes. This section expands upon that by examining how useful different subsets of features are for classification on their own. While we found that the optimal subset according to automatic feature subset selection is 13 and 19 features for manual and ASR, respectively, it is still interesting to examine performance using only certain classes of features on this data. We therefore divide the features into five categories of **prosodic** features, **length** features, **speaker** features, **structural** features and **lexical** features. Note that we do not consider DA duration to be a prosodic feature.

Figure 4 shows the ROC curves and AUROC values for each feature subset for the manual transcriptions. We find that no individual subset matches the classification performance found by using the entire feature set, but that several classes exhibit credible individual performance. The length and term-weight features are clearly the best, but we find that prosodic features alone perform better than structural or speaker features.

Figure 5 shows the ROC curves and AUROC values for each feature subset for the ASR transcriptions. The trend is largely the same as above: no individual feature type is better than the combination of feature types. The principal difference is that prosodic features alone are worse on ASR, likely due to extracting prosodic features aligned to erroneous word boundaries, while term-weight features are about the same as on manual.

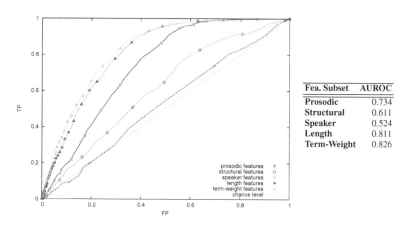

Fea. Subset	AUROC
Prosodic	0.734
Structural	0.611
Speaker	0.524
Length	0.811
Term-Weight	0.826

Fig. 4. AUROC Values, Manual Transcripts

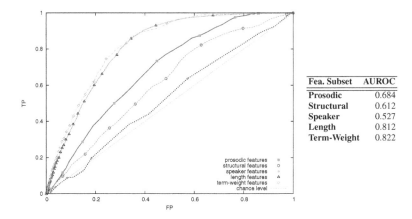

Fea. Subset	AUROC
Prosodic	0.684
Structural	0.612
Speaker	0.527
Length	0.812
Term-Weight	0.822

Fig. 5. AUROC Values, ASR Transcripts

4.4   Summary Evaluation

Figure 6 presents the weighted F-measures using the novel extractive labelling, for the new meta summaries as well as for the summaries created and evaluated in the first experiment. For manual transcripts, the new summaries outperform the old summaries with an average F-measure of 0.17 versus 0.12. The reason for the scores overall being lower than the F-measures reported in the previous chapter using the original formulation of weighted precision/recall/F-measure is that there are now far fewer positive instances in each meeting since we are restricting the positive class to the "meta" subset of informative DAs. The meta summaries are significantly better than the previous summaries on this evaluation according to paired t-test ($p < 0.05$).

For ASR, we find both the new meta summaries and older non-meta summaries performing slightly better than on manual transcripts according to this evaluation. The meta summaries again are rated higher than the non-meta summaries, with an average F-measure of 0.19 versus 0.14 and are significantly better according to paired t-test ($p < 0.05$).

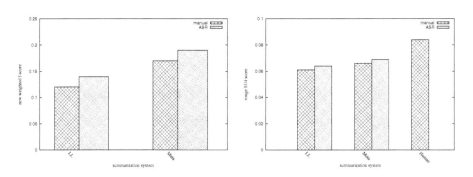

Fig. 6. New Weighted F-measures   **Fig. 7.** ROUGE-SU4 Scores

LL=low-level summaries from first experiment, **Meta**=novel meta summaries

We would expect the new meta extractive summaries to perform better in terms of weighted F-measure with respect to the new extractive labelling, since the classifiers were trained in a consistent manner. However, when using the old extractive labelling the weighted F-measures for these new summaries are also slightly higher than the F-measures reported in the previous section. The F-measure for manual transcripts is 0.23 compared with 0.21 previously, and 0.24 for ASR compared with 0.22 earlier. This is a surprising and encouraging result, that our new annotation and subsequent "meta" DA extraction experiments have led not only to finding areas of high-level meta comments in the meetings but also to improved general summary informativeness. Kappa statistics also suggest that it is easier for annotators to agree on DAs that meet these specific meta criteria (κ=0.45) than DAs that simply support the general abstract portion of the human summary (κ=0.40).

We also evaluate the meta summaries using the ROUGE-2 and ROUGE-SU4 metrics [13], which have previously been found to correlate well with human judgements in the DUC summarization tasks [4, 12]. We calculate precision, recall and F-measures for each, and ROUGE is run using the parameters utilized in the DUC conferences, plus removal of stopwords.

Again the meta summaries outperform the summaries created in the first experiments. For ROUGE-2, using manual transcripts, the meta summaries average a score of 0.039, compared with 0.033 for the previous non-meta summaries.On the ASR transcripts, the meta summaries scored slightly higher with an average of 0.041 compared with 0.032 for the non-meta summaries, which is significant at $p<0.05$. According to ROUGE-SU4, on manual transcripts the meta summaries outperform the low-level summaries with an average of 0.066 compared with 0.061, respectively. On ASR transcripts, the meta summaries average 0.069 compared with 0.064 for the low-level summaries. Both differences are significant at $p<0.05$. Figure 7 shows the ROUGE-SU4 scores for meta and non-meta summaries compared with human extracts of the same length.

The following two DAs from meeting TS3003c are examples of DAs that are extracted for the meta summary but not for the previously generated non-meta summary of the same meeting.

- **Speaker A:** So the industrial designer and user interface designer are going to work together on this one
- **Speaker D:** I heard our industrial designer talk about flat, single- and double-curved.

4.5 Discussion

According to multiple intrinsic evaluations, our novel meta summaries are superior to the previously generated summaries. We believe that the criteria for *informativeness* are more meaningful, that the output is more flexible, and that these high-level summaries would be more coherent from the perspective of a third-party end user.

Of the two novel feature types in the expanded features database, abstractive cuewords are found to be very good indicators of meta DAs, while the presence of filled pauses is much less useful. It may be the case that the presence of filled pauses would be a helpful feature for a general extraction task but is simply not indicative of meta DAs.

There are interesting possibilities for new directions with this research. For example, by training on individual classes one could create a complex extractive summary that first lists DAs relating to decisions, followed by DAs that identify action items for the following meeting. A hierarchical summary could also be created, with high-level DAs at the top, linked to related lower-level DAs that might provide more detail. It is also possible that these meta summary DAs would lend themselves to further interpretation and generation of automatic abstracts.

5 Conclusion

The aim of this work has been two-fold: to help move the state-of-the-art in speech summarization further along the extractive-abstractive continuum, and to determine the most effective feature subsets for the summarization task. We have shown that informative meta DAs can be reliably identified, and have described the effectiveness of various feature sets in performing this task. While the work has been firmly in the extractive paradigm, it has moved beyond previously used simplistic notions of "informative" versus "uninformative" in order to create more informative and high-level summary output.

Acknowledgements. This work is supported by the European IST Programme Project AMIDA (FP6-0033812). Thanks to the AMI-ASR team for providing the ASR.

References

1. Carletta, J., Ashby, S., Bourban, S., Flynn, M., Guillemot, M., Hain, T., Kadlec, J., Karaiskos, V., Kraaij, W., Kronenthal, M., Lathoud, G., Lincoln, M., Lisowska, A., McCowan, I., Post, W., Reidsma, D., Wellner, P.: The AMI meeting corpus: A pre-announcement. In: Renals, S., Bengio, S. (eds.) MLMI 2005. LNCS, vol. 3869, pp. 28–39. Springer, Heidelberg (2006)
2. Chen, Y.-W., Lin, C.-J.: Combining SVMs with various feature selection strategies. In: Guyon, I., Gunn, S., Nikravesh, M., Zadeh, L. (eds.) Feature extraction, foundations and applications. Springer, Heidelberg (2006)
3. Christensen, H., Gotoh, Y., Renals, S.: A cascaded broadcast news highlighter. IEEE Transactions on Audio, Speech and Language Processing 16, 151–161 (2008)
4. Dang, H.: Overview of duc 2005. In: Proc. of the Document Understanding Conference (DUC) 2005, Vancouver, BC, Canada (2005)
5. Dielmann, A., Renals, S.: DBN based joint dialogue act recognition of multiparty meetings. In: Proc. of ICASSP 2007, Honolulu, USA, pp. 133–136 (2007)
6. Galley, M.: A skip-chain conditional random field for ranking meeting utterances by importance. In: Proc. of EMNLP 2006, Sydney, Australia, pp. 364–372 (2006)
7. Hain, T., Burget, L., Dines, J., Garau, G., Wan, V., Karafiat, M., Vepa, J., Lincoln, M.: The AMI system for transcription of speech in meetings. In: Proc. of ICASSP 2007, pp. 357–360 (2007)
8. Hori, C., Furui, S.: Speech summarization: An approach through word extraction and a method for evaluation. IEICE Transactions on Information and Systems E87 D(1), 15–25 (2004)
9. Hori, T., Hori, C., Minami, Y.: Speech summarization using weighted finite-state transducers. In: Proc. of Interspeech 2003, Geneva, Switzerland, pp. 2817–2820 (2003)

10. Janin, A., Baron, D., Edwards, J., Ellis, D., Gelbart, D., Morgan, N., Peskin, B., Pfau, T., Shriberg, E., Stolcke, A., Wooters, C.: The ICSI meeting corpus. In: Proc. of IEEE ICASSP 2003, Hong Kong, China, pp. 364–367 (2003)
11. Koumpis, K., Renals, S.: Automatic summarization of voicemail messages using lexical and prosodic features. ACM Transactions on Speech and Language Processing 2, 1–24 (2005)
12. Lin, C.-Y.: Looking for a few good metrics: Automatic summarization evaluation - how many samples are enough. In: Proc. of NTCIR 2004, Tokyo, Japan, pp. 1765–1776 (2004)
13. Lin, C.-Y., Hovy, E.H.: Automatic evaluation of summaries using n-gram co-occurrence statistics. In: Proc. of HLT-NAACL 2003, Edmonton, Calgary, Canada, pp. 71–78 (2003)
14. Maskey, S., Hirschberg, J.: Comparing lexial, acoustic/prosodic, discourse and structural features for speech summarization. In: Proc. of Interspeech 2005, Lisbon, Portugal, pp. 621–624 (2005)
15. Murray, G., Renals, S.: Term-weighting for summarization of multi-party spoken dialogues. In: Popescu-Belis, A., Renals, S., Bourlard, H. (eds.) MLMI 2007. LNCS, vol. 4892, pp. 155–166. Springer, Heidelberg (2008)
16. Murray, G., Renals, S., Carletta, J.: Extractive summarization of meeting recordings. In: Proc. of Interspeech, Lisbon, Portugal, pp. 593–596 (2005)
17. Murray, G., Renals, S., Moore, J., Carletta, J.: Incorporating speaker and discourse features into speech summarization. In: Proc. of the HLT-NAACL 2006, New York City, pp. 367–374 (2006)
18. Reithinger, N., Kipp, M., Engel, R., Alexandersson, J.: Summarizing multilingual spoken negotiation dialogues. In: Proc. of ACL 2000. Association for Computational Linguistics, Hong Kong, pp. 310–317. Morristown, NJ (2000)
19. Valenza, R., Robinson, T., Hickey, M., Tucker, R.: Summarization of spoken audio through information extraction. In: Proc. of the ESCA Workshop on Accessing Information in Spoken Audio, Cambridge, UK, pp. 111–116 (1999)
20. Zechner, K.: Automatic summarization of open-domain multiparty dialogues in diverse genres. Computational Linguistics 28(4), 447–485 (2002)
21. Zhang, J., Chan, H., Fung, P., Cao, L.: Comparative study on speech summarization of broadcast news and lecture speech. In: Proc. of Interspeech 2007, Antwerp, Belgium, pp. 2781–2784 (2007)
22. Zhu, X., Penn, G.: Summarization of spontaneous conversations. In: Proc. of Interspeech 2006, Pittsburgh, USA, pp. 1531–1534 (2006)

A Generic Layout-Tool for Summaries of Meetings in a Constraint-Based Approach

Sandro Castronovo, Jochen Frey, and Peter Poller

Deutsches Forschungszentrum für Künstliche Intelligenz GmbH
Stuhlsatzenhausweg 3, 66123 Saarbrücken, Germany
sandro.castronovo@dfki.de
jochen.frey@itemis.de
peter.poller@dfki.de

Abstract. We present SuVi - Summary Visualizer -, a generic layout-tool which displays a multimodal summary of a meeting in either a story-board style or newspaper-style. The system relies on constraint solving techniques in such a way that the two layouts have been extensively modeled in a series of constraints representing the underlying design knowledge. While the story-board aims to give the reader an overview of the chronological sequence of the meeting, the newspaper-layout focuses on presenting the topics of a meeting depending on their relevance. We also show two methods for connecting the whole AMI meeting corpus as a large input resource for the story-board part of SuVi and present a first end-to-end implementation of our system.

1 Introduction

One of the main goals of the AMIDA project[1] is the automatic generation of multimodal meeting summaries. Apart from their generation, there are many ways of presenting these summaries to the user. A very appealing presentation style has been realized by the SuVi-tool (Summary Visualizer). Based on actual audio and video data it generates a story-board layout or displays the meeting in the style of a newspaper.

The major task of SuVi was the modeling of the necessary design knowledge for the layout process of the respective output presentation style. Consequently, we implemented SuVi based on hand-generated input data for just a single meeting. The primary goal of the development was to show the general feasibility of a constraint-based layout approach. Later on, in order to greatly extend the number of available input resources, we developed M2SuVi, a generic interface to the whole AMI meeting corpus. In the compound system it is even possible to implement different ways of filling the story-board layout with content very quickly giving us the flexibility to adapt the system to completely new domains in a very short amount of time.

---

[1] Augmented Multiparty Interaction with Distance Access (AMIDA) is an Integrated Project funded by the ECs 6th Framework Program FP6-0033812, Publication ID - AMIDA-26, jointly managed by IDIAP (CH) and the University of Edinburgh (UK).

A. Popescu-Belis and R. Stiefelhagen (Eds.): MLMI 2008, LNCS 5237, pp. 248–259, 2008.

This paper presents first the SuVi system in section 2 and the layout constraints used for the story-board part of SuVi in section 3. We elaborate the generic interface which makes the whole AMI meeting corpus accessible for SuVi in section 4 and show the robustness of our implementation by a batch-run over the whole AMI corpus in section 5. Our first online end-to-end implementation of the compound system which was configured to generate a story-board layout of a selected part of the first AMIDA review meeting is presented in section 6. Finally, section 7 lists related work and gives an overview of the future work in this context.

2   SuVi

SuVi - Summary Visualizer is a constraint based layout system for the automatic visualization of multimodal meeting summaries either in a multimedia story-board style or in the style of a newspaper. While the newspaper component focuses on the hierarchical topic presentation, e.g., showing more relevant topics more prominently on the page, the story-board layout aims to represent the chronological sequence of a meeting. Figure 1 depicts the resulting layout for the newspaper style and an example of the story-board layout is shown in figure 4. In this section we give a general introduction to our constraint-based layout approach and explain the story-board layout component of SuVi.

Fig. 1. Example of a newspaper layout

2.1 Architecture of SuVi

From a functional point of view, the constraint-based layout-system SuVi is a self-contained, generic and parameterizable layout generator for multimodal meeting summaries. It realizes a broad spectrum of functionalities:

- Full automatic layout generation of meeting summaries
- API for different layout-specifications
- User adaptivity by offering a variety of parameters for layout generation

Figure 2 shows the architecture of SuVi from the story-board point of view. SuVi consists of three main components which are coordinated by a central distributor component. The central architecture is the same as for the newspaper layout. The major difference is the constraint based modeling of the target domain, the different layout objects and the varying layout manager.

The input data consists of meeting topics, speaker utterances and parameters for the layout generation. The user can exert an influence on the topics used in the layout and the parameters of the generation, e.g., the number of panels on a page. Speaker utterances are used to fill the layout objects, namely text-boxes and balloons. All of this data is analyzed and appropriately represented by the **input reader**. Based on that representation, the **constraint solver** derives the necessary constraint variables which are stored within corresponding layout objects. These are are shown in the resulting layout in figure 4. The layout objects that are used in the story-board implementation of SuVi are balloons, panels and text-boxes. Like the input data for the layout objects, the background images were hand-set in SuVi.

The constraint solver is comprised of the mechanisms needed to process the layout knowledge by initially producing and then solving appropriately defined general constraints for all layout objects. More details of these different constraints are given in the following section.

Finally, the **layout manager** component creates a corresponding layout representation in XML-format from the instantiated layout objects. This format is then processed by Comiclife©, a commercial software which is used by SuVi to render the resulting story-board layout.

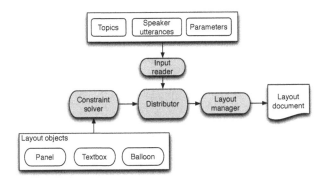

Fig. 2. Architecture of SuVi

3 Constraints

Story-board generation by SuVi distinguishes between two types of layout constraints: Page layout constraints and panel layout constraints. Furthermore, all constraints are split into hard and soft constraints. The former have to be fulfilled by the constraint solver in order to find a solution at all. The latter represent optimizations but do not necessarily have to be fulfilled. They are used to optimize found solutions with respect to the story-board specific design knowledge, e.g., how it's layout elements are organized in general. For example, be aware of the effect that appropriate locations of the balloons in a panel must consider the fact, that these locations "imply" a reading order for them, e.g., left to right vs. top down.

The system relies on Choco[2] , a constraint solver implemented in the programming language JAVA. Below we describe the most important constraints in more detail.

3.1 Hard Page Layout Constraints

These constraints model the alignment of the story-board panels on a single page.

Page border constraints: A panel must not poke out the page margins.

Beginning constraint: The first panel is always placed on the top left position of a page.

Panel width constraint: The panel width is determined by the panel type, e.g., the width of a panorama panel is larger than a portrait panel, because the first one shows the whole meeting room, while the latter shows a close-up of a participant.

Brick wall constraint: A brick wall is the typical layout of a story-board and modeled by this constraint. Its purpose is to emphasize the reading direction, e.g., from left to right. Thus the leftmost panels in subsequent rows must not have the same width. Figure 3 shows a typical brick wall layout.

Maximum balloon constraint: Every panel must not contain more than five balloons.

Fig. 3. A typical brick wall layout

---

[2] http://choco-solver.net

3.2 Hard Panel Layout Constraints

These constraints control the positioning of text-boxes and speech balloons inside a single panel.

Balloon border constraint: Balloons must not exceed the borders of a panel.

Text-box placement constraint: The alignment of the speech balloons must reflect the natural reading direction of the user, e.g., from the top left corner to the bottom right corner.

3.3 Soft Constraints

Soft constraints are variables defined over a range of values. Their optimization is used to find the best layout solution out of a number of valid solutions.

End of line constraint: In order to exploit the available space of each line, the horizontal gap between the last panel of a line and the right border of the page should be minimized.

End of page constraint: The vertical gap between the last panel (i.e., last line) of a page and the bottom of that page should also be minimized. This constraint is used for for the optimal utilization of the available space on a page.

3.4 Resulting Layout

The story-board that results from the application of all the constraints shown above on the hand-generated input is shown in figure 4. Text-boxes are rendered

Fig. 4. Story-board layout of meeting IS1003b

in green in the upper left corner of the panels which fulfills the text-box placement constraint. The panels are positioned according to the brick wall constraint,
e.g., the first two panels in the first row have different widths unlike the first
two panels in the second row. Also, all balloons fit into the panels as required
by the balloon border constraint. The tails of all balloons are statically set in
dependence of the panel type. The problem of overing the faces of the speakers
is addressed in section 7.

4   M2SuVi

The AMI meeting corpus offers a huge amount of annotated meetings and several
video streams for each meeting but not explicitly contains story-board annotations. In order to use the data as input for SuVi, we need to find a mapping
between the available corpus resources and the layout objects we described in
the previous chapter. Therefore, we developed M2SuVi - meeting to SuVi. The
following layout elements need to be filled automatically:

- The content of the text-boxes
- The content of the balloons
- Background images for the panels

SuVi needs the content for the balloons and text-boxes as complete sentences
which are not available in the AMI corpus. Second, SuVi uses all sentences which
are fed into the system for the layout. It is impossible to use all the data in a
meeting and therefore a selection of relevant data for a story-board layout has
to be made. We elaborate and implement two promising approaches for filling
the layout objects with content taken from the AMI corpus.

First, we give an overview of the general system architecture in section 4.1.
Then we describe the two approaches to make AMI corpus data available for
automatic summary generation in section 4.2 and 4.3, respectively.

4.1   Architecture of M2SuVi

Figure 5 depicts the architecture of M2SuVi. The Input Reader of the system
needs appropriate input data in the Nxt-Format[3] from the AMI corpus. Depending on the particular Content Creator the data are then extracted and converted
into a special internal content representation which is depicted in figure 6. The
linked Hash-map shown on the left contains the content for each topic. Every
topic in turn comprises the contents for the text-box shown in green in figure
4 and the content for the assigned balloons. We additionally store the speaker,
time and topic for each balloon to preserve the reading order. For filling the
panels with appropriate pictures the Image Extractor uses the available video
streams of a meeting and take time synchronized still-pictures. Otherwise, it uses
a default picture. As a fallback for cases in which the required video stream is not

---

[3] http://www.ltg.ed.ac.uk/NITE/index.html

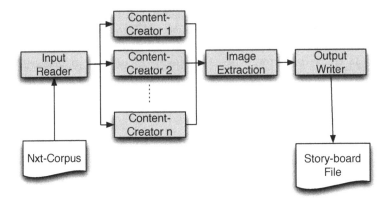

Fig. 5. Architecture of M2SuVi

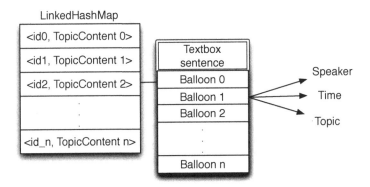

Fig. 6. Internal representation of the content

available. Section 4.4 describes this extraction process in more detail. Finally, the Output Writer uses the resulting data to output the story-board file which is understood by SuVi.

4.2   Content Creation with Abstract Summaries

Our first implementation gathers input data for the story-board generation from the AMI-corpus based on the abstract summaries of a meeting. Abstract in that sense, that they contain a hand written summary of the whole meeting. They are divided in the sections "abstract", "decisions", "action points" and "problems". In order to cover the whole meeting, we use the abstract-section of a summary for our approach. In the corpus, each sentence of the abstract summary is linked to a series of actually uttered sentences in the meeting. Moreover, it summarizes all these linked sentences.

The idea is to transform this type of annotation into a story-board layout by taking the sentence from the abstractive summary for a text-box while all

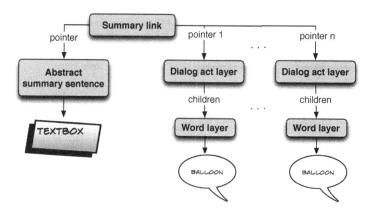

Fig. 7. Following the links in the abstractive summaries

linked sentences are taken for filling the balloons. Figure 7 illustrates the relation between a summary link from the abstractive summary, its linked sentences and the role they play in the story-board layout. In order to restrict the number of balloons for each summary sentence, the maximum number of links to follow can simply be set by a system parameter.

4.3   Content Creation with Extractive Summaries

Our second implementation of a story-board generation out of the AMI-corpus is based on the extractive summaries and the topic segmentation. The advantage of this approach is that there are already automatic tools that produce this kind of data. However, this implementation is more complex because the extractive summaries are not linked in the corpus. Therefore, we cannot benefit from existing corpus structures. Instead, we have to compute the relations of the story-board elements to each other, e.g., which topic a sentence of an extractive summary belongs to.

Figure 8 shows the strategy for filling the balloons and text-boxes in this case. Every word in a meeting is assigned to a topic and stored in an appropriate data-structure. The corpus contains a set of default-topics, which are used throughout for annotation. We use these default-topics in the order in which they occur in a meeting and map every word to the topic it belongs to (see the left part of figure 8).

Every balloon is filled by one sentence of the extractive summary. Again, every sentence of the summary is used for the content of the story-board but in this case every extractive summary sentence fills one balloon. Remember that in the previous section we used the sentences of the abstract summary for the text-boxes, not the balloons. Since we have to build a mapping from every word to a topic, we can in turn assign a topic to every sentence because topics do not change within a sentence.

To fill the text-boxes with content we simply take the topic description as it exists for each topic of the AMI corpus. To augment the content of the text-boxes,

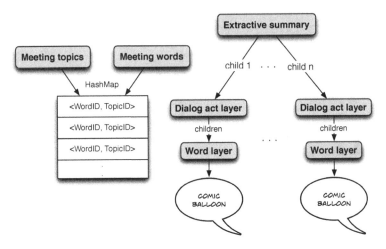

Fig. 8. Creating story-board content with extractive summaries

one could simply extend these topic descriptions manually by providing more elaborated sentences.

4.4 Still-Pictures Extraction

The extraction of still pictures is a procedure running independently of the content extraction step. There are two types of panels in SUVI: Portrait-panels and Panorama-panels The first type of panel is a close-up of a single speaker. It is chosen if SUVI identifies a dominant speaker for one panel (i.e., the speaker who made most of the utterances in a panel). In the corpus, there is an individual video stream available for each speaker from which we extract a time synchronous still-picture. Depending on the dominant speaker of a panel, the appropriate video stream is selected for still-picture extraction. The second type of panel is used if no dominant speaker can be identified. We then choose the video stream which shows the general view, e.g., the meeting room and all participants. If one of the video files cannot be found, e.g., if a reduced version of the system is running offline on a small mobile device, we implemented a simple fallback and use previously stored default pictures for the missing stream.

5   Batch-Run over the AMI-Corpus

In order to prove the robustness of the two components of our system, we did a batch-run over all available meetings in the AMI-meeting corpus. We did this for the two strategies we described in the previous two sections (extractive and abstractive summaries).

M2SUVI generated at most six topics per page and used a maximum of eight balloons per topic. For reasons of simplicity, we used default pictures for the

Table 1. Batch-run results

Mode	avg. runtime (s)	result	no result	total	successful layouts in %
Extractive	48.8	120	3	123	97.6
Abstractive	86.1	86	12	98	87.8

layout. The batch-run was done on an Intel Core2Duo processor running at 2.2 GHz with 2 GB of working memory.

Table 1 shows the results for both of our components and demonstrates that a solution is possible for nearly every input as shown in the sixth column. There were a few meetings, however, for which no layout was possible because of errors in the corpus, e.g., dead links. Furthermore, an abstract summary is not available for every meeting, which explains the difference of total meetings in the fifth column. The average runtime in seconds of the constraint solver is shown in the second column.

6   Automatic End-to-End Story-Board Generation

In order to show the applicability of our generic approach in an end-to-end implementation for a completely different domain and in a different use case, we tested the system on a selected part of the first AMIDA review meeting. Here is a short description of this special approach:

In contrast to the data in the AMI-corpus, the review meeting data was completely processed by automatic tools from The University of Sheffield (ASR), The University of Edinburgh (topic segmentation & labeling) and The IDIAP Research Institute in Martigny (recordings). An ASR engine provided the raw data and the necessary foundation for further processing. After that, the ASR output was automatically converted into the required NXT-format and segmented into topics.

Both components of our system, SuVi and M2SuVi, proved to be very robust under the new input data and in a completely new domain. Although the data was previously unknown, after resolving some minor formating issues it was possible to do a provisional

Fig. 9. Story-board layout of the first AMIDA review meeting

story-board layout of the review meeting. However, we realized, that the balloons got too large and covered the whole panel. A newly invented "spurts"-layer linked far more words per comic-balloon than the original data, i.e. the links in the abstractive and extractive summaries. We quickly limited the content-size of the comic-balloons and added "..." at the end of each comic-balloon to indicate that there is more text available. Due to technical problems, there were no video streams available. However, we could benefit from our fallback strategy here by simply using default pictures which were taken during the meeting with a digital camera. Figure 9 shows the resulting story-board layout of the first AMIDA review meeting.

7   Conclusion and Future Work

In this paper we described SuVi, an automatic layout tool for meeting summaries. Due to the initial restrictions of the input for this tool, M2SuVi was developed which made the complete AMI meeting corpus accessible for story-board generation.

The generation of layouts is robust and works fairly well, even in a completely new domain as described in section 5 and 6. But too often the faces of the speakers are superposed by the balloons. In the next version of SuVi, we will make use of image processing techniques to detect faces and set dynamic constraints in such a way, that the faces are kept free of balloons. The detection of the face positions will also give us the possibility to optimize the positioning of the balloon tails and adjust them to the mouth of the person. Actually, they are statically set simply depending on the panel type. SuVi now uses a one page layout by default. Depending on the number of how many topics/balloons available, we will implement a multi page layout automatically.

With our project partner Philips we are currently implementing a server-version of our system which takes the user input from a web page, generates the story-board in the background and sends back the result as a Scalable Vector Graphic (SVG) using a newly developed proprietary display component. The http-client will run on an embedded platform making it necessary to replace the proprietary ComicLife©-format. The final version will feature output formats in jpeg, png, pdf and plain svg.

We are also in negotiation with industrial partners for commercial use of this technology.

References

1. Frey, J.: Constraint-basierte Generierung parametrisierbarer, multimodaler Comic-Layouts für verlaufsorientierte Meeting-Zusammenfassungen, Master's thesis, Saarbrücken (2007)
2. Lang, B.: Parameterisierbares Layout inhaltsorientierter, multimodaler Zusammen-fassungen von Meetings anhand der Zeitungsmetapher in einem Constraint-basierten Ansatz. Master's thesis, Saarbrücken (2007)

3. Kleinbauer, T., Becker, S., Becker, T.: Indicative Abstractive Summaries of Meetings. Saarbrücken (2007)
4. Rendering software Comiclife© by plasq, http://plasq.com/comiclife/
5. Carletta, J., Ashby, S., Bourban, S., Flynn, M., et al.: The AMI Meeting Corpus. In: Proceedings of the Measuring Behavior 2005 symposium on, Annotating and measuring Meeting Behaviour(2005)
6. AMIDA: "Augmented Multiparty Interaction with Distance Access", Deliverable D5.2: Report on multimodal content abstraction. Technical report, Brno University of Technology, DFKI, ICSI, IDIAP, TNO, University of Edinburgh, University of Twente and University of Sheffield (2007)
7. Carletta, J., Evert, S., Heid, U.: The NITE XML Toolkit: data model and query language. Language Resources and Evaluation Journal (2006)
8. Apt, K.R.: Principles of Constraint Programming. Cambridge University Press, Cambridge (2003)

A Probabilistic Model for User Relevance Feedback on Image Retrieval

Roberto Paredes[1], Thomas Deselaers[2], and Enrique Vidal[1]

[1] Pattern Recognition and Human Language Technology Group
Instituto Tecnológico de Informática
Universidad Politécnica de Valencia, Spain
rparedes@iti.upv.es, evidal@iti.upv.es
[2] Human Language Technology and Pattern Recognition Group
Computer Science Department, RWTH Aachen University
Aachen, Germany
deselaers@cs.rwth-aachen.de

Abstract. We present a novel probabilistic model for user interaction in image retrieval applications which accounts for consistency among the retrieved images and considers the distribution of images in the database which is searched for. Common models for relevance feedback do not consider this and thus do not incorporate all available information. The proposed method is evaluated on two publicly available benchmark databases and clearly outperforms recent competitive methods.

1   Introduction

This work presents a probabilistic model to handle user interaction in information retrieval applications. This user interaction is usually accomplished using some feedback regarding the relevance of the information retrieved by the system. The model presented is for general information retrieval systems but here we focus on image retrieval. Image retrieval has been investigated since the 80's and, in the 90's, content-based image retrieval (CBIR) became an active area of research. In CBIR, the objective is to find relevant images where the query is often described by an example image of the type of images that the user is looking for. In practice, CBIR is still far away from being a solved problem. One way to increase retrieval performance is to consider user feedback, i.e. a user starts his query with an example image and is then presented with a set of hopefully relevant images; from these images the user selects those images which are relevant and which are not (possibly leaving some images unmarked) and then the retrieval system refines its results, hopefully leading to better results after each iteration of user feedback.

Related Work. Relevance feedback has been under investigation in the field of image retrieval and information retrieval nearly as long as the field of information retrieval exists [1]. An overview of the early related work on relevance feedback in image retrieval is given in [2]. Most approaches use the marked images as

A. Popescu-Belis and R. Stiefelhagen (Eds.): MLMI 2008, LNCS 5237, pp. 260–271, 2008.
© Springer-Verlag Berlin Heidelberg 2008

individual queries and combine the retrieved results. More recent approaches follow a query-instance-based approach [3] or use support vector machines to learn a two-class classifier [4]. All approaches have in common that only the feedback-images are considered and the database to be searched for relevant images is not considered. In this work, we use a set of images from which images are retrieved in a fully probabilistic way to determine the relevance probability of candidate image sets. This leads to a significant boost in performance and also opens new ways to integrate consistency checks into the retrieval procedure. Another related field of research is browsing of image and video databases. The approach most closely related to the approach presented here is Bayesian browsing [5]. The formulation presented here, follows the concepts for interactive pattern recognition proposed in [6].

2   Methodology

This section presents the methodology followed in the present work. First, a basic notation is introduced followed by our proposed probabilistic model and a greedy algorithm. Notation and modelling are particularized for the image retrieval problem but they can be easily adapted to any information retrieval system.

2.1   Notation and Probabilistic Model

Let U be the universal set of images and let $C \subset U$ be a fixed, finite *collection* of images. The initial query image proposed by the user is $q \in U$. We assume the user "has in mind" some *relevant set* of images $R \subset C$. This set is unknown and the system's objective is to discover n images of it, among the images in C. The interactive retrieval process starts with the user proposing a particular *query image*, $q \in U$. Then the system provides an initial set $X \subset C$ of n images that are "similar" to q according to a suitable distance measure. These images are judged by the user who provides a *feedback* by selecting which images are relevant (and, implicitly, which are not relevant). Such feedback information is used by the system to obtain a new set of images X and the process is repeated until the user is satisfied, which means that he/she considers all images X to be relevant.

At any step of this process, let the user feedback be denoted by $F = (Q^+ \cup Q^-) \in C^m$, where $m \geq n$ is the number of images supervised by the user[1], $Q^+ \subset R$ are the images that the user has considered to be relevant and $Q^- \subset C - R$ are the images that the user has considered to be non-relevant. Let $C_F = C - F$ be the set of the images in the collection that have not been retrieved. Usually the initial query is considered to be in the set of relevant images, $q \in Q^+$. In the following notation, m, r and $\bar{r}$ are the sizes of F, Q^+ and Q^-, respectively.

---

[1] As F can be obtained as a result of *several* feedback iterations, the total number of supervised images m, can be greater than the number of images retrieved in each iteration n.

To optimize the user experience, we propose to maximize the probability that the images in X are relevant according to F. That is, the images in X should be "similar" to the images in Q^+ (and may also be similar among each other) and "different" from images in Q^-. Formally:

$$\hat{X} = \arg \max_{X \in C^n} Pr(X \mid C, q, F) \tag{1}$$

Since C and q are fixed, to simplify notation we will drop these conditions from now on. Now, applying Bayes' rule,

$$\hat{X} = \arg \max_{X \in C^n} Pr(F \mid X) \cdot Pr(X) \tag{2}$$

For the first term of (2) we can use a model directly based on image distances:

$$Pr(F \mid X) \propto \prod_{x \in X} P(F \mid x) \tag{3}$$

where each term in the product[2] is a *smooth* version of the classical class-conditional probability estimate based on nearest neighbors [7] using a suitable image distance $d(\cdot, \cdot)$:

$$P(F \mid x) = \frac{\sum_{q \in Q^+} d(q, x)^{-1}}{\sum_{q \in F} d(q, x)^{-1}} \tag{4}$$

Note that we use a product to combine probabilities in (3) (rather than a sum). This enables using the greedy search strategy proposed in Section 3 to find approximate solutions to (2).

For the second term of (2), we assume that the prior probability of a set X should be high if it is *"consistent"*; that is, if all its images are similar among them. Applying the chain rule, we obtain:

$$\begin{aligned} Pr(X) &= Pr(x_1, x_2, \ldots, x_n) \\ &= Pr(x_1) \, Pr(x_2 \mid x_1), \ldots, Pr(x_n \mid x_1 \ldots x_{n-1}) \end{aligned} \tag{5}$$

As before, each term of this product can be adequately modeled in terms of image distances:

$$Pr(x_i \mid x_1 \ldots x_{i-1}) \propto \frac{P(x_1 \cdots x_i)}{P(x_1 \cdots x_{i-1})} \tag{6}$$

where

$$P(x_1 \cdots x_i) = \frac{1}{i(i-1)} \sum_{j=1}^{i} \sum_{k \neq j, k=1}^{i} d(x_j, x_k)^{-1} \tag{7}$$

---

[2] Note that only the notation Pr() stands for true probabilities; we abuse the notation by letting P() denote arbitrary functions used as a models.

Intuitively, equations (4) and (6), respectively, measure *relevancy* and *consistency* of images in X. Therefore, in practice, it is convenient to balance the importance of both factors by means of a parameter α, where $\alpha = 1$ denotes that no consistency information is used and $\alpha = 0.0$ denotes that only consistency information is considered. Taking this into account, equation (2) can be expanded as:

$$\hat{X} \approx \arg\max_{X \in C^n} P(F \mid x_1) Pr(x_1) \prod_{i=2}^{n} P(F \mid x_i)^\alpha \left(\frac{P(x_1 \cdots x_i)}{P(x_1 \cdots x_{i-1})} \right)^{1-\alpha} \quad (8)$$

In the following sections we describe an efficient procedure to find an approximately optimal set of images X.

3 Greedy Approximation Relevance Feedback Algorithm

We propose an algorithm to approximate the maximization presented in (8). This algorithm works as follows. First of all the r images in Q^+ are selected as the first r images in $\hat{X}$. The remaining $n - r$ images are to be selected from the set C_F since the images in Q^+ and Q^- have just been supervised by the user. This approximation entails a slight modification of the maximization in (8):

$$\hat{X} \approx Q^+ \cup \arg\max_{X \in C_F^{n-r}} P(F \mid x_{r+1}) Pr(x_{r+1}) \prod_{i=r+2}^{n} P(F \mid x_i)^\alpha \left(\frac{P(x_1 \cdots x_i)}{P(x_1 \cdots x_{i-1})} \right)^{1-\alpha}$$

$$(9)$$

We assume that $Pr(x)$ follows an uniform distribution, so the term $Pr(x_{r+1})$ is constant in the maximization process and can be dropped. To solve the maximization, the *t-best* images, $t \geq (n - r)$, with the highest values of $P(F \mid x_i)$ are determined, we refer to this set as $\mathcal{B}$. Each image that belongs to $\mathcal{B}$ is tentatively hypothesized to be the first image, x_{r+1}. Subsequently, the following images can be determined by greedy maximization of the index (9), using the GARF algorithm shown in Figure 1.

3.1 A Simplified Version of GARF

If $\alpha = 1$, image consistency is not taken into account and thus the expression to maximize becomes

$$\hat{X} = Q^+ \cup \arg\max_{X \in C_F^{n-r}} \prod_{i=r+1}^{n} P(F \mid x_i), \quad (10)$$

which further simplifies the procedure. To maximize this expression, only those images with maximum values for $P(F \mid x_i)$ have to be chosen, yielding the GARFs algorithm shown in Figure 2.

Due to this simplification, GARFs is no longer a greedy algorithm but it is an exact solution to (10) instead. We prefer to refer to this algorithm as GARFs because it can be considered as a simplified version of GARF. The computational complexity of GARFs is the same as the relevance feedback baseline methods presented in section 4.2.

$\hat{X}$=**GARF**(C, Q^+, Q^-)
{
    for each $x \in C_F$
        $V_x = P(F \mid x)$
    end for
    $\mathcal{B} = select(V, t)$
    $max = -\infty$
    for each $x \in \mathcal{B}$
        $x_{r+1} = x$
        $S = \{x_{r+1}\}$
        for $i = r + 2 \ldots n$
            $x_i = \arg\max_{x \in \mathcal{B}-S} P(F \mid x)^\alpha \left(\frac{P(x_{r+1}, \ldots, x_{i-1}, x)}{P(x_{r+1}, \ldots, x_{i-1})}\right)^{1-\alpha}$
            $S = S \cup \{x_i\}$
        end for
        $sc = P(F \mid x_{r+1}) \prod_{i=r+2}^{n} P(F \mid x_i)^\alpha \left(\frac{P(x_{r+1} \ldots x_i)}{P(x_{r+1} \ldots x_{i-1})}\right)^{1-\alpha}$
        if $(sc > max)$ {
            $max = sc$
            $SBest = S$
        }
    end for
    $\hat{X} = Q^+ \cup SBest$
    return $\hat{X}$
}

Fig. 1. GARF: Greedy approximative algorithm to determine the most relevant and consistent images. The value of t has to be tuned empirically.

$\hat{X}$=**GARFs**(C, Q^+, Q^-)
{
    for each $x \in C_F$
        $V_x = P(F \mid x)$
    end for
    $\mathcal{B} = select(V, n - r)$
    $\hat{X} = Q^+ \cup \mathcal{B}$
    return $\hat{X}$
}

Fig. 2. GARFs: Simplified GARF algorithm not considering image consistency

4   Experiments

The proposed algorithm is evaluated using the two well know data sets, Corel/Wang and MSRC published by the Machine Learning and Perception Group from Microsoft Research, Cambridge, UK. For the sake of experimental clarity and reproducibility, in all the experiments, relevance feedback was simulated, i.e. no real users where involved. Nevertheless the methods proposed here

Fig. 3. Example images from (a) the WANG database and (b) the MSRC database

can directly be used with any user interface that allows users to mark images as relevant and/or non-relevant in interactive retrieval processes such as those presented in [8,9].

WANG Database. It consists of a subset of 1,000 images of the Corel stock photo database which have been manually selected and which form 10 classes of 100 images each. Example images are shown in Figure 3 (a). The WANG database can be considered similar to common stock photo retrieval tasks with several images from each category and a potential user having an image from a particular category and looking for similar images which have cheaper royalties or which have not been used by other media. The 10 classes are used for relevance estimation: given a query image, it is assumed that the user is searching for images from the same class, and therefore the remaining 99 images from the same class are considered relevant and the images from all other classes are considered irrelevant.

MSRC Database. It was published by the Machine Learning and Perception Group from Microsoft Research, Cambridge, UK and is available online[3]. It consists of 4320 from 33 classes such as aeroplanes, bicycles/general, bicycles/sideview, sheep/general, sheep/single and is generally considered a difficult task [10]. Some example images from this database are shown in Figure 3 (b). We use this database in two different setups. In the first setup, we use 10% of the data as query images and the rest is used as image collection C. In the second setup, we use all images from classes with less than 50 images as queries in a leaving-one-out manner. The latter setup allows for investigating the effects that occur on larger databases where only a small fraction of all images are considered relevant.

4.1   Image Feature Extraction

For our experiments, we choose to represent our images using color histograms and Tamura texture histograms. Although there are image descriptors that

---

[3] http://research.microsoft.com/research/downloads/Details/b94de342-60dc-45d0-830b-9f6eff91b301/Details.aspx

perform far better for special applications, it was recently shown that these features are a very reasonable baseline for general image databases [11]. Furthermore, the probabilistic model for relevance feedback investigated here, can be applied on top of any image descriptor that allows for distance calculation between images. In the following, we describe how these features are compared and obtained.

The features used are represented as histograms, as it is described in the next sections. To compare the histograms, we use L_1 distance, which was shown to be identical to histogram intersection if the histograms share the same bins

$$d(h, h') = \sum_{i=1}^{I} |h_i - h'_i|,\tag{11}$$

where h and h' are two histograms to be compared and h_i and h'_i are the i-th bins.

Color Histograms. Color histograms are among the most basic approaches and widely used in image retrieval [12,13,14]. To show performance improvements in image retrieval, systems using only color histograms are often used as a baseline. The color space is partitioned and for each partition the pixels with a color within its range are counted, resulting in a representation of the relative frequencies of the occurring colors. We use the RGB color space for the histograms, and split each dimension into 8 bins leading to an $8^3 = 512$ dimensional histogram. We observed only minor differences with other color spaces which was also observed in [15].

Tamura Features. In [16] the authors propose six texture features corresponding to human visual perception: *coarseness, contrast, directionality, line-likeness, regularity,* and *roughness*. From experiments testing the significance of these features with respect to human perception, it was concluded that the first three features are very important. Thus, in our experiments we use coarseness, contrast, and directionality, calculate each of these values in a neighborhood for each pixel, quantize each of these values into 8 discrete values and create a 512-dimensional joint histogram for each image. In the QBIC system [13] histograms of these features were used as well.

4.2   Baseline Methods

The proposed approach is compared with some baseline methods:

Simple Method. The simple method is accomplished by performing the next search of $n - r$ images among the set of images in C_F, keeping the relevant images, and performing the next search exactly equal as the initial one but over this reduced collection C_F.

Relevance Score. Relevance score (RS) was proposed by [3], and has been inspired by the nearest neighbor classification method. Instead of only finding the best match for each query image among the database images, for each database image only the best matching query image is considered among the positive and negative query images. The ratio between the nearest relevant and the nearest non-relevant image is considered for ranking the images. In [3], the RS is computed as

$$RS(x, (Q^+, Q_-)) = \left(1 + \frac{\min\limits_{q_+ \in Q^+} d(x, q_+)}{\min\limits_{q_- \in Q^-} d(x, q_-)}\right)^{-1} \tag{12}$$

and then images are ranked such that the images with smallest relevance score are presented first.

Rocchio Relevance Feedback. Rocchio's method for relevance feedback [1] can be considered a de facto standard in textual information retrieval. In CBIR, it has been investigated in the context of the GIFT system [17]. In Rocchio relevance feedback, the individual query documents are combined into a single query according to

$$\hat{q} = q + w_+ \left(\sum_{q_+ \in Q^+} q_+\right) - w_- \left(\sum_{q_- \in Q^-} q_-\right), \tag{13}$$

where $\hat{q}$ is the new query, q is the query from the last feedback iteration and w_+ and w_- are weighting factors to determine the influence of relevance feedback, commonly the parameters are chosen $w_+ = |Q^+|, w_- = |Q^-|$.

Once, $\hat{q}$ is determined it is used to query the database and find the most similar images.

4.3   Results

In all the experiments, we set the number of images to be retrieved to $n = 20$ and the query image is always contained in set of retrieved images. Up to four feedback iterations were performed. The precision was measured for each iteration obtaining 5 values for each method $P_1, \ldots, P_5$. The precision is the ratio of the relevant images among the n retrieved ones and is given in percentage.

WANG database. For the evaluation of the different relevance feedback methods on this database a Leaving-One-Out approach has been followed. Every image is used as query and the rest of images are used as reference set C.

The results for the database are shown in Table 1. The simplified version of GARF obtains the best results. It is worth to mention that the user is interested to obtain high precision values for the first feedback iterations, and in this case, GARFs is the best method.

Figure 4 shows the results of the GARF algorithm for the first feedback iteration (P_2) with varying α-parameter and the size of the set $\mathcal{B}$. The α parameter is varied from 0 (no consistency information considered, simplified GARF) to 1 (only consistency information considered). The size of the set $\mathcal{B}$, t-parameter, is

Table 1. Experimental results on the WANG database

Method	P_1	P_2	P_3	P_4	P_5
Simple	73.6	83.2	88.0	91.0	92.9
Rocchio	73.6	92.7	97.3	99.2	99.8
RS	73.6	92.2	97.8	99.5	99.9
GARFs	73.6	94.5	98.9	99.9	99.9

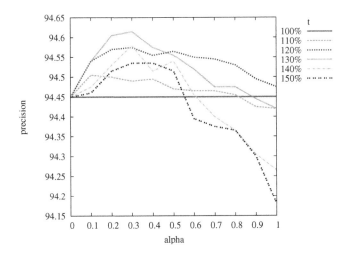

Fig. 4. Results on the WANG database using different values of α and t

given relatively to the number of relevant images still needed $n - r$. The results obtained for $t = 100\%$ does not vary with respect to α because this value means that $\mathcal{B}$ has only $n - r$ images. The highest precision for the first feedback iteration is 94.62 and is obtained using GARF with $\alpha = 0.3$ and $t = 140\%$.

MSRC database. First we consider the setup where 10% of the images are used as queries and the rest as reference set. The results for this database are shown in Table 2. Again, the simplified version of GARF obtains the best results. The improvement of the proposed approach becomes more significant as more interaction steps are used. This effect is probably due to the additional relevant samples which allow for much better probability estimation.

Figure 5 shows the results of the algorithm GARF for the first feedback iteration (P_2), varying the parameter α and the size of the set $\mathcal{B}$.

The highest precision for the first feedback iteration is 62.92 and is obtained using GARF with $\alpha = 0.1$ and $t = 140\%$. In this case the use of GARF does not produce any significant improvement over the simplified version. This is due to the fact that in this database images from the same class may differ significantly and so the consistency factor of the probabilistic model does not help to improve the precision of the system. An example of images that belongs to some of the classes is showed in Figure 6.

Table 2. Results using different relevance feedback methods on the MSRC database

Method	P_1	P_2	P_3	P_4	P_5
Simple	45.5	55.2	61.0	65.3	68.4
Rocchio	45.5	60.8	69.6	75.1	78.8
RS	45.5	60.6	68.5	75.0	79.9
GARFs	45.5	62.9	73.4	80.0	84.2

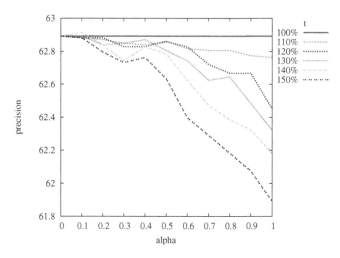

Fig. 5. Results on the MSRC database using different values of α and t

Fig. 6. MSRC example of the differences among images of the same class. (a) office (b) benches and chairs.

MSRC database few relevant images. A more challenging experiment has been performed for the MSRC dataset considering as query images only those images that belong to classes with less than 50 images. In this case we used only 263 images from 9 different classes. This experiment aims at simulating a real scenario when the user is interested in images which are seldom among the searched database and thus this task is more closely related to searching images

Table 3. Results using different relevance feedback methods on the MSRC subset with few relevant images

Method	P_1	P_2	P_3	P_4	P_5
Simple	18.4	23.7	27.7	31.1	33.7
Rocchio	18.4	26.5	32.1	36.3	39.8
RS	18.4	24.4	30.1	35.4	39.8
GARFs	18.4	27.0	35.4	42.6	48.5

in the internet. The results for these experiments are show in Table 3 for the different methods from the literature and for the simplified GARF algorithm.

Again, GARFs obtains the best results but opposed the experiments presented in the previous section, here the difference between GARFs and the other methods is much bigger, which underlines the effectiveness of the proposed model. The relative improvement of GARFs in the fifth feedback iteration is higher than 25% over the second best technique (RS). The proposed approach entails a good technique for image search problems on real conditions.

5   Conclusions

We present a novel probabilistic model for relevance feedback in image retrieval. In contrast to other approaches, we incorporate consistency among the retrieved images in a theoretically sound way. A simpler model which does not take into account such consistency is also proposed.

The results obtained by this simplified version are already clearly better than the results obtained by the state-of-the-art techniques tested. On the other hand the incorporation of the consistency model can increase the performance of the retrieval system even further. The improvements contributed by this consistency model have shown to be effective mainly when the classes of the images are *consistent* enough under an *appearance* point of view.

While these improvements are really marginal, they show that the novel approach to information retrieval proposed here provides a suitable framework to develop new techniques that better take advantage of all the information sources available.

References

1. Rocchio, J.: Relevance feedback in information retrieval. In: Salton, G. (ed.) The SMART Retrieval System: Experiments in Automatic Document Processing, pp. 313–323. Prentice-Hall, Englewood Cliffs (1971)
2. Zhou, X.S., Huang, T.S.: Relevance feedback in image retrieval: A comprehensive review. Multimedia Systems 8, 536–544 (2003)
3. Giacinto, G., Rolli, F.: Instance-based relevance feedback for image retrieval. In: Neural Information Processing Systems (NIPS), Vancouver, Canada (December 2004)

4. Setia, L., Ick, J., Burkhardt, H.: Svm-based relevance feedback in image retrieval using invariant feature histograms. In: IAPR Workshop on Machine Vision Applications (MVA), Tsukuba Science City, Japan (May 2005)
5. Vasconcelos, N., Lippman, A.: Bayesian modeling of video editing and structure: Semantic features for video summarization and browsing. In: ICIP, Chicago, IL, USA, pp. 153–157 (1998)
6. Vidal, E., Rodríguez, L., Casacuberta, F., García-Varea, I.: Interactive pattern recognition. In: Popescu-Belis, A., Renals, S., Bourlard, H. (eds.) MLMI 2007. LNCS, vol. 4892, pp. 60–71. Springer, Heidelberg (2007)
7. Duda, R., Hart, P.: Pattern Recognition and Scene Analisys. John Wiley, New York (1973)
8. Rooij, O., Snoek, C.G.M., Worring, M.: Query on demand video browsing. In: ACM Int. Conf. on Multimedia, Augsburg, Germany, pp. 811–814 (2007)
9. Moënne-Loccoz, N., Bruno, E., Marchand-Maillet, S.: Interactive Retrieval of Video Sequences from Local Feature Dynamics. In: Detyniecki, M., Jose, J.M., Nürnberger, A., van Rijsbergen, C.J. (eds.) AMR 2005. LNCS, vol. 3877. Springer, Heidelberg (2006)
10. Winn, J., Criminisi, A., Minka, T.: Object categorization by learned universal visual dictionary. In: International Conference on Computer Vision 2005, Beijing, China, vol. 2, pp. 1800–1807 (October 2005)
11. Deselaers, T., Keysers, D., Ney, H.: Features for image retrieval: An experimental comparison. Information Retrieval (2008) (in press)
12. Smeulders, A.W.M., Worring, M., Santini, S., Gupta, A., Jain, R.: Content-based image retrieval at the end of the early years. IEEE Transactions on Pattern Analysis and Machine Intelligence 22(12), 1349–1380 (2000)
13. Faloutsos, C., Barber, R., Flickner, M., Hafner, J., Niblack, W., Petkovic, D., Equitz, W.: Efficient and effective querying by image content. Journal of Intelligent Information Systems 3(3/4), 231–262 (1994)
14. Swain, M.J., Ballard, D.H.: Color indexing. International Journal of Computer Vision 7(1), 11–32 (1991)
15. Smith, J.R., Chang, S.F.: Tools and techniques for color image retrieval. In: SPIE Storage and Retrieval for Image and Video Databases, vol. 2670, pp. 426–437 (1996)
16. Tamura, H., Mori, S., Yamawaki, T.: Textural features corresponding to visual perception. IEEE Transaction on Systems, Man, and Cybernetics 8(6), 460–472 (1978)
17. Müller, H., Müller, W., Marchand-Maillet, S., Squire, D.M.: Strategies for positive and negative relevance feedback in image retrieval. In: Sanfeliu, A., Villanueva, J., Vanrell, M., Alquezar, R., Eklundh, J.-O., Aloimonos, Y. (eds.) Proceedings of the International Conference on Pattern Recognition (ICPR 2000), Barcelona, Spain. Computer Vision and Image Analysis, vol. 1, pp. 1043–1046 (2000)

The AMIDA Automatic Content Linking Device: Just-in-Time Document Retrieval in Meetings

Andrei Popescu-Belis[1], Erik Boertjes[2], Jonathan Kilgour[3], Peter Poller[4],
Sandro Castronovo[4], Theresa Wilson[3], Alejandro Jaimes[5,*], and Jean Carletta[3]

[1] Idiap Research Institute, P.O. Box 592
CH-1920 Martigny, Switzerland
andrei.popescu-belis@idiap.ch
[2] TNO ICT, Brassersplein 2
NL-2612 CT Delft, The Netherlands
erik.boertjes@tno.nl
[3] HCRC and CSTR, University of Edinburgh
2 Buccleuch Place, Edinburgh, EH8 9LW, UK
{jonathan,jeanc,twilson}@inf.ed.ac.uk
[4] DFKI GmbH, Stuhlsatzenhausweg 3
D-66123 Saarbruecken, Germany
{peter.poller,sandro.castronovo}@dfki.de
[5] Telefonica Research, C/Emilio Vargas 6
ES-28403 Madrid, Spain
ajaimes@tid.es

Abstract. The AMIDA Automatic Content Linking Device (ACLD) is a just-in-time document retrieval system for meeting environments. The ACLD listens to a meeting and displays information about the documents from the group's history that are most relevant to what is being said. Participants can view an outline or the entire content of the documents, if they feel that these documents are potentially useful at that moment of the meeting. The ACLD proof-of-concept prototype places meeting-related documents and segments of previously recorded meetings in a repository and indexes them. During a meeting, the ACLD continually retrieves the documents that are most relevant to keywords found automatically using the current meeting speech. The current prototype simulates the real-time speech recognition that will be available in the near future. The software components required to achieve these functions communicate using the Hub, a client/server architecture for annotation exchange and storage in real-time. Results and feedback for the first ACLD prototype are outlined, together with plans for its future development within the AMIDA EU integrated project. Potential users of the ACLD supported the overall concept, and provided feedback to improve the user interface and to access documents beyond the group's own history.

Keywords: just-in-time retrieval, meeting assistants, meeting processing, real-time document retrieval.

---

* Work performed while at Idiap Research Institute.

A. Popescu-Belis and R. Stiefelhagen (Eds.): MLMI 2008, LNCS 5237, pp. 272–283, 2008.

1   Introduction

Participants in a meeting often mention documents containing facts that are currently discussed, but only few documents are at hand. Searches could be performed within a document management system for the right piece of information, but the participants in a meeting usually do not have the time to perform such operations frequently during the meeting. Moreover, even where they do have their documents available, few groups have access to recordings of their past meetings, much less an efficient device for searching them. And when browsing through the recordings of previous meetings, users do not have the time to search for additional information among the meeting documents.

Therefore, a system that would provide tailored access to potentially relevant documents or recorded meetings, based on ongoing discussions, could be very valuable in improving group decision-making. Such an *Automatic Content Linking Device (ACLD)* could be applied to at least two scenarios [1]: the device could be used online during a meeting to display potentially relevant documents in real time (*meeting assistant*), or it could be used offline to browse a past meeting that was recorded, enriching it with potentially relevant documents (*meeting browser*). These scenarios are broadly related to the following options observed in the literature. Conceptually, the content linking mechanism is the same in both cases, only the resources that are available and the constraints of producing results in real-time are different.

1. *Just-in-time retrieval* [2,3,4]: participants to a meeting are constantly given suggestions about documents (including excerpts of previous meetings) that are potentially relevant to the ongoing discussion. Participants are free to ignore them, or to start using them to enhance the discussion, e.g. with figures, precise facts, or decisions made in previous meetings.
2. *Document/speech alignment for meeting browsers* [5,6,7]: users of a meeting archive can view the recordings of previous meetings augmented with related documents, regardless of whether the participants to the meeting referred to them explicitly or not. This can be essential for meetings whose main purpose is to discuss a long document, e.g. a report, and might provide a quicker understanding of the meeting context.

The AMIDA Content Linking Device (ACLD) demonstrates the basic concept of tailored access to a group's history using a set of four meetings from one of the groups recorded in the AMI Meeting Corpus [8]. Although the primary use of such a device would be during live meetings, we need to be able to demonstrate the concept even when there is no meeting happening. Our demonstration replays the group's last meeting (ES2008d) to simulate a live meeting, treating segments from the three previous meetings (ES2008a-c) and associated documents as the group history to be linked. In the recordings, the group carries out a role-playing exercise in which they pretend to be a design team specifying a new kind of remote control. Each group member is given a unique role to play in the team and carries out individual work as well as taking part in the four meetings. Final design decisions are made in the last meeting, which is ES2008d, therefore a number of project documents and fragments of previous meetings are relevant to the discussions in this meeting. The past documents available for linking include reports, emails, and presentations given during the first three meetings, plus segments derived from the first three meetings by dividing them into 200 second chunks.

The remainder of the paper is organized as follows. Section 2 outlines the concept, architecture, and components of the ACLD, which are described in detail in the various subsections of Section 3. Brief implementation notes for the proof-of-concept prototype appear in Section 4, while evaluation results and perspectives for future work are given in Sections 5 and 6 respectively.

2   Concept and Architecture

The Automatic Content Linking Device performs searches at regular intervals over a database of meeting-related documents and pseudo-documents. The search criterion is constructed based on the words that were recognized automatically from the meeting discussion, thanks to online or offline automatic speech recognition (ASR)[1]. The audio signal is captured in an instrumented meeting room [9] or elsewhere, but recording conditions have a strong influence on the recognition accuracy. If some pre-specified terms or keywords are recognized, then they receive greater weight in the subsequent query.

The results are presented as a list of document names ordered by relevance, which can be empty if no document matches enough the words that were recognized. A persistence (smoothing) mechanism ensures that documents which are often retrieved remain some time at the top of the list. A user interface offers the participants quick access to the content of the documents that are retrieved, if they need to search them for valuable information.

These functionalities are supported by a number of modules that communicate through a subscription-based client/server architecture called 'the Hub' [10]. The Hub allows the connection of heterogeneous software modules, which may operate remotely, and ensures that data exchange is extremely fast – a requirement for real-time processing of human interaction. Data circulating through the Hub is formatted as timed triples (time, object, attribute, value), and is also stored in a special-purpose database, which was designed to deal with large-scale, real-time annotation of audio and video recordings. 'Producers' of annotations send triples to the Hub, which are received by the 'consumers' that subscribed to the respective types; consumers can also query the Hub for past annotations and metadata about meetings.

The architecture of the ACLD is shown in Figure 1, while the main components are first outlined below and then described in the following subsections.

Document Bank Creator (DBC): Gathers documents that are of potential interest for an upcoming meeting. In the current implementation, this is

---

[1] An online ASR module was recently developed in the AMIDA project, and its connection to the ACLD is under work at the time of writing.

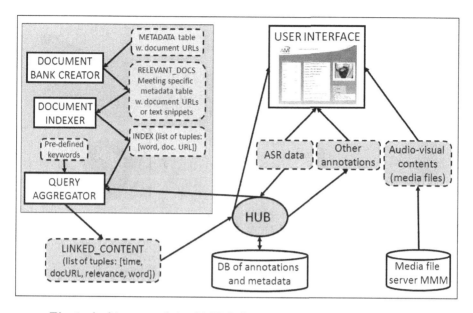

Fig. 1. Architecture of the AMIDA Automatic Content Linking Device

done semi-automatically from IDIAP's multimodal media file server (MMM, see http://mmm.idiap.ch), which gives access to the entire AMI Meeting Corpus, including media files, documents, metadata and annotations.

Document Indexer (DI): Creates an index over the document bank prepared by the DBC for the upcoming meeting.

Query Aggregator (QA): Performs document searches at regular time intervals, using words and terms that are recognized automatically from the meeting discussion, and produces a list of document names, ordered by relevance, based on the search results and on the persistence model explained below.

User Interface (UI): Displays results from the QA and offers quick access to text, HTML and source versions of documents, as well as to metadata and summaries for past meetings.

3 Components of the Automatic Content Linking Device

3.1 User Interface

We start the description of the ACLD with the User Interface, as this encompasses most of the functionalities of the system. In the online scenario of use, a connection must initially be established between the ASR device and a live meeting that is captured in a smart meeting room. In the offline scenario (or to demonstrate the online one from past recordings), the only information initially given to the UI is the identifier of a completed meeting to display. This allows the UI to retrieve via the Hub all the pointers to the related media, and to subscribe

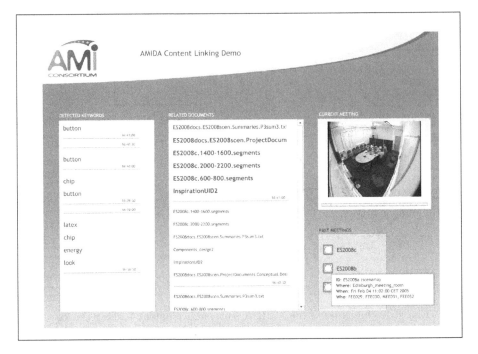

Fig. 2. Snapshot of AMIDA ACLD's user interface

to all the annotations that will be displayed, including the `Content_Linking` annotations produced by the Query Aggregator. For demonstrations and for meeting browsing, it is more convenient for repeatability reasons to use a completed meeting (ES2008d in the present version), hence, a number of metadata variables are hard-coded into the UI.

Figure 2 shows a snapshot of the UI over meeting ES2008d, three minutes from the beginning of the meeting. On the left, a list of keywords, referring to important concepts for the group's activity, reassures the user about the search terms being used, as they were recognized from the audio. Every 30 seconds, a newly recognized keyword set is added at the top, with the timestamp shown as a horizontal line. The central column, which scrolls in the same way as the keywords, shows the six most relevant documents for that time in the meeting, with font size chosen to reflect the hypothesized degree of relevance. At the bottom right there is a static display showing the three meetings in the history – giving access to their contents, metadata and summaries – and above that, the room-view video of the ongoing meeting (with the audio in the case of past meetings).

The UI displays at any given moment in a meeting at most N documents ordered by relevance, based on the data it receives from the QA, which contains information about the documents' URL, their type and relevance, meeting time and detected keywords. This list is constantly updated as the meeting proceeds. The interface offers the users several possibilities for interacting with documents, depending on each document type. For a meeting fragment, hovering over its label displays its extractive summary (obtained on-the-fly by the UI from the Hub), while clicking on the label displays the ASR transcript. For documents, clicking on their label displays their content in a text window, from where a version formatted in HTML can also be obtained. This file format was selected as it preserves a significant part of the original document's formatting, and is much quicker to visualize than opening the source document with its dedicated program, which is quite slow for MS Office documents.

3.2 Document Bank Creator

The Document Bank Creator is run offline before a meeting to create the bank of documents and pseudo-documents that will be searched during the meeting. This is a preparation task, which copies documents in a separate folder, in preparation for the Document Indexer (alternatively, a metadata layer with pointers to documents could be generated to avoid copying). In a less supervised scenario for the future, the DBC could determine automatically the documents that are potentially relevant, based on the project or series the meeting belongs to.

The DBC includes documents, fragments of previous meetings, slides, and emails. The fragments of past meetings are currently 200-second chunks of the ASR transcript, but a more logical segmentation based for instance on topics [11] is under study. The DBC accepts heterogeneous file formats, and extracts text from them using calls to the proprietary software that created the files. In the process, the module also generates HTML versions of each document, which are easier and quicker to visualize than the original MS Office versions.

3.3 Document Indexer

The Document Indexer uses the text version of the files associated to the current meeting by the DBC to construct an index, i.e. a data structure that optimizes word-based search over the document set, which can become quite large over time. The index can also be conceived of as a new annotation layer, represented logically as a list of tuples (meeting, keyword, doc_type, URL), where the URLs are used as unique identifiers of the documents. The DI uses a state-of-the-art system, Apache Lucene in its Perl implementation called Plucene, using all words as keywords and building an optimized index using word stemmers and the TF*IDF weighing scheme.

In the present implementation, the index is accessed directly by the Query Aggregator as a set of files in native Plucene format. However, as the index is a permanent layer of information concerning the documents related to a meeting, it could be stored in a declarative format in the Hub's main database, from where it could be retrieved at the beginning of the demo by the Query Aggregator, which is constantly using it.

3.4 Query Aggregator

The Query Aggregator periodically extracts from the speech of a given meeting a list of keywords that are mentioned, using the ASR, or even a manual transcript for the offline scenario or for development purposes. The QA gets the words via the Hub and processes them in batches corresponding to time frames of fixed size, currently every 30 seconds. This size is a compromise between the need to gather enough words for search, and the need to refresh the search results reasonably often. Instead of the fixed time frame, information about audio segmentation into spurts or utterances could be used for a more natural segmentation of the ASR input.

The QA uses the words to build a query string for the Apache Plucene engine, which searches the index to retrieve relevant documents. These documents are sent as new `Linked_Content` annotations to the Hub, from where they can be used by the UI to display the document labels and give access to them via their URLs. This task has thus a similar goal as speech/document alignment [7,12], except that alignment is viewed here as the construction of sets of relevant documents for each meeting segment, and not only as finding the document that the segment "is about". The retrieval techniques that are employed are therefore quite different too, as speech/document alignment relies on precise matching between a referring expression and one of the elements of a document.

An offline version of the QA generates static XML and HTML views for completed meetings, which are used for debugging and for evaluation. The HTML view shown in Figure 3 displays on the left the ASR for the current meeting segment t_n, and on the right up to six most relevant documents (using their HTML version) with their relevance scores. The keywords are highlighted in red, both within the meeting transcript and in the documents. The words from the transcript are highlighted in blue, but only in the documents where they are

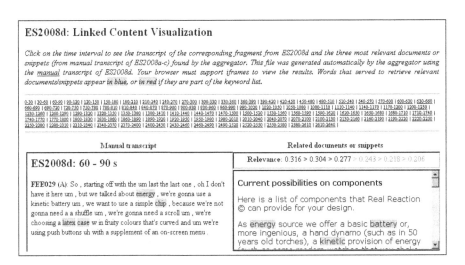

Fig. 3. HTML view of the offline output of the Query Aggregator – only the best document is shown (bottom right). Keywords are highlighted both in the transcript (left) and in the documents (right): e.g., 'energy', 'chip' or 'latex'. Words from the transcript that appear in the retrieved documents are highlighted only in the documents (right): e.g., 'kinetic' or 'battery'.

found – otherwise the entire meeting segment would be highlighted in blue, which is not very informative. The upper frame of the interface in Figure 3 allows the user to select a segment of the current meeting based on its timing in seconds.

Role of Pre-specified Keywords. Existing knowledge about the important terminology of a project can be used to increase the impact of specific words on search. A list of pre-specified keywords can be defined, and in case any of them is detected in the audio input from the meeting, their importance is increased when doing the search, using Plucene's boosting mechanism. The weight of the keyword boosting is currently set at five times the weight of non-boosted words. A specific list was defined by the user-study group for the meetings under study, and at present it contains words or expressions such as 'cost', 'energy', 'component', 'case', 'chip', 'interface', 'button', 'L_C_D', 'material', 'latex', 'wood', 'titanium', and so on, for a total of about 30 words. However, the QA works also without a list of boosted terms.

In addition, the words from the ASR or transcript are filtered for stopwords, so that mostly content words are used for search. Our list has about 80 words, including the most common function words, interjections and discourse markers.

The QA performs document search by matching the query words from the ASR with those from the index constructed by the DI and returns the most relevant set of documents for the respective time frame, more specifically a list of tuples such as (meeting, time, keyword, relevance, doc_type, pointer). It is useful to include in this annotation the keywords that were matched (i.e. the ones that helped to retrieve the specific document) as well as a relevance score produced by the search engine, to allow the interface to sort the relevant documents as needed. This annotation, of the Linked_Content type, is sent to the Hub (and also stored in the Hub's database), from where it is retrieved by consumers that have subscribed to Linked_Content, such as the user interface.

Persistence and Filtering Mechanisms. To avoid inconsistent results from one time frame to another, due to the fact that word choice varies considerably in such small samples, and therefore search results vary as well, a *persistence (smoothing) mechanism* was defined. This mechanism was partly inspired by the notion of perceptual salience of entities, used for reference resolution, and more specifically from techniques that were implemented to compute salience in texts or in multimodal settings [7,13,14]. In the present case, the relevance of the documents amounts to a form of conceptual salience that evolves in time.

The persistence mechanism adjusts the current relevance scores for each document returned by the search engine, considering also the documents from the previous time frame and their own adjusted relevance scores. If t_n denotes the current time frame and t_{n-1} the previous one, and if $r(t_n, d_k)$ is the raw relevance of document d_k computed by the search engine after a query at time t_n, then the *adjusted relevance* $r'(t_n, d_k)$ computed using the persistence (smoothing) mechanism, is $r'(t_n, d_k) = r(t_n, d_k) + \alpha * r'(t_{n-1}, d_k)$, where α is a smoothing factor. Roughly, a larger value of α denotes a larger persistence – but α should be set below 1, because if $\alpha > 1$ then $r(t_n)$) keeps increasing even if the document is no longer retrieved. In our experiments, a typical value of $\alpha = 0.8$ was used. The intuition behind the choice of this formula (as opposed to a more traditional $r'_n = \alpha * r_n + (1 - \alpha) * r'_{n-1}$) is a correction of the relevance score returned by the search engine, possibly increasing it if the document was already present, but without multiplying it from the start by an α factor.

Additionally, a filtering mechanism deletes the least relevant of the documents sent to the UI, returning at most N documents (currently $N = 6$), or fewer, depending on the following constraints. Given the list of all documents that were retrieved, sorted by decreasing relevance, the QA sends to the UI the documents that have an adjusted relevance above a certain threshold (currently 0.2), and the list of results is truncated where relevance decreases sharply, typically when $r'(t_n, d_{k+1}) \leq 0.5 * r'(t_n, d_k)$.

4 Implementation

The first version of the AMIDA Automatic Content Linking Device is now operational, and a second version is in preparation at the time of writing. Both the UI and the QA are implemented using two components: a Java front-end ensuring communication with the Hub – as a consumer for the UI or as a producer and consumer for the QA – and a separate piece of code in a different programming language – Flash for the UI and Perl for the QA.

The ACLD runs on a single Windows PC or over a network, and other operating systems will be considered in the future. The main software prerequisite is the Hub itself, which requires a MySQL database with one table for timed triples. To run the QA, Perl and the Plucene search and indexing modules are required. Compilation of all source files is centrally managed by a `build.xml` file in the top level directory of the repository, which requires the Apache Ant build tool. A number of variables can be set by modifying the initial lines of `build.xml`. The same `build.xml` file also executes the following groups of actions required to start the ACLD on meeting ES2008d, once all source code is compiled:

1. Start the Hub and roll back its database to the state that holds after meetings ES2008a-c and before ES2008d.
2. Start the QA and the UI, which subscribe to the Hub.
3. Stream the words obtained by the ASR for ES2008d to the Hub.

As both the QA and UI "listen" to the Hub, the words are sent to the QA, which sends back `Content_Linking` data, which is used by the UI to display the results.

5 Evaluation

The execution tests of the first prototype have been satisfactory: the communication between the modules using the Hub works smoothly, and the logs show that modules connect properly, and that annotation triples are correctly sent and received. The documents that are retrieved contain the expected words and keywords, as we carefully checked using the static HTML representation of Linked_Content produced by the QA (Figure 3). The functionalities offered by the UI over these documents are available as described in Section 3.1. The nature of Perl scripting makes it easy to change many of the parameters of the QA, even while the system is running, which allows experimenting with various values of the persistence and filtering model, and with various lists of keywords and stopwords.

The performance evaluation of the ACLD is the topic of future work. One can test the performance of the retrieval system in terms of precision and recall, but this requires the definition of a ground truth document set for each time interval of a meeting, which is the main difficulty for such an evaluation. Three approaches to the ACLD evaluation problem are planned: (1) construct ground truth data using human annotators who associate documents to meeting segments; (2) evaluate the ACLD by judging the relevance of each document it returns; and (3) test the ACLD *in use* on the participants to an ongoing meeting, by measuring how often they consult the proposed documents.

The ACLD was demonstrated to potential industrial partners, namely about thirty representatives of companies that are active in the field of meeting technology. A series of sessions, lasting 30 minutes each, started with a presentation of the ACLD and continued with a discussion, during which notes were taken by the first author. The participants found that both online and offline application scenarios are promising, as well as both individual and group uses. The ACLD received very positive verbal evaluation, as well as useful feedback and suggestions for future work.

6   Future Work

The first implementation of the ACLD served as a demonstration or proof-of-concept, and enabled the authors to collect feedback indicating the most important developments that are required to turn it into a real-world application.

The **graphical layout of the interface** will be improved by allowing a larger part of the screen to be used for displaying the documents, using larger overviews of each document, and discarding past documents more quickly. This would also help to reduce the number of mouse clicks required to access the content of documents. Color-coding the document types and displaying their relations to the words from the ASR would also improve user experience.

Another line of suggestions concerns the **document repository**, which can be extended in various ways. The repository could include documents from larger sets, which are not entirely known to users, so that the interface brings new knowledge into a meeting. These sets could be private, personalized and better structured. A significant extension would be the connection to a Web search engine, which could be limited to a sub-domain to avoid potential noise in the results.

A number of **additional functionalities** were suggested. For instance, keeping a record of the documents that were consulted during a meeting might help users who want to go back to them after the meeting. Detecting similarities with previous discussions would help alerting users that they already had this discussion before. Retrieval could be improved by including a relevance feedback mechanism for the returned documents, by representing keywords in a structured manner, e.g. using tag clouds, and by using word sense disambiguation to improve the precision of the retrieval.

Finally, the ACLD could be part of a **broader-scope meeting assistant**, which would not only help local participants with their documents, but would also improve the engagement of remote participants that attend a meeting using a mobile device [15]. In this case, document sharing would be one of the factors that improve the participants' engagement in a meeting.

Acknowledgments

This work was supported by the European Union's IST Programme, through the AMIDA Integrated Project FP6-0033812, Augmented Multiparty Interaction with Distance Access.

References

1. Nijholt, A., Rienks, R., Zwiers, J., Reidsma, D.: Online and off-line visualization of meeting information and meeting support. The Visual Computer 22(12), 965–976 (2006)
2. Hart, P.E., Graham, J.: Query-free information retrieval. IEEE Expert: Intelligent Systems and Their Applications 12(5), 32–37 (1997)
3. Budzik, J., Hammond, K.J.: User interactions with everyday applications as context for just-in-time information access. In: IUI 2000 (5th International Conference on Intelligent User Interfaces), New Orleans, LA (2000)
4. Henziker, M., Chang, B.W., Milch, B., Brin, S.: Query-free news search. World Wide Web: Internet and Web Information Systems 8, 101–126 (2005)
5. Rhodes, B.J., Maes, P.: Just-in-time information retrieval agents. IBM Systems Journal 39(3-4), 685–704 (2000)
6. Franz, A., Milch, B.: Searching the Web by voice. In: Coling 2002 (19th International Conference on Computational Linguistics), Taipei, pp. 11–15 (2002)
7. Popescu-Belis, A., Lalanne, D.: Reference resolution over a restricted domain: References to documents. In: ACL 2004 Workshop on Reference Resolution and its Applications, Barcelona, pp. 71–78 (2004)
8. Carletta, J., Ashby, S., Bourban, S., Flynn, M., Guillemot, M., Hain, T., Kadlec, J., Karaiskos, V., Kraaij, W., Kronenthal, M., Lathoud, G., Lincoln, M., Lisowska, A., McCowan, I., Post, W., Reidsma, D., Wellner, P.: The AMI Meeting Corpus: A pre-announcement. In: Renals, S., Bengio, S. (eds.) MLMI 2005. LNCS, vol. 3869, pp. 28–39. Springer, Heidelberg (2006)
9. Moore, D.J.: The IDIAP Smart Meeting Room. Communication 02-07, IDIAP Research Institute (July 2002)
10. AMIDA: Commercial component definition. Deliverable 7.2, AMIDA Integrated Project (Augmented Multi-party Interaction with Distance Access) (November 2007)

11. Hsueh, P.Y., Moore, J.D.: Combining multiple knowledge sources for dialogue segmentation in multimedia archives. In: ACL 2007 (45th Annual Meeting of the Association of Computational Linguistics), Prague, pp. 1016–1023 (2007)
12. Mekhaldi, D., Lalanne, D., Ingold, R.: From searching to browsing through multimodal documents linking. In: ICDAR 2005 (8th International Conference on Document Analysis and Recognition), Seoul, pp. 924–928 (2005)
13. Huls, C., Claassen, W., Bos, E.: Automatic referent resolution of deictic and anaphoric expressions. Computational Linguistics 21(1), 59–79 (1995)
14. Kehler, A., Martin, J., Cheyer, A., Julia, L., Hobbs, J., Bear, J.: On representing salience and reference in multimodal human-computer interaction. In: AAAI 1998 workshop on Representations for Multi-modal Human-Computer Interaction, Madison, WI, pp. 33–39 (1998)
15. Matena, L., Jaimes, A., Popescu-Belis, A.: Graphical representation of meetings on mobile devices. In: MobileHCI 2008 Demonstrations (10th International Conference on Human-Computer Interaction with Mobile Devices and Services), Amsterdam (2008)

Introducing Additional Input Information into Interactive Machine Translation Systems

Germán Sanchis-Trilles, Maria-Teresa González,
Francisco Casacuberta, Enrique Vidal, and Jorge Civera

Instituto Tecnológico de Informática,
Camino de Vera s/n,
46020 Valencia, Spain
{gsanchis,fcn,evidal,mgonzalez}@dsic.upv.es
jorcisai@iti.es
http://www.iti.es

Abstract. Statistical Machine Translation (SMT) has been receiving a very great amount of attention in recent years. However, translations provided by SMT systems are still far from being perfect. This fact leads to the necessity of including a human expert in the translation process to assure high quality translations. Among the possible ways to incorporate human knowledge in a translation process, we adopt the Interactive-Predictive (IP) framework. In this framework, we show how the mouse actions that the expert performs offer information to the IP system, and can be used to automatically improve the translation even before the user introduces a correction. In addition, we present an improved user interface, which introduces mouse actions as a novel, additional, input information source for the underlying SMT engine.

Keywords: Interactive MT, Computer Assisted Translation.

1 Introduction

Machine Translation (MT) is a research field that has been receiving a great amount of attention during the last years, both in official institutions such as the European Parliament and the United Nations, and in private environments such as to translate user manuals or correspondence. Hence, a breakthrough in this area would have an important socio-economic impact.

Classical MT systems require an important human effort [1], whereas *Statistical Machine Translation* (SMT) has proved to be an efficient framework for building MT systems automatically with little or no human effort, whenever suitable parallel corpora are available.

The statistical approach to the MT problem was described by [2] as follows: given an input sentence $\mathbf{x}$ from a certain source language, an adequate sentence $\hat{\mathbf{y}}$ that maximises the posterior probability is to be found. Such a statement can be specified with the following equation:

$$\hat{\mathbf{y}} = \underset{\mathbf{y}}{\mathrm{argmax}}\, Pr(\mathbf{y}|\mathbf{x}) \tag{1}$$

A. Popescu-Belis and R. Stiefelhagen (Eds.): MLMI 2008, LNCS 5237, pp. 284–295, 2008.

Applying Bayes' theorem on this definition, one can easily reach the next equation

$$\hat{\mathbf{y}} = \underset{\mathbf{y}}{\operatorname{argmax}} \frac{Pr(\mathbf{x}, \mathbf{y})}{Pr(\mathbf{x})} = \underset{\mathbf{y}}{\operatorname{argmax}} Pr(\mathbf{x}, \mathbf{y}) \qquad (2)$$

where the denominator has been neglected because it has no effect when maximising over $\mathbf{y}$.

In this paper, we consider the joint probability $Pr(\mathbf{x}, \mathbf{y})$, instead of the widely used decomposition $Pr(\mathbf{y}) \cdot Pr(\mathbf{x}|\mathbf{y})$, because we model the translation process according to the stochastic finite-state framework described in [3], following previous work on *Interactive Machine Translation* (IMT) [4] and for comparison purposes in this work.

Nevertheless, current MT systems are far from perfect. Because of this fact, those who are in need of such software often have to choose between the (potentially flawed) translation provided by a MT system and the use of *Computer Assisted Translation* (CAT) [5] software. In the first case, the user must correct the errors produced by the MT system in a post-editing step. In the second case, the user cannot take advantage, or only partially, of the potential of MT systems.

After such arguments, it seems only obvious that SMT systems should be merged into CAT systems, in order to obtain flawless translations while reducing significantly the effort performed by the human translator. This is the idea behind the IMT [4] paradigm, in which the human translator is integrated *into* the translation process, in the spirit of merging both the efficiency of SMT systems and the correctness of human translators, achieving an effective interaction between both actors. The IMT paradigm fits well within the *Interactive Pattern Recognition* framework introduced in [6].

Within the IMT paradigm, the user is given an input sentence $\mathbf{x}$ and a candidate translation $\mathbf{y}$, obtained via an implementation of Equation 2. Then, the user validates a prefix $\mathbf{p}$ of $\mathbf{y}$ as correct by positioning the cursor in a certain position of $\mathbf{y}$. Note that it may also be an empty prefix, in case the first word of the sentence is not appropriate. Implicitly, he is also marking the rest of the sentence, the suffix $\mathbf{s}_l$, as potentially incorrect. Next, he introduces a new word k, which is assumed to be different from the first word s_{l_1} in the suffix $\mathbf{s}_l$ which was not validated, $k \neq s_{l_1}$. This being done, the system suggests a new suffix hypothesis $\hat{\mathbf{s}}_h$, subject to $\hat{s}_{h_1} = k$. Again, the user validates a new prefix, introduces a new word and so forth. The process continues until the whole sentence is correct.

This process is illustrated in Figure 1. In this example, the interactive-predictive process starts by the system first suggesting a translation in which the word order is not the one preferred by the user. Hence, the user validates the prefix "*To print a*", introduces the word "*list*", and the system suggests the correct suffix. Finally, the user validates the whole sentence and marks the sentence as correct by introducing the special character "*#*". The system then retains as final prefix the whole translation. In this case, the user just needed

SOURCE (x):   Para imprimir una lista de fuentes postscript:
REFERENCE (y): To print a list of postscript fonts:

ITER-0	(p) ($\hat{\mathbf{s}}_h$)	( ) (*To print a postscript font list:*)
ITER-1	(p) ($\mathbf{s}_l$) (k) ($\hat{\mathbf{s}}_h$)	(To print a) (*postscript font list:*) (list) (*of postscript fonts:*)
ITER-2	(p) ($\mathbf{s}_l$) (k) ($\hat{\mathbf{s}}_h$)	(To print a list of postscript fonts:) ( ) (#) ( )
FINAL	($\mathbf{p} \equiv \mathbf{y}$)	(To print a list of postscript fonts:)

Fig. 1. Example of typical interactions in the IMT paradigm, for translating a Spanish sentence into English

to interact once, whereas in a post-editing scenario he would have needed to interact perhaps four times.

The above ideas can be formalised as follows [7]:

$$\hat{\mathbf{s}}_h = \operatorname*{argmax}_{\mathbf{s}_h} Pr(\mathbf{s}_h | \mathbf{x}, \mathbf{p}, k) \tag{3}$$

Following the same process that led us from 1 to 2:

$$\hat{\mathbf{s}}_h = \operatorname*{argmax}_{\mathbf{s}_h} Pr(\mathbf{x}, \mathbf{p}, k, \mathbf{s}_h) \tag{4}$$

being more appropriate for an SMT system based on stochastic finite-state transducers (SFST).

When observing Equations 2 and 4, the difference between them can be seen as a search problem, in which we need to constrain the search space to only consider those translation hypotheses which contain a prefix $\mathbf{p}$ and suffix $\mathbf{s}_h$ that begins with word k provided by the user.

Since the problem of finding $\hat{\mathbf{s}}_h$ is most probably NP-hard because of its similarity to other problems described as such in [8], we will approximate $\hat{\mathbf{s}}_h$ using the Viterbi algorithm as done in [4]. To decrease the computational cost of the search for the optimal suffix $\hat{\mathbf{s}}_h$ in Equation 4, a word graph with translations of $\mathbf{x}$ available in the SFST (a pruned Viterbi trellis) is generated in the first iteration.

Now, the search for the optimal $\hat{\mathbf{s}}_h$ in each iteration is carried out on the above described word graph, instead of performing a conventional search with the stochastic finite-state transducer.

2   Mouse Actions as Additional Information Provided by the User

Until now, however, the only interface between the underlying SMT engine and the user was the keyboard, i.e. when the user introduced or corrected a word, the system provided a new translation hypothesis composed by the prefix validated

SOURCE (**x**):   Para imprimir una lista de fuentes postscript:
REFERENCE (**y**): To print a list of postscript fonts:

ITER-0	(**p**)	|( )
	($\hat{\mathbf{s}}_h$)	(*To print a postscript font list:*)
ITER-1	(**p**)	(To print a)
	($\mathbf{s}_l$)	(*postscript font list:*)
	($\hat{\mathbf{s}}_h$)	(*list of postscript fonts:*)
ITER-2	(**p**)	(To print a list of postscript fonts:)
	($\mathbf{s}_l$)	()
	(k)	(#)
	($\hat{\mathbf{s}}_h$)	()
FINAL	($\mathbf{p} \equiv \mathbf{y}$)	(To print a list of postscript fonts:)

Fig. 2. Example of non-explicit MA which solves an error of a missing word. In this case, the system produces the correct suffix $\mathbf{s}_h$ immediately after the user validates a prefix **p**, implicitly indicating that we wants the suffix to be changed, without need of any further action.

by the user, the new word introduced, and a suffix suggested by the translation engine. Hence, the only utility of Mouse Actions (MA) was to position the cursor in the appropriate place before typing in a word.

In this work, we present the MAs as a new input interface between the user and the SMT engine. In this context, we will be considering two types of MA:

1. *Non-explicit* MA: Whenever the user wants to correct the translation hypothesis, he needs to first click on the position he intends to correct, in order to place the cursor in the appropriate position. By doing so, the user is already providing some useful information: he is validating a prefix up to the position where he has set the cursor, and, moreover, he is indicating that whatever comes after that cursor position is incorrect and he wants it to be replaced. Hence, at this point the system can already provide a new translation hypothesis, in which the first word of the suffix must be different to the first word of the previous suffix. Of course, this does not ensure that the new suffix provided will be the one the user has in mind. However, given that we have the certainty that the previous suffix was incorrect, the worst thing we can do by changing it is that it remains incorrect. We are naming this kind of MA *non-explicit* because it does not require an additional action from the user: the user is performing a MA to position the cursor, which is taken advantage of by the system to suggest another (potentially correct) suffix. Hence, we only consider as non-explicit MA the one that implies a change in cursor position, i.e. if the cursor is already in the correct position (e.g. after correcting the previous word), the user does not perform a MA, and the suffix remains unchanged. Figure 2 illustrates an example in which a non-explicit MA is enough to correct the error described in Figure 1. In this example, when the user is positioning the cursor after "*To print a*", the system already knows that, in this case, the word "*postscript*" should not be placed after word "*a*", and suggests a new suffix, which happens to be correct. Hence, the user does not need to introduce the word "*list*", as was the case in Figure 1, and just needs to validate the whole sentence and proceed to next sentence.

SOURCE (x):   Seleccione el tipo de instalación.
REFERENCE (y): Select the type of installation.

ITER-0	(**p**) ($\hat{s}_h$)	( ) (*Select the installation wizard.*)
ITER-1	(**p**) (s_l) ($\hat{s}_h$)	(Select the) (*installation wizard.*) (*install script.*)
ITER-2	(**p**) (k) ($\hat{s}_h$)	(Select the) (*type*) (*installation wizard.*)
ITER-3	(**p**) (s_l) ($\hat{s}_h$)	(Select the type) (*installation wizard.*) (*of installation.*)
FINAL	($\mathbf{p} \equiv \mathbf{y}$)	(Select the type of installation.)

Fig. 3. Example of explicit MA which solves an error of an erroneous suffix. In this case, after a non-explicit MA is performed **ITER-1**, with no success. Then, the user introduces word "*type*" in **ITER-2**, which leaves the cursor position located immediately after word "*type*". Hence the user would not need to perform a MA to re-position the cursor and continue typing in order to further correct the remaining errors. However, since he has learned the potential benefit of MAs, he performs an explicit MA, after which the system changes the suffix and corrects the error.

2. *Explicit* MA: If the system is efficient, and provides suggestions which are good enough, another scenario one could easily picture is the one in which the user would like the suffix to be changed, ignoring where the cursor position is located. Hence, the user would always click before an incorrect word, the cursor position being irrelevant. We are naming this kind of MA *explicit*, because it is not completely transparent to the user: it requires additional actions than those he would normally perform. However, if the MT engine providing the suffixes is good enough, the user could quickly realise that performing a MA is less costly than introducing a whole new word, and would take advantage of this fact by systematically clicking before introducing a word. An example of such a MA is illustrated in Figure 3.

At this point, we would like to emphasise that improvements in performance achieved with explicit MAs may be arguable, since they imply a trade-off between MAs and key strokes. On the other hand, improvements obtained with non-explicit MAs constitute improvements *per se*, since they do not require any additional action from the user.

3   Mouse Actions as a Constrained Search Problem

Now, we are considering two possible situations. The first one, in which a user validates a prefix **p** by positioning the cursor before the first wrong word in the hypothesis generated by the system. In this situation, the equation that describes the search that has to be performed evolves to

$$\hat{s}_h = \operatorname*{argmax}_{s_h : s_{h_1} \neq s_{l_1}} Pr(\mathbf{x}, \mathbf{p}, s_h | s_l) \tag{5}$$

where s_l is the suffix generated in the previous iteration, already discarded by the user, and s_{l_1} is the first word in s_l.

If such a search is successful and returns a suffix that satisfies the user, at least in its first word, then the user validates a new prefix, and a new search with the same form of Equation 5 takes place.

However, if the user does not like the new suffix provided and decides to type in a new word, we have a different situation, which is the same one as described in Equation 4.

The main difference between the situations described in Equations 4 and 5 is that, in the second case, the user does not type in any new word whatsoever.

4   Experimental Setup

4.1   System Evaluation

System evaluation is a difficult issue in MT. In contrast with other fields of Natural Language Processing such as speech recognition and text recognition, in MT there is no unique ground truth, i.e. given a system input $\mathbf{x}$, the system could produce several *correct and different* outputs. This implies a huge difficulty when evaluating automatically whether a translation produced by a given system is correct. This problem has given rise to its own research field, where several automatic evaluation metrics have been proposed. By extension, this problem is also applicable to IMT.

In this paper, we will be reporting results measured in *Word Stroke Ratio* (WSR) [4], which is a ratio between the number of word-strokes a user would need in order to achieve the reference translation and the total number of words in the reference.

However, given that in this paper we are also introducing MAs as a user action, we will also present a *Mouse Action Ratio* (MAR), which, analogously to WSR, is a ratio between the number of MAs required by the user to achieve the final reference sentence and its total number of words.

It must be noted, however, that these measures are, because of their nature, pessimistic, since they are only taking into account one single possible ground truth translation. One could easily picture a situation in which the system would produce a perfectly acceptable translation, which would happen to be different to the sentence considered ground truth. This would imply that a (possibly) high WSR measure would be returned, whereas the translation would not "deserve" this evaluation.

4.2   Corpora

Part of the experiments reported here were carried out on the Xerox corpora [9], which is a compendium of user manuals for Xerox printers and photocopiers. English being the source language, the reference translations in Spanish, French and German were provided by Xerox's language services. The corpora were divided into two subcorpora, one for training the transducers and one reserved for

Table 1. Characteristics of the Xerox corpora. "K" means that the numbers are given in thousands, and "OOVs" stands for "Out Of Vocabulary" words.

		Es–En		Fr–En		De–En	
		Spanish	English	French	English	German	English
	Sentences (K)	55		52		49	
	Avg. length	13	11	13	11	10	11
Training	Vocabulary (K)	11	7	9	7	19	7
	Singletons (K)	3	1	2	1	7	1
	Run. words (K)	752	665	686	632	534	587
	Sentences	1000		1000		1000	
	Avg. length	8	7	12	11	11	12
Test	OOVs	69	49	118	82	426	81
	Run. words (K)	10	8	11	11	11	12
	Perplexity	32.9	47.0	50.4	69.1	85.9	49.2

Table 2. Characteristics of the EU corpora. "K" means that the numbers are given in thousands, and "OOVs" stands for "Out Of Vocabulary" words.

		Es–En		Fr–En		De–En	
		Spanish	English	French	English	German	English
	Sentences (K)	214		215		222	
	Avg. length	27	24	27	24	24	25
Training	Vocabulary (K)	97	83	91	83	152	86
	Singletons (K)	42	37	39	37	74	38
	Run. words (K)	5845	5203	5806	5283	5348	5698
	Sentences	800		800		800	
	Avg. length	28	25	28	25	23	25
Test	OOVs	82	58	64	60	182	58
	Run. words (K)	22	19	21	19	18	19
	Perplexity	45.8	57.7	45.2	57.8	86.9	56.7

the automatic evaluation of the IMT systems built. The characteristics of these corpora can be seen in Table 1.

The other corpus used for this paper is the *EU* corpus, built of the Bulletin of the European Union, which exists in all official languages of the European Union [10] and is publicly available on the internet. In this case, we also performed our experiments on the French↔English, German↔English and Spanish↔English subcorpora. In this case, as well, the corpora were subdivided into training and evaluation sets. The characteristics of these corpora can be seen in Table 2.

4.3   Experimental Results

The results of both non-explicit and explicit MA types can be seen in Tables 3 and 4. In these tables, the baseline system presents the same MAR as when introducing non-explicit MAs precisely because of the definition of non-explicit

Table 3. Experimental results with the Xerox corpus, when considering both non-explicit and explicit Mouse Actions. The last column is given in terms of WSR relative improvement with respect to the baseline. All results are in percentage.

	baseline		non-explicit			explicit		
	MAR	WSR	MAR	WSR	WSR red.	MAR	WSR	WSR red.
En–Es	10.0	27.4	10.0	24.3	11.3	27.1	21.6	21.2
Es–En	13.5	31.7	13.5	27.0	14.8	31.3	23.8	24.9
En–De	12.6	65.1	12.6	63.2	2.9	65.0	59.2	9.1
De–En	13.5	58.5	13.5	56.2	3.9	58.4	51.9	11.3
En–Fr	13.6	55.4	13.6	52.1	6.0	54.9	48.3	12.8
Fr–En	15.7	55.0	15.7	51.5	6.4	54.6	47.1	14.4

Table 4. Experimental results with the EU corpus, when considering both non-explicit and explicit Mouse Actions. The last column in given in terms of WSR relative improvement with respect to the baseline. All results are in percentage.

	baseline		non-explicit			explicit		
	MAR	WSR	MAR	WSR	WSR red.	MAR	WSR	WSR red.
En–Es	15.9	52.1	15.9	49.0	6.0	52.3	44.9	13.8
Es–En	13.8	48.5	13.8	45.5	6.2	48.2	40.8	15.9
En–De	23.5	62.2	13.5	60.6	2.6	62.3	56.4	9.3
De–En	14.4	60.5	14.4	58.5	3.3	60.5	53.4	11.7
En–Fr	15.6	49.6	15.6	47.0	5.2	49.8	43.1	13.1
Fr–En	14.4	44.0	14.4	40.3	8.4	43.8	36.3	17.5

MA: the baseline MAs are those the user needs to perform in order to position the cursor before introducing a new word, and are the same as those taken into account when considering non-explicit MAs. It can be seen that, throughout all the language pairs and for both corpora, considering non-explicit MAs, which do not require any additional action from the user, obtains a relative improvement of at least 2.9%, ranging up to a very significant relative improvement of 14.8%. In addition, considering explicit MAs further improves the baseline system, and even the system obtained when considering only non-explicit MAs. Although in this case it does require additional actions from the user, and the MAR increases significantly as well, we have the conviction that a MA is less costly for the user than typing in a word.

Moreover, it must be noted that, according to these results, it seems that the lower the baseline WSR, the higher the relative improvement when introducing both non-explicit and explicit MAs. This is due to the fact that a higher baseline points towards a better translation model, which will, in turn, be able to provide a more useful suffix hypotheses when asking it to return a new $\hat{s}_h$ such that $s_{h_1} \neq s_{l_1}$. If the translation model is not complex enough, it will most probably return an empty suffix, since the only suffix hypothesis which it is able provide is the one the user already discarded. This (inverse) relation is illustrated in Figure 4.

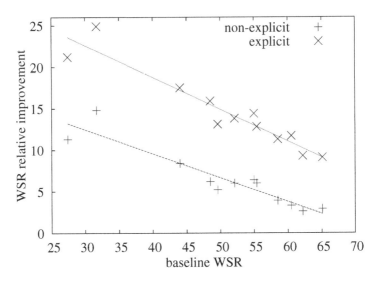

Fig. 4. Plot evidencing the inverse relation between baseline WSR and WSR relative improvement when considering both non-explicit and explicit MAs

5   Development of a User Interface

As the main aim of an IMT system is its final utilisation by a user, we developed a user interface for our system. The great advantage of having such an interface is that users can test how it works, providing useful feedback about its practical functionality. Having somebody use the interface allowed us to see that considering MAs as additional input information is a very intuitive improvement for the user.

An important point about this interface is how the user interacts with the system. In this section we will explain how this interaction is carried out.

Firstly, the user selects a source sentence to translate ($\mathbf{x}$). At real time speed, the system returns a suggestion for this translation. In that moment, the user can accept (with a MA) the complete sentence, or he can position the cursor before the word which is regarded as incorrect. In this latter case, the system returns automatically another suffix suggestion subject to the constraint described in Equation 5. Hence, the user might not need to introduce the next word. If a new error appears at the same place or the user does not like the new suggestion, he can simply type in the word he has in mind without further ado. This being done and the error being corrected, the process is repeated again until we have obtained a correct translation.

For example, let the source sentence be *"Select the print line that you want to use"*, which has as reference translation *"Seleccione la línea que desea usar"*. At the beginning, the system will return the suffix hypothesis *"Seleccione el línea que desea usar"*. The user accepts *"Seleccione"* and the system returns the new suffix hypothesis *"la línea que desea usar"*. Then, the user accepts the suggestion and the translation process is finished.

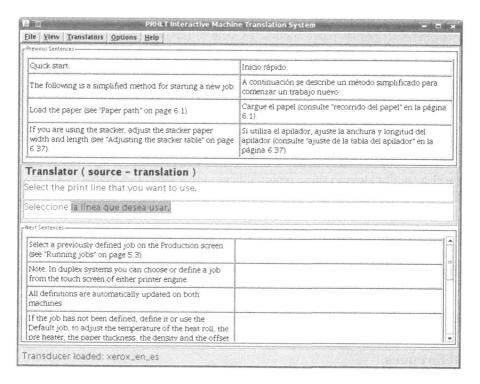

Fig. 5. User interface window of the IMT system built. The upper frame displays the list of processed sentences. The middle frame presents the sentence being currently worked on, where the current source sentence and its corresponding translation, which is currently being built, are shown. Note that suggestions are differently coloured, in order to distinguish them better. Finally, the lower frame lists the sentences that are yet to be translated.

6   Conclusions and Future Work

In this paper we have considered new input sources for IMT systems. By introducing Mouse Actions as a new information source for the IMT system, we have shown that we can significantly improve the performance of the human translator, as measured by WSR, when dealing with such a system. Although the results show important improvements, they highly depend on how suitable the SMT model on which the IMT system relies is.

A lot of future work remains to be done. First, we would like to extend these results to the character level, i.e. that the user may click on the middle of a word and signal in such a way that only part of the word is correct. By doing so, we would be able to reduce the human effort even further, and, moreover, we would be able to measure the effort of the human translator more accurately, by computing the amount of key-strokes he needs to type, instead of word-strokes.

Furthermore, we also intend to exchange the underlying SMT model by a state-of-the-art phrase-based model. To achieve this, we first need to obtain a word graph from the phrase-based decoding process.

In addition, we also plan on investigating the effect on WSR of several consecutive MAs on the same spot, i.e. allowing the user to click several times before a given translation error so that several hypotheses cycle before he needs to introduce a word.

And finally, we also plan to perform a human evaluation that verifies the goodness of the improvements pointed by the WSR measure.

The work reported on this paper is closely related to the work reported by [11], in which similar ideas to those reported here were applied to Computer Assisted Text Recognition, yielding satisfactory results as well.

Acknowledgements

This work has been partially supported by the Spanish MEC under scholarship AP2005-4023 and under grants CONSOLIDER Ingenio-2010 CSD2007-00018 and TIC2003-08681-C02-02, and by the EC (FEDER) and the Spanish MEC under grant TIN2006-15694-CO2-01.

References

1. Hutchings, J., Somers, H.: An introduction to machine translation. In: Ed. Academic Press, London (1992)
2. Brown, P., Pietra, S.D., Pietra, V.D., Mercer, R.: The mathematics of machine translation. Computational Linguistics 19, 263–311 (1993)
3. Casacuberta, F., Vidal, E.: Learning finite-state models for machine translation. Machine Learning 66(1), 69–91 (2007)
4. Barrachina, S., Bender, O., Casacuberta, F., Civera, J., Cubel, E., Khadivi, S., Ney, A.L.H., Tomás, J., Vidal, E.: Statistical approaches to computer-assisted translation. Computational Linguistics, (in press, 2008)
5. Isabelle, P., Church, K.: Special issue on new tools for human translators. Machine Translation 12(1–2) (1997)
6. Vidal, E., Rodríguez, L., Casacuberta, F., García-Varea, I.: Interactive pattern recognition. In: Popescu-Belis, A., Renals, S., Bourlard, H. (eds.) MLMI 2007. LNCS, vol. 4892, pp. 60–71. Springer, Heidelberg (2008)
7. Casacuberta, F., Civera, J., Cubel, E., Lagarda, A., Lapalme, G., Macklovitch, E., Vidal, E.: Human interaction for high quality machine translation. Communications of the ACM, (in press, 2008)
8. Casacuberta, F., de la Higuera, C.: Computational complexity of problems on probabilistic grammars and transducers. In: Oliveira, A.L. (ed.) ICGI 2000. LNCS (LNAI), vol. 1891, pp. 15–24. Springer, Heidelberg (2000)
9. Esteban, J., Lorenzo, J., Valderrábanos, A., Lapalme, G.: Transtype2 - an innovative computer-assisted translation system. In: The Companion Volume to the Proceedings of 42st Annual Meeting of the Association for Computational Linguistics, Barcelona, Spain, pp. 94–97 (July 2004)

10. Khadivi, S., Goute, C.: Tools for corpus alignment and evaluation of the alignments (deliverable d4.9). In: Technical Report, TransType2 (IST-2001-32091) (2003)
11. Romero, V., Toselli, A., Civera, J., Vidal, E.: Improvements in the computer assisted transcription of handwritten text images system. In: 8th International Workshop on Pattern Recognition in Information Systems. 10th International Conference on Enterprise Information Systems, 12-13 June (submitted, 2008)

Computer Assisted Transcription of Text Images and Multimodal Interaction[*]

Alejandro H. Toselli[1], Verónica Romero[2], and Enrique Vidal[2]

[1] Institut Tecnològic d'Informàtica
[2] Departament de Sistemes Informàtics i Computació
Universitat Politècnica de València
Camí de Vera s/n, 46071 - València, Spain
{ahector,vromero,evidal}@iti.upv.es

Abstract. Current automatic handwriting text image recognition systems are far from being perfect and, in general, human intervention is required to check and correct the results of such systems. This is both inefficient and uncomfortable to the user. As an alternative to this post-editing process, a multimodal interactive approach is proposed, where user feedback is provided by means of touch-screen pen strokes and/or more traditional keyboard and mouse operation. Experiments suggest that, using this approach, significant amounts of user effort can be saved with respect to the conventional, non-interactive, post-editing process.

1 Introduction

Lately, the paradigm for Pattern Recognition (PR) systems design has been shifting from the concept of full-automation to systems where the decision process is conditioned by human feedback [1]. A task where this paradigm shift particularly applies is the transcription of handwritten text images.

State-of-the-art handwritten text recognition systems (HTR) can not suppress the need of human work when high quality transcriptions are needed. HTR systems can achieve fairly high accuracy for restricted applications with rather limited vocabulary and/or form-constrained handwriting [2,3]. However, in the case of unrestricted text, current HTR technology typically fails to achieve results which are directly acceptable in practice. Therefore, once the full recognition process of one document has finished, heavy human expert revision is required to really produce a transcription of standard quality. Such a *post-editing* solution is rather inefficient and uncomfortable for the human corrector.

An interactive scenario allows for a more effective approach. Here, the automatic HTR system and the human transcriber cooperate to generate the final transcription, thereby combining the accuracy provided by the human operator with the efficiency of the HTR system. We call this approach "Computer Assisted Transcription of Text Images" (CATTI) [4,5].

[*] This work has been supported by the EC (FEDER), the Spanish MEC under grant TIN2006-15694-C02-01 and the research programme Consolider Ingenio 2010 MIPRCV (CSD2007-00018).

A. Popescu-Belis and R. Stiefelhagen (Eds.): MLMI 2008, LNCS 5237, pp. 296–308, 2008.

In our previous works, human feedback for CATTI has been assumed to come in the form of keyboard and mouse actions. Nevertheless, at the expense of loosing the deterministic accuracy of this traditional input modality, more ergonomic multimodal interfaces are possible. It is worth noting, however, that this increased ergonomy comes at the cost of new errors expected from the decoding of the feedback signals. Therefore, solving the *multimodal interaction problem* requires adequate techniques to achieve a *modality synergy* where both main and feedback data streams help each-other to optimize overall accuracy. These ideas have recently explored in the context of computer assisted translation, where speech signals are used for feedback [1]. Among many possible feedback modalities, we focus here on touch-screen operation, which is perhaps the most natural feedback modality for CATTI. This way, the user corrective feedback can be quite naturally provided by means of on-line text or pen strokes which are exactly registered over the text produced by the system (see fig. 2).

We will employ the words "HTR system" (or just HTR) to mean the *off-line* HTR system which processes the main text images, whereas "handwritten feedback recognition subsystem" (or just HFR) will be employed for the *on-line* HTR system used in multimodal correction. In the present work, both HTR and HFR are based on Hidden Markov Models (HMMs) [6], in a similar way as HMMs are currently used in Automatic Speech Recognition [7].

In this paper we briefly review the CATTI framework (section 2) and formally introduce the multimodal version of this framework discussed above (section 3). After an overview of the HTR and HFR systems used (section 4), experiments are presented (section 5) to assess the capabilities of the proposed techniques using a well-known and publicly available corpus of off-line handwritten text images (IAMDB [8]) and another public corpus of on-line handwritten text (UNIPEN [9]) to simulate the user feedback touchscreen data.

2   Review of the CATTI Framework

In the CATTI framework, the user is directly involved in the transcription process since he/she is responsible of validating and/or correcting the HTR output. The process starts when the system predicts an initial whole transcription of (some adequate segment of) the input image. Then, the user reads this prediction until finding (and correcting) an error. This generates a new, extended prefix (the previous validated prefix, plus the user amendments), which is used by the HTR system to attempt a new prediction hypothesis, thereby starting a new cycle that is repeated until a final correct transcription is achieved.

Formally, CATTI fits within the *Interactive Pattern Recognition* (IPR) paradigm proposed in [1], in which a best system hypothesis is expressed as:

$$\hat{h} = \arg \max_{h} Pr(h \mid x, f) \tag{1}$$

where x is the input signal or data and f stands for the feedback, user-interaction derived informations.

In CATTI, in addition to the given input (image) x, a user-validated *prefix p* of the transcription is available, which corresponds to the feedback f in eq. (1)). It contains information from the previous system's prediction, plus user's actions in the form of amendment keystrokes. The HTR system should try to complete this prefix by searching for the most likely *suffix* $\hat{s}$ ($\hat{h}$ in eq. (1)), according to:

$$\hat{s} = \arg\max_{s} Pr(s \mid x, p) = \arg\max_{s} Pr(x \mid p, s) \cdot Pr(s \mid p) \tag{2}$$

Therefore, the search must be performed over all possible suffixes s of p and the language model probability $Pr(s \mid p)$ must account for the words that can be written *after the prefix p*. As discussed in [4], the image $x \equiv x_1^m$ can be considered split into two fragments, x_1^b and x_{b+1}^m and (2) can be rewritten as:

$$\hat{s} \approx \arg\max_{s} \max_{0 \le b \le m} Pr(x_1^b \mid p) \cdot Pr(x_{b+1}^m \mid s) \cdot Pr(s \mid p) \tag{3}$$

This optimization problem entails finding an optimal boundary point, $\hat{b}$, associated with the optimal suffix decoding, $\hat{s}$. Therefore, the search can be performed just over segments of the image corresponding to the possible suffixes and, on the other hand, we can take advantage of the information coming from the prefix to implement the language model constraints involved in $Pr(s \mid p)$.

The probabilities $Pr(x_1^b \mid p)$ and $Pr(x_{b+1}^m \mid s)$ are modelled by HMM morphological words models [4,6,10] whereas, for $Pr(s \mid p)$, an n-gram model conditioned by the prefix p is needed. In what follows, modelled probabilities will be written as $P()$, while $Pr()$ is reserved for true probabilities. As discussed in [4], the conventional n-gram language model estimated for (non-interactive) off-line HTR is adapted to cope with the prefix p in $Pr(s \mid p)$:

$$Pr(s \mid p) \simeq \prod_{j=1}^{n-1} P(s_j \mid p_{k-n+1+j}^k, s_1^{j-1}) \cdot \prod_{j=n}^{l} P(s_j \mid s_{j-n+1}^{j-1}) \tag{4}$$

where $p = p_1^k$ is a consolidated prefix and $s = s_1^l$ is a possible suffix. The first term of (4) accounts for the probability of the $n-1$ words of the suffix whose probability is conditioned by words from the validated prefix, while the second term is the usual n-gram probability for the rest of the words in the suffix.

As in [4], we can explicitly rely on eq. (3) to implement a decoding process in one step, as in conventional HTR systems. The decoder should be forced to match the previously validated prefix p and then continue searching for a suffix $\hat{s}$ according to the constraints (4). This can be achieved by building a special language model which can be seen as the "concatenation" of a *linear* model which strictly accounts for the successive words in p and a "suffix language model" as in (4). This is illustrated in figure 1. Owing to the finite-state nature of this special language model, the search involved in eq. (3) can be efficiently carried out using the well known Viterbi algorithm [10].

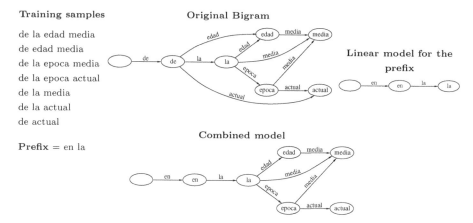

Fig. 1. Example of CATTI dynamic language model building. First, a bigram for the training set of the figure is obtained. Then, a linear model which accounts for the prefix *"en la"* is constructed. Finally, these two models are combined into a single *prefix-constrained model*.

3 Multimodal Computer Assisted Transcription of Handwritten Text Images (MM-CATTI)

As discussed in Section 2, traditional peripherals like keyboard and mouse can be used to unambiguously provide the user feedback required for the validation and correction of the successive system predictions. Nevertheless, providing the system with more ergonomic multimodal interfaces should result in an easier and more comfortable human-machine interaction, at the expense of the feedback being less deterministic to the system. Here we will focus on *touchscreen* communication, which is perhaps the most natural modality to provide the required feedback in CATTI systems.

The proposed multimodal interaction process is formulated in two steps. Let x be the input text image and p a user-validated prefix of the transcription. In the first step a CATTI system solves the problem (2), yielding an optimal continuation (or suffix) $\hat{s}$ of p. In the second step, the user enters some (may be null) on-line touchscreen pen-strokes, t, to correct the first error in $\hat{s}$ and an *on-line* HTR feedback subsystem (or HFR) is used to decode t into a word (or word sequence), $\hat{d}$:

$$\hat{d} = \arg\max_d Pr(d \mid x, p, \hat{s}, t) \tag{5}$$

Finally, the user can enter additional amendment keystrokes κ, if necessary, and produce a new consolidated prefix, p, based on the previous p, $\hat{d}$, κ and parts of $\hat{s}$. The process continues in this way until p is completely accepted by the user as a full correct transcription of x.

	x	*opposed*	*the*	*Government*	*Bill*	*which*	*brought*
STEP-0	p						
	$\hat{s} \equiv \hat{w}$	opposite	this	Comment	Bill	in that	thought
	p',t	*opposed*	this	Comment	Bill	in that	thought
STEP-1	$\hat{d}$	opposed					
	κ						
	p	opposed					
	$\hat{s}$		the	Government	Bill	in that	thought
	p',t	opposed	the	Government	Bill	*which*	thought
STEP-2	$\hat{d}$					whack	
	κ					ich	
	p	opposed	the	Government	Bill	which	
	$\hat{s}$						brought
	p',t	opposed	the	Government	Bill	which	brought
FINAL	κ						#
	$p \equiv T$	opposed	the	Government	Bill	which	brought

Fig. 2. Example of typewriter and on-line touchscreen interaction with a MM-CATTI system, to transcribe an image of the text segment: *"opposed the Government Bill which brought"*. Each interaction step starts with a transcription prefix p that has been fixed in the previous step. First, the system suggests a suffix, $\hat{s}$, from which the user defines a longer correct prefix, p', and handwrites some touchscreen data, t, to correct the first error in $\hat{s}$. Taking advantage of p', the *on-line* HTR subsystem decodes t into $\hat{d}$ and, then, the user may type some keystrokes, κ, possibly aimed to amend $\hat{d}$ (and/or maybe other errors in $\hat{s}$). A new prefix, p, is built from the previous prefix p', along with the decoded handwritten data, $\hat{d}$, and the typed text, κ. The process ends when the user types the special character "#". In the final transcription, T, text obtained from on-line handwriting decoding is marked in red color, while typed text is underlined.

An example of this inter-related off-line image recognition and on-line touchscreen interaction is shown in figure 2. The potential increase in user comfort comes at expense of a hopefully small number of additional interaction steps. Assuming, for simplicity, that the cost of correcting an on-line decoding error is just similar to that of another on-line touchscreen interaction, in this example the user would need 3 interaction steps using MM-CATTI, compared with 2 corrections that would have needed a pure keyboard-and-mouse-based CATTI system. Both compare very favorably with the 6 corrections required to post-edit the original, non-interactively recognized hypothesis.

Let us now focus on eq. (5). Assuming independence between t and $x, p, \hat{s}$ given d, it can be approximated as:

$$\hat{d} \approx \underset{d}{\arg\max} \, Pr(x, p, \hat{s} \mid d) \cdot Pr(t \mid d) \cdot Pr(d)$$

$$= \underset{d}{\arg\max} \, Pr(d \mid x, p, \hat{s}) \cdot Pr(t \mid d) \qquad (6)$$

This independence assumption, in some sense, results natural considering that t is a signal of on-line touchscreen pen-strokes and x an image.

As in Section 2, $Pr(t \mid d)$ is modelled by HMM morphological models of the words in d. On the other hand, here, $Pr(d \mid x, p, \hat{s})$ can be provided by a language model constrained by the input image x, by the previous prefix p and by the suffix $\hat{s}$ produced at the beginning of the current interation step. From these constraints, only the information provided by the prefix p and the produced suffix $\hat{s}$ is considered in the present work. More specifically, the HFR subsystem should find adequate transcriptions of the touchscreen data t, which are also suitable continuations of the prefix $p' = p\,\hat{s}_a$ (formed by the given prefix p and the part $\hat{s}_a$ of the system-suggested suffix $\hat{s}$ which the user accepts as correct) and depending on $\hat{s}_e$, the remaining (wrong) word(s) in the suffix $\hat{s}$ (which the user tries to correct using touchscreen strokes); that is, $Pr(d \mid x, p, \hat{s})$ $\equiv Pr(d \mid p', \hat{s}_e)$.

3.1   Language Model and Search for MM-CATTI

To find an expression for the on-line language model $P(d \mid p', \hat{s}_e)$, we first find one for $P(d \mid p')$. The problem is similar to that of eq. (4). In this case, the prefix is p' (the length of which is assumed to be k'); that is, $p' = p\,\hat{s}_a = p_1^{k'}$. If we further assume the user only handwrites one word per interaction, then the length of d is 1 and eq. (4) simplifies to:

$$Pr(d \mid p') \simeq P(d \mid p_{k'-n+2}^{k'}) \tag{7}$$

Now, excluding the wrong-recognized word $\hat{s}_e$ from the model, we have:

$$Pr(d \mid p', \hat{s}_e) \simeq \begin{cases} 0 & d = \hat{s}_e \\[2mm] \dfrac{P(d \mid p_{k'-n+2}^{k'})}{1 - P(\hat{s}_e \mid p_{k'-n+2}^{k'})} & d \neq \hat{s}_e \end{cases} \tag{8}$$

It is worth noting that $Pr(d \mid p', \hat{s}_e)$ is directly derived from the original (n-gram) language model used in the non-interactive off-line HTR system and no further parameters need to be estimated.

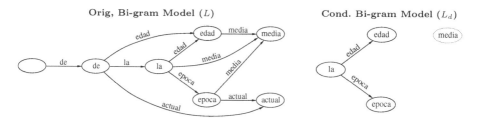

Fig. 3. Example of MM-CATTI dynamic bi-gram language model generation. L is the original bi-gram model used by off-line HTR system, whereas L_d is the bi-gram sub-model, derived from L, which takes as initial state the one corresponding to the prefix "la". This derived language model is used by the HFR subsystem to recognize the handwritten word "edad" intended to replace the off-line misrecognized word "media", which was disabled from L_d.

A simple implementation of eq. (8) is shown in figure 3. This example assumes the user wants to correct the off-line misrecognized word "media" by handwriting the word "edad" (for example). Hence, the HFR bi-gram model is conditioned by the prefix context word "la" and has the word transition "media" disabled.

As shown in the example, and unlike it happened in CATTI, no "linear language model" of the prefix p' is concatenated with the bi-gram model L starting at the labelled node "la", because the on-line touchscreen data corresponding to p' do no exist in this case. Moreover, as we assume that at most one feedback word is handwritten per interaction step, only the transitions from the starting node ("la" node in the example) need to be considered.

4   Off- and On-Line HTR Systems Overview

A similar conceptual architecture is adopted for both the off- and the on-line basline HTR systems. It is composed of three modules: *preprocessing, feature extraction* and *recognition*. The first two entail different techniques depending on the data type, but the last one is identical for both subsystems.

On the one hand, off-line HTR preprocessing [11] is aimed at correcting image degradations and geometry distortions: skew and slant corrections and size normalization. On the other hand, on-line handwriting preprocessing [12] involves only two simple steps: repeated points elimination and noise reduction.

Feature extraction in the off-line case, transforms a preprocessed text line image into a sequence of 60-dimensional feature vectors (see [13] for details); whereas a touchscreen coordinates sequence is transformed into a new speed- and size-normalized temporal sequence of 15-dimensional real-valued feature vectors as in [14].

As mentioned in section 1, the recognition process is based on HMMs. Thus, characters are modeled by continuous density left-to-right HMMs, using 6 states for all HMMs in the off-line case, and a variable number of states for the different character classes in the on-line case. In the latter case, the number of states of a particular HMM is in function of the average length of of feature vector sequences used to train it. A Gaussians mixture serves as a probabilistic law to model the emission of feature vectors of each HMM state. In the off-line case, 64 Gaussian mixture components were used per state, while 16 Gaussians were employed in the on-line case. The optimum number of HMMs states as well as the number of Gaussian densities per state were tuned empirically on the corpora explained in the section 5.2.

Each lexical word is modelled by a stochastic finite-state automaton (SFS), which represents all possible concatenations of individual characters to compose the word. On the other hand, text sentences are modelled using word *bi-grams* with Kneser-Ney back-off smoothing [15], estimated directly from the training transcriptions of the text line images. These bi-grams are directly used in the baseline, non-interactive HTR systems and are the basis for the "dynamic", prefix-conditioned CATTI and MM-CATTI language models for $Pr(s \mid p)$ and $Pr(d \mid p', \hat{s}_e)$, respectively.

All these finite-state (HMM character, word and sentence) models can be easily *integrated* into a single *global* model on which a search process is performed for decoding the input feature vectors sequence into an output sequence of words. This search is efficiently carried out by using the Viterbi algorithm [10], which can be adapted also for the search required in both CATTI and MM-CATTI interactive frameworks. As discussed in Section 3, MM-CATTI language modelling and search, are simpler in this case because, we have restricted our present study to single whole-word touchscreen corrections.

5   Experimental Framework

In order to test the effectiveness of both CATTI and MM-CATTI approximations, different experiments were carried out. The performance measures and the different corpora used in the experiments are explained bellow.

5.1   Assessment Measures

Two kinds of measures have been adopted. On the one hand, the quality of conventional, non-interactive transcription is given by the well known word error rate (WER), which is a good estimate of user post-editing effort.

On the other hand, the effort (number of interactions/corrections) needed by a human transcriptor to produce correct transcriptions using the CATTI system is estimated by the *word stroke ratio* (WSR). Using a reference transcription of each text image, the WSR is computed as the number of (word level) user interactions that are necessary to achieve the reference transcription of the text image considered, divided by the total number of reference words. This makes WSR comparable with WER. Moreover, the relative difference between WER and WSR gives us an estimation of the reduction in human effort that can be achieved by using CATTI with respect to using a conventional HTR system followed by human post-editing.

Apart from these measures, the conventional classification error rate (ER) will be used to assess the accuracy of the on-line HFR subsystem under the different constraints entailed by the MM-CATTI interaction process.

5.2   Corpora

Both CATTI and MM-CATTI were evaluated on the off-line handwritten sentences from IAMDB corpus. In addition, for MM-CATTI, the on-line UNIPEN corpus was employed to simulate the production of touchscreen HFR data.

IAMDB Corpus: This publicly accessible corpus[1] was compiled by the Research Group on Computer Vision and Artificial Intelligence (FKI) at Institute

---

[1] http://iamwww.unibe.ch/~fki/iamDB/

Number of:	Training	Test	Total	Lexicon
writers	448	100	548	–
phrases	2,124	200	2,324	–
words	42,832	3,957	46,789	8,938
characters	216,774	20,726	237,500	78

Fig. 4. Left: Basic statistics of the IAMDB corpus and its standard partition. Right: examples of IAMDB handwritten sentences.

Number of:	Train	Test	Total	lexicon
digits (1a)	9,032	6,921	15,953	10
letters (1c)	39,354	18,894	58,248	26
symbols (1d)	10,321	6,849	17,170	32
All Together	58,707	32,664	91,371	68

Fig. 5. Left: Basic statistics of the UNIPEN categories `1a,1c` and `1d` in the `Train-R01/V07` dataset and their corresponding partition definitions. Right: Some examples from these categories.

of Computer Science an Applied Mathematics (IAM). The acquisition was based on the Lancaster-Oslo/Bergen Corpus (LOB).

The last released version (3.0) is composed of 1,539 scanned text pages, handwritten by 657 different writers. No restriction was imposed related to the writing style or with respect to the pen used. The database is provided at different segmentation levels: characters, words, lines, sentences and page images. In our case, the sentence segmentation level is considered (see figure 4 right).

The corpus was partitioned into training and test sets. The former is composed of 5,799 text lines, handwritten by 448 different writers, which add up to 2,124 sentences, whereas the latter comprises 200 sentences, written by 100 different writers. Figure 4 (left) summarizes all this information.

In order to determine a baseline performance figure, an experiment using the basic non-interactive off-line HTR system (outlined in section 4) was performed. After some parameter tuning, a 25.8% WER was obtained. This compares reasonably well with state-of-the art, non-interactive results on this data-set [16].

UNIPEN Corpus: The UNIPEN `Train-R01/V07` dataset[2] comes organized in several categories: lower and upper-case letters, digits, symbols, isolated words and full sentences. However, the UNIPEN isolated words category does not contain all (or almost none of) the required word instances to be handwritten by the user in the MM-CATTI interaction process with the IAMDB text images. Therefore, they were generated by concatenating random character instances from three UNIPEN categories: `1a` (digits), `1c` (lowercase letters) and `1d` (symbols). Some character examples from these categories are shown in figure 5.

---

[2] For a detailed description of this dataset, see http://www.unipen.org

In order to tune the parameters of the 68 on-line character HMMs, experiments were carried out on each of these UNIPEN categories, partitioned into the training and a test sets shown in the table of figure 5. All on-line character samples were previously preprocessed using the preprocessing and feature extraction modules outlined in section 4. The classification error rates (ER(%)) obtained for digits, letters, symbols and merging-all-sets were 3.3%, 15.8%, 24.9% and 22.5%, respectively. These results are comparable with the state-of-the-art results obtained for this dataset [17].

Moreover, in order to establish a performance baseline for the HFR subsystem, a word recognition experiment was carried out. All the 778 words that will be needed in the MM-CATTI experiments were generated and 11.3% of them were misclassified by the plain on-line HTR system without using any CATTI-derived contextual information.

6   Results

Different experiments have been carried out to assess the feasibility and potential of the CATTI and MM-CATTI approaches. For the CATTI approximation, two types of results are reported: the conventional WER (first column of table 1), and the WSR (second column of table 1). The relative difference between them is called Estimated Effort-Reduction (EER, sixth column of table 1).

The 21.8% WSR in the table 1 corresponds to a total 778 words that the user has had to correct. In the MM-CATTI approximation, these words would have had to be handwritten by the user on the touchscreen. As discussed in section 5.2, this is simulated here through the concatenation of character samples from the UNIPEN corpus.

The 778 on-line words obtained in this way, were used to assess the on-line handwritten word decoding accuracy under increasingly constrained MM-CATTI language models explained in section 3.1. The left panel in fig. 6 plots

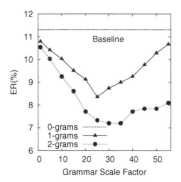

#Corrections		778
GSF		30
ER(%)	0-grams	11.3
	1-grams	8.7
	2-grams	7.2

Fig. 6. Left: On-line Word Error Rates (ER(%)) for different prefix-constrained language models and grammar scale factor values. Right: Best global ER(%) reported for 0-grams, 1-grams and 2-grams language models using a GSF=30.

Table 1. From left-to-right: word error rate (WER) and word stroke ratio (WSR); contributions of both modalities: on-line touch-sccreen input (TS) and keybord input (KBD); MM-CATTI total interaction steps; and overall estimated effort reduction (EER) for both approaches

WER(%)	WSR(%)	On-Line		MM-CATTI	Overall EER(%)	
		TS(%)	KBD(%)	Total Iter.(%)	CATTI	MM-CATTI
25.8	21.8	20.2	1.6	23.4	15.5	9.3

word error rates (ER) as a function of the *grammar scale factor* (GSF), and shows a table (right-panel) summarizing the results of ER for a GSF=30.

On the other hand, table 1 shows the CATTI WSR decomposed into a part corresponding to successful on-line touch-screen handwritten decoding input (TS) and another corresponding to the words that required typed input (KBD) (third and fourth columns respectively). Furthermore, the fifth column shows the MM-CATTI total interactions (in %) resulting from adding the part corresponding to keyboard input (KBD) to the CATTI WSR. Finally, the last column shows the overall estimated effort reduction (EER) in the MM-CATTI approach, computed from the relative difference between WER and MM-CATTI total interaction rate. As mentioned in section 3, MM-CATTI overall effort reduction is estimated under the simplifying (but reasonable) assumption that the cost of keyboard-correcting a feedback on-line decoding error is similar to that of another on-line touchscreen interaction step.

7   Remarks and Conclusions

We have reviewed a recently introduced interactive approach for off-line handwritten text recognition (CATTI [4,5]). In this approach user feedback is provided by means of keystroke corrections, which are used to consolidate increasingly longer correct prefixes of the final transcription. These prefixes are used by CATTI to to suggest new suffixes that the human transcriber can accept or modify until a full, correct target transcription is finally produced.

Furthermore, based on the CATTI approach we have proposed to use on-line touch-screen handwritten pen strokes as an alternative means to input the required word corrections. We have called this new approximation "multimodal CATTI" (MM-CATTI). From the results, we observe that this much more ergonomic feedback modality can be implemented without significantly increasing the number of interaction steps due to errors caused by the decoding of the feedback signals. This is achieved thanks to the constraints derived from the interative process.

In future works, we plan to carry out field experiments with real users (expert transcribers) to show whether this kind of systems can actually save significant amounts of human effort under the considered assumptions.

References

1. Vidal, E., Rodríguez, L., Casacuberta, F., García-Varea, I.: Interactive pattern recognition. In: Popescu-Belis, A., Renals, S., Bourlard, H. (eds.) MLMI 2007. LNCS, vol. 4892, pp. 60–71. Springer, Heidelberg (2008)
2. Srihari, S., Keubert, E.: Integration of Handwritten Address Interpretation Technology into the United States Postal Service Remote Computer Reader System. In: Fourth International Conf. Document Analysis and Recognition, Ulm, Germany, vol. 2, pp. 892–896 (August 1997)
3. Dimauro, G., Impedovo, S., Modugno, R., Pirlo, G.: A new database for research on bank-check processing. In: 8th Int. Workshop on Frontiers in HandwritingRecognition, pp. 524–528 (2002)
4. Toselli, A.H., Romero, V., Rodríguez, L., Vidal, E.: Computer Assisted Transcription of Handwritten Text. In: 9th International Conference on Document Analysis and Recognition (ICDAR 2007), pp. 944–948. IEEE Computer Society Press, Curitiba (2007)
5. Romero, V., Toselli, A.H., Rodríguez, L., Vidal, E.: Computer Assisted Transcription for Ancient Text Images. In: Kamel, M., Campilho, A. (eds.) ICIAR 2007. LNCS, vol. 4633, pp. 1182–1193. Springer, Heidelberg (2007)
6. Bazzi, I., Schwartz, R., Makhoul, J.: An Omnifont Open-Vocabulary OCR System for English and Arabic. IEEE Trans. on PAMI 21(6), 495–504 (1999)
7. Rabiner, L.: A Tutorial of Hidden Markov Models and Selected Application in Speech Recognition. Proc. IEEE 77, 257–286 (1989)
8. Marti, U., Bunke, H.: A full English Sentence Database for Off-line Handwriting Recognition. In: 5th International Conference on Document Analysis and Recognition, pp. 705–708 (1999)
9. Guyon, I., Schomaker, L., Plamondon, R., Liberman, M., Janet, S.: UNIPEN Project of On-Line Data Exchange and Recognizer Benchmarks. In: Proc. of the 14th International Conference on Pattern Recognition, Jerusalem (Israël), pp. 29–33 (1994)
10. Jelinek, F.: Statistical Methods for Speech Recognition. MIT Press, Cambridge (1998)
11. Drira, F.: Towards restoring historic documents degraded over time. In: DIAL 2006: Proceedings of the Second International Conference on Document Image Analysis for Libraries (DIAL 2006), pp. 350–357. IEEE Computer Society, Los Alamitos (2006)
12. Huang, B.Q., Zhang, Y.B., Kechadi, M.T.: Preprocessing techniques for online handwriting recognition. In: ISDA 2007: Proceedings of the Seventh International Conference on Intelligent Systems Design and Applications, pp. 793–800. IEEE Computer Society Press, Washington (2007)
13. Toselli, A.H., Juan, A., Keysers, D., González, J., Salvador, I.: Integrated Handwriting Recognition and Interpretation using Finite-State Models. Int. Journal of Pattern Recognition and Artificial Intelligence 18(4), 519–539 (2004)
14. Tosellli, A., Pastor, M., Vidal, E.: On-Line Handwriting Recognition System for Tamil Handwritten Characters. In: Martí, J., Benedí, J.M., Mendonça, A.M., Serrat, J. (eds.) IbPRIA 2007. LNCS, vol. 4477, pp. 370–377. Springer, Heidelberg (2007)

15. Kneser, R., Ney, H.: Improved backing-off for n-gram language modeling. In: International Conference on Acoustics, Speech and Signal Processing (ICASSP), vol. 1, pp. 181–184 (1995)
16. Zimmermann, M., Chappelier, J.C., Bunke, H.: Offline grammar-based recognition of handwritten sentences. IEEE Transactions on Pattern Analysis and Machine Intelligence 28(5), 818–821 (2006)
17. Ratzlaff, E.H.: Methods, Report and Survey for the Comparison of Diverse Isolated Character Recognition Results on the UNIPEN Database. In: Proc. of the Seventh International Conference on Document Analysis and Recognition (ICDAR 2003), Edinburgh, Scotland, August 2003, vol. 1, pp. 623–628 (2003)

Designing and Evaluating Meeting Assistants, Keeping Humans in Mind

Patrick Ehlen, Raquel Fernandez, and Matthew Frampton

Center for the Study of Language and Information
Stanford University, 210 Panama Street
Stanford, California, USA
{ehlen,raquel.fernandez,frampton}@stanford.edu

Abstract. Meeting assistants pose some interesting and unique challenges to the enterprise of software design and evaluation. As the technology reaches greater levels of development, we must begin to consider methods of evaluation that reach beyond regarding meeting browsers as signal replay and information search tools, and begin to assess the dimensions in which meeting assistants and browsers can augment or hinder human cognition and interaction. Some of these dimensions are considered, inasmuch as they were encountered during development of the DARPA CALO Meeting Assistant and Meeting Browser.

Keywords: meeting browser, meeting assistant, multimodal, evaluation, design, user requirements, CALO.

1 Introduction

Meetings are an important aspect of modern life. Sometimes people miss a meeting or forget exactly what happened in one, and it would be handy if those people could just ask a computer to tell them the things they need to know. It would be even handier if that computer could find and re-create the relevant parts of the meeting, from any perspective in the room, like computers do on *Star Trek*. Unless, of course, the computer goes berserk and starts to make up things that never happened. But let's not worry about that yet.

Of more pressing concern is the question of how we can develop meeting assistance tools that render meetings more productive and the information exchanged in them more durable and accessible. From a high-level perspective, there are two dimensions on which meeting participants may be aided: *participation* and *memory*. The dimension of participation includes finding ways to help people to interact efficiently and constructively and to exchange the right kinds of information at the right moments. The dimension of memory includes finding ways to make meeting information "stick," so to speak, either by making it more accessible in people's heads (their "organic memory") or by making it more accessible somewhere else, such as in the notes they've taken (or "prosthetic memory") [1].

The relation between these two dimensions of participation and memory is fairly orthogonal—which means they don't always work hand-in-hand, and a tool that helps

A. Popescu-Belis and R. Stiefelhagen (Eds.): MLMI 2008, LNCS 5237, pp. 309–314, 2008.

one does not necessarily help the other. Efforts at aiding participation can hinder memory by failing to encourage information consolidation. Likewise, tools designed to help memory can hinder participation. But participation and memory can sometimes be tapped in tandem, as happens when videoconferencing tools aid memory by promoting cross-modal encoding. So when faced with the task of evaluating meeting assistance tools, we cannot in good conscience invoke only one of these dimensions as grounds for appraisal. Rather, as designers of meeting assistants and meeting browsers, we must consider how both of these dimensions of participation and memory can be evaluated, and develop tools and methods for striking the right balance between the two, given the varying circumstances in which such tools may be used.

One further consideration should not be missed when designing tools that broker in human interaction and language: Any tool that interacts with people ultimately has the potential to change the way those people behave, and thus may alter the effectiveness of—or even break—the tool itself. For example, a system that identifies people's spoken commitments during a meeting and creates a record of them may eventually cause people to be more specific and deliberate when speaking about commitments, or may make them less likely to commit to things using speech. In the same way that laptops, PDAs, and presentation software have changed the way people act during meetings over the past few decades, so will the meeting assistant technologies we develop today change the behavior of tomorrow's meeting-goers. Any technology that aims to endure must be flexible enough to adapt to changing patterns of interactive behavior.

The aforementioned sensitivity of such tools to the vagaries and reactivity of human behavior throws a spanner in the works of typical software development cycles that tend to progress iteratively, basing the next iteration's set of development requirements on the failures of the prior iteration. This is the *iterative Catch-22* of development for meeting assistants, and the only way out of the mire is to design tools that adapt to their circumstances the way people do. Let us keep these thoughts in mind as we review a couple instances of interfaces designed for the DARPA CALO Meeting Assistant (CALO-MA).

2 Meeting Assistance Tools

Meeting assistance tools come in two flavors: *online* and *offline*. An online tool allows participants to interact with it during the meeting. This would include anything from traditional notepads and whiteboards to a virtual secretary that interacts with the participants. An offline tool, by contrast, is designed to be used at some point outside the meeting. It might help participants prepare for a meeting, or it might allow them to revisit aspects of the meeting after it's finished. Such tools would include browsable video recordings or transcripts, or a daemon that quietly identifies the tasks people agree to do during a meeting and places them on participants' to-do lists when they return to their desks. (A review of online and offline approaches can be found in [2]).

Each of these two flavors of meeting assistance tools has its advantages and disadvantages. Online tools have the advantage of allowing people to specify and lock in information while it's fresh in their minds, and can foster immediate feedback regarding the quality and accuracy of information as it is stored. But the presence of the technology in the ongoing meeting can distract from normal interaction and from the decision-making process. As a simple example, when people take notes during a meeting, they must either tune out of a conversation for a moment, or halt the conversation process as they write their notes. Offline interfaces, on the other hand, have the advantage of allowing meeting participants to focus on participation, and encourage feedback to happen at a more leisurely pace (such as later in the day, when participants return to their desks). If an offline tool is part of a wider suite of applications, it can help to integrate information established during meetings with other desktop tools, such as to-do lists, calendars, e-mail, or project planners. However, many management-level workers of our era rightfully smirk at the idea of attending to meeting-related interfaces after "returning to the desk," since their workdays often consist of a series of one meeting after another, with no desk to be seen until the end of the day, by which time a great deal of information may be degraded or completely forgotten.

Each of these options poses challenges to design and evaluation. We'll first consider the offline interface experience for CALO-MA.

2.1 The CALO Offline Meeting Assistant and Browser

As part of a wider DARPA CALO research project effort, the CALO-MA group inherited a mandate to design a meeting assistance system that would not only be effective and usable, but also would learn to improve over time, preferably in a personalized manner. This mandate nudged development toward two simultaneous efforts: (1) an effort to create models of speech and behavior that begin as functioning generalized models, but can adaptively evolve into personalized ones; and (2), an effort to solicit and incorporate user feedback that can retrain those models and improve and personalize them over time. These models include ASR language models, gesture and handwriting models, topic models, and models to classify sets of ASR-transcribed spoken utterances into dialogue acts, question and answer pairs, action items, and decision discussions.

A second, self-imposed mandate of CALO-MA was that the system under development should not include any type of in-meeting dialogue system, since such a system could prove disruptive to the natural flow of meeting dialogue. So maintaining natural *participation* was prioritized over the possible benefits of having a system that participants could explicitly address. Each participant is given a wireless headset that sends audio to a VoIP client. The VoIP client also provides a small suite of software collaboration tools, such as chat, notes, and a shared whiteboard. The system is designed to work equally well for remote, distributed meetings as for meetings carried out with all participants at the same table.

Post-Meeting Process. When participants finish their meeting, audio is delivered to a server that begins a chain of processes, such as producing an ASR transcript and detecting topics, question-answer pairs, and action items. When complete, an e-mail is sent to the participants, who may then review the transcript and extracted information in an offline meeting browser. This browser displays the transcript, with audio playable from any point. But more importantly, it displays hypotheses for the distilled information that users would be likely to want to retain a record of, such as action items and decisions (see [4] and [5] for more extensive descriptions of the CALO-MA meeting browser and its workings).

These hypotheses, as results of machine learning, are far from perfect. So the meeting browser is designed to harvest the implications of ordinary user actions as *implicit user feedback* that can be used to retrain classifier models without explicitly asking the user for feedback. For example, action items from the browser that a user adds to a to-do list are marked as valid positive instances for future retraining, while action items that are explicitly rejected are tagged as negative instances for retraining. If a user changes the description or responsible party of an action item, these actions are also harvested for future retraining, so the system will improve over time. Action item detection models retrained on even a few meetings' worth of feedback data can show reasonable improvements [5].

Humans in the Loop. Even though this offline system is designed to be unobtrusive and essentially invisible during the meeting process, aspects of the system's design had a discernable effect on people's behaviors during meetings, which in turn affected the system's behavior—resulting in the aforementioned iterative Catch-22. For example, an action item detection system was initially trained on transcripts from a diverse set of meetings (collected from the ICSI and ISL corpora, as well as some meetings recorded at SRI and CSLI). Participants' action items were detected by this model during test meetings at SRI and posted to an "Action Items" section of the offline meeting browser which participants could review a few hours after each meeting.

But the action item detection system did not work as well as expected for some participants, who expressed surprise after they diligently and explicitly stated declarations of action items during meetings, using statements along the lines of, "So here is an action item for you, to write up a plan before the next meeting." Not surprisingly, the original utterance data used to train the action item classifiers did not tend to contain such explicit statements of task commitments; and the words "action item" were not present in a single training meeting. So why did these new participants suddenly speak this way? Most likely because they were now aware that action items were being explicitly noted by some external entity, and because the meeting browser itself displayed a rather prominent section labeled "Action Items," which primed the participants to use that term. The detection system thus needed to be retrained on a set that included meetings that contained these types of utterances, so such explicit talk about "action items" would also be detected as such.

By contrast, a later iteration of the system actually worked better than expected, but for a similar reason: For each action item detected, the meeting browser displayed fields for the person(s) responsible for the action item, as well as the timeframe in which the action item should be completed, and these fields were populated when such information could be identified. But the presence of those fields in the browser prompted meeting participants to produce more utterances that specified not only what tasks needed to be done, but who would do them and when. Since these types of utterances contribute to the success of overall action item detection, this unexpected change in behavior led to better detection of action items than prior iterations [5].

2.2 Online Meeting Assistants

If people's behavior during meetings can be influenced by interfaces that do not actively participate in the meeting, we must wonder about the extent to which their behavior will change when different types of meeting assistance interfaces are introduced into the meeting room itself, and what effects these interfaces will have on participation and memory. As mentioned earlier, the tools people currently use during meetings—such as laptops and notepads—incur a certain level of cognitive load which can require people to "check out" of the meeting (even if only briefly) as they attend to the tools that promise to help them remember more information down the line.

The current state of technology, as demonstrated by the existing CALO-MA system, shows potential for different types of in-meeting interfaces that could help or hinder both participation and memory. For example, consider the cognitive load incurred by a person engaged in ordinary note-taking: While listening, that person must select information from dialogue that is salient, then distill and consolidate that information into a sensible chunk, and must finally exert the language and motor skills required for production of that distilled information onto a piece of paper (or keyboard). It's no wonder that many people have a hard time participating in a conversation while simultaneously taking notes. But if a real-time ASR transcript were generated during a meeting in progress and scrolled before each participant, participants could take notes simply by marking or highlighting the portions of the transcript they wish to revisit later. Such a process could aid participation by removing the cognitive load involved in note-taking; only listening and selection would be required. (Note that lawyers and judges in the courtroom have had access to this sort of technology advantage for years, thanks to digital networks that link their stations to electronic transcripts produced by professional stenographers.)

An even simpler interface might be to give each participant some type of "button" which could be pressed whenever a salient event happens during the meeting. Once a region of the meeting is indicated as containing salient information, machine learning techniques could attempt to extract that salient information and save it for the participant to access later, or even to act on it in some way. In either case, participants are freed from a good-deal of "record-keeping" and allowed to engage in more productive interactions.

But would these interactions necessarily be more productive? From the standpoint of participation, such interfaces may indeed allow people to participate more. But more is not always better. From the standpoint of the dimension of memory, we may arrive at a different perspective: Because such interfaces can provide a substitute for the cognitive process of consolidation that would normally take place during note-taking, they could actually lead to meetings where people talk more, but walk away remembering less.

Of course, this type of question can only be answered through an empirical study, and an experiment designed to provide that answer is now underway. Cognitive measures for participation and cognitive load can be obtained through both subjective measures, such as questionnaires given to meeting participants, and objective measures, such as comparative statistics on the contributions people make during meetings when using different types of interfaces. For measures of memory, the best method may be to test how well people remember the things that happened during a meeting by asking them to recall events and decisions at later intervals.

3 Final Thoughts

This brief discussion has covered some real-world attempts to develop meeting assistant and browser interfaces over the past two years, as part of the CALO-MA project. We have discussed possibilities for both offline and online interfaces, and looked at how the dimensions of participation and memory must ultimately figure into evaluations of such interfaces, pointing the way to a (perhaps foggy) realm of evaluation beyond gold-standard annotations and F-scores. We have also discussed some examples of how the typical software design process can result in an iterative Catch-22, which hints at a need for design methods that treat meeting assistant software as part of the interactive process, and not an appendix to it. Only software that can adapt to the behaviors and variations of its users will prove flexible enough to avoid that iterative loop.

Other methods of evaluation for meeting browsers have been put forward, such as the BET [6,7], and these methods work well for evaluating browsers of automatically-generated meeting information repositories that will be searched by users who did not necessarily participate in the meeting. But when it comes to evaluating tools that are more "embedded" in the process of meeting participation and incorporating information and decisions into the everyday work cycle, there are many more possibilities left to consider.

Acknowledgments. This material is based upon work supported by the Defense Advanced Research Projects Agency (DARPA) under Contract No. NBCHD030010. Any opinions, findings, and conclusions or recommendations expressed in this material are those of the authors and do not necessarily reflect the views of DARPA or the Department of Interior-National Business Center.

References

1. Kalnikaite, V., Whittaker, S.: Software or Wetware? Discovering When and Why People Use Digital Prosthetic Memory. In: CHI 2007, pp. 71–80. ACM Press, New York (2007)
2. Rienks, R., Nijholt, A., Barthelmess, P.: Pro-Active Meeting Assistants: Attention Please! AI & Soc (2008)
3. Voss, L.L., Ehlen, P.: The CALO Meeting Assistant Team: Multimodal Meeting Capture and Understanding with the CALO Meeting Assistant. In: Popescu-Belis, A., Renals, S., Bourlard, H. (eds.) MLMI 2007. LNCS, vol. 4892, Springer, Heidelberg (2008)
4. Ehlen, P., Purver, M., Niekrasz, M.: A Meeting Browser that Learns. In: Proc. AAAI (2007)
5. Ehlen, P., Purver, M., Niekrasz, J., Lee, K., Peters, S.: Meeting Adjourned: Off-line Learning Interfaces for Automatic Meeting Understanding. In: Proc. IUI (2008)
6. Wellner, P., Flynn, M., Tucker, S., Whittaker, S.: A Meeting Browser Evaluation Test. In: Proc. CHI 2005. ACM Press, New York (2005)
7. Tucker, S., Whittaker, S.: Accessing Multimodal Meeting Data: Systems, Problems and Possibilities. In: Bengio, S., Bourlard, H. (eds.) MLMI 2004. LNCS, vol. 3361, pp. 1–11. Springer, Heidelberg (2005)

Making Remote 'Meeting Hopping' Work: Assistance to Initiate, Join and Leave Meetings

Anita H.M. Cremers, Maaike Duistermaat, Peter L.M. Groenewegen,
and Jacomien G.M. de Jong

TNO Human Factors, P.O. Box 23, 3769 ZG Soesterberg, The Netherlands
{anita.cremers,maaike.duistermaat,peter.groenewegen,
jacomien.dejong}@tno.nl

Abstract. Recently, it has become more and more common for colleagues and project teams to cooperate at a distance. In order for cooperation at a distance to really boom, it should be made easier to have ad hoc, short, informal meetings. Here it is important to receive cues about the availability of the person you wish to speak to. These cues are usually apparent in a situation of physical proximity, but they are not readily accessible at a distance. Also, attending formal meetings should be made more efficient and attractive, by allowing participants to just attend those parts of the meeting that are relevant to them. This 'meeting hopping' should be organized in a way not detrimental to the ongoing meeting. This paper provides an exploration of how a virtual 'meeting assistant' that could support remote meeting participants to initiate, join and leave both formal and informal meetings in a natural, non-obtrusive way should be designed, in the form of a scenario and some examples of user interfaces.

Keywords: Availability cues, remote meetings, meeting assistant, user interface, scenario.

1 Introduction

Recently, it has become more and more common for colleagues and project teams to cooperate at a distance. This is partly caused by the fact that more people have started teleworking, i.e. "working in a location away from the main office or production facilities, without personal contact with colleagues, but instead through electronic communication (Cascio, 2000)". Another important reason is internationalization of work, for instance in the context of the European Union or multinational companies. Allowing people to be still able to cooperate when not co-located physically, is made possible through the advance of multiple Information and Communication Technology (ICT) applications, such as teleconferencing, electronic meeting rooms, chat, shared (network) disks and electronic cooperation spaces.

Cooperation at a distance offers many advantages to the society, organization as well as employee, such as less traveling, a higher productivity and a higher work satisfaction. However, part of the other side of the medal is the fact that people who cooperate at a distance feel they lack personal contact with colleagues, diminishing social

A. Popescu-Belis and R. Stiefelhagen (Eds.): MLMI 2008, LNCS 5237, pp. 315–324, 2008.

commitment, cohesion and team spirit, and find it hard to tune work to one another (Bailey & Kurland, 2002). Despite the availability of various ICT applications, people still experience a threshold for participation in remote meetings. Important causes of this threshold are that remote meetings need to be planned and tend to be rather formal and long, allowing limited support for having *ad hoc*, more informal and shorter meetings. This latter type of meeting is much easier to organize in the traditional workplace. During informal communication not only information transfer takes place (as addition or correction to the formal information provided), but it is also a way of finding a connection with colleagues. A lack of informal contact also strengthens the 'feeling of distance' (Kraut et al., 1998; Mulder, 2004).

In order for cooperation at a distance to boom, it should be made easier to have these informal meetings, e.g. similar to having a short conversation in the corridor of the office. Here it is important to receive cues about the availability of the person you wish to speak to, for instance about whether the person is currently in another meeting. These cues are usually apparent in a situation of physical proximity, but they are not accessible at a distance. Also, attending formal meetings should be made more efficient and attractive, by allowing participants to just attend those parts of the meeting that are relevant to them. This 'meeting hopping' should be organized in a way not detrimental to the ongoing meeting. For example, the participant should be able to receive cues about: when it is a good time to join the meeting (when the meeting is 'available' to him) in order not to interrupt the meeting; to be up-to-date about what has been discussed during his absence, to avoid the meeting participants having to interrupt the meeting to inform him about the proceedings so far; and to indicate when he is leaving the meeting (ending his availability to the meeting, but becoming available to other people, for instance for an informal meeting).

The advance of novel multi-media and automatic recognition and processing technologies is now mature enough to start making it possible to check the availability of both people and meetings in an intuitive manner, and to provide real-time updates of (parts of) meetings for participants who are late join the meeting. In this paper we explore the possibilities of applying these novel technologies to create a virtual 'meeting assistant' that supports remote meeting participants to initiate, join and leave both formal and informal meetings in a natural, non-intrusive way. This type of meeting support is argued to be a first step towards making remote meetings more dynamic, and hopefully also more efficient, effective and satisfactory for participants.

First, we further elaborate on the ideas of supporting initiating and joining/leaving a meeting, based on an analysis of how this is accomplished in situations of physical proximity. The notions of both availability and participant status play important roles here. Then a scenario is presented in which two situations are explicated: a situation in which a person is late joining a meeting, and one in which an expert is *ad hoc* invited to join an on-going meeting. Both scenarios are illustrated by user interface concepts of a virtual project environment. Further, some initial comments on the scenarios are provided, which resulted from a focus group discussion on future meeting support tools. The paper finishes with an outlook on future work on the meeting assistant functionalities presented here as well as suggestions on how these functionalities can be extended.

2   Assistance for Remote Meetings

Both when initiating a remote meeting and when joining a meeting that has already started, the potential meeting participant should receive cues about the availability of the person(s) he wants to meet with or the meeting he wants to join. Additionally, in the case of joining a meeting, the person should get an overview of the proceedings so far. Once the meeting has started or the person has joined, all participants are assumed to be fully available to the meeting and, consequently, not available to the outside world. However, a person from the outside world may still try to contact a person who is attending a meeting, if the urgency is high. These outside persons may or may not have access to the proceedings of the meeting, depending on their statuses.

2.1   Initiating a Meeting

Before initiating a meeting with someone, an assessment should be made of whether the person is available for communication. In situations of physical proximity, people make use of various cues, which together form an impression of the availability for communication. In general, humans are remarkably skilled at using subtle social cues about the presence and activities of others to govern their interactions (Erickson & Kellogg, 2000). For example, particular availability cues are linked to the person one tries to contact, the current situation of the person, the relationship between the two people and additional (digital) information on the current activity:

- *Person cues:* Background information (status, knowledge, experience, skills, interests, private information); activity and behaviour (in a conversation, in a formal meeting, working, pausing, absent, medium use); location and body (sitting behind desk, in the vicinity of the desk, somewhere else in the room, posture, gestures); appearance (conspicuous clothing or accessories, symbols or insignia, dress code); emotional constitution (character, mood);
- *Situation cues*: Type of room ((in)formal, own office, meeting room); place and time (in a situation of physical vicinity there is no difference in place and time, but time can be seen in the context of an activity: almost finished, not started yet, etc.); dimensions, acoustics and appearance (size of the room, quality of interior, audibility of what goes on in the room, lighting); atmosphere and accessibility (door ajar, music, laughter, tone of a conversation, type of lighting); other persons present ((un)known colleague, (un)known customer, unknown person).
- *Relationship cues (between the two people)*: Shared knowledge and experience (stories, media (photo's, video); shared culture (company culture, subculture, e.g., what does it mean if the door is closed); forms of address; relationship in the communicative context (type of relationship: work, project-specific, old/new, colleague, private, friend, intimate, family, acquaintance, unknown), hierarchy (superior, subordinate, equal).
- *Additional information cues*: (Public) electronic agenda, use of shared (network) disks and electronic cooperation spaces.

The cues are multidimensional, in the sense that someone on the basis of one cue may not seem to be open to communication (someone is talking to another person), but on the basis of another cue, he is (the door is open). The combination of the cues leads to an initial assessment of the availability. Subsequently, the contact seeker weighs the assessment against the importance or urgency of the communication, and then acts upon it. The act can take several forms: refrain from communication and possibly try later or find somebody else; ask whether the person is available for communication; or start communicating (barge in). The latter two situations may result in the desired communication, or in a kind of 'negotiation', which can again lead to cancellation, postponement or referral to somebody else.

In situations of trying to initiate remote *ad hoc* communication most of the aforementioned cues unfortunately are not readily accessible to the contact seeker. This makes it harder to assess whether it is the right moment to contact someone, and which communication means are best suited for that. Some existing informal communication means, such as chat or messaging applications offer the possibility to give an indication of the availability for communication. This availability is presented in different ways in different applications (e.g., iChat, GTalk, MSN, ICQ and Skype), but can roughly be subdivided into 'available', 'busy', 'away' and 'offline'. The number of indications for availability in current applications is significantly smaller than the number of cues we display in a physical situation. Also, these indications are always univocal, and one always has to take the initiative to set one's availability. The advantage is that one can control which indication to communicate and has the possibility to be slightly dishonest about it. Unfortunately, this means that the contact seeker can never be sure about the real status, which can form a threshold for trying to get in touch.

In future applications, it should be easier to make a more realistic assessment of the availability of the potential remote communication partner, assuming that working at a distance should become more similar to working in a situation of physical proximity. In this vision, there is no need for people to actively indicate their availability status, but a potential contact seeker can derive the availability from cues that are displayed. These cues may stem from the existing digital information sources mentioned above, but may be supplemented with additional information, e.g., media usage (computer, telephone), specific document and application usage, indication of workload (based on, e.g., number of open documents, keyboard hit frequency), and live audio and video (web cam) of the person (possibly blurred).

2.2 Joining (or Leaving) a Meeting

For a person wishing to join (or leave) a meeting, a list of similar availability cues as the ones described above can be composed, in this case not related to an individual person but to the meeting as a whole. Whether or not a person who wants to join the meeting has access to these cues and in which form they are presented to him, depends on his status. In the envisioned dynamic remote meetings of the future, at different points in time, participants may have different statuses. A first division is between people who are not invited and people who are invited to the meeting. People who are *not invited* are not aware of the meeting, but may receive an ad hoc invitation to join the meeting at a certain point in time, e.g. for giving an expert opinion on a certain matter that is being discussed. People who are *invited* may either be absent or present at the meeting. If they are currently *absent*, they may have *declined* the invitation, they may be *late* to arrive, or they may have *left the meeting temporarily* or *definitely.* Also, people may be *standby,* i.e., they know they could be asked to join at some point during the meeting, or they may have indicated to be *only interested in certain parts of the meeting,* at which points they will be alerted. Finally, people who are *present* may either be just *listening in* or (supposedly) actively *participating* (which may vary from having the floor, listening, paying attention to not paying attention at all) in the meeting. It is important for all of these statuses to be clear to the participants of the meeting. The question is how the meeting assistant should indicate these different statuses to the meeting participants.

Also, the meeting assistant should automatically provide information on the proceedings of the meeting so far, for catching up purposes when a person is late, is only interested in parts of the meeting, or asked to join a meeting only for a specific part. This requires real-time processing of meeting information, which could be made possible through the application of novel multi-media and automatic recognition and processing technologies that create real-time digital, annotated recordings of meetings (AMI, 2003). This functionality builds further on previous work on off-line meeting browsers, i.e., applications that supports users in finding elements of interest in (multimedia) digital recordings that have been captured during meetings (Tucker & Whittaker, 2004; Cremers et al, 2005). Existing research prototypes of these innovative meeting browsers, such as Ferret (Wellner et al., 2005) provide synchronized access to, among other things, videos of participants, presentations held, loggings of who speaks when, transcripts of dialogues and summaries (minutes). How to present this type of information to people with various meeting statuses is an open question.

3 A scenario

3.1 A Project Team Spread Geographically

A project team, consisting of eight persons, is cooperating in a project. Because of the geographical distribution they are dependent of ICT facilities for information exchange and communication. The project team has access to a virtual project environment, which helps them to communicate more effectively with each other, formally as well as informally. An important characteristic of the environment is that team members can show each other their current statuses, allowing others to judge whether they can disturb them at a certain moment in time. Also, the environment provides meeting updates for people who have missed parts of meetings.

The scenario shows two situations. The first is a situation where one of the participants, Frank, arrives late for a formal meeting which has been planned ahead of time. The second situation is a more ad hoc decision during a meeting to ask someone to join the meeting, where it is of relevance whether this person is available to the meeting or not.

3.2 Frank Arrives Late (Joining a Meeting)

A meeting is being held for which Frank is invited, but he is late. At arrival, Frank 'listens' at the door to make a quick assessment of the situation, to decide whether it is a right time to enter the meeting room. The information presented to him (see

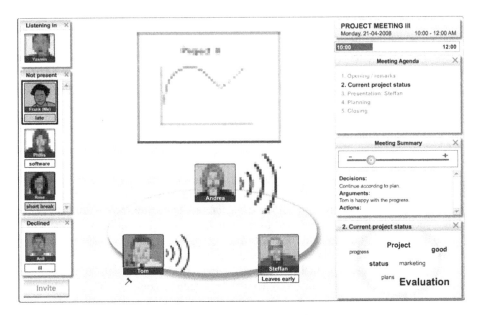

Fig. 1. Frank is late for a meeting

Figure 1) can be personalized, where only information relevant to his personal inter-est, role and status is shown.

Frank can see that a part of the project team, Tom (the chairman, with a hammer), Steffan (who has indicated he will leave early) and Andrea, is present in the virtual project room. Frank overhears blurred audio and sees blurred video of the people in the room as well as a blurred graphic. Apparently an intense discussion is going on.

Also, in the left bar he sees all invited but not present project members in blurred pictures. Their current statuses can be either 'listening in' (not being able to contrib-ute), 'not present' (yet or anymore) and 'declined' the meeting invitation. His own virtual representation is still 'not present', with a 'late' message attached to it by Tom, whom he had already contacted about his late arrival. Other people have appropriate messages attached to their representations. Phillis has indicated that she is only inter-ested in software issues and will receive a warning from the meeting assistant when this has become the current topic of the meeting. Rose is currently having a short meeting break and Anil is ill.

Subsequently, Frank looks at the right part of the room which provides information on the current meeting. On top, the meeting agenda with its past, current and planned agenda items is shown. By clicking on a past agenda item, the summary of that item is shown. By default, in the middle, an overall summary of the meeting up till now is presented. The summary also includes the global meeting atmosphere, indicated by a circle positioned on a negative-positive scale, where the size of the circle indicates the intensity of the interaction. Below, the current agenda item is presented with an overview of automatically recognized current topics, prioritized through size.

Frank is not very interested in the current topic and does not feel like entering in the middle of the discussion, so he decides to wait another minute, gets some coffee

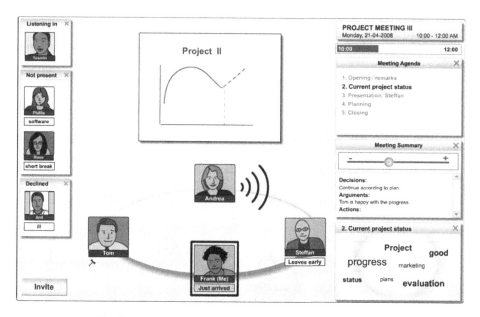

Fig. 2. Frank has joined the meeting, indicating 'Just arrived'

and then enters the room. To enter the room he drags his image to the table at which point the comment 'late' is removed. Chairman Tom receives a message of his arrival and greets Frank. After entering the room (see Figure 2) all four participants, including himself are visible in a live streaming image. The fact that they all participate in the same meeting is represented by the oval 'table' connecting all of them.

3.3 Chairman Tom Invites Expert Peter to the Meeting (Initiating a Meeting)

During the meeting an expert opinion is needed on a certain matter that is being discussed. Tom knows a person named Peter, who is an expert on the subject. They decide to invite Peter to the meeting. First Tom opens Peters profile from his list of contacts, using the invite button, to check his availability and to be able to initiate contact (see Figure 3).

Peter's profile shows indications of his availability: his calendar showing he is in the office and not in a meeting, his current level of activity and mood (e.g. based on his media usage, specific document and application usage, workload (e.g. based on number of open documents, keyboard hit frequency) and a blurred video created by a web cam. Tom can derive form the information that Tom is on the phone and his mood is not very positive. However, he can see that Tom still has quite some time available before he has to join another meeting. Since Tom is a personal acquaintance, he decides to wait for Peter's phone conversation to end, and to take the chance to invite him to join the meeting. In the mean time, he still monitors the current meeting, to stay up to date with the proceedings.

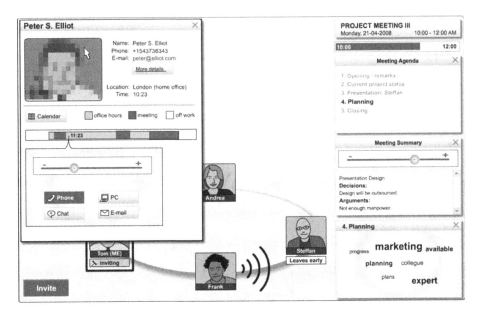

Fig. 3. Chairman Tom views marketing expert Peter's profile in order to invite him

4 Initial Evaluation of the Concept

An evaluation session was organized to get initial feedback on the functionalities and the designs. The scenario was presented to eight persons who were all experienced meeting participants, as part of a focus group discussion on future meeting support tools. Both the scenarios and the designs were presented to them and the various proposed functionalities were explained.

In general, the scenarios were received well. Participants acknowledged the idea that participants of meetings could have different statuses, for instance in meetings with primary participants and 'back benchers'. They could even imagine participating in two meetings at the same time, possibly with different statuses in each meeting. With respect to joining a meeting, the 'catching up' functionality was liked. Also, knowing about the current agenda item was considered useful, since they could all imagine wanting to join a meeting just at the point where an agenda item of interest starts. The possibility of calling in an expert was considered useful as well, since having to look up information afterwards tends to delay proceedings. In addition, participants suggested it would be useful to have access to areas of expertise of all meeting participants, as well as their roles, in particular for catching up purposes. A final suggestion was to offer the possibility of private communication between the meeting particants during the meeting, similar to whispering in a face-to-face situation. A concern was raised however on making meetings tóo efficient; sometimes it just takes time to think things over to reach better results.

5 Conclusions and Further Work

The functionalities of the meeting assistant discussed in this paper focus on 'meeting hopping': making it possible to efficiently organize and participate in remote meetings. Main functionalities of the meeting assistant are the possibility to remotely assess a person's current availability to attend a meeting, to smoothly join and leave ongoing meetings, without having to miss important information exchanged in periods of absence. This could be seen as a combination of support for balancing the workload and 'catching up' (Post & Lincoln, 2008). To fully benefit from this dynamic way of meeting, it should also be possible for an outside person to check the 'availability' of a person attending a meeting for joining another meeting, if the urgency is high. Outside persons may or may not have access to the virtual meeting room, depending on their statuses. It could be possible for them to check the engagement of the person attending the meeting: is the person currently speaking, listening or not paying attention at all. These engagement cues could help the outside person weighing whether or not to disturb the meeting participant.

The ideas presented in this paper should be further developed to meet requirements of persons who are experienced in remote cooperation and meeting. Also, user interface versions of the meeting assistant should be developed to evaluate how interactions that minimalize interruption of the ongoing meeting should be designed. In order to actually build these functionalities, real-time performance of relevant technologies should be assessed. Further, other possible functionalities of a meeting assistant should be explored (Post & Lincoln, 2008), such as goal orientation (e.g., agenda management and leadership support) and engagement *enhancement* (e.g., compensating for bandwidth problems, and social phenomena such as commitment loss).

A reliable proof of the ideas can only be achieved in a real professional environment, in which true adoption and appreciation of functionalities should first be demonstrated. It can be expected that real life issues not yet discussed here, such as privacy issues, will play an important role in these investigations.

Acknowledgments

This work was partly supported by the European Union 6th FWP IST Integrated Project AMIDA (Augmented Multi-party Interaction Distant Access).

References

AMI, Augmented Multi-party Interaction (AMI). Sixth Framework Programme, Priority 2, Information Society Technologies, Integrated project Annex 1 – "Description of Work" (2003)

Bailey, D.E., Kurland, N.B.: A review of telework research: Findings, new directions, and lessons for the study of modern work. Journal of Organizational Behavior 23, 383–400 (2002)

Cascio, W.F.: Managing a virtual workplace. Academy of Management Executive 14, 81–90 (2000)

Cremers, A.H.M., Hilhorst, B., Vermeeren, A.P.O.S.: What was discussed by whom, how, when and where?: personalized browsing of annotated multimedia meeting recordings. HCI International, Las Vegas, July 22-27 (2005)

Erickson, T., Kellogg, W.A.: Social translucence: An approach to designing systems that mesh with social processes. Transactions on Computer-Human Interaction 7(1), 59–83 (2000)

Kraut, R., Egido, C., Galegher, J.: Patterns of contact and communication in scientific research collaboration. In: Proceedings of the 1988 ACM conference on Computer-supported cooperative work, Portland, Oregon, United States, pp. 1–12 (1988)

Mulder, I.: Understanding designers, designing for Understanding - Collaborative learning and shared understanding in video-based communication, Dissertation University of Enschede, The Netherlands (2004)

Post, W.M., Lincoln, M.: Developing and evaluating a meeting assistant test bed. 'User requirements and evaluation of multimodal meeting assistants/browsers. In: 5th Joint Workshop on Machine Learning and Multimodal Interaction, Utrecht, The Netherlands (September 2008) (submitted)

Tucker, S., Whittaker, S.: Accessing multimodal meeting data: systems, problems and possibilities. In: Fourth Joint AMI/PASCAL/IM2/M4 workshop on multimodal interaction and related machine learning algorithms, June 21-2, Martigny (2004)

Wellner, P., Flynn, M., Guillemot, M.: Browsing Recorded Meetings with Ferret. In: Bengio, S., Bourlard, H. (eds.) MLMI 2004. LNCS, vol. 3361, pp. 12–21. Springer, Heidelberg (2005)

Physicality and Cooperative Design

Dhaval Vyas, Dirk Heylen, and Anton Nijholt

Human Media Interaction Group, Dept. of Computer Science, University of Twente,
P.O. Box 217, 7500 AE Enschede, The Netherlands
d.m.vyas@ewi.utwente.nl

Abstract. CSCW researchers have increasingly come to realize that the material work setting and its population of artefacts play a crucial part in coordination of distributed or co-located work. This paper uses the notion of physicality as a basis to understand cooperative work. Using examples from an ongoing fieldwork on cooperative design practices, it provides a conceptual understanding of physicality and shows that material settings and co-workers' working practices play an important role in understanding the physicality of cooperative design.

Keywords: Physicality, Cooperative Design, Artefacts, CSCW.

1 Introduction

Amongst its several definitions, the term *physical*[1] means something that has "material existence" or a thing that is "perceivable through senses" and "subject to the laws of nature". And the term *physicality* can be seen as an attribute or characteristic of a physical nature. The basis of human physicality (embodiment) allows us to see, talk and perform collaborative activities when we are in a shared physical space. In this case, human physicality makes the perceptual resources (visibility, sound, touch, smell or taste – any of the applicable) available to form the basis of human-to-human interaction. However, when humans do not share a common physical space, it is necessary to mediate these perceptual cues to establish human interaction via technological or other support.

People use languages and other means when they are involved in group activities. In fact, from the historical and evolutionary point of view, languages have emerged from joint activities of individuals working in small groups [4]. However, Clark [3] suggests that in everyday group activities, our coordination acts are not limited only to the linguistic signals but also the 'material' signals – signals in which we communicate through material artefacts, locations and our embodied actions. Keeping Clark's argument as a central theme, this paper explores the importance of physicality in the field of computer supported cooperative work (CSCW). Using examples from naturalistic cooperative design practices, we show that both the material settings and co-workers' working practices play an important role in understanding physicality in work environments.

---

[1] Merriam-Webster Collegiate Dictionary. HarperCollins; 11th Edition.

A. Popescu-Belis and R. Stiefelhagen (Eds.): MLMI 2008, LNCS 5237, pp. 325–337, 2008.
© Springer-Verlag Berlin Heidelberg 2008

Despite its importance, the role of physicality in cooperative work has been under explored within the HCI and CSCW communities. Often, studies have shown a certain analytic primacy to the conversations people engage in and in particular the verbal language. Despite the rich ethnographic tradition within CSCW and interest in analyzing technology-in-practice [15], the ways in which material artefacts are used remains surprisingly neglected [26]. We believe that an analysis of seemingly simple activities with artefacts may have important implications for our understanding of collaborative work. This is even more relevant when teams are from domain such as design, engineering and architecture – teams that use a variety of tools, objects and artefacts to support their synchronized work. The skilled and timely use of these artefacts, their availability, exchange and manipulation, is an integral feature of the accomplishment of complex collaborative activities that these domains represent.

The interest in understanding and designing for physicality has grown in recent time [5]. A handful of studies have indeed shown that material aspects play an important role in coordinating co-located and distributed activities. Several CSCW and design studies have approached materiality as supporting accountability [7], affordances [23] and coordination [10]. It has been shown that in architectural practices [22], medical hospitals [2] and meeting rooms [19], a considerable part of work is coordinated through material artefacts, like paper documents, notice boards, architecture plans and drawings. In a recent work, it is shown that materiality can play performative, persuasive and experiential roles in coordinating collaborative design work [13].

Within the AMIDA project, we have been focusing on understanding the role of physicality in meeting practices [28] and designing new ways to support remote collaboration. In this paper, we aim to provide a conceptual understanding of physicality, showing how 1) the materiality of work settings and 2) co-workers' working practices can contribute towards the collaboration of teams involved in co-located design practices. We illustrate this, using examples from our ongoing fieldwork of naturalistic design practices. We believe that a thoughtful consideration of these two aspects can contribute to the design of new technological tools for collaborative work without impoverishing what individuals do in their day to day working lives.

In the following sections we first describe the reason for our take on physicality. We then describe the conceptual understanding of physicality for supporting collaborative work. In the end we discuss the usefulness of the physicality approach.

2   Why Turn to Physicality

We describe several aspects that motivated us to look at physicality for understanding cooperative work of designers.

Utilizing materiality. Materiality of artefacts has a wide range of physical properties such as, spatial (size, shape, proportion, location in space), material (weight, rigidity, plasticity), energy (temperature, moisture), texture (roughness or smoothness, details) as well as other dynamic properties [13]. The role of materiality in coordinating team work has been echoed by several researchers in HCI and CSCW [7, 10, 23]. Several field studies of collaborative work have shown that materiality expands communicative and collaborative resources, e.g. the study of paper use in large organizations [23]. For example, Jaccuci and Wagner [12] show that in case of design practice different design materials and artefacts allow direct and bodily engagement and hence broaden communicative resources by evoking sensual experiences. Additionally, materiality of a physical object supports wider resources for actions compared to what current desktop-based applications support [9]. However, there is a lack of understanding about how to utilize material and physical aspects for design purposes within CSCW. Schmidt and Wagner [22] argue that conceptual frameworks of understanding contexts (such as distributed cognition and activity theory) do not adequately address the usefulness of materiality. For example, within the framework of Distributed Cognition (DCog), Hutchins [10] shows that information migrates from the minds of actors to artefacts and back to mind without any 'change', maintaining unity and integrity across several instances of physicality, minds and time. The DCog framework does not address how the materiality of artefacts may affect the affordances of the actors. (Read [22] for a discussion)

The design domain. Several CSCW studies have focused on designing systems with a view to support the cooperative work practices of specialized knowledge workers like designers, architects, engineers and doctors [16, 17, 19, 22, 25, 26]. Because of the nature of design practices, the interest in physicality in design work is pretty obvious. Designers, whose intention is to produce tangible products, communicate through a varied set of design representations often involving different materials, modalities and scale. To an extent, the whole design practice progresses through the use and manipulations of these representations and iterative refinements of both the conceptual and physical designs of products to be designed. Jacucci and Wegner [12] look at the creative and experiential side of physicality. In their work on understanding the design practices of students, they suggest that physicality spurs designers' thinking, helps them communicate ideas that would be difficult to communicate through words alone. Schön's [20] work on *the reflective practitioners* also emphasizes the 'conversational relationship' of designers with the medium they are interacting with.

Awareness and coordination. Understanding how material artefacts within a work environment are organized, configured, manipulated and handled could enhance the awareness of co-workers' activities and coordination of work. Awareness has been an important issue in supporting cooperative work. Taking a phenomenological stance, Robertson [18] has shown that physicality sheds light on establishing an understanding of awareness as a continuous and lived phenomenon. She suggests that if the participants in a cooperative process can be aware of what other people are doing, or have done, then the agency for structuring interaction and cooperative processes in the workplace can be claimed and practiced by the people using the technology [17]. In the case of design practice, the arrangement or configuration of material artefacts used in design process provide some useful perceptual resources that could allow participants to anticipate and structure a set of action.

Ubiquitous applications. Our particular interest in physicality is intended towards augmenting artefacts with computing capabilities taking into account co-workers natural practices. We believe that in order to develop efficient and effective ubiquitous technologies [29] we need to have a wide range of understandings of the ways in which the mundane artefacts are used within the everyday practical design activities. A large part of the CSCW research has focused on the mediaspaces applications – supporting remote communication through audio-video links [1]. It has been argued that because of the impoverished understanding of 'collaborative work' [8, 21], researchers could not achieve efficient and seamless coordination between distributed teams. New approaches like tangible interfaces [27] have emerged within this theme but they are mainly for 'one' user and do not support much collaboration [9]. In some cases when these applications support collaboration, they are mainly for supporting the co-located activities, using, for example, tabletop interfaces [e.g. 24]. Ishii's work on TeamWorkStations allows a shared drawing space for distant participants to coordinate their work [11]. However, the use of work practice studies to inform the design of ubiquitous applications is still lacking in the current research.

3 Physicality and Cooperative Work

Cooperative work involves supporting communication between two or more actors by establishing mutual understanding ("common ground") about the subject of conversation [6]. This mutual or shared understanding is not a precondition of cooperative work but it is obtained and maintained only as a result of articulation efforts. The distributed activities of the actors in a cooperative situation are *interdependent* in the sense that they contribute to the overall process of a shared practice of work. In order to contribute purposefully to the cooperative effort, each actor needs access to information pertaining to the state of the work: what is the situation, what has happened, what is happening currently, what might happen, and so on. We consider successful coordination in co-located and distributed teams as the situation where all participants can monitor, notify, share, allocate, mesh, or interrelate each other's distributed individual activities in an effective manner. As an example from a non-computing domain, Dix [6] discusses, in his framework of CSCW, how two actors trying to move a piano coordinate their activities. Even though the two actors cannot see each other very well the feedback that they receive from each other's activities – mediated through the material properties of the piano – help them make sense of each other's moving process. In the case of computer mediated communication the same process occurs. Actors who cannot see each other can be aware of each other's actions as mediated in different ways.

We discuss physicality at two levels: the materiality of the work setting and the social practices of the co-workers involved in the interaction. What seems to make an artefact meaningful to an actor is the interplay of its materiality and the practice within which the artefact is used or developed. Figure 1 provides our initial understanding of physicality as a lens to understand cooperative work. In order to support effective coordination (C), we need to understand both the materiality (A) of the overall work setting and the practice within which this materiality is utilized (B). Here (A) and (B) are mutually dependent: sometimes facilitating and sometimes constraining each other.

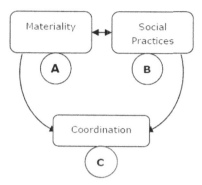

Fig. 1. A conceptual understanding of physicality for understanding cooperative work. The interplay between the materiality of the work setting and social practices of the co-workers could support coordination of work.

In the following sub-sections, we will discuss issues related to the materiality of work environments and the social practices of co-workers and how both contribute towards the collaborative work. We also provide examples from our ongoing fieldwork of co-located design practices to support our discussion.

3.1 Materiality of Work Setting

Design practitioners use a plethora of material artefacts to support their work. In order to understand designers' collaborative work practices one needs to take into account how these artefacts play a role in their work. As such, the use and manipulation of these artefacts is not a given, neither do these artefacts exist objectively in designers' everyday practices, but they are constructed in and through the process of design. Additionally, the materiality of artefacts can be seen in two different ways: materiality as a tool to support work and, materiality as representations of work. Artefacts such as a drawing board, scale, pencil and others are used as tools to support designers' work. Whereas artefacts such as a design sketch, clay or 3D model can be considered as representations of the design process. In the following, we provide several characteristics of materiality of a cooperative design setting, supported by some examples from our own fieldwork with designers.

We use a specific case in our discussion, where student designers were involved in designing a health-care system for supporting everyday medical care of the elderly. The students developed a software interface of a television set-top box and a specialized remote control that can be used on a normal television set. We captured their complete design cycle and analyze the role of artefacts in the design process.

Representation. Material artefacts often used and produced during design practices such as paper drawings, physical or graphical models can serve as representations of a cooperative work. In Bruno Latour's [14] terms, these representations have the characteristics of immutability and mobility. I.e. these artefacts can work as a persistent form of information as well as a carrier for information that can be moved in or out of the work space in order to support efficient collaboration amongst

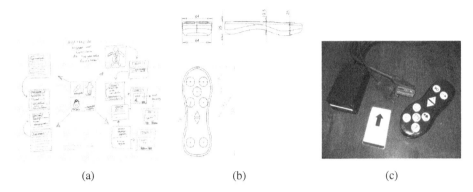

(a)   (b)   (c)

Fig. 2. Examples of different levels of design representations: (a) Information architecture of the health-care system, (b) Detailed design of the remote control and (c) Final product

different co-workers. For example, Sellen and Harper [23] have utilized the concept of affordances of papers. They showed that the physical properties of paper (being thin, light, porous, opaque, flexible, and so on) afford many different human actions, such as grasping, carrying, manipulating, folding, and in combination with a marking tool, writing on. Central to their notion of affordance is the materiality of artefacts. The immutability and mobility of artefacts, designed or used during a design process, allow co-workers to collaborate and coordinate work amongst themselves.

From our fieldwork we observed several examples of design representations depicting different stages of design (figure 2). These representations, in the form of a design sketch or a detailed design, carry a great number of conventions, notations and layers that can be very useful when designers collaborate with each other and allow them to extract information they need. Designers can also extract the details of notation, format, and syntax underlying their form and use, such as the specific techniques involved in working with maps, charts or matrices. The important issue here is that the materiality of different design representations can afford and trigger different collaborative actions in the design team.

Multi-modality. The multi-modality supported by material artefacts can provide a better understanding of a design practice as opposed to the sequential text or speech. Considering different stages of any design process, designers produce different models of the product they are trying to build. This could range from a conceptual stage in a sketch, to a card-board model, to a full prototype. Figure 3 shows some examples from our fieldwork that provides indication about different levels of multi-modality of the design artefacts. As can be seen in the figure, the multi-modality of these artefacts involves two-dimensional hand-made drawing (3a), three-dimensional physical object (3b) and a software-based representation (3c). It is important to note that these variations influence the properties of a representation and suggest or enable different usages, interaction styles and variations in meaning, even when they represent the same object, idea or concept. Each of these models can be seen as having a specific 'mode' of expression, when put together these model form a multi-modal representation of the design concept. The materiality of these artefacts connote

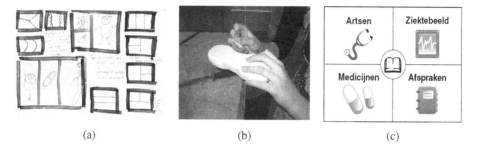

(a)   (b)   (c)

Fig. 3. Examples of different design modalities: (a) A drawing of design scenario, (b) Physical remote control created in the studio and (c) Software interface of the final product

a variety of qualities that are connected to the designers' senses (vision, sound, smell or touch) and vary with parameters such as weight, thickness, transparency, and so on. It is this multi-modality that turns the materiality of an artefact into a source of multiple channels of interactions that could lead to rich experiences.

Temporality. The temporality of different material artefacts could help establishing an understanding of the process that is used in the cooperative design work. Figure 4 shows three different stages of the design of the remote control used to operate the set-top box of the elderly-care system. Because of the iterative nature of a design process, temporality becomes especially relevant since there will be a need to understand, explain and mediate the design activities involved in it. The temporal dimension of the materiality of artefacts points to different time frames as well.

Additionally, designers produce different models and representations throughout the different stages of design such as, text, diagrams, comics, and video clips to sketch models, virtual models, and physical prototypes. The materiality of these represent-tational artefacts could provide a great deal of information about the way they are created, used and manipulated, conveying the process that is applied in designing. Importantly, the temporality serves not only as indicative of different stages of a design process, it also serves for accountability (planning, managing, budgeting, and so on) of the design work. A thorough insight into different artefacts produced during a design process could lead to some indication about change of plan, change of methods or any other deviations during the cooperative work. Especially in the collaborative design processes, these artefacts provide cues and signals for the co-workers to appreciate the

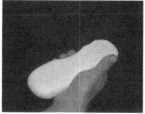

Fig. 4. Different stages of the design of remote control

intention of colleagues and the challenges and problems that are faced by the others. The temporality is indicative of the design-in-progress which is of a great importance in cooperative work.

Spatiality. The use and design of artefacts is often connected to their specific physical form and positioning in an environment. In addition the way a set of artefacts is organized could provide useful information about their relevance in the design process. Spatiality is not only a practical property of an artefact but it supports interactions and communications amongst several co-workers and is often used as a thinking tool. For example, in a brain storming session (normally, early in the design process) designers collect their ideas in sticky-notes and position them and group them in a certain way that allows co-workers to articulate the current understanding of a design project and generate new ideas for design. In this case, the spatiality of material artefacts such as sticky notes plays a role in explaining the order, relationship and overview of different activities of designers. In addition, the spatiality of artefacts also serves as a source of inspiration, especially in the case of designers.

3.2 Social Practices

One of the important issues to take into account when understanding physicality is that the role of physicality is not limited to providing the external tool support (specialized tools used to design products) or the material itself that is used for designing the product, but physicality is both what is produced and the process that is used in producing it.

In addition to the material aspects within the work environment, the social practices that are applied to support cooperative design is also an important aspect to understand physicality of design work. These two aspects of physicality: materiality of work environments and co-workers' social practices are dependent on each other and co-evolve over time. This has also been proven by the work of Sellen and Harper [23] on understanding the use of paper documents in organizations. They showed that some specific use of papers is not replaceable by other means (e.g. organizational policies and changes), as papers have become so integral to an organization's work practices.

Our fieldwork of design practices was limited to co-located design meetings. Figure 5 shows two different sessions of design meetings. In co-located design

Fig. 5. Two different sessions of design meetings

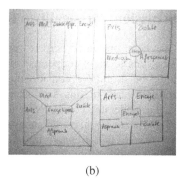

(a)   (b)

Fig. 6. Brainstorming processes used in the design team at different stages of their design project. (a) At concept development stage and (b) During interface design stage.

environment the perceptual resources (visibility, sound, touch, smell or taste – any of the applicable) are readily available. During design processes, designers accomplish activities and tasks utilizing not only their internal cognitive processes but via the combination of different cooperative 'embodied' actions [17]. The public availability of embodied actions of one designer enables others to organize their own actions accordingly, to support a cooperative activity in design. Cooperation is achieved by the mutual perception of these actions as the basis for the ongoing creation of shared meaning. Designers align and integrate their activities with those of their colleagues in a seamless manner by asking, suggesting, requesting, ordering or reminding others of some specific activities. From our fieldwork, we found several examples (figure 6) of designers' brainstorming process that provide indications about how designers collected ideas amongst themselves at different stages of design. Figure 6b is an indication of different interface design mockups that these designers considered and discussed during the process.

Public availability, central to many CSCW studies [7, 18, 21], of actions and material artefacts allow co-workers to appropriate their own actions. In other words, while carrying out the individual part of a cooperative work, actors typically modulate their own actions such that their colleagues are provided with cues and other kinds of perceptual resources relevant to their monitoring these activities. This calls for a consideration not just of human perception but also an understanding of how human perception relates to the way in which the significance of artefacts and actions is negotiated and conveyed in practice.

The communicative function of actions and artefacts is of particular importance here, as it goes beyond perceptions. People can only shape their own actions so that they are meaningful in relation to those of others if the ongoing activity is publicly available to each of the participants; i.e. if they are aware of each other. Moreover, it is important to note that the significance of the artefacts and actions is negotiated in different ways by different people within the same workplace. As Schmidt [21] suggests that 'awareness' of x may or may not entail the same practices as 'awareness' of y.

4 Discussion: Physicality – Beyond Communication

What has been presented here is our conceptual understanding of physicality that is used as a lens to view cooperative work. However, there are some important issues that could be useful for consideration when designing new technologies to support cooperative work. In this section we discuss the benefits of taking a physicality approach to understand cooperative work.

In cooperative work, establishing a shared perspective or common ground between the co-workers is the most important aspect. A recent review [31] shows that mediating visual information about work related artefacts is more efficient to support coordination than information about the participants involved in a cooperative work. This means that the artefacts – used or designed during cooperative work are a source of supporting and mediating interactions amongst the distributed or co-located workers. The physicality of these artefacts could support rich understandings of cooperation between co-workers.

Directness. The physicality of artefacts allows direct engagement with the artefacts and provides direct feedback, which in turn leads to shared resources for coordination and expression. Since the designers are in direct touch with their artefacts, the engaging nature of these artefacts can support better ways of collaboration. The issue of directness has been utilized by the research theme of Tangible Interaction [27]. Hornecker [9] has utilized this aspect and provided several guidelines to design new technology for supporting collaborative work. For example, she suggests utilizing physical constraints to facilitate the distribution of work and help co-work in coordinating each other's actions.

Affordance. The physicality of a material artefact allows a rich set of possibilities of actions. For example, Sellen and Harper [23] show that paper documents, because of their material properties, allow an array of collaborative practices amongst co-workers, such as: providing a flexible medium for the display of real-time information, a mechanism for team coordination, providing support for face-to-face interactions, and so on. Designers can think about new systems that allow multiple points of interaction, providing simultaneous access or establishing access control within the design of these systems.

Configurability. The spatial flexibility supported by physicality of an artefact allows co-workers to configure the artefacts and importantly the inherent signals that are conveyed by the positioning of these artefacts. For example, in a meeting room, papers can be positioned in such a way that can make them 'public' or 'private'. Additionally, the spatiality of material artefacts has a specific design narrative. The way different artefacts are positioned, along with their multi-modal expressions and behaviors could inform us about the design process and activities that are applied to it.

Experiential aspects. Again, the multi-modality and ability to support and convey information through all senses, makes the use of an artefact experientially rich. In the case of joint design activities, co-workers don't just interact with these artefacts when they are designing, they actually get the feeling and experience each other's activities through these artefacts. This really helps in the process of collaborative design in which the designers are always in search of new, creative and inspirational ideas. The communication channels that are established by these multi-modal artefacts go beyond facilitating and satisfying the basic task-oriented activities.

5 Conclusions

We highlight that the issues that are presented here are conceptual and are used here mainly to generate awareness about the issues related to physicality. However, these issues adequately point to the importance of physicality in understanding cooperative work – a perspective different from other face-to-face or linguistically oriented approaches. We believe that in the future a take on physicality is inevitable as the ubiquitous technologies are emerging. At the current stage, a thorough insight into the notion of physicality could help us foresee the future trends of ubiquitous technologies.

What has been discussed in this paper, in a nutshell, shows that in order to support efficient coordination amongst different co-workers we have to understand the real – material world and the world that we have created with our social and cultural practices. They are both the product as well as the mediator of each other. These aspects related to physicality are important to understand how co-workers make sense of each other's collaborative activities.

Overall, physicality is an important notion to understand cooperative design practices. It captures several important aspects that may not be easily extracted through other means, such as speech.

Acknowledgments. This work is supported by the European IST Programme Project FP6-0033812 (Publication ID: AMIDA-81). This paper only reflects the authors' views and funding agencies are not liable for any use that may be made of the information contained herein.

References

1. Bly, S., Harrison, S., Irwin, S.: Media Spaces: Bringing People Together in a Video, Audio, and Computing Environment. CACM 36(1), 28–46 (1993)
2. Bardram, J.E., Bossen, C.: A web of coordinative artefacts: collaborative work at a hospital ward. In: Proceedings of the 2005 international ACM SIGGROUP Conference on Supporting Group Work. GROUP 2005, pp. 168–176. ACM, New York (2005)
3. Clark, H.H.: Coordinating with each other in a material world. Discourse and Society 7, 507–525 (2005)
4. Croft, W.: Explaining Language Change: An Evolutionary Approach. Longman, Harlow (2000)
5. Dix, A.: First Steps in Physicality. In: Ghazali, M., et al. (eds.) Preface to Physicality 2006: First International Workshop on Physicality, pp. ii–v (2006)
6. Dix, A.: Computer Supported Cooperative Work: A framework. In: Rosenberg, D., Hutchinson, C. (eds.) Design Issues in CSCW. Springer, Berlin (1994)
7. Heath, C., Luff, P.: Collaboration and Control: Crisis Management and Multimedia Technology in London Underground Line Control Rooms. Computer Supported Cooperative Work 1(1), 24–48 (1992)

8. Heath, C., Luff, P., Sellen, A.: Reconsidering the virtual workplace: flexible support for collaborative activity. In: Proceedings of ECSCW 1995, pp. 83–99. Kluwer Academic Publishers, Norwell (1995)

9. Hornecker, E.: A design theme for tangible interaction: embodied facilitation. In: Proceedings of ECSCW 2005, pp. 23–43. Springer, New York (2005)

10. Hutchins, E.: Cognition in the wild. MIT Press, Cambridge (1995)

11. Ishii, H.: TeamWorkStation: Towards a Seamless Shared Workspace. In: Proceedings of Conference on Computer-Supported Cooperative Work (CSCW 1990), pp. 13–26. ACM SIGCHI and SIGOIS, New York (1990)

12. Jacucci, G., Wagner, I.: Supporting Collaboration Ubiquitously: An Augmented Learning Environment for Design Students. In: Proceedings of ECSCW 2003, pp. 139–158. Kluwer Academic Publishers, Dordrecht (2003)

13. Jacucci, G., Wagner, I.: Performative roles of materiality for collective creativity. In: Proceedings of C&C 2007, pp. 73–82. ACM, New York (2007)

14. Latour, B.: Visualization and cognition: thinking with eyes. Knowledge and Society - Studies in the Sociology of Culture Past and Present 6, 1–40 (1986)

15. Orlikowski, W.: Using technology and constituting structures: A practice lens for studying technology in organizations. Organ. Sci. 11(4), 404–428 (2000)

16. Perry, M., Sanderson, D.: Co-ordinating joint design work: the role of communication and artefacts. Design Studies 19(3), 273–288 (1998)

17. Robertson, T.: Cooperative Work and Lived Cognition: A Taxonomy of Embodied Actions. In: Proceedings of ECSCW 1997, pp. 205–220. Kluwer Academic Publishers, Dordrecht (1997)

18. Robertson, T.: The Public Availability of Actions and Artefacts. Computer Supported Cooperative Work: The Journal of Collaborative Computing 11(2-3), 299–316 (2002)

19. Ramduny-Ellis, D., Dix, A., Rayson, P., Onditi, V., Sommerville, I., Ransom, J.: Artefacts as designed, Artefacts as used: resources for uncovering activity dynamics. In: Jones, P., et al. (eds.) Cognition Technology and Work, pp. 76–87. Springer, Heidelberg (2005)

20. Schön, D.: The Reflective Practitioner: How Professionals Think in Action. Basic Books (1983)

21. Schmidt, K.: The problem with 'awareness': Introductory remarks on 'Awareness in CSCW. In: Computer Supported Collaborative Work, vol. 11, pp. 285–298. Springer, Heidelberg (2002)

22. Schmidt, K., Wagner, I.: Coordinative artefacts in architectural practice. In: Blay-Fornarino, M., et al. (eds.) Proceedings of the Fifth International Conference on the Design of Cooperative Systems (COOP 2002), pp. 257–274. IOS Press, Amsterdam (2002)

23. Sellen, A., Harper, R.: The Myth of the Paperless Offices. MIT Press, MA (2002)

24. Shen, C., Vernier, F.D., Forlines, C., Ringel, M.: DiamondSpin: an extensible toolkit for around-the-table interaction. In: Proceedings of the CHI 2004, pp. 167–174. ACM Press, New York (2004)

25. Suchman, L.: Embodied Practices of Engineering Work. Mind, Culture, and Activity 7(1&2), 4–18 (2000)

26. Svensson, M., Heath, C., Luff, P.: Instrumental action: the timely exchange of implements during surgical operations. In: Proceedings of the 10th European Conference on Computer-Supported Cooperative Work, pp. 41–60. Springer, Heidelberg (2007)

27. Ullmer, B., Ishii, H.: Emerging frameworks for tangible user interfaces. IBM Syst. J. 39(3-4), 915–931 (2000)

28. Vyas, D., Dix, A.: Artefact Ecologies: Supporting Embodied Meeting Practices with Distance Access. In: Krumm, J., Abowd, G.D., Seneviratne, A., Strang, T. (eds.) UbiComp 2007. LNCS, vol. 4717, pp. 117–122. Springer, Heidelberg (2007)
29. Weiser, M.: The computer for the 21st century. Scientific American 9, 933–940 (1991)
30. Whittaker, S.: Things to talk about when talking about things. Human-Computer Interaction 18, 149–170 (2003)

Developing and Evaluating a Meeting Assistant Test Bed

Wilfried Post[1] and Mike Lincoln[2]

[1] TNO Human Factors,
Kampweg 5 3769ZG Soesterberg
wilfried.post@tno.nl
[2] CSTR, University of Edinburgh,
2 Buccleuch Place, Edinburgh, EH8 9LW United Kingdom
mlincoll@inf.ed.ac.uk

Abstract. A test bed has been developed in which participants are tasked to work in simulated, scenario based, projects in which face-to-face and remote meetings of about 45 minutes have to be held. Measures on performance, team factors and remote aspects are automatically collected with electronic questionnaires. The sensitivity and reliability of these questionnaires are positively evaluated. The test bed is now ready to be used for evaluating how well meeting assistants support collocated meetings and videoconferencing.

Keywords: remote meetings, meeting assistant, audio-video capture, evaluation, questionnaires.

1 Introduction

This paper reports on work carried out in the context of the AMIDA project, the successor of AMI (IST FP6-0033812, http://www.amiproject.org). AMI (Augmenting Multi-party Interaction) was aimed at enhancing a meeting, or series of meetings, by developing tools for capturing, processing, searching and browsing multi-modal meeting information. The aim of AMIDA (AMI – Distant Access) is to incorporate this technology into a *meeting assistant* that supports not only at the content level (e.g. capturing, searching and browsing), but also at the process level (e.g., meeting guidance) and at the communication level (e.g., enhancing remote participation).

To collect data for learning to understand what is going on in a (remote) meeting (i.e., for developing machine learning algorithms that can recognize meeting phenomena) and for determining the effect of such a meeting assistant (i.e., to know whether it really leads to better collaboration, efficiency and outcomes), we developed a meeting assistant test bed. The test bed allows us to run both face to face and remote meetings in a controlled manner, with participants using the available meeting assistant technologies, and to collect various measures. This paper reports on the development of this test bed and the evaluation of it on a large set of participants.

Independent of ongoing multimodal technology developments in general and user requirements studies for meeting assistants in particular (such as [1]), we have identified a number of generic functionalities that our meeting assistant test bed should be able to evaluate. Figure 1 illustrates these functionalities. It shows firstly

A. Popescu-Belis and R. Stiefelhagen (Eds.): MLMI 2008, LNCS 5237, pp. 338–348, 2008.
© Springer-Verlag Berlin Heidelberg 2008

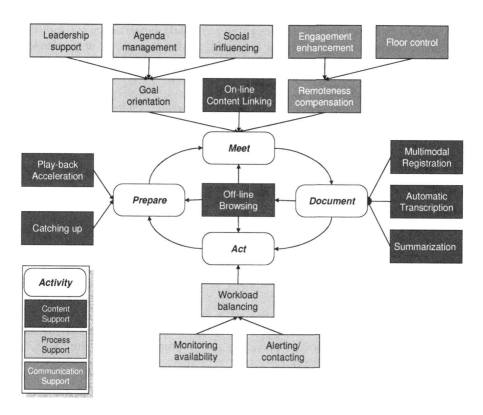

Fig. 1. Potential Meeting Assistant functionalities, associated to the meeting cycle

that the functionalities are related to a meeting cycle, consisting not only of a meeting itself but also of documenting the meeting outcome, of acting upon the result of that meeting (e.g., to carry out the actions that have been agreed on), and of preparing a next meeting, and so on. AMI was focused on supporting documenting (e.g. Multimodal Registration, Automatic Transcription, Summarization), browsing and preparation (e.g., speeding up meeting play-back). AMIDA focuses firstly on support during the meeting, such as with goal orientation (e.g., agenda management and leadership support), and compensating remoteness (e.g., to handle engagement and floor control problems and Floor control). Secondly, it will focus on workload balancing: how to tune one's meetings with all other work that has to be done in an organization. This aspect has to do with monitoring availability for interaction and ways to alert or contact people to start an interaction. Thirdly, AMIDA will support a specific type of meeting preparation which we call "Catching up": when you are late or asked to join a meeting only for a specific part, and need to be pre-briefed. The test bed should include all those meeting cycle situations.

The meeting assistant test bed builds on earlier work [2]. This paper describes the adaptations to that work to enable the evaluation of all functionalities presented in Figure 1, and not only meeting browsing (such as described in [3]). The test bed follows an approach in which participants are placed in a simulated organization and are tasked to carry out a particular design project, while supported or not with the particular meeting functionality to be evaluated. During their work, at preplanned points in time, they receive by e-mail information about their job, as well as electronic questionnaires for collecting various evaluation measures. The scenario is described in more detail in section 2.4.

In the remainder of this paper we will describe the evaluation method, present the results of the evaluation, and discuss our findings.

2 Method

This section describes how the test bed was evaluated. The participants that carried out the design projects are described, as well as the apparatus that was used to run and control the scenario, and how the meetings, including remote conferencing, was captured. Further, an overview is provided of the measures that were taken and a more detailed explanation of the procedure.

2.1 Participants

Data from 12 project teams consisting of 4 participants were collected in the instrumented meeting room at Edinburgh. Most of the 36 subjects were undergraduate students taken from the Edinburgh University student populous. They were paid £20 for approximately 4 hours of work.

2.2 Apparatus

The meetings were conducted in the Instrumented Meeting Room at the University of Edinburgh. The equipment used for the collection of the data is an extension to that used in the collection of the original AMI corpus, as documented in [5]. Some modifications have been made to permit remote participation and the capture of participant's use of the meeting assistant tools.

A second, smaller office for use by the remote participant has been instrumented in addition to the meeting room. This office contains a camera giving a close up view of the participant, an 8 element microphone array, and a lapel and headset microphone for the remote participant. These 'high quality' capture channels are fully synchronized to the audio and video recordings from the meeting room. The video conference system (Figure 1), which connects the remote participant room to the meeting room, uses a Visual Nexus multipoint control unit and EConf software endpoints from France Telecom. The conference is run at 4cif resolution, essentially the same as the resolution used for the 'high quality' video capture (PAL) which allows algorithms developed for the high quality signals to be used on the conference recordings. The conference is captured by means of a Codian IPVCR, which independently captures the streams from each endpoint. The use of software based endpoints allows the time code used for synchronization of the high quality video to be inserted into the conference video streams before they are sent, allowing the effect of delays in the videoconference on participant behavior to be studied.

In order for the participants to share presentations during the meetings, a simple remote collaboration system, based on VNC [6], has been implemented (Figure 2).

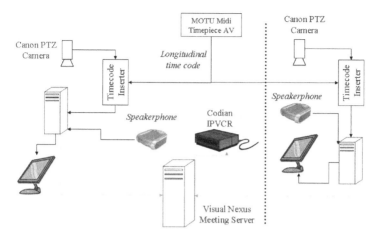

Fig. 2. Video Conferencing System

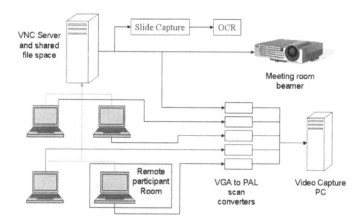

Fig. 3. Remote Collaboration System

The system consists of a central VNC server attached to the beamer in the meeting room, which the participants connect to from VNC clients on their personal laptops. PowerPoint presentations are transferred to the server prior to the meetings and shown on the VNC server. Participants in the meeting room see the presentation on the projector screen while the remote participant can see the presentation via the VNC client on their laptop.

To allow the observation of the participants' use of the various meeting assistant tools, screen capture of their laptops is performed. While dedicated screen capture software which would run on the machines is available, it was found that the software slowed the machines unacceptably when used alongside the meeting browser software and led to unreliable capture. Instead a hardware based solution has been used. A 'scan converter' converts the VGA output of the laptops to a PAL video signal, and this is subsequently recorded as an MPEG video, for later observation and annotation.

The scenario itself is fully automated – the timing is controlled by a simple crontab script which lists the times and contents of the emails which are sent to the participants.

2.3 Measures

The scenario also specifies the timings of e-mails for automatic measurement by means of electronic questionnaires. They are sent out before and/or after each meeting (see Table 2 for the details). Measures have been taken in the categories *Performance*, *Team Factors* and *Remote Aspects*. Performance and team factors are refined measurements from the questionnaires described in [2]. Except for mental effort (for which a validated 150pt rating scale was used), all measures has been taken by questionnaires (with for each factor 4 items, measured on a 7pt Likert scale). The remote aspects questionnaire has been developed to measure possible shortcomings in collaboration when one or more participants meet though videoconferencing. It also uses 4 items for each factor, measured on a 7pt Likert scale. The first three factors (commitment, social loafing and paying attention) are aimed at measuring the level of engagement. The latter two measure how the fluency and clarity of communication is perceived. Table 1 shows an overview and some example items.

Table 1. Overview of the measures, taken by questionnaires (except for Mental Effort). For each measure, one of the four items is provided as an example.

	Example questions
Performance	
Mental effort	*Validated 150 pt rating scale*
Info processing	We shared the necessary information well.
Proc. satisfaction	I am satisfied with the process by which the group made its decision.
Work pace	I had too much work to do.
Team efficacy	On my own I would have never been able to find such a good solution
Team efficiency	The meetings could have been done in less time.
Team satisfaction	I am satisfied with the way we worked together
Outcome satisfac.	In all, I am satisfied with the solution for the design.
Team factors	
Leadership	The meeting was well-run.
Dominance	*Dominance rating (1-7) for each participant.*
Cohesiveness	I find the members of the group pleasant to be with.
Communication	I had difficulty with understanding my coworkers.
Support. behavior	We corrected each others mistakes.
Remote aspects	
Commitment	I feel jointly responsible for the project outcome.
Social loafing	It appears to me that some team members add more than other.
Paying attention	Not every team member pays full attention.
Address./ turn tk.	I can clearly see when to interrupt a fellow team member.
Clear Communic.	I can recognize non-verbal signals easily

2.4 Procedure

In a scenario that has been developed to control this evaluation process, four participants acting as employees of a consumer electronics company, join a project to

Table 2. Mean values for 12 project teams at various project stages (carried out individually, face-to-face or partially remote), significant differences between stages (p =), and questionnaire reliability results (reliability coefficients α 1,2 and 3, for subsequent measurements). N R: not reliable. [1]N=6 instead of N=12. *statistical significant at 0.05 level.

	At start	Pre-pare	Kick-off	Pre-pare	Conc. design	Pre-pare	Detail. design	P=	α 1	α 2	α 3
			Project stages					**Sign.**	**Reliability**		
Face-face:remote		Ind.	4:0	Ind.	3:1	Ind/1:1	3:0/3:1				
Performance											
Mental effort	41	56	49	52	54	47	56	.043*			
Info processing			4.94[1]		5.99[1]		6.07[1]	.006*	.82	.85	
Proc. satisfaction			5.15[1]		5.93[1]		5.86[1]	.041*	.87	.91	
Work pace							4.08		.81		
Team efficacy							5.52		.73		
Team efficiency									n r		
Team satisfaction							5.64		.76		
Outcome satisfac.							5.60		.90		
Team factors											
Leadership			4.84[1]		5.82[1]		5.80[1]	.007*	.83	.91	
Dominance			3.94		4.41		4.48	.001*			
Cohesiveness			5.69[1]		6.07[1]		6.15[1]	.011*	.82	.75	
Communication							5.72		.70		
Support. behavior							5.84		.83		
Remote aspects											
Commitment			5.57		5.90		5.95	.001*	.89	.96	.94
Social loafing			4.50		3.56		3.51	.002*	.78	.37	.87
Paying attention			5.36		5.88		5.57	.001*	.66	.87	.82
Address./ turn tk.			5.22		5.36		` 5.33	.230	.74	.66	.77
Clear Communic.			5.21		5.40		5.55	.058	.87	.67	.82

design an innovative TV remote control. They are told that to shorten the time-to-market, and to increase the possibility of having a better quality product, a number of design teams are going to work in parallel, in a competitive way. The best resulting design will be selected for production. The participants are assigned a particular role within the team: project manager (PM), marketing expert (MA), user interface designer (UD) or industrial designer (ID). The overall project method that has to be followed has four phases: project start-up, functional design, conceptual design, and detailed design. Each phase is followed by a meeting.

In this adapted version for meeting assistant evaluation, the participants are asked to prepare and carry out the last two phases, with one participant working remotely. In order to do this they are provided with materials from the first two project phases which have been completed by a different design team. The materials include email correspondence between the previous team members, word and power-point documents they produced, and recordings of their meetings which are made available via a meeting browser. Figure 4 illustrates the project method.

To understand what the project is about, in addition to the final two phases of the design method, the participants are first asked by e-mail to prepare and carry out an initial meeting prior to the conceptual design phase. Preparing for this additional

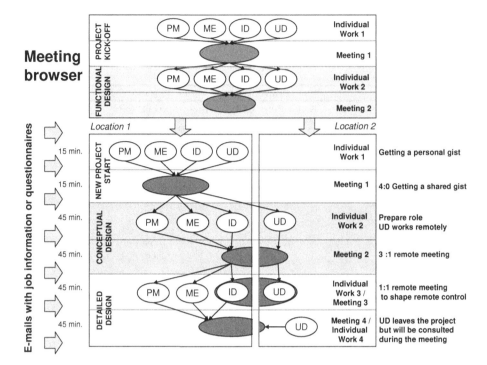

Fig. 4. Schematic overview of the scenario

meeting consists of getting a personal gist of the project, using the meeting browser and other information from the previous team for information and guidance.

During their first meeting their task is getting a shared gist: discussing what the project is about and collectively formulating the objective of the project. After this meeting, the User Interface Designer moves to a remote location (the instrumented 'remote participants room' detailed in section 2.2) where he stays for the remainder of the project, and all the participants individually prepare for the second meeting on conceptual design. In the second meeting, the participants present the results of their individual work (the UD joining by video conference) and collectively come to a conceptual design.

The participants then prepare for the final project meeting, the 'detailed design' phase. For the User Interface Designer and Industrial Designer, preparation consists of holding a videoconference in which they make a mock-up of the remote control using modeling clay provided to the Industrial Designer. Because they are remote, the User Interface Designer must communicate any ideas about the design to the Industrial designer using the videoconference, so that they may be included in the clay mock-up. The other participants prepare the last meeting individually.

Immediately prior to the final meeting, the UD receives an email instructing him not to participate in the meeting. He briefly calls the other participants to explain that he is not permitted to participate, and then closes the connection to the meeting room. To manipulate his availability, the UD is then occupied with another task - to define a usability program. While he is working on this task he can indicate his availability (e.g. using the 'presence' system integrated in the video conference system, or later on through an AMIDA functionality). The other participants present their individual work and the clay prototype is presented and evaluated. The scenario is designed such that the remote control cannot be made within the budget constraints initially supplied, however, at a certain point during the final meeting the participants in the meeting room receive new information. They are told that a new, cheap, interface component has been developed which may solve the budget issue, however, only the UD has specific information required about the device. The UD must therefore be consulted before it can be used, requiring them to asses his availability and call him using the video conference for more information. Finally, after the meeting, the PM will detail the finished remote control in the Product Specification Document.

The scenario allows the integration and evaluation of a number of the meeting assistant technologies outlined in section 1: New meeting browsers may be evaluated during preparation for the first meeting; Technologies for improving goal orientation may be useful during meeting 1 while the participants familiarize themselves with the project; engagement enhancement technologies can be evaluated while the participants use the video conference; The UD could use software to indicate his availability when he has to withdraw from the final meeting; The UD could use meeting catch up software to quickly find out what has been going on in the final meeting when he is consulted about the new interface component.

3 Results

From a technically viewpoint, the scenario performed well. Once the participants were instructed on the use of the video conference and remote collaboration systems, they had little difficulty in using them as required.

The existing questionnaires on performance and team factors that were refined and the questionnaire on remote aspects that have been newly developed have been tested on reliability. Table 1 shows the measured values and the reliability of the instrument on the individual factors. The values are collected after the different stages in the scenario (i.e., at the start, and after preparing and after carrying out the kick-off meeting, the conceptual design meeting and the detailed design meeting). Some are measured only once, and others repeatedly (for which more alpha's are shown). The setting changes during the scenario. Preparation is mostly done individually (except the preparation of the detailed design meeting, which is done together by the UID and the ID; the PM and the ME prepare individually. This is indicated by "Ind/1:1"). The Kick-off meeting is done all together ("4:4"), the Conceptual Design meeting with one remote participant ("3:1") and the detailed design meeting initially with three, face-to-face, but halfway with a consultation of the remote participant ("3:0/3:1).

Apart from team efficiency, all appeared to be reliable: all reliability coefficients (alpha's) are at least .70. Further, for those factors that were repeatedly measured, the instrument was able to show significant differences between the project stages (i.e., the three meetings), except for the factors addressing / turn taking and clear communication. From this, we can expect most of the instrument is able to detect differences within the stages as well, when we are comparing meetings assistant variants in the future.

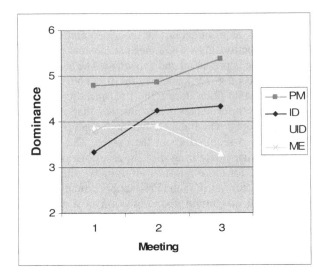

Fig. 5. An interaction effect of the factors role and meeting on dominance

The data allows more detailed analysis, as is shown by the factor dominance. We related dominance not only to project stage but also to the particular role (PM, ID, UD and ME). As shown in Table 1, a significant difference on dominance between the three meetings was found $(F(2,22)=9.831;$ p .001). Not shown in the table is a significant difference on dominance between the four roles $(F(3,33)=5.862;$ p .003). Moreover, there happens to be an interesting interaction effect between the factors role and meeting: $(F(6,66)=5.072;$ p .000). Figure 5 shows that particular roles tend to be more dominant than others (i.e., the PM). It also shows that for each role, dominance increases during the project, except for the UD, whose dominance decreases during the project. Remember that the UD starts face-to-face in the first meeting, next meets remotely, and then doesn't share the third meeting, until (s)he is consulted half way that last meeting. Working at a distance seems to have a clear effect, but such a conclusion may not be drawn directly, since the tasks of each participant are changing during the project too. The value of this approach arises when we compare the project meetings in which the participants are or are not supported by meeting assistants that, for example, can help with goal direction (e.g., based on dominance indicators, influence the meeting thought explicit floor control), or may be able to increase the level of engagement (e.g., by providing the remote participant information on the focus of attention, which is often difficult to obtain from a remote location).

4   Discussion

The main goal of this work is to be able to systematic evaluate meeting assistants that support meetings on the aspects of goal orientation, catching up meetings, engagement enhancement and workload balancing. Building on previous work, we extended our previous developed test bed for face-to-face meetings, in particular meant for meeting browser evaluation. We are now able to evaluate a wide range of meeting assistants that support not only face-to-face but also remote meetings.

For measuring the level of engagement, we developed questions on commitment, social loafing and paying attention. There are more options to define engagement. Curtlan and Pentland, for example, successfully operationalized engagement as the influence that individual turn-taking patters have on one another [7]. In our future work, we will try to relate these two objective and subjective measures.

One of our measures is about addressing and turn taking. Although this part of the questionnaire was found to be reliable, it didn't measure any difference between face-to-face and remote meetings, which are expected to exist. A possible explanation is that people are not able to perceive these subtle cues consciously to be able to answers questions about it. More research needs to be done on this aspect.

Further research will also include the relation between engagement and team factors such as dominance and supporting behavior, and also between engagement and meeting outcome: can too much engagement become unproductive? Answers to these questions are also useful for the development of other meeting assistants such as for goal orientation. Can engagement and dominance be actively balanced? Of course, once the relevance of these features have been demonstrated, work needs to be done to automatically detect them. Researchers in this area are invited to make use of our captured material and collected data, either to train their algorithms or to test them out.

A final remark on our approach. We let participants work with (or without) meeting assistants within a simulated, but quite realistic, project in which several interrelated meetings needs to be prepared and carried out. During their work, we took various measures on performance, team factors and remote aspects. Our approach is costly and labor intensive. For each observation session, multiple participants have to work for four hours, and to statistically compare meeting agents, many sessions are required, with, as a heuristic, a minimum amount of 5 to 6 and a preferred amount of 10 to 12 observation sessions per condition. There are less time-consuming ways to evaluate group support systems, such as expert review, collaboration usability analysis [7], Interaction Process Analysis [8], and relating performance to an expert defined gold standard [9]. Less expensive is also an evaluation at the individual level [10]. However, we think that user-centered-designed meeting assistants can best be evaluated through experimentally controlled collective user experience.

Acknowledgments. This work was partly supported by the European Union 6th FWP IST Integrated Project AMIDA (Augmented Multi-party Interaction Distant Access, FP6-0033812, publication AMIDA-106). Melissa Kronenthal and Anja Langefeld contributed importantly to this work.

References

1. Cremers, A.H.M., Groenewegen, P.L.M., De Jong, J.G.M.: Making remote "meeting hopping" work: assistance to initiate, join and leave meetings. In: Popescu-Belis, A., Stiefelhagen, R. (eds.) MLMI 2008. LNCS, vol. 5237, pp. 315–324. Springer, Heidelberg (2008)
2. Post, W.M., Huis In't Veld, M.A.A., van den Boogaard, S.A.A.: Evaluating Meeting Support Tools. Personal & Ubiquitous Computing 12, 223–235 (2008)

3. Post, W.M., Elling, E., Cremers, A., Kraaij, W.: Experimental comparison of multimodal meeting browsers. In: Proceedings of the HCII 2007, Beijing, July 22-27 (2007)
4. Carletta, J., Ashby, S., Bourban, S., Flynn, M., Guillemot, M., Hain, T., Kadlec, J., Karaiskos, V., Kraaij, W., Kronenthal, M., Lathoud, G., Lincoln, M., Lisowska, A., McCowan, I., Post, W., Reidsma, D., Wellner, P.: The AMI Meetings Corpus. In: Proceedings of the Measuring Behavior 2005 symposium on Annotating and measuring Meeting Behavior (2005)
5. VNC - Virtual Network Computing, http://www.realvnc.com/index.html
6. Curtlan, J.R., Pentland, A.: Thin slices of negotiation: Predicting outcomes from conversational dynamics within the first 5 minutes. Journal of Applied Psychology 92(3), 802–811 (2007)
7. Pinelle, D., Carl Gutwin, C.: Evaluating teamwork support in tabletop groupware applications using collaboration usability analysis. Personal and Ubiquitous Computing 12, 237–254 (2008)
8. Pianesi, F., Zancanaro, M., Not, E., Leonardi, C., Falcon, V., Lepri, B.: Multimodal support to group dynamics. Personal and Ubiquitous Computing 12, 181–195 (2008)
9. Ehlen, P., Purver, M., Niekrasz, J., Lee, K., Peters, S.: Meeting Adjourned: Off-line Learning Interfaces for Automatic Meeting Understanding. In: Proceedings of IUI (2008)
10. Wellner, P., Flynn, M., Tucker, S., Whittaker, S.: A Meeting Browser Evaluation Test. In: Proceedings of CHI 2005. ACM Press, New York (2005)

Extrinsic Summarization Evaluation: A Decision Audit Task

Gabriel Murray[1], Thomas Kleinbauer[2], Peter Poller[2], Steve Renals[3],
Jonathan Kilgour[3], and Tilman Becker[2]

[1] University of British Columbia, Vancouver, Canada
[2] German Research Center for Artificial Intelligence, Saarbrücken, Germany
[3] University of Edinburgh, Edinburgh, Scotland

Abstract. In this work we describe a large-scale extrinsic evaluation of automatic speech summarization technologies for meeting speech. The particular task is a decision audit, wherein a user must satisfy a complex information need, navigating several meetings in order to gain an understanding of how and why a given decision was made. We compare the usefulness of extractive and abstractive technologies in satisfying this information need, and assess the impact of automatic speech recognition (ASR) errors on user performance. We employ several evaluation methods for participant performance, including post-questionnaire data, human subjective and objective judgments, and an analysis of participant browsing behaviour.

1 Introduction

In the field of automatic summarization, machine summaries are often evaluated *intrinsically*, i. e., according to how well their information content matches the information content of multiple reference summaries. A more comprehensive and reliable evaluation of the quality of a given summary, however, is the degree to which it aids a real-world *extrinsic* task: an indication not just of how informative the summary is, but how useful it is in addressing a real information need. While intrinsic evaluation metrics are indispensable for development purposes and can be easily replicated, they ideally need to be chosen based on whether or not they are good predictors for extrinsic usefulness, e.g. whether they correlate to a measure of real-world usefulness.

We therefore design an extrinsic task that models a real-world information need, create multiple experimental conditions and enlist subjects to participate in the task. The chosen task is a *decision audit*, wherein a user must review previously held meetings in order to determine how a given decision was reached. This involves the user determining what the final decision was, which alternatives had previously been proposed, and what the arguments for and against the various proposals were. The reason this task was chosen is that it represents one of the key applications for analyzing multimodal interactions - that of aiding *corporate memory*, the storage and management of a organization's knowledge, transactions, decisions, and plans. A organization may find itself in the position

A. Popescu-Belis and R. Stiefelhagen (Eds.): MLMI 2008, LNCS 5237, pp. 349–361, 2008.

of needing to review or explain how it came to a particular position or why it took a certain course of action. We hypothesize that this task will be made much more efficient when meetings are archived and summarized.

The decision audit represents a complex information need that cannot be satisfied with a simple one-sentence answer. Relevant information will be spread throughout several meetings and may appear at multiple points in a single discussion thread. Because the decision audit does not only involve knowing *what* decision was made but also determining *why* the decision was made, the person conducting the audit will need to understand the evolution of the meeting participants' thinking and the range of factors that led to the ultimate decision. Because the person conducting the decision audit does not know which meetings are relevant to the given topic, there is an inherent relevance assessment task built into this overall task. As time is limited, they cannot hope to scan the meetings in their entirety and so must focus on which meetings and meeting sections seem most promising.

2   Related Extrinsic Evaluation Work

This section describes previous extrinsic evaluations relating either to summarization or to the browsing of multi-party interactions. We then describe how our decision audit browsers fit into a typology of multi-media interfaces.

2.1   Previous Work

In the field of text summarization, a commonly used extrinsic evaluation has been the *relevance assessment* task [1]. In such a task, a user is presented with a description of a topic or event and then must decide whether a given document (e.g. a summary or a full-text) is relevant to that topic or event. Such schemes have been used for a number of years and on a variety of projects [2, 3, 4]. Due to problems of low inter-annotator agreement on such ratings, Dorr et. al [5] proposed a new evaluation scheme that compares the relevance judgment of an annotator given a full text with that same annotator given a condensed text.

Another type of extrinsic evaluation for summarization is the *reading comprehension* task [1, 6, 7]. In such an evaluation, a user is given either a full source or a summary text and is then given a multiple-choice test relating to the full source information. A system can then calculate how well they perform on the test given the condition. This evaluation framework relies on the idea that truly informative summaries should be able to act as substitutes for the full source.

In the speech domain, there have been several large extrinsic IR evaluations in the past few years, though not necessarily designed with summarization in mind. Wellner et. al [8] introduced the Browser Evaluation Test (BET), in which *observations of interest* are collected for each meeting, e.g. the observation "Susan says the footstool is expensive." Each observation is presented as both a positive and negative statement and the user must decide which statement is correct by browsing the meetings and finding the correct answer. It is clear that such a set-up could be used to evaluate summaries and to compare summaries with other information sources. We choose not to use this evaluation paradigm, however, because the observations of interest tend to be skewed towards a keyword search approach, where it would always be simpler just to search for a word such as "footstool" rather than read a summary.

The Task-Based Evaluation (TBE) [9] evaluates multiple browser conditions containing various information sources relating to a series of meetings. Participants are brought in four at a time and are told that they are replacing a previous group and must finish that group's work. In essence, the evaluation involves re-running the final meetings of the series with new participants. The participants are given information related to the previous group's initial meetings and must finalize the previous group's decisions as best as possible given what they know. There are several reasons we have chosen not to use the TBE for this summarization evaluation. One is that the TBE relies primarily on post-questionnaire answers for evaluation. While we do incorporate post-questionnaires in our evaluation, we are also very interested in the objective participant performance in the task and browsing behaviour during the task. Two, the TBE is more costly to run than our decision audit task, as it requires having groups of four people spend an afternoon reviewing previous meetings and conducting their own meetings, which are also recorded, whereas the decision audit is an individual task.

The SCANMail browser [10, 11] is an interface for managing and browsing voicemail messages, with multi-media components such as audio, ASR transcripts, audio-based paragraphs, and extracted names and phone numbers. To evaluate the browser and its components, the authors compared the SCANMail browser to a state-of-the-art voicemail system on four key tasks: scanning and searching messages, extracting information from messages, tracking the status of messages (e.g. whether or not a message has been dealt with), and archiving messages. Both in a think-aloud laboratory study and a larger field study, users found the SCANMail system outperformed the comparison system for these extrinsic tasks. The field study in particular yielded several interesting findings. In 24% of the times that users viewed a voicemail transcript with the SCANMail system, they did not resort to playing the audio. This testifies to the fact that the transcript and extracted information can, to some degree, act as substitutes for the signal, which user comments also back up. On occasions when users did play the audio, 57% of the time they did not play the entire audio. Most interestingly, 57% of the audio play operations resulted from clicking within the transcript. The study also found that users were able to understand the transcripts even with recognition errors, partly by having prior context for many of the messages.

Whittaker et. al [12] described a task-oriented evaluation of a browser for navigating meeting interactions. The browser contains a manual transcript, a visualization of speaker activity, audio and video streams with play, pause and stop commands, and artefacts such as slides and whiteboard events (the slides, but not the whiteboard events, are indices into the meeting record). Users were given two sets of questions to answer, the first set consisting of general "gist" question about the meeting, and the second set comprised of questions about specific facts within the meeting. There were 10 questions in total to be answered. User responses were subsequently scored on correctness compared with model answers. While general performance was not high, users found it much easier to answer specific questions than "gist" questions using this browser setup. This has special relevance for our work, as certain types of information needs might be easily satisfied without recourse to derived data such as summaries or topic segments, but getting the general gist of the meeting seems to be much more difficult. Very interestingly, users often felt that they had performed much better than they actually had. Specifically, users seemed to be unaware that they had missed relevant or vital information and felt that they had provided comprehensive answers. Across the board, participants focused on reading the transcript rather than beginning with the audio and video records directly.

2.2   Multimodal Browser Types

Tucker and Whittaker [13] provided an overview of the mechanisms available for browsing multimodal meetings. They established a four-way browser classification: audio-based browsers, video-based browsers, artefact-based browsers, and derived data browsers. In light of this classification scheme, our decision audit browsers are video browsers incorporating derived data forms. Although other incarnations of our browsers contain meeting artefacts such as slides, we simplify the browsers as much as possible for this task by putting the focus on derived data forms and their usefulness for browsing the meeting records. Each version of the experimental browser is built using JFerret [14], an easily modifiable multi-media browser framework[1].

3   Task Overview

The experiment consists of five different conditions, described below. We recruited 10 subjects per condition for a total of 50 subjects, all native speakers of English. For each condition, 6 participants were run in Edinburgh and 4 were run at Saarbrücken, the experimental setups for the two locations being as identical as possible.

As our underlying data we chose four meetings from the AMI Meeting Corpus [15]. The meeting series ES2008 was selected because the participant group in that series worked well together on the task of designing a new remote control. The group took the task seriously and exhibited deliberate and careful decision-making processes in each meeting and across the meeting series as a whole.

The basic task for the participants was to write a summary of the decision making process in the meetings for separating often and rarely used functions of the remote control. This particular information need was chosen because the relevant discussion manifested itself throughout the 4 meetings, and the group went through several possibilities before designing an eventual solution to this portion of the design problem. A participant in the decision audit task therefore

---

[1] http://www.idiap.ch/mmm/tools/jferret

would have to consult each meeting to be able to retrieve the full answer to the task's information need.

Each participant in our task was first given general instructions explaining the meeting browser used in the experiment, the specific information need they were meant to satisfy in the task, and a notice of the allotted time, 45 minutes, which included both searching for the information and writing up the answer. This amount of time was based on the result of an individual pilot task for Condition EAM (s. 3.1). After reading the task instructions, each participant is briefly shown how to use the browser's various functions for navigating and writing in the given experimental condition. They are then given several minutes to familiarize themselves with the browser using unrelated meeting data, until they state that they were comfortable and ready to proceed.

3.1 Experimental Conditions

There are five conditions run in total: one baseline condition, two extractive conditions and two abstractive conditions, all of which come with audio/video recordings and either a manual or automatic meeting transcript. Table 1 lists the experimental conditions. The three-letter ID for each condition corresponds to keywords/extracts/abstracts, automatic/semi-automatic/manual algorithms, and automatic/manual transcripts.

Table 1. Experimental Conditions

Condition	Description
KAM	Top 20 keywords
EAM	Extractive summary of manual transcripts
EAA	Extractive summary of ASR transcripts
AMM	Human abstracts
ASM	Semi-Automatic abstracts

The baseline condition, Condition KAM, consists of a browser with manual transcripts and a list of the top 20 keywords in the meeting. The keywords are determined automatically using $su.idf$ [16]. Though this is a baseline condition, the fact that it utilizes manual transcripts gives users in this condition a possible advantage over users in conditions with ASR. In this respect, it is a challenging baseline. There are other possibilities for the baseline, but we choose the top 20 keywords because we are interested in comparing different forms of derived content from meetings, and because a facility such as keyword search would likely be problematic for a participant who is uncertain of what to search for because they are unfamiliar with the meetings.

Condition AMM is the gold-standard condition, a human-authored abstractive summary. Each summary is divided into subsections: abstract, actions, decisions and problems. Because of the distinct "decisions" subsection, this is considered a challenging gold-standard to match for a decision audit task.

Conditions EAM and EAA present the user with an extractive summary of each meeting, with the difference between the conditions being that the latter is based on ASR and the former on manual transcripts. Condition EAA is the only experimental condition using ASR output. These summaries were generated by training a support vector machine (SVM) with an RBF kernel on the AMI training data, using 17 features from five broad feature classes: prosodic, lexical, length, structural and speaker-related. The classifier was run on the four meetings of interest, ranking dialogue acts in descending order of informativeness according to posterior probability, extracting until we reach the desired summary length, approximately 1000 words for the first meeting, 1900 words each for the second and third meetings, and 2300 words for the final meeting. These lengths correlate to the lengths of the meetings themselves and represent compressions to approximately 40%, 32%, 32% and 30% of the total meeting word counts, respectively. These summary lengths were based on the compression rates of the human extracts for these meetings.

Condition ASM presents the user with a semi-automatically generated abstractive summary, as described in [17]. This method utilizes hand-annotated topic segmentation and topic labels available in the AMI corpus. In addition, the meeting transcript was manually annotated with content items from a taxonomy for the domains *project*, *meeting* and *product*. A sentence is generated for each meeting topic based on the annotated topic label. It may also mention the three most frequent content items, indicating roughly what was discussed.

3.2   Browser Setup

The meeting browsers are kept essentially the same in all conditions to eliminate any potential confounding factors relating to the user interface. In each browser, there are 5 tabs for the 4 meetings and a writing pad, provided for the participant to author their decision audit answer. As a consequence, the participant cannot view the meeting tabs while typing the answer; they are restricted to tabbing back and forth as needed.

Fig. 1. Condition AMM Browser

This was designed deliberately so as to be able to discern when the participant was working on formulating or writing the answer on the one hand and when they were browsing the meeting records on the other. In each meeting tab, the videos displaying the four meeting participants are laid out horizontally with the media controls beneath. The transcript is shown in the lower left of the browser tab in a scroll window.

In Condition KAM, each meeting tab contains buttons corresponding to the top 20 keywords. Pressing a button highlights the first instance of the associated keyword in the transcript, as well as opening a list of hyperlinks to all occurrences of that word in the transcript. In Conditions AMM and ASM, the abstractive summary is presented next to the meeting transcript. Clicking on a summary sentence opens a list of hyperlinks similar to Condition KAM, linking to dialogue acts in the transcript that support the particular summary sentence. In addition to an abstract, Condition ASM displays three extra tabs with bullet points for the subsections mentioned above (s. fig. 1). In Conditions EAM and EAA, the extractive summary is displayed with each dialogue act hyperlinked to the point in the transcript it was extracted from.

3.3   Evaluation Features

For evaluation of the decision audit task, there are three types of features to be analyzed: answers to questionnaires, human ratings of the users' written answers, and features extracted from logfiles. In all conditions, we log with time stamps mouse clicks on the transcript, the play-, pause-, stop buttons, changing tabs, and characters entered into the typing tab.

Upon completion of the decision audit task, we present each participant with a post-task questionnaire consisting of 10 statements with which the participant can state their level of agreement or disagreement via a 5-point Likert scale, such as *I was able to efficiently find the relevant information*, and two open-ended questions about the specific type of information available in the given condition and what further information they would have liked. Of the 10 statements evaluated, some are re-wordings of others with the polarity reversed in order to gauge the users' consistency in answering.

In order to gauge the participant accomplished the decision audit task, we enlist two human judges to do both *subjective* and *objective* evaluations. For the subjective portion, the judges first read through all 50 answers to get a view of the variety of answers. They then rate each answer using a 1-8 Likert-scale on criteria roughly relating to the precision, recall and f-score of the answer, as well as effort, comprehension and writing style (s. table 3). The results are averaged to yield a single score. For the objective evaluation, three judges constructed a gold-standard list of 25 items that should be contained in an ideal answer to the decision audit task. Two of them then checked off individually how many of the gold-standard items were contained in each participant answer. In a second step, they identified those participant answers where their ratings diverged by more than two points. There were 12 out of 50 ratings pairs that needed revision in this manner. After the judges' consultation on those 12 pairs of ratings, each experiment was given a single objective rating.

4   Results

Post-Questionnaires. An analysis of the *post-questionnaires* reveals that participants in general find the task to be challenging, as evidenced by the average answers on questions 4, 6 and 7 in Table 2. The task was designed to be challenging and time-constrained, because a simple task with a plentiful amount of

Table 2. Post-Questionnaire Results

Question	KAM	EAM	EAA	AMM	ASM
Q1: *I found the meeting browser intuitive and easy to use*	3.8	4.0	3.02_{AMM}	$4.3^{EAA,ASM}$	3.7_{AMM}
Q2: *I was able to find all of the information I needed*	2.9_{AMM}	3.8	2.9_{AMM}	$4.1^{KAM,EAA,ASM}$	3.0_{AMM}
Q3: *I was able to efficiently find the relevant information*	2.8_{AMM}	3.4^{ASM}	2.5_{AMM}	$4.0^{KAM,EAA,ASM}$	$2.65_{EAM,AMM}$
Q4: *I feel that I completed the task in its entirety*	2.3_{AMM}	3.1	2.3	3.2^{KAM}	2.9
Q5: *I understood the overall content of the meeting discussion*	3.8	**4.5**	3.9	4.1	3.9
Q6: *The task required a great deal of effort*	3.0	2.6^{EAA}	3.9_{EAM}	3.1	3.2
Q7: *I had to work under pressure*	3.3	**2.6**	3.3	2.7	3.1
Q8: *I had the tools necessary to complete the task efficiently*	3.1_{EAM}	$4.3^{KAM,EAA,ASM}$	3.0_{EAM}	4.1	3.5_{EAM}
Q9: *I would have liked additional information about the meetings*	3.0_{EAM}	2.0^{KAM}	2.4	2.6	2.7
Q10: *It was difficult to understand the content of the meetings...*	2.1	$1.5^{EAA,ASM}$	2.7_{EAM}	2.0	2.3_{EAM}

For each score in the table, that score is significantly better than the score for any conditions in superscript, and significantly worse than the score for any condition in subscript (according to t-test).

allotted time would allow the participants to simply read through the entire transcript or listen and watch the entire audio/video record in order to retrieve the correct information, disregarding other information sources. The task as designed requires efficient navigation of the information in the meetings in order to finish the task completely and on time.

Participants in condition AMM found the gold-standard human abstracts and specifically the summary subsections to be very valuable sources of information. One participant remarked "Very well prepared summaries. They were adequate to learn the jist [sic] of the meetings by quickly skimming through... I especially liked the tabs (Decisions, Actions, etc.) that categorised information according to what I was looking for."

Condition ASM rated quite well on questions regarding ease of use and intuitiveness, but slightly less well in terms of using the browser to locate the important information. It does consistently rate better than KAM and EAA.

For overall comprehension of the information in the meetings, extractive summaries were rated the highest of all. Extractive summaries of manual transcripts (EAM) were also rated the best in terms of the effort required to conduct the task. Perhaps the most compelling result is that Condition EAM not only rated the best in a question relating to having the tools necessary to complete the task, but it is *significantly better* than all conditions except the gold-standard human abstracts (according to t-test).

However, it is quite clear that the errors within an ASR transcript adversely affect user satisfaction in such an information retrieval task. For the questions relating to the effort required, the tools available, and the difficulty in understanding the meetings, Condition EAA tends to perform the worst of all, on par or even lower than the baseline condition. It should be noted however, that a baseline such as Condition KAM is working off of *manual* transcripts and would be expected to be worse when applied to ASR. As mentioned earlier, the baseline is a challenging baseline in that respect. Judging from the open-ended questions

Table 3. Human Evaluation Results - Subjective and Objective

Criterion	KAM	EAM	EAA	AMM	ASM
Q1: *overall quality*	3.0_{AMM}	4.15	3.05_{AMM}	$4.65^{KAM,EAA}$	4.3
Q2: *conciseness*	$2.85_{EAM,AMM,ASM}$	4.25^{KAM}	3.05_{AMM}	$4.85^{KAM,EAA}$	4.45^{KAM}
Q3: *completeness*	2.55_{AMM}	3.6	2.6_{AMM}	$4.45^{KAM,EAA}$	3.9
Q4: *task comprehension*	$3.25_{EAM,AMM}$	$5.2^{KAM,EAA}$	$3.65_{EAM,AMM}$	$5.25^{KAM,EAA}$	4.7
Q5: *participant effort*	4.4	5.2^{EAA}	$3.7_{EAM,AMM,ASM}$	5.3^{EAA}	4.9^{EAA}
Q6: *writing style*	4.75	5.65^{EAA}	$4.1_{EAM,AMM,ASM}$	5.7^{EAA}	5.8^{EAA}
Q7: *objective rating*	4.25_{AMM}	7.2	5.05_{AMM}	$9.45^{KAM,EAA}$	7.4

For each score in the table, that score is significantly better than the score for any conditions in superscript, and significantly worse than the score for any condition in subscript (according to t-test).

in the post-questionnaires, it's clear that at least two participants found the ASR so difficult to work with that they tended not to use the extractive summaries, let alone the full transcript, relying instead on watching the audio/video as much as possible.

Subjective Evaluation. Table 3 shows the results of the *subjective* evaluation. Condition AMM is clearly a challenging gold-standard, and Conditions EAM and ASM are roughly comparable to each other. Subjective ratings drop off sharply for Condition EAA incorporating ASR, particularly for comprehension and writing style. We presume that the ASR errors cause participants in that condition to have a lower understanding of the meeting content, which in turn leads to lower coherence and inferior writing quality in their responses. Interestingly, the scores on each criterion and for *every* condition tend to be somewhat low on the Likert scale, due to the difficulty of the task.

Objective Evaluation. According to the objective evaluation, Condition AMM is superior, with an average more than two points higher than the next best condition. The worst overall is the baseline Condition KAM, averaging only 4.25 hits (of a maximum possible 25). However, while the worst two conditions are significantly worse than the best overall condition, there are no significant differences between the other pairs of conditions, e.g. Condition EAA incorporating ASR is not significantly worse than Conditions EAM and ASM. So even with an errorful transcript, participants in Condition EAA are able to retrieve the relevant pieces of information at a rate not significantly worse than participants with a manual transcript. The quality may be worse from a subjective standpoint, as evidenced in the previous section, but the decision audit answers are still informative and relevant.

For the objective evaluation, in any given condition there is a large amount of variance that is simply down to differences between users. For example, even in the gold-standard Condition AMM there are some people who can only find one or two relevant items whilst others find 16 or 17. Given a challenging task and a limited amount of time, some people may have simply felt overwhelmed in trying to locate the informative portions efficiently.

Browsing Evaluation. A result gleaned from close analysis of participants' browsing behaviours shows an interesting strategy of people in Condition EAA faced

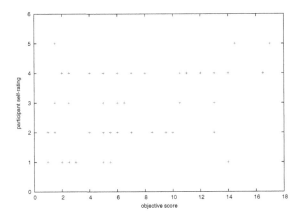

Fig. 2. Objective Scores and Post-Questionnaire Scores

with ASR transcripts. While they still frequently use the summary dialogue acts as indices into the meeting record, they subsequently utilize the audio/video record much more frequently than in the other conditions, presumably to disambiguate the errors encountered. This shows that, to some extent, participants can compensate for the noisy transcript by altering their browsing strategies, using the summaries in tandem with the audio/video in order to find the relevant items from the meetings.

The analysis of browsing behaviour also shows that participants in the gold-standard Condition AMM are able to begin answering the question much earlier in the task, write longer answers overall, and have more time for editing before times expires.

Questionnaire/Objective Evaluation Correlation. Figure 2 shows the relationship between the objective ratings and participant self-ratings for all 50 participants. While the positive correlation is evident, an interesting trend is that while there are relatively few people who score highly on the objective evaluation but score low on the self-ratings, there are a fair number of participants who have a low objective score but rate themselves highly on the post-questionnaire. A challenge with this type of task is that the participant simply may not have a realistic idea of how much relevant information is out there. After retrieving four or five relevant items, they may feel that they've completed the task entirely. This result is similar to the finding by Whittaker et. al [12], mentioned in the discussion of previous work, where participants often feel that they performed better than they really did.

5   Discussion

Although the semi-automatic abstracts got average reviews in the post-questionnaire, both the subjective and objective evaluation rate them second after the gold standard for most ratings, or even better (writing style). For task comprehension and participant effort, they come in third after EAM, however, the difference in rating is not significant. These are encouraging results for further research in automatic abstracting.

Overall the results are also very good news for the extractive summarization paradigm. Users find extractive summaries to be intuitive, easy-to-use and efficient, are able to employ such documents to locate the relevant information in a timely manner according to human evaluations, and users are able to adapt their browsing strategies to cope with ASR errors. While extractive summaries might be far from what people conceptualize as a traditional meeting summary, they are intuitive and useful documents in their own right.

Perhaps the most interesting result from the decision audit overall is regarding the effect of ASR on carrying out such a complex task. While participants using ASR find the browser to be less intuitive and efficient, they nonetheless feel that they understand the meeting discussions and do not desire additional information sources. In a subjective human evaluation, the quality of the answers in Condition EAA suffers according to most of the criteria, including writing style, but the participants are still able to find many of the relevant pieces of information according to the objective human evaluation. We find that users are able to adapt to errorful transcripts by using the summary dialogue acts as navigation and then relying much more on audio/video for disambiguating the conversation in the dialogue act context. Extractive summaries, even with errorful ASR, are useful tools for such a complex task, particularly when incorporated into a multi-media browser framework. There is also the possibility of creating browsing interfaces that minimize the user's direct exposure to the ASR transcript (e.g. audio summaries with limited textual accompaniment).

6   Conclusion

We have presented an extrinsic evaluation paradigm for the automatic summarization of spontaneous speech in the meetings domain: a decision audit task. In each condition of the experiment, users were able to utilize the derived content in order to find and extract information relevant to a specific task need. The largely positive results for the extractive conditions justify continued research on this summarization paradigm. However, the considerable superiority of gold-standard abstracts in many respects also support the view that research should begin to try to bridge the gap between extractive and abstractive summarization.

It is widely accepted in the summarization community that there should be increased reliance on extrinsic measures of summary quality. It is hoped that the decision audit task will be a useful framework for future evaluation work. Intrinsic and extrinsic methods should be used hand-in-hand, with the former as a valuable development tool and predictor of usefulness and the latter as a real-world evaluation of the state-of-the-art.

Acknowledgements. This work is supported by the European IST Programme Project FP6-033812.

References

1. Mani, I.: Summarization evaluation: An overview. In: Proc. of the NTCIR Workshop 2 Meeting on Evaluation of Chinese and Japanese Text Retrieval and Text Summarization, Tokyo, Japan, pp. 77–85 (2001)
2. Jing, H., Barzilay, R., McKeown, K., Elhadad, M.: Summarization evaluation methods: Experiments and analysis. In: Proc. of the AAAI Symposium on Intelligent Summarization, Stanford, USA, pp. 60–68 (1998)
3. Mani, I., House, D., Klein, G., Hirschman, L., Firmin, T., Sundheim, B.: The TIPSTER SUMMAC text summarization evaluation. In: Proc. of EACL 1999, Bergen, Norway, pp. 77–85 (1999)
4. Harman, D., Over, P.: Document understanding conference 2004. In: Proc. of the DUC 2004, Boston, USA (2004)
5. Dorr, B., Monz, C., President, S., Schwartz, R., Zajic, D.: A methodology for extrinsic evaluation of text summarization: Does ROUGE correlate? In: ACL 2005, MTSE Workshop, Ann Arbor, USA, pp. 1–8 (2005)
6. Hirschman, L., Light, M., Breck, E.: Deep read: A reading comprehension system. In: Proc. of ACL 1999, College Park, MD, USA, pp. 325–332 (1999)
7. Morris, A., Kasper, G., Adams, D.: The effects and limitations of automated text condensing on reading comprehension performance. Information Systems Research 3, 17–35 (1992)
8. Wellner, P., Flynn, M., Tucker, S., Whittaker, S.: A meeting browser evaluation test. In: Proc. of the SIGCHI Conference on Human Factors in Computing Systems 2005, pp. 2021–2024. ACM Press, New York (2005)
9. Kraaij, W., Post, W.: Task based evaluation of exploratory search systems. In: Proc. of SIGIR 2006 Workshop, Evaluation Exploratory Search Systems, Seattle, USA, pp. 24–27 (2006)
10. Hirschberg, J., Bacchiani, M., Hindle, D., Isenhour, P., Rosenberg, A., Stark, L., Stead, L., Whittaker, S., Zamchick, G.: SCANMail: Browsing and searching speech data by content. In: Proc. of Interspeech 2001, Aalborg, Denmark, pp. 1299–1302 (2001)
11. Whittaker, S., Hirschberg, J., Amento, B., Stark, L., Bacchiani, M., Isenhour, P., Stead, L., Zamchick, G., Rosenberg, A.: Scanmail: a voicemail interface that makes speech browsable, readable and searchable. In: Proc. of the SIGCHI 2002, Minneapolis, Minnesota, pp. 275–282. ACM, New York (2002)
12. Whittaker, S., Tucker, S., Swampillai, K., Laban, R.: Design and evaluation of systems to support interaction capture and retrieval. Personal and Ubiquitous Computing (to appear)
13. Tucker, S., Whittaker, S.: Accessing multimodal meeting data: Systems, problems and possibilities. In: Bengio, S., Bourlard, H. (eds.) MLMI 2004. LNCS, vol. 3361, pp. 1–11. Springer, Heidelberg (2005)
14. Wellner, P., Flynn, M., Guillemot, M.: Browsing recorded meetings with Ferret. In: Bengio, S., Bourlard, H. (eds.) MLMI 2004. LNCS, vol. 3361, pp. 12–21. Springer, Heidelberg (2005)
15. Carletta, J., Ashby, S., Bourban, S., Flynn, M., Guillemot, M., Hain, T., Kadlec, J., Karaiskos, V., Kraaij, W., Kronenthal, M., Lathoud, G., Lincoln, M., Lisowska, A., McCowan, I., Post, W., Reidsma, D., Wellner, P.: The AMI meeting corpus: A pre-announcement. In: Renals, S., Bengio, S. (eds.) MLMI 2005. LNCS, vol. 3869, pp. 28–39. Springer, Heidelberg (2006)

16. Murray, G., Renals, S.: Term-weighting for summarization of multi-party spoken dialogues. In: Popescu-Belis, A., Renals, S., Bourlard, H. (eds.) MLMI 2007. LNCS, vol. 4892, pp. 155–166. Springer, Heidelberg (2008)
17. Kleinbauer, T., Becker, S., Becker, T.: Combining multiple information layers for the automatic generation of indicative meeting abstracts. In: Proc. of ENLG 2007, Dagstuhl, Germany (2007)

Author Index

Lecture Notes in Computer Science

Sublibrary 3: Information Systems and Application, incl. Internet/Web and HCI

For information about Vols. 1– 4803
please contact your bookseller or Springer

Vol. 5005: V. Christophides, M. Collard, C. Gutierrez (Eds.), Semantic Web, Ontologies and Databases. VII, 153 pages. 2008.

Vol. 4997: B. Monien, U.-P. Schroeder (Eds.), Algorithmic Game Theory. XI, 363 pages. 2008.

Vol. 4993: H. Li, T. Liu, W.-Y. Ma, T. Sakai, K.-F. Wong, G. Zhou (Eds.), Information Retrieval Technology. XIII, 685 pages. 2008.

Vol. 4976: Y. Zhang, G. Yu, E. Bertino, G. Xu (Eds.), Progress in WWW Research and Development. XVIII, 699 pages. 2008.

Vol. 4969: R. Kronland-Martinet, S. Ystad, K. Jensen (Eds.), Computer Music Modeling and Retrieval. XII, 508 pages. 2008.

Vol. 4956: C. Macdonald, I. Ounis, V. Plachouras, I. Ruthven, R.W. White (Eds.), Advances in Information Retrieval. XXI, 719 pages. 2008.

Vol. 4952: C. Floerkemeier, M. Langheinrich, E. Fleisch, F. Mattern, S.E. Sarma (Eds.), The Internet of Things. XIII, 378 pages. 2008.

Vol. 4950: A. Kerren, J.T. Stasko, J.-D. Fekete, C. North (Eds.), Information Visualization. IX, 177 pages. 2008.

Vol. 4947: J.R. Haritsa, R. Kotagiri, V. Pudi (Eds.), Database Systems for Advanced Applications. XXII, 713 pages. 2008.

Vol. 4936: W. Aiello, A. Broder, J. Janssen, E.E. Milios (Eds.), Algorithms and Models for the Web-Graph. X, 167 pages. 2008.

Vol. 4932: S. Hartmann, G. Kern-Isberner (Eds.), Foundations of Information and Knowledge Systems. XII, 397 pages. 2008.

Vol. 4928: A.H.M. ter Hofstede, B. Benatallah, H.-Y. Paik (Eds.), Business Process Management Workshops. XIII, 518 pages. 2008.

Vol. 4918: N. Boujemaa, M. Detyniecki, A. Nürnberger (Eds.), Adaptive Multimedia Retrieval: Retrieval, User, and Semantics. XI, 265 pages. 2008.

Vol. 4903: S. Satoh, F. Nack, M. Etoh (Eds.), Advances in Multimedia Modeling. XIX, 510 pages. 2008.

Vol. 4900: S. Spaccapietra (Ed.), Journal on Data Semantics X. XIII, 265 pages. 2008.

Vol. 4892: A. Popescu-Belis, S. Renals, H. Bourlard (Eds.), Machine Learning for Multimodal Interaction. XI, 308 pages. 2008.

Vol. 4882: T. Janowski, H. Mohanty (Eds.), Distributed Computing and Internet Technology. XIII, 346 pages. 2007.

Vol. 4881: H. Yin, P. Tino, E. Corchado, W. Byrne, X. Yao (Eds.), Intelligent Data Engineering and Automated Learning - IDEAL 2007. XX, 1174 pages. 2007.

Vol. 4877: C. Thanos, F. Borri, L. Candela (Eds.), Digital Libraries: Research and Development. XII, 350 pages. 2007.

Vol. 4872: D. Mery, L. Rueda (Eds.), Advances in Image and Video Technology. XXI, 961 pages. 2007.

Vol. 4871: M. Cavazza, S. Donikian (Eds.), Virtual Storytelling. XIII, 219 pages. 2007.

Vol. 4868: C. Peter, R. Beale (Eds.), Affect and Emotion in Human-Computer Interaction. X, 241 pages. 2008.

Vol. 4858: X. Deng, F.C. Graham (Eds.), Internet and Network Economics. XVI, 598 pages. 2007.

Vol. 4857: J.M. Ware, G.E. Taylor (Eds.), Web and Wireless Geographical Information Systems. XI, 293 pages. 2007.

Vol. 4853: F. Fonseca, M.A. Rodríguez, S. Levashkin (Eds.), GeoSpatial Semantics. X, 289 pages. 2007.

Vol. 4836: H. Ichikawa, W.-D. Cho, I. Satoh, H.Y. Youn (Eds.), Ubiquitous Computing Systems. XIII, 307 pages. 2007.

Vol. 4832: M. Weske, M.-S. Hacid, C. Godart (Eds.), Web Information Systems Engineering – WISE 2007 Workshops. XV, 518 pages. 2007.

Vol. 4831: B. Benatallah, F. Casati, D. Georgakopoulos, C. Bartolini, W. Sadiq, C. Godart (Eds.), Web Information Systems Engineering – WISE 2007. XVI, 675 pages. 2007.

Vol. 4825: K. Aberer, K.-S. Choi, N. Noy, D. Allemang, K.-I. Lee, L. Nixon, J. Golbeck, P. Mika, D. Maynard, R. Mizoguchi, G. Schreiber, P. Cudré-Mauroux (Eds.), The Semantic Web. XXVII, 973 pages. 2007.

Vol. 4823: H. Leung, F. Li, R. Lau, Q. Li (Eds.), Advances in Web Based Learning – ICWL 2007. XIV, 654 pages. 2008.

Vol. 4822: D.H.-L. Goh, T.H. Cao, I.T. Sølvberg, E. Rasmussen (Eds.), Asian Digital Libraries. XVII, 519 pages. 2007.

Vol. 4820: T.G. Wyeld, S. Kenderdine, M. Docherty (Eds.), Virtual Systems and Multimedia. XII, 215 pages. 2008.

Vol. 4816: B. Falcidieno, M. Spagnuolo, Y. Avrithis, I. Kompatsiaris, P. Buitelaar (Eds.), Semantic Multimedia. XII, 306 pages. 2007.

Vol. 4813: I. Oakley, S.A. Brewster (Eds.), Haptic and Audio Interaction Design. XIV, 145 pages. 2007.

Vol. 4810: H.H.-S. Ip, O.C. Au, H. Leung, M.-T. Sun, W.-Y. Ma, S.-M. Hu (Eds.), Advances in Multimedia Information Processing – PCM 2007. XXI, 834 pages. 2007.

Vol. 4809: M.K. Denko, C.-s. Shih, K.-C. Li, S.-L. Tsao, Q.-A. Zeng, S.H. Park, Y.-B. Ko, S.-H. Hung, J.-H. Park (Eds.), Emerging Directions in Embedded and Ubiquitous Computing. XXXV, 823 pages. 2007.

Vol. 4808: T.-W. Kuo, E. Sha, M. Guo, L.T. Yang, Z. Shao (Eds.), Embedded and Ubiquitous Computing. XXI, 769 pages. 2007.

Vol. 4806: R. Meersman, Z. Tari, P. Herrero (Eds.), On the Move to Meaningful Internet Systems 2007: OTM 2007 Workshops, Part II. XXXIV, 611 pages. 2007.

Vol. 4805: R. Meersman, Z. Tari, P. Herrero (Eds.), On the Move to Meaningful Internet Systems 2007: OTM 2007 Workshops, Part I. XXXIV, 757 pages. 2007.

Vol. 4804: R. Meersman, Z. Tari (Eds.), On the Move to Meaningful Internet Systems 2007: CoopIS, DOA, ODBASE, GADA, and IS, Part II. XXIX, 683 pages. 2007.